Catholic Culture

in Early Modern England

Edited by

Ronald Corthell,
Frances E. Dolan,
Christopher Highley,
and
Arthur F. Marotti

University of Notre Dame Press
Notre Dame, Indiana

Notre Dame, Indiana 46556
www.undpress.nd.edu

Designed by Wendy McMillen
Set in 11.3/13.6 Fornier by Four Star Books
Printed on 60# Williamsburg Recycled Paper by Versa Press

Library of Congress Cataloging-in-Publication Data

Catholic culture in early modern England / edited by Ronald Corthell . . . [et al.].
p. cm.
Includes bibliographical references and index.
ISBN-13: 978-0-268-02294-5 (pbk. : alk. paper)
ISBN-10: 0-268-02294-1 (pbk. : alk. paper)
1. Catholic Church—England—History—16th century.
2. Catholic Church—England—History—17th century. 3. Catholic Church—Customs and practices. 4. England—Church history—16th century.
5. England—Church history—17th century. I. Corthell, Ronald, 1949–
BX1493.2.C38 2007
282'.4209031—dc22

2007033429

This book is printed on recycled paper.

Catholic Culture in Early Modern England

Contents

Catholic Culture in Early Modern England

Introduction

Ronald Corthell, Frances E. Dolan,
Christopher Highley, and Arthur F. Marotti

In the early modern period, many kinds of cultural and political struggles that would be articulated later in a more clearly secular vocabulary were couched in religious language and perceived as religious conflicts. After Henry VIII's break with Rome, the more radical Protestant reign of Edward VI, and the accession of the Protestant Queen Elizabeth I, who succeeded her Catholic half-sister, Queen Mary, Protestant-Catholic hostility was exacerbated by the 1570 Papal Bull excommunicating the queen. Sectarian conflict continued with varying intensities, culminating in the 1688 "Glorious Revolution" against the last English Catholic monarch, James II. Anti-Catholic propaganda poured from the English presses, especially at times of political crisis such as the post-Armada era of the late 1580s and 1590s, the years immediately following the 1605 Gunpowder Plot, the events of the Irish Rebellion (1641–49) and of the English Civil Wars (1642–49), the 1678–81 "Popish Plot" era, and the political upheaval of 1688–89. Even as England's identity as a Protestant nation was being forged throughout this period, a Catholic subculture survived in a religiously divided land. The "old faith" was sustained initially by nonconforming priests from Mary's reign and later by missionary priests trained in the foreign seminaries that were at the center of a vibrant exile community. Despite the penal laws against Catholics and the waves of persecution, a steady stream of Catholic texts circulated in England in manuscript and print—some produced and/or printed domestically, some produced on the Continent, some disseminated by being quoted at length or wholesale in Protestant polemical rejoinders.

Despite the strong presence of both a residual and continuing Catholic culture, a more or less official "Whig," Protestant, anti-Catholic version of English history long flourished as the dominant one (although, building on earlier Catholic oppositional narratives, the early-nineteenth-century historian John Lingard and his successors offered a Catholic counternarrative).[1] This teleological narrative of English nationhood and cultural supremacy celebrates the "inevitable" triumph of English Protestantism and of the anti-absolutist politics related to it. One of the consequences of this historical process and of its representation in a national mythology has been the marginalization of English Catholicism (except as a threat) both within sixteenth- and seventeenth-century England and beyond that era in historical accounts of that period. Partly in response to the serious and balanced reexamination of English Protestant history by Patrick Collinson and others,[2] scholars are questioning the assumption that the Reformation was a decisive and wholly positive change and reimagining Catholics as participants in, rather than obstacles to or exiles from, post-Reformation English history.

This project, in which our volume participates, builds on determined efforts on the part of scholars to write the post-Reformation history of English Catholics, initially by collecting documentary materials necessary for the project. The monumental collection of English Jesuit records by Henry Foley, S.J.;[3] the books on English Catholic martyrs by John Hungerford Pollen, S.J.;[4] Richard Simpson's nineteenth-century biography of Edmund Campion;[5] Dom Bede Camm's studies of Catholic houses and the experiences of early modern Catholics;[6] Philip Caraman's biographical and historical narratives;[7] the volumes on Elizabethan and Jacobean religious controversies by Peter Milward, S.J.;[8] A. C. Southern's study of recusant prose;[9] and the many volumes published by the Catholic Record Society over the last hundred years[10] all testify to this activity. These scholars have assembled a rich body of evidence and brought a hermeneutic of suspicion to once-dominant assumptions, thereby forming the foundation for subsequent work.

More recently, John Bossy, Eamon Duffy, and Christopher Haigh have studied the complex manifestations of post-Reformation Catholic culture, with special attention to ways the "old religion" changed and adapted to survive in a hostile environment at a time when the authorities, if not the mass of the population, espoused the Reformed faith.[11] Scholars such as Frances Dolan, Peter Lake, Michael Questier, Alexandra Walsham, and Anthony Milton have analyzed English Catholicism and anti-Catholicism in relation to both political struggles and cultural change, pointing out, for example, the multivalent uses of anti-Catholic codes in Protestant/Catholic polemical conflicts and in internal English Protestant factionalism.[12] Anne Dillon, Susannah Monta, and Brad S. Gregory have reexamined the phenomenon of martyrdom, the last in a pan-European context.[13] Claire Walker has reconstructed the remarkable histories of the many English women who entered English contemplative houses on the Continent after the Reformation.[14] Alison Shell, Raymond Tumbleson, and Arthur Marotti have analyzed religious discourse and highlighted the importance of Catholic texts, situating them in the context of the religious conflicts of the period.[15] Some recent essays and essay collections, part of a new turn to religion in literary studies, have signaled the renewed interest in both Catholicism and anti-Catholicism.[16] Alison's and Rogers's bibliography of English Catholic writing and Rogers's 374-volume facsimile series of Catholic writing—a collection that contains an even larger number of published texts, since many of the volumes contain multiple items[17]—are now being exploited extensively by scholars. Increasingly, scholars have been using British, Irish, and continental archives for their rich trove of Catholic manuscript materials. New anthologies of early modern Catholic writing are in progress.[18] The recent establishment of the Society for Early Modern Catholic Studies also signals increased scholarly interest in post-medieval Catholicism.

Despite the increase in historical, as well as literary, attention to early modern Catholic culture and history, as recently as the year 2002 Christopher Haigh could say, "The study of Catholic history and literature is still an intellectual backwater."[19] Clearly there is much work to be done to bring to this subject area the attention it deserves. To this end, the editors of this volume organized the conference "Early Modern English Catholic Culture," held at the Newberry Library in Chicago in October 2002. The term *culture* as used both in the conference title and in this volume is broad: in Raymond Williams's discussion of it as one of his "keywords," one of the three basic meanings he distinguishes is most relevant, culture as "a particular way of life, whether of a people, a period, a group, or humanity in general."[20] In relating the use of the word and its derivatives to particular disciplines, Williams notes that "in history and *cultural studies* the reference is primarily to *signifying* or *symbolic* systems."[21] When we look at the various manifestations of early modern English Catholic culture, we encounter a complex entity, containing residual medieval practices (especially on the level of folk beliefs); newer forms of Counter-Reformation doctrines, rules, and devotional practices; and forms of social and religious hybridity. It has separate, but interconnected, social histories on the popular and elite levels: although English Catholicism found protection within the English aristocracy, it also, through the seventeenth century, grew within the lower social strata. Within the embattled English Catholic community, there were struggles for leadership and dominance (between, for example, the Jesuits and the secular priests), different rationales for the choices of open recusancy and church papistry, different degrees of acceptance of or resistance to coercion, local and regional variations of practical toleration and persecution, and distinctly different modes of private and communal practice of the faith on different social levels and in different regions. While a term like *Catholic culture* embraces all of these, it is clear that the variations within the field of observation are marked and many.

At the Newberry conference, a group of twenty-one literary and historical scholars from both sides of the Atlantic presented papers on a wide variety of topics, treating English Catholic culture in an international context and historically examining written texts as well as other material artifacts. The speakers, who included the eleven contributors to this volume, were all committed to widening the scope of what we mean by early modern English Catholic culture in its many religious, social, political, literary, visual, and material forms. They are therefore part of the ongoing project of writing the cultural history of post-Reformation English Catholicism, especially in relation to the symbolic forms in which Catholic culture expressed itself in the early modern period. This collection represents a selection of the papers presented at the conference, the authors having been asked to develop further their original talks. The result, we think, is a collection of studies that has scholarly originality, historical and geographical range, topical variety, and interdisciplinary richness.

Peter Davidson sets the tone for our collection's aim of rethinking what we mean by Catholic culture by attending to its physical and material dimensions. He studies what might be termed early modern Catholic "places of identity," positing a relationship between "spaces and structures" and "the kinds of mental or interior space articulated in contemporary books of devotion." His work is thus linked to essays in the collection by Mark Netzloff, Sophie Holroyd, and Anne Myers. Anticipating the argument of Netzloff, Davidson begins by locating an important version of Englishness in the chapels of the English Colleges in Rome and Valladolid. Both he and Sophie Holroyd identify Henry Hawkins's *Partheneia Sacra* as an important guide to reading the symbolic language of space. Particularly suggestive is the range of Davidson's investigation—from temporary spaces created by the use of hangings and inscriptions to Sir Thomas Tresham's Triangular Lodge, which Davidson describes as a kind of protest building whose nearly invisible placement behind Tresham's house at Rushton itself evokes a semihidden recusant subject position. Through its careful analysis of material evidence, Davidson's paper produces new knowledge about active, oppositional signifying practices and self-fashioning on the part of early modern English Catholics.

Many of the essays in this volume explore the roles played by women and concepts of gender in the English Catholic community and the Protestant imagination. The central figures for Catholicism in contemporary polemic were often feminine, whether the beloved Virgin and female saints or the reviled Whore of Babylon and Pope Joan.[22] Certain historical persons such as Mary Stuart or Henrietta Maria came to stand as figureheads for all that was to be feared in Catholicism: its seductive power; its insinuation into families, households, and the court; its subordination of the intellect to the emotions and senses; its exoticism; its fecundity. Anti-Catholic discourses relied on gendered invective as an adaptable, resonant vocabulary for describing and condemning Catholicism as both the traitor within and the exotic, foreign seductress.[23] The association of Catholicism with the feminine might also work positively, positioning the "old faith" as a mother, a nurse, or an object of desire. While it is important to recognize the positive associations that the feminization of Catholicism could activate, it is equally important to remember that such associations were unstable. Given the pervasive anxiety evoked by maternal figures, for instance, casting the church as a blessed mother raised as many questions as it answered. Some people in post-Reformation England must certainly have felt nostalgia for lost intercessors, such as the Virgin Mary. But it oversimplifies attitudes toward both Catholicism and women to suggest that such nostalgia was widespread or unambivalent.

Feminized figures seem to have populated the dreams and nightmares of those who longed for or feared Catholicism. But women were also important players in the daily struggles of preserving and propagating the faith. As custodians of household religion, women presided over household worship, catechized their children and sometimes servants, and in some cases sustained a family's identity as Catholic by recusing themselves from Church of England services while their husbands conformed. Women often took risks to hide priests from pursuivants. This was a felony and led to heart-stopping searches and architectural transformations of houses to accommodate priest holes.[24] But harboring priests also involved a more mundane grind of finding secular roles for them to play in the household and keeping them fed and sheltered. While all of these contributions took place at home, recusant women also ventured outward: entering convents abroad or sending their children to seminaries or convents; founding orders; serving as abbesses, which in the case of someone like Mary Knatchbull, abbess of the English Benedictine convent at Ghent for forty-six years (1650–96), included actively supporting the Royalist cause and the Restoration;[25] going to jail as prisoners or as visitors; in some cases, dying for their faith. Finally, women read, translated, wrote, and circulated devotional texts; in at least one case a woman harbored a press.[26] Although scholars are aware of the importance of women in post-Reformation Catholicism, there is much more to be learned about specific cases. Several of the essays in this collection contribute to that project.

Jane Stevenson presents evidence for the influence of Latin culture on the formation of early modern Catholic Englishwomen. Her essay locates identifiable traditions of Latin education for women in a number of recusant families (not only that of St. Thomas More), and it opens prospects for further study of both convent life and marriage as experienced by early modern Englishwomen. The particular situation for Englishwomen aspiring to the religious life lends an international dimension to their acculturation and points to an understudied component of the Catholic diaspora, discussed in this collection by Mark Netzloff with respect to the English Colleges. Latin literacy appears to be yet another potentially empowering feature of early modern convent life that challenges assumptions regarding virginity and the cloister. Perhaps even more suggestive is Stevenson's elucidation of a tradition in elite families of Catholic humanist marriage that supported the ideal of companionate marriage typically associated with Puritanism. Evidence that Catholic women's education in such households depended on mothers, and that Latinity for women was not restricted to court circles, further enriches and complicates our understanding of women, literacy, and religion in the period.

Sophie Holroyd's essay draws our attention to the fates of female relatives of the Gunpowder Plotters, many of whom entered convents, and pays particular attention to the remarkable achievement of Helena Wintour, the daughter of a man executed for his involvement in the plot. Wintour remained unmarried, lived in retirement, and dedicated herself to prayer, self-sacrifice, works of charity, and support of the Catholic Church through her remarkable, and remarkably well-preserved, group of vestments that used as its central conceit the notion of the Virgin Mary as garden. Participating in recent work about the needle, not as opposed to the pen but as a kind of pen or paintbrush, Holroyd shows how Wintour stitches a unique devotional vision that both resembles Henry Hawkins's Jesuit emblem book *Partheneia Sacra* (1633) in its vocabulary and its set of emphases for Marian devotion and stands out as distinctive. Holroyd demonstrates the depth and inventiveness of Wintour's devotion, the importance of her aesthetic achievement, the value of these vestments as historical evidence, and their complexity as texts. The vestments were not only rich material for scholars. They were also a valuable legacy her heirs disputed; as a result they were divided between the Jesuits for whom she made the vestments and her heir, the widow of her nephew. One question lingers at the end of this essay: How did Wintour, unmarried woman and the daughter of an executed traitor, obtain the "diamonds, rubies, garnets and hundreds of large pearls" with which she ornamented these vestments?

Helena Wintour worked alone for years on her vestments and left little evidence behind except for them; she is an artist whose work will be new to most readers of this collection. In contrast, Henrietta Maria, wife of Charles I, was one of the most visible and notorious Catholic women in Stuart England. Although there has been considerable scholarly work on the queen and how she was represented, much remains to be learned. Caroline Hibbard's essay offers fresh insight into the much-maligned queen. Hibbard shifts our attention away from anxious fantasies about Henrietta Maria and toward the details of her presence and practices as a historical person and English queen who engaged in particular actions, held specific opinions, and imported particular objects and fashions. "Restoring contingency to the narrative," Hibbard invites us to forget the end of the story in order to see the possibility that English political and religious conflict, and the queen's role in it, might have unfolded somewhat differently. Hibbard also challenges us not to adopt the perspective of the queen's enemies by overstating the threat she supposedly embodied and oversimplifying its nature. Questioning the very notion of English Catholicism, Hibbard shows that Catholicism was inevitably and institutionally cosmopolitan. In what ways, then, did Henrietta Maria's foreignness matter? How did its significance change over time? How did contemporaries associate it with her Catholicism and, later, her "Spaniolized" policies?

While the social/culturalist turn in early modern literary studies has tended to displace devotional literature and poetics from the center of scholarship on religion and literature in the period, several contributors to this volume return to the subject of devotion, influenced, to be sure, by more recent work on ideology and culture. Gary Kuchar's essay on Southwell's *Mary Magdalene's Funeral Tears* is perhaps the piece most directly engaged with devotional writing, and it details at length the psychic conflicts in Southwell's poetry and prose. Such an analysis of devotional practice departs from earlier studies of both Catholic and Protestant traditions of meditation that insisted that powerfully unifying theories and practices informed the literature of devotion. What is more, Kuchar argues for a connection between Southwell's moving representations of Magdalene's struggles with "radical self-division" and a recusant subject position. Kuchar's essay, then, brings devotional writing into discussions of the process of subjectification. Kuchar complicates his assessment of Southwell's politics by also arguing for a gendered resistance on Southwell's part to Magdalene as a model of religious subjectivity. Drawing on both historical research on recusant women and contending Aristotelian and Augustinian ethics, Kuchar detects in Southwell's devotions male anxieties regarding female desire and "the devotional power of women." Thus the English Catholic devotional subject is doubly divided by politics and gender.

Heather Wolfe's essay on the Benedictine nun Dame Barbara Constable is a case study illuminating some important aspects of the English Catholic exile community—here through the transcription and editing activities of an extraordinarily industrious woman. Though living a cloistered life distant from her English home, Constable—as Wolfe demonstrates—not only had a significant impact on her immediate religious environment and on the devotional practices of the exiled religious community but also maintained contact with her family and the Catholic community in England, serving them in a "missionary" role. Through her work, she forged links between the Catholic community abroad and the dispersed Catholic population in England, helping also to sustain a long tradition of English spirituality through an ambitious antiquarian project of textual recovery whose purpose was to disseminate both medieval and contemporary works of devotion, meditation, and mysticism. Constable helped to preserve the valuable writings of the Benedictine Augustine Baker, who had been, before her arrival, spiritual director at her convent at Cambrai and who himself tried to maintain the devotional traditions of the medieval mystical writers Constable then compiled. Part of a collective effort on the part of exiled nuns "to provide the Catholics of England with an institutional memory" through transcription and compilation of these works, Barbara Constable transcended the physical and social limitations of enclosure and of female subordination to "contribute to the survival and flourishing of medieval English Catholic contemplative culture." She even exercised moral and social authority in her fearless criticism of contemporary monks and nuns in positions of authority by "pointing them to examples from the past." Finally, as Wolfe argues, she struggled "to justify her wide learning within a contemplative environment that stressed the exercise of the will over that of the understanding." Although Barbara Constable might not offer the kind of example of female agency modern feminist scholars have traditionally sought, within the context of early modern English Catholic culture this intelligent and strong-willed woman had a crucial social and cultural role. Wolfe's study of Constable, based on original research in American, English, and continental archives, helps broaden our understanding of the international scope of English Catholicism, of how the "old religion" was preserved in the face of efforts to eradicate all of its traces, and of the relationship of religious exiles to the community of Catholics in England.

Molly Murray's study of Catholic conversion accounts, which concentrates on the serial convert William Alabaster's narrative of his sudden conversion to Catholicism in the late Elizabethan era, sets that remarkable document in two main contexts. The first is that of the *responsa scholarum,* the autobiographical answers to a set of questions posed to the would-be seminarians entering the English College, Rome. She cites a number of these short narratives to prove, among other things, the existence of a Catholic form of spiritual autobiography in the early modern period. The second context is that of St. Augustine's *Confessions,* which offers an imitable model of conversion that involves responding to a particular text and that belongs to a tradition of conversion narratives from St. Paul onward. Murray contrasts Catholic conversion, which she defines as a kind of denominational shift or "revised outward affiliation" and a "fitting in" to a receptive church, with the

Protestant spiritual autobiographical model of inner spiritual change. As practiced by Alabaster and others, the Catholic conversion takes the form of, on the one hand, a "literary" experience of being "moved" by a particular text (rather than being convinced by particular arguments) and, on the other, an experience of being affected by "specific outward influences . . . family members, friends, and priests." Catholic, as opposed to Protestant, conversion is an "adherence" (to a church) rather than an "aversion" (to the world). William Alabaster's extended conversion narrative, which has not received either the literary or the historical attention it deserves, is a text "reflecting the unmistakable influence of the *Confessions* in form as well as 'spirit,'" "a work of artful self-representation" designed both as a personal apologia and as a model for other readers' experience. Murray attends closely to Alabaster's imitation of Augustine's narrative and to the intertextual continuity of such conversion accounts.

Anne Myers's essay on the Latin autobiography written by the Jesuit priest John Gerard primarily for a Catholic audience on the Continent concentrates on the uses of relics and other objects circulated in the Catholic community as means of preserving the identity and continuity of English Catholicism in the times of persecution. Myers demonstrates how Gerard's "preoccupation with the persistence and preservation of relics and other objects central to Catholic devotion" is related to "the continued survival of the Catholic community in England" and to "the special threats [especially of imprisonment and martyrdom] faced by Reformation Catholics in general and Jesuit missionaries in particular." Gerard uses relics and other valued objects associated with both long-dead and recently martyred Catholics to prove the "survival and resiliency" of the persecuted English Catholic community within the context of the long history of English Christianity, but instead of focusing on the authenticity of these objects themselves he treats them as signs of the vitality of Catholic belief and religious resistance. Myers notes Gerard's emphasis on the circulation of relics and related materials, including writings of martyrs, for belief in such objects "function[ed] like a language that identifie[d] its speakers as members of the Catholic community" and "[a]s long as Gerard ha[d] others to whom he [could] circulate the illicit objects of Catholic devotion, Catholicism [was] not a dead language in England." Myers analyzes Gerard's "coded orange juice writing" and his crafting in prison of religious artifacts such as rosaries from orange peels as material practices all of a piece with the traditional Catholic uses of physical objects in devotional and religious social life—part of what has been called elsewhere an "incarnational aesthetic"[27] at odds with a Protestant language-based religion and sensuous minimalism. In Catholic practice, holy or valued objects mediated not only sacred experience but also social relations within the Catholic community. Set in the context of its primary audience of continental Jesuit seminarians, many of whom were preparing for frightfully hazardous missionary service in England, Gerard's *Autobiography,* as Myers shows, served to prepare these young men for the experience both by assuring them of a receptive English Catholic community and by idealizing the heroic deeds and models of those who had recently suffered and died for the faith.

The experience and consequences of exile for both lay and religious Catholics are recurrent issues in many of the essays in this collection. From early in Elizabeth's reign, Catholic and Protestant propagandists struggled for control of how the exiles were perceived. In government proclamations they were labeled "unnatural subjects" or "Hispaniolized" Englishmen. Exiles themselves projected different self-images and expressed their condition in various ways. Gary Kuchar sees the predicament of Southwell's Mary Magdalene before the empty tomb of Jesus as paradigmatic of the exile's agony in having to choose between staying and going: "If I stay here where he is not, I shall never finde him. If I would go further to seeke, I know not whether. . . . I am left free to choose whether I will stay without helpe, or go without hope." Many refugees expressed homesickness and nostalgic longing for an England often imagined in idealized ways: "I finde the saying so true *Dulcis odor patriae,*" wrote the exiled Thomas Copley at the thought of returning home, "that alreadie me seemith, the ayer I shall breathe on the hills neere to Roan, looking towards Ingland, wilbe sweeter than I can drawe from any other parte."[28] Displacement from an ancestral home was frequently understood by Catholic exiles as emblematic of the sinner's distance—even banishment—from the presence of God.

But if exile was a cause for lamentation and grief (and analogized to the diaspora of the Old Testament Jews), it was also a culturally enabling and productive condition, providing Catholics from all parts of the British Isles and Ireland with opportunities to organize, fund-raise, write, and publish. As Alexandra Walsham has argued, post-Tridentine Catholicism was as much invested in print culture as Protestantism, the so-called religion of the book.[29] Exiles had access to Catholic presses across Europe at St. Omer in northern France, and at Louvain, Antwerp, Douai, and elsewhere. Some of the texts discussed in this volume remained part of a system of manuscript circulation and publication that existed alongside print culture. William Alabaster's conversion narrative, composed at the English College in Rome, was subsequently translated by Robert Parsons from the vernacular into Latin for a larger European readership, although never printed. John Gerard's manuscript *Autobiography* was written at Louvain as a guidebook for the circumscribed audience of future Jesuit missionaries, warning them of the dangers that awaited them in England but also reassuring them about the survival of a robust Catholic subculture there. We might think of the Benedictine nun Dame Barbara Constable as doubly exiled, her enclosure inside the walls of a convent superimposed on her external exile from England. Yet Constable, too, made exile an opportunity for outreach, collecting texts, reading, transcribing the works of others, and composing her own devotional works for circulation beyond her immediate enclosed community at Cambrai.

Mark Netzloff's chapter addresses most directly the experience of exile by examining the English Colleges on the Continent. Netzloff is interested in how "the Catholic polemical texts written from the position of continental diaspora offered their own formulations of English identity." As the writings of three prominent exiles—William Allen, Robert Persons, and Richard Verstegan—reveal, these formulations were varied and nuanced. Allen, who established the first college at Douai in 1568, defended the colleges against Protestant characterizations of their members as vagrants, deviants, and traitors. Netzloff shows how Allen defends travel from Protestant associations of it with error and spiritual waywardness, conceiving of Englishness not in ethnic or geographical terms but as an adherence to certain religious and legal principles. Robert Persons, on the other hand, constructs in his writings on diaspora a Catholic identity based on "cosmopolitanism and cultural hybridity," a conceit that refuses the Protestant emphasis on English "isolationism and exceptionalism." In Persons's accounts, the colleges, far from being novel innovations, help restore England's historical ties with Iberia and the rest of Europe. Netzloff uses the cosmopolitanism of the English Colleges to challenge influential modern narratives about nation formation. Citing the speeches delivered in multiple languages to Philip II by the English students at Valladolid, Netzloff questions Benedict Anderson's equation of the modern state with the dominance of the vernacular. Netzloff's final case study is of exiled Catholic Richard Verstegan and his antiquarian work *A Restitution of Decayed Intelligence in Antiquities*. For Netzloff, Verstegan's racialized view of English identity as Germanic-Saxon in origin stressed England's ties to continental Europe and preserved an essential identity for Catholics that could not be invalidated by geographical displacement or religious and political affiliation. Such a racialized imagining of English identity, however, did little to encourage cooperation between English, Welsh, Scottish, and Irish Catholics. Indeed, Verstegan's work fueled English Catholics' conviction in their preeminence over co-religionists from neighboring regions.

It was from continental centers of resistance like Louvain, Rome, and Douai that exiled Catholics took on Protestants in ecclesiastical arguments about the origins, continuity, and identity of the true church and its relation to Rome. John Jewel's Protestant *Apology for the Church of England* (1564), the work that ignited this polemical battle, drew responses from exiled Catholic intellectuals like Thomas Harding and Thomas Stapleton, who conscripted the Venerable Bede for the modern Catholic cause by translating and publishing an edition of the *Ecclesiastical History*. Intimately related to arguments about the history of the church as an institution were the attempts by different factions to claim Christianity's roll call of saints and martyrs. The Catholic writing of hagiography, like the collecting, preserving, translating, and transcribing of medieval spiritual texts, was a way of safeguarding a religious heritage that the passage of time and the iconoclastic phases of the reformation threatened to erase. In her chapter "*The Lives of Women Saints of Our Contrie of England*: Gender and Nationalism in Recusant Hagiography," Catherine Sanok shows how Catholics were just as invested as Protestants in forging national narratives and myths designed to validate their status as custodians of an authentic Englishness. While Reformation governments revised the religious calendar and drastically curtailed the number of officially recognized saints and their festivals, Catholics produced legendaries of native saints that asserted the antiquity and legitimacy of their faith and insisted upon England's status as a Catholic nation. Sanok further shows how the legendary's reconciliation of Catholic and nationalist discourses is inflected by issues of gender. Overturning the misogynistic stereotypes found in anti-Catholic polemic (the church as the Whore of Babylon, for instance), the Catholic hagiography that Sanok studies celebrates these pious women as representatives of a distinctly English Catholic nationalism. Ironically, this hortatory vision of an ancient Catholic England figured as feminine is used to shame and thus motivate the present-day English Catholic community of timid and backsliding men. Sanok shows how in *The Lives of Women Saints*

England's identity as a Catholic nation transcends political formations but is inscribed on the land itself—a land in which the bodies of martyred virgins are interred and from which springs of fresh water issue, miraculously marking the site of these martyrdoms.

Just as stay-at-home recusants looked outside England for support from Europe's Catholic powers, so, argues Donna Hamilton, writers like Anthony Munday insinuated a Catholic agenda into their writings by looking outside England to texts from a continental Catholic literary tradition. Discussing works that have been all but ignored by recent scholars, Hamilton shows how Munday's translations of a cluster of Iberian romances, including *Palmerin of England*, constituted interventions in ongoing controversies about confessional practices and England's ties to an idea of Christendom embodied in Catholic Europe. Hamilton's treatment of Munday is all the more remarkable in that it represents a bold reassessment of a figure who has until now had a reputation as a staunch anti-Catholic for works like *The English Roman Life* (1582) and his continuation of John Stow's *Chronicles.*[30] Scholars have long recognized the political implications attending the act of translation; Munday's translations are notable, however, for preserving more than they change in their originals. Munday's translations might have excised obvious references to Catholic devotional practices, but they retained an essentially Catholic worldview, thus unobtrusively importing heterodox ideas and fantasies into a Protestant state that tried to seal its borders against such infiltration. Munday's translation project implicitly rejected myths of England's exceptionalism and status as a Protestant *hortus conclusus* by inviting readers to remember in a positive light their country's earlier connections to the wider world of Christendom and the loss of community and security that had resulted from severing those ties.

Hamilton's study raises many fascinating questions that require further study, not the least of which is what religious label we should give Munday. *Catholic loyalist* and *church papist* are two that might fit, but they are only two possible ways to name the multiple, shifting, overlapping, perhaps uncategorizable subject positions that Catholics could occupy. The case of Munday—a figure once firmly rooted in the Protestant camp and now claimed for the Catholic—should remind us of the problems inherent in trying to fix individual religious identity in this period according to a single set of binary categories.[31] Recent scholarship is creating an increasingly complex account of early modern English Catholic culture. In this collection alone, we encounter a broad range of Catholics—laymen and laywomen, a queen, a Benedictine nun, Jesuit missionaries, and Catholic exiles; recusants, church papists, and loyalists—working and writing within widely varying contexts and communities. Catholic activities and cultural products emerged from special combinations of conflicts that contributed in a positive, not just oppositional, way to the construction of new religious identities in early modern England. It is our hope that the essays gathered here will encourage an ongoing reappraisal of early modern English Catholic culture and the complex religious orientations of the men and women of the period.

Notes

1. See the discussion of Whig historiography, for example, in Kevin Sharpe, *Remapping Early Modern England: The Culture of Seventeenth-Century Politics* (Cambridge: Cambridge University Press, 2000), 4–9. See Lingard's multivolume, multiple-edition, expanding *History of England* (the first through fifth editions published during his lifetime in 1819–51, the sixth and seventh published posthumously in 1854–55 and 1883 respectively).

2. See, for example, Patrick Collinson, *The Religion of Protestants: The Church in English Society, 1559–1625* (Oxford: Clarendon Press, 1982) and *The Birthpangs of Protestant England: Religion, Society and Cultural Change in the Sixteenth and Seventeenth Centuries* (Basingstoke: Macmillan, 1988).

3. Henry Foley, S.J., ed., *Records of the English Province of the Society of Jesus*, 7 vols. (London: Burns and Oates, 1877–83).

4. See, for example, John Hungerford Pollen, S.J., *Unpublished Documents Relating to the English Martyrs*, vol. 1, *1584–1603*, Catholic Record Society 5 (London: J. Whitehead and Sons, 1908), and *The Ven. Philip Howard Earl of Arundel, 1557–1595*, vol. 2 of *English Martyrs*, Catholic Record Society 21 (London: Harrison and Sons, 1919).

5. Richard Simpson, *Edmund Campion: A Biography* (London: J. Hodges, 1867).

6. See, especially, Dom Bede Camm, *Forgotten Shrines: An Account of Some Old Catholic Halls and Families in England and of Relics and Memorials of the English Martyrs* (London: MacDonald and Evans, 1910).

7. These include [John Gerard, S.J.], *The Autobiography of an Elizabethan*, trans. Philip Caraman (London: Longmans, Greene, 1956); and Philip Caraman's *Henry Garnet, 1555–1606 and the Gunpowder Plot* (London: Longmans, 1964), *The Other Face: Catholic Life under Elizabeth I* (New York: Sheed and Ward, 1960), and *The Years of Siege: Catholic Life from James I to Cromwell* (London: Longmans, 1966).

8. Peter Milward, *Religious Controversies of the Elizabethan Age* (Lincoln: University of Nebraska Press, 1977) and *Religious Controversies of the Jacobean Age* (Lincoln: University of Nebraska Press, 1978).

9. A. C. Southern, *English Recusant Prose: 1559–1582* (London: Sands, n.d.).

10. These include not only some eighty volumes in the Records series, six volumes in the monograph series, and two occasional publications but also the journal *Recusant History* (called *Biographical Studies* during its first three years of publication).

11. John Bossy, *The English Catholic Community, 1570–1850* (London: Darton, Longman and Todd, 1975); Eamon Duffy, *The Stripping of the Altars: Traditional Religion in England c. 1400–c. 1580* (New Haven: Yale University Press, 1992); Christopher Haigh, *English Reformations: Religion, Politics, and Society under the Tudors* (Oxford: Clarendon Press, 1993).

12. Frances Dolan, *Whores of Babylon: Catholicism, Gender, and Seventeenth-Century Print Culture* (1999; reprint, Notre Dame, IN: University of Notre Dame Press, 2005); Peter Lake, "Anti-Popery: The Structure of a Prejudice," in *Conflict in Early Stuart England: Studies in Religion and Politics, 1603–1642,* ed. Richard Cust and Ann Hughes (New York: Longman, 1989), 72–106; Peter Lake, with Michael Questier, *The Antichrist's Lewd Hat: Protestants, Papists and Players in Post-Reformation England* (New Haven: Yale University Press, 2002); Alexandra Walsham, *Church Papists: Catholicism, Conformity and Confessional Polemic in Early Modern England* (Woodbridge: Royal Historical Society and Boydell Press, 1993) and *Providence in Early Modern England* (Oxford: Oxford University Press, 1999); Anthony Milton, *Catholic and Reformed: The Roman and Protestant Churches in English Protestant Thought, 1600–1640* (Cambridge: Cambridge University Press, 1995). See also Thomas McCoog, S.J., *The Society of Jesus in Ireland, Scotland, and England, 1541–1588: "Our Way of Proceeding?"* (Leiden: E. J. Brill, 1996); Scott R. Pilarz, S.J., *Robert Southwell and the Mission of Literature, 1561–1595* (Aldershot: Ashgate, 2004); Lisa McClain, *Lest We Be Damned: Practical Innovation and Lived Experience among Catholics in Protestant England, 1559–1642* (London: Routledge, 2003); and Ethan H. Shagan, ed., *Catholics and the "Protestant Nation": Religious Politics and Identity in Early Modern England* (Manchester: Manchester University Press, 2005).

13. Anne Dillon, *The Construction of Martyrdom in the English Catholic Community, 1535–1603* (Aldershot: Ashgate, 2002); Susannah B. Monta, *Martyrdom and Literature in Early Modern England* (Cambridge: Cambridge University Press, 2005); Brad S. Gregory, *Salvation at Stake: Christian Martyrdom in Early Modern Europe* (Cambridge, MA: Harvard University Press, 1999).

14. Claire Walker, *Gender and Politics in Early Modern Europe: English Convents in France and the Low Countries* (New York: Palgrave, 2005).

15. Alison Shell, *Catholicism, Controversy and the English Literary Imagination, 1558–1660* (Cambridge: Cambridge University Press, 1999); Raymond D. Tumble-

son, *Catholicism in the English Protestant Imagination: Nationalism, Religion and Literature, 1600–1745* (Cambridge: Cambridge University Press, 1998); Arthur F. Marotti, *Religious Ideology and Cultural Fantasy: Catholic and Anti-Catholic Discourses in Early Modern England* (Notre Dame, IN: University of Notre Dame Press, 2005). See also the cross-confessional study of devotional literature in Gary Kuchar, *Divine Subjection: The Rhetoric of Sacramental Devotion in Early Modern England* (Pittsburgh: Dusquesne University Press, 2005).

16. See Arthur F. Marotti, ed., *Catholicism and Anti-Catholicism in Early Modern English Texts* (Basingstoke: Macmillan, 1999); Arthur F. Marotti, "John Donne's Conflicted Anti-Catholicism," *Journal of English and Germanic Philology* 101 (July 2002): 358–79; Paul Voss, "The Catholic Presence in Renaissance Literature," *Ben Jonson Journal* 7 (2000): 1–26; Richard Dutton, Alison Gail Findlay, and Richard Wilson, eds., *Region, Religion and Patronage: Lancastrian Shakespeare* (Manchester: Manchester University Press, 2003) and *Theatre and Religion: Lancastrian Shakespeare* (Manchester: Manchester University Press, 2003); Ken Jackson and Arthur F. Marotti, "The Turn to Religion in Early Modern English Studies," *Criticism* 46 (Winter 2004): 167–90. See also Christopher Highley, Catholics Writing the Nation in Early Modern Britain and Ireland (forthcoming).

17. A. F. Allison and D. M. Rogers, eds., *The Contemporary Printed Literature of the English Counter-Reformation between 1558 and 1640: An Annotated Catalogue*, 2 vols. (Aldershot: Scolar Press, 1989); D. M. Rogers, ed., *English Recusant Literature, 1558–1640* (Aldershot: Scolar Press, 1968–79). Both projects assemble a canon of Catholic print texts that are still underrepresented in the English Short Title Catalogue and Early English Books Online databases, which are biased toward English imprints and thus against many Catholic texts printed abroad. Alison's and Rogers's bibliography expands an earlier one published in the journal *Biographical Studies*, the forerunner of the valuable journal *Recusant History*, which has been publishing important studies of Catholic history for over a half-century. See also Thomas H. Clancy, S.J., ed., *English Catholic Books, 1641–1700: A Bibliography* (Chicago: Loyola University Press, 1974).

18. Both Annabel Patterson and Robert Miola are compiling soon-to-be-published anthologies of early modern Catholic writing, the former in the context of a large collection of religious writing from the period. These would be the first such anthologies since Louise Guiney's *Recusant Poets* (New York: Sheed and Ward, 1939) and John Roberts's *A Critical Anthology of English Recusant Devotional Prose, 1589–1603* (Pittsburgh: Dusquesne University Press, 1966).

19. Christopher Haigh, "Catholicism in Early Modern England: Bossy and Beyond," review article, *Historical Journal* 45, no. 2 (2002): 493.

20. Raymond Williams, *Keywords: A Vocabulary of Culture and Society* (New York: Oxford University Press, 1976), 90.

21. Ibid., 91.

22. Huston Diehl, *Staging Reform, Reforming the Stage: Protestantism and Popular Theater in Early Modern England* (Ithaca: Cornell University Press, 1997); Claire McEachern, *The Poetics of English Nationhood, 1590–1612* (Cambridge: Cambridge University Press, 1996).

23. Alastair Bellany, *The Politics of Court Scandal in Early Modern England: News Culture and the Overbury Affair, 1603–1660* (Cambridge: Cambridge University Press, 2002); Dolan, *Whores of Babylon*; Peter Stallybrass, "The World Turned Upside Down: Inversion, Gender, and the State," in *The Matter of Difference: Materialist Feminist Criticism of Shakespeare,* ed. Valerie Wayne (Ithaca: Cornell University Press, 1991), 201–20; David E. Underdown, *A Freeborn People: Politics and the Nation in Seventeenth-Century England* (Oxford: Clarendon Press, 1996).

24. For a recent discussion of priest holes, see Julian Yates, *Error, Misuse, Failure: Object Lessons from the English Renaissance* (Minneapolis: University of Minnesota Press, 2003), 139–207.

25. Claire Walker, "Prayer, Patronage, and Political Conspiracy: English Nuns and the Restoration," *Historical Journal* 43 (2000): 1–23.

26. Arthur F. Marotti, "Alienating Catholics in Early Modern England: Recusant Women, Jesuits and Ideological Fantasies," in Marotti, *Catholicism and Anti-Catholicism,* 1–34; Marie B. Rowlands, "Recusant Women, 1560–1640," in *Women in English Society, 1500–1800,* ed. Mary Prior (London: Methuen, 1985), 149–80; Alexandra Walsham, "'Domme Preachers'? Post-Reformation English Catholicism and the Culture of Print," *Past and Present* 168, no. 1 (2000): 72–123.

27. The term is used by Michael O'Connell, "The Idolatrous Eye: Iconoclasm, Antitheatricalism, and the Image of the Elizabethan Theater," *ELH* 52 (1985): 279–310.

28. Richard Copley Christie, ed., *The Letters of Sir Thomas Copley* (London, 1897), 140.

29. Walsham, "'Domme Preachers'?" 72–123.

30. See the essay on Stow's continuators in J. F. Merrit, ed., *Imagining Early Modern London: Perceptions and Portrayals of the City from Stow to Strype, 1598–1720* (Cambridge: Cambridge University Press, 2001).

31. David L. Smith, "Catholic, Anglican or Puritan? Edward Sackville, Fourth Earl of Dorset, and the Ambiguities of Religion in Early Stuart England," in *Religion, Literature, and Politics in Post-Reformation England, 1540–1688,* ed. Donna B. Hamilton and Richard Strier (Cambridge: Cambridge University Press, 1996), 115–37.

I

Recusant Catholic Spaces in Early Modern England

Peter Davidson

The Catholic spaces that I would like to consider here are not restricted to priest holes or secret chapels, although these, of course, survive as moving and eloquent spaces in their own right. (One of the most beautiful of these is the little porch room at Grange Farm, Abbey Dore, Herefordshire, with its repeated "IHS" in the plasterwork, belief woven into the fabric of the house.)[1] I am not attempting to describe Townley Hall in Lancashire or Baddesley Clinton in Warwickshire as somehow distinct from the other country houses of Tudor or Stuart England as a consequence of their recusant histories. These are both haunting and thought-provoking structures: Townley especially for its extraordinary, post-nineteenth-century location, which has left it poised between industrial and rural England. Baddesley Clinton is a house that has undergone at least two major restorations in the nineteenth and twentieth centuries, each of which has left this modest moated house, rich in priest holes, slightly more Elizabethan than it was in the sixteenth century. (If space permitted, we might also consider the extraordinary Catholic ménage who lived there in the nineteenth century, who seem to have derived so much innocent pleasure from dressing up as their recusant predecessors.) But in this essay I am concerned with houses as more than associational places of memory. The elegiac view of the recusants originated by Newman, and quoted as definitive by Dom Bede Camm in his early-twentieth-century work on recusant houses, is certainly not the only possible view: "a few adherents of the Old Religion, moving silently and sorrowfully about as memorials of what had been. . . . An old-fashioned house of gloomy appearance, closed in with high walls, with an iron gate and yews, and the report attaching to it that 'Roman Catholics' lived there."[2]

The spaces in England and Scotland that I consider here are those that retain some palpable traces of their recusant Catholic identity in decoration, layout, or inscription. Among these, the particular focus of this investigation is on what might be called *symbolically articulated spaces,* such as the study room at Norbury in Derbyshire, or Sir Thomas Tresham's buildings in Northamptonshire, spaces and structures that bear, in reality, a demonstrable relation to the kinds of mental or interior space articulated in contemporary books of devotion.

To use space symbolically is not specifically Catholic, of course, although I hope to argue that there are indeed specifically Catholic articulations of space. It is useful to remember here that the symbolic language of place was a widespread, if now partially forgotten, aspect of the European late Renaissance world. Indeed, we should also remember that one of the most heavily inscribed houses in England belonged to the hard-line Protestants Nicholas Bacon and his wife Anne Cooke Bacon. The latter seems also to have commissioned the programs for elaborate allegorical painted schemes that survive among the Sloane manuscripts in the British Library. Coincidentally, it seems to have been a dependent of the Bacon family, the translator Robert Dallington, who brought the classic Renaissance text of symbolic place, the *Hypnerotomachia Poliphili,* to the notice of Sir Thomas Tresham, the deviser of three-dimensional articulations of statements of Catholic allegiance.

It seems likely that these symbolic rooms and buildings were a casually central part of early modern thought and experience: we seem to have lost sight of them to a considerable extent. A reconsideration of a classically northern Renaissance symbolic garden can be found in Erasmus, in the *Convivium religiosum* of 1522, which describes an ideal humanist house and garden heavily inscribed and emblematized in a way that is common to many of the recusant places considered in this essay.[3] For the present, it is enough to point out that these recusant symbolic rooms and structures are a coherent part of a whole that would embrace such diverse texts and artifacts as Colonna's *Hypnerotomachia,* the country-house poems of Baroque Holland, Andrew Marvell's *Upon Appleton House*, and Montaigne's study at the Chateau de Montaigne, as well as innumerable descriptions of symbolically charged house and garden layouts forgotten in those vast romances that were the preferred reading of the early modern elite. These Catholic spaces speak in a universal language, but perhaps, as I hope to demonstrate, with a recognizably recusant intonation.

We will see that many of the places and inscriptions that can be identified as recusant bear a double signification. There is an apprehensible degree of encoding: sentiments that appear at first to be nothing more than unexceptionable Scripture quotations can acquire a covert sense, apprehensible to the initiated. Indeed, one of the questions that arises as we begin to think about these Catholic spaces in Reformation Britain is, Why construct them at all? Why not rest content with paper houses, or at most with discreet upper rooms that can function as chapels? Why go to the length (and, very often, the considerable expense) of constructing a painted room or a sculptured or engraved building to declare an illegal allegiance, which structure or decorative scheme can then return upon the owner as evidence in times of particular confessional tension?

Among the answers to that question might be counted the desire to act as a confessor, to refute any possible charge of denial of the faith. There is also a deeper, more complex current (central, I think, to all considerations of the culture of the English Catholics) of an internalized recusant refusal to admit the legitimacy of the new order. Although Tresham and many other recusant builders may have been scrupulous in their loyalty to Queen Elizabeth (or to the more accommodating James) to the point of offering themselves as hostages for the good behavior of their co-religionists, there is no indication that they compromised in any way a belief in their own identity as Catholic Englishmen. On the contrary, they saw themselves as the true English who remained loyal to the old patterns of belief in the face of those new varieties of religion that they perceived as pernicious foreign innovations. Conversely, of course, the Elizabethan establishment was at pains to articulate Catholicism itself as a new religion, born of Tridentine innovations, visibly administered by the new order of the Society of Jesus, and irredeemably tainted by alien associations. (This is in opposition to the Church of England theory that the Anglican settlement is the true inheritor of the primitive church generally and of the church of Aelfrich and Bede in particular.)

I do not know of any instance of a recusant being specifically charged with displaying a defiant iconography, although several were charged with owning treasonable iconographies, and in fact the display of certain images such as the Agnus Dei was specifically illegal. It is a difficulty as yet unreconciled in this subject that while some recusant communities met in upland barns and remote farmhouses, there were still elite recusants like the Northamptonshire Treshams, the Oxfordshire Stonors, and the Cumbrian Hudlestons who went to lengths to proclaim their allegiance in stone, physically and immediately identifying their houses as Catholic. Local conditions varied: recusants certainly composed a powerful elite bloc in Lancashire and Herefordshire. Not all Protestant neighbors were inevitably hostile; indeed, evidence is beginning to emerge that in many parts of England (and possibly in northeastern Scotland) old class loyalties proved in practice stronger than new confessional loyalties. Despite this, we should be constantly aware of the risk and deliberation that attends the encoding of proscribed religious belief in carving or inscription.

Inevitably, these considerations lead to others that will probably attend all further deliberations on this subject: considerations of the degree to which recusant culture is an apologetic culture that is, however, in the modern sense, unapologetic. Even more importantly, we must begin to think about how recusant culture concerns itself with questions of Englishness or Scottishness, how it confronts questions of precedent and heritage, how it disputes with the "New Religion" for what we might call the ownership of history. There can be little doubt that the statement made by many of the rooms and buildings discussed here is that adherence to the Roman Church is adherence also to the ancient and rooted church of the British Isles.

British Catholic Spaces on the Continent

I will now consider two British Catholic spaces that can be said to set forth symbolically a recusant perception of the new order in Britain. Inevitably, these frankly oppositional schemes are found in continental Europe in the two exiled Catholic colleges of Rome and Valladolid. They make statements that could not be made so confrontationally in even the most remote regions of Catholic Lancashire or Aberdeenshire. The scheme of decoration of the chapel of the Venerable English College in Rome was certainly available to English recusants in engraved form in the *Ecclesiae Anglicanae trophaea* of 1582, but what is most important is to remember the degree to which the symbolic language of both these exiled Catholic spaces formed the minds of generations of mission priests and also thereby influenced the attitudes expressed by the Catholic laity living under penalty in Britain, although the expression of Catholic loyalties in Britain was of necessity discreet or encoded.

Both of these heavily symbolic chapels (and the enacted ceremonial that attended them in the early modern period) assert a startling reversal of the status quo as it was officially perceived in Britain and vehemently contradict Protestant nationalist propaganda. The schemes of decoration of both chapels assert that the true England is itself in exile and that the Venerable English College at Rome and the College of St. Alban at Valladolid are the sites of authenticity, the cells, the seedbeds (or literally "seminaries") out of which true Englishness may be restored to England itself. For the time of exile, for the time of the Schism, England is articulated as a partial, diminished place, violent, lost, reduced, untrue to itself. It is no accident that Valladolid and other exiled religious houses commissioned paintings of the ancient sovereigns of England, asserting their continuity with ancient English tradition, and that the Valladolid library contains to this day Protestant histories with manuscript erasures and refutations.[4]

If we begin with the chapel of the Venerable English College, we find a powerful articulation of the violent lostness of Schismatic England: before the rebuilding of the chapel in the nineteenth century, the walls were painted with scenes of all the martyrdoms for the Christian religion in England, from St. Alban to the first Henrician martyrs. The rebuilding exiled these images of carnage to the upper gallery, thus diluting their message that England had grown untrue to itself and become a place from which truth was exiled with only destruction remaining. The altarpiece of the chapel, painted by Durante Alberti and placed there in 1580, is a complex spatial and pictorial expression of the nature of the exiled recusant project and of the purpose of the English mission (fig. 1). The Trinity are above in the heavens, and Christ's blood falls onto the dim map of England, below which an angel holds up the banderole with the fine defiant motto "I come to set the world on fire." Immediately below the figure of Christ is a gateway with the figures of St. Edmund and St. Thomas à Becket flanking it. Angels hold the martyrs' palms over their heads, and on the ground at their feet lie the disregarded attributes of royal or ecclesiastical dignity. Behind them a gateway with a landscape beyond occupies the center of the composition, directly below the figure of Christ, proximate to the banderole and the map of England. It is the Flaminian gate, the

Fig. 1. Durante Alberti, "The Martyrs' Picture," Venerable English College, Rome. From *Ecclesiae Anglicanae trophaea*, 1582. Courtesy of Ohio State University Library, Rare Book Room.

beginning of the road north from Rome, the road back to England and the martyrdom that awaits on the English mission. The martyrs of England point the way (the just king and the archbishop who defied the unjust king), and the blood of those who stand before the picture as students may in time be unified with the blood of Christ and the depictions on the walls around them of all the blood shed in England for the faith. Whenever news came to Rome that a former student had died a martyr in England, the college gathered before the picture to sing a Te Deum. Mentally, another image was added to the carnage on the walls, and symbolically blood from more English veins mingled with the blood in the Martyrs' Picture.

Originally the High Altar at Valladolid was also flanked with the statues of the martyred King Edmund and Archbishop Thomas, with the representation of the proto-martyr of England, Alban, in the middle. But historical circumstance presented the new College at Valladolid with a ready-made emblem of the wounds that history had inflicted on the church and on England itself. In the course of the Earl of Essex's abortive 1596 expedition against Spain, his troops had sacked a church at Cadiz and mutilated the statue of the Virgin and Child. This image, in its mutilated state under the name of *Nuestra Señora Vulnerata,* was transported to Valladolid and installed with great ceremony in the College Chapel in 1601 in the presence of the queen of Spain (fig. 2). In this context, the Vulnerata becomes the image of England self-wounded by the ignorance and blindness of her children, and the image interweaves with two familiar tropes attaching to Our Lady: the medieval idea that England is her dowry and the ideas of exile and return at the end of the Salve Regina ("Tuos miscricordes oculos ad nos converte, Ut Jesum fructum benedictum ventris tui nobis post hoc exilium ostende"). It is England that is in exile from its true place. England is no homeland but a barbarous place. This is all enacted in the image itself in which the Christ Child has been destroyed (a world with no Incarnation, therefore with no hope), and the gashes on the sacred image are a reflection of the state of those who desecrated the image in the first place. This interpretation is kept constantly before the viewer by the sequence of later seventeenth-century paintings around the dome of the chapel that show the history of the image, with a final panel of the image being adored by the Spanish royal family.

Complex ideas of fall and exile are prominent in the ceremonial that accompanied the installation of the image in 1601: the emblems displayed included the palm as an emblem of resilience and ultimate victory and Our Lady Star of the Sea as a beacon guiding the ship of the church back to England. In the English-language oration for the Vulnerata, the opposition is made very clear:

> Enter O triumphant queene of martyrs enter into this your college as into a fertill soyle of martyrdome, that by your coming the number of those victorious martyrs may daily encrease. Remayne with us, most gratious

Fig. 2. St. Alban's College chapel, Valladolid, "La Vulnerata." Photo by author.

> lady, in this our solitude and tyme of banishment until the clouds of heresy be dispenced and the desryed day appear. That day I meane when our England shall be lightened again and renewed againe with the true sonne of the catholicke religione and you returning tryumphant and victorious with us to take possession of your ancient dowry.[5]

These two chapels (with their flaunting, defiant iconographies) are different in scale and in kind from the allusive and secretive declarations of allegiance inscribed, painted, sewn, or carved in England. But the version of history and truth that they propound formed the generations of missionary priests and, as a consequence, the self-perception of the recusant Catholics to whom they ministered upon return to Britain.

Spatial Symbolism in Counter-Reformation Devotion

Before we turn to the consideration of those Catholic spaces that survive in England and Scotland, we must explore, however briefly, the rich tradition of thinking about symbolic space that is set forth in Counter-Reformation devotional manuals. This is again to consider in full ways of thinking and representing that are mostly hinted or encoded in recusant spaces in Britain.

A detailed interior garden is set forth in the Marian hortulan meditations, the *Partheneia Sacra*, published by the English Jesuit Henry Hawkins in 1633.[6] This is a complex, transitional book. Hawkins's readings of objects perform a complex act of balance between traditions: of crypto-Ignatian meditation, *ars memorativa*, and emblematics, as well as medieval allegory. Hawkins's mental garden is constructed in an imagined space that alters as the devout reader progresses through the book. Initially it is offered by Hawkins in small, broken-down sections, emblem by emblem, but at the very end he simply sets devout souls free to ramble at their own speed in the interior garden that has been constructed under his direction as if it were a place now susceptible of infinite deepening, infinite recessions of new meaning, a place capable of containing everything that the devout mind can feel.

The engraved frontispiece of the book suggests the degree to which Hawkins is working from an established tradition: the enclosed garden with its roses and lilies is a constant in the tradition that applies the praises of the Song of Songs to the praise of Our Lady: the house of gold and the tower of ivory of the Litany of Loreto, the palm and olive that are figures in Ecclesiasticus for the Holy Wisdom. It is not hard to discern the essential Edenic nature of the circular walled garden depicted here. What is fascinating in the *Partheneia Sacra*, however, is the use Hawkins makes of these garden elements.

Readers are invited to participate in the progressive interior imagination of the garden, so that by the end of each section they are ready to possess, as their own, the closing address, adding their voices and their assent to the words of the author. Hawkins describes a lavish and contemporary garden layout rather than the simple *hortus conclusus* pictured in the frontispiece. The imaginary garden is Baroque both in the way in which it is apprehended and in its collection of fashionable bulbous plants and florists' flowers, canals and fountains. It becomes clear that we are contemplating indeed a Baroque garden on a vast scale, perhaps not unlike the semisacred Paradise garden of Valsanzibio in the Veneto. For the meditating reader, this garden is internalized, and at the same time a habit is formed of reading external gardens in terms of sacred symbolism.

This latter element is all-important in the work of Louis Richeome, S.J., particularly in his *Peinture spirituelle* of 1611, which deals with the buildings and gardens of the Jesuit house of Sant Andrea al Quirinale in Rome. The same perceptions and allegorizations are applied, but, crucially, they are applied to a real and known garden.[7] The book consists of an interpreted walk through various parts of the Jesuit House for Novices on the Quirinal, continually demonstrating how everything that meets the eye in its progression through a real building and garden can be allegorized in a spiritual sense, from the obelisks in the gardens to the sick brothers and novices in the infirmary. To Richeome every visible thing has a spiritual resonance.

He is patently aware of all Renaissance modes of symbolic discourse: he was himself an emblematist and well aware of the debate on hieroglyphics, on the history of speaking pictures. It is clear also that he was aware of the kinds of medieval traditions of interpretation to which Hawkins also had access. All these traditions, as well as allegorical traditions of reading Scripture, combine to give him the reservoir of material with which he can interpret the material world.

One brief example, from the last book that deals with the gardens, must suffice. The fountains of the lower garden are read as symbols of the humility and usefulness of water; then the weeping tree, the *arbre triste* of Goa (presumably sent back to Rome by the established Jesuit mission there), is read as a symbol of the true Christian in penitence, in that it casts its night-born flowers at the moment when the sun rises. Thus it represents the triumph of penitence in the religious soul. To summarize, these two works suggest that symbolic layouts, most specifically gardens, can bear a weight of devotional meaning or can be constructed within the mind to function as a place of meditation. The relation between these interior places and the realized structures that form my central subject is a rich one.

Recusant Spaces in England and Scotland

We must begin by recognizing that many of the rooms that may have articulated a recusant positioning of self were evanescent. The most common form of early modern wall decoration in England was the painted-canvas hanging. Of these once-ubiquitous artifacts only a handful remain. Another way of making a temporary room was with woven or appliqué textile hangings, a sphere particularly open to women, as in the Hardwick "black tapestries" that Elizabeth, Countess of Shrewsbury, the Protestant jailer of Mary Queen of Scots, produced in her household in the mid-sixteenth century. If these were hung as the Hardwick inventories record, all in one room, a symbolic space would be produced that was devoted to the contemplation of women as figures of virtue and authority.[8]

The Catholic and oppositional content of the needleworks of Mary Queen of Scots is uncontestable: if we consider the celebrated hanging, now at Oxburgh Hall in Norfolk, posthumously assembled from the small emblematic panels that she worked on during her long imprisonment, it is not hard to identify some images intended to convey a very clear message about Mary's perception of her status and fortunes. We have to begin by focusing on the center square, which shows a hand with a pruning knife and the motto *Virescit vulnere virtus* (Virtue grows strong by being wounded). The application of this is fairly clear—Mary's adversities are but rendering her stronger, spiritually if not materially. There are other implications in the device—that the tree cut back by God is to be favored by God in eternity if not in this world. But she is also rendered stronger, more vigorous, more ready to assume command, if providence should direct it. The tree that is pruned is also fruitful—I don't think the force of that would be lost on anyone in England considering the succession to the throne after Elizabeth.

Interest in the content of Mary Stuart's embroideries survived her death. A French-language inventory of the emblems on her bed curtains, dating probably from 1587, survives in a manuscript in the Public Record Office, Kew.[9] William Fowler, the (Protestant) poet and secretary to the (Catholic) Queen Anne, preserved two versions of the devices on the state bed after it had been transported to Edinburgh.[10] In the early seventeenth century the same curtains were described in a letter from Drummond of Hawthornden to Ben Jonson, thus implying that the matter was still of interest, as we may assume it would be to the (intermittently) Catholic Jonson, himself a great user of "hierogyphicks" and the personifications of Cesare Ripa in his court masques and entertainments.[11] If Drummond's description is accurate, there were on this bed a tissue of emblems (or, strictly, *imprese*), many derived from Claude Paradin's *Devices heroiques* of 1557, all stating the same self-perception: that Mary would triumph in adversity, that God had a care for her, that Elizabeth was sterile (one emblem shows a woman with a javelin as opposed to one with a cornucopia) whereas she herself was fruitful.

Another kind of temporary Catholic space is central to the experience of oppositional recusancy: temporary inscriptions or decorations on the walls of prison cells. These often chose the same texts from the Vulgate that were used in recusant inscriptions in other contexts. Inscribing these words on prison walls in one sense made the cell a sacred space, expressing the commonplace that no regime, however coercive, can control the mind. It also made the cell a potentially welcoming place for subsequent Catholic prisoners. The inscription made by S. Philip Howard in his cell in the Tower of London and dated June 22, 1584, is typical: "Quanto plus afflictionis pro Christo in hoc saeculo tanto plus gloria cum Christo in futuro. . . . In memoria aeterna erit justus." (The more suffering for Christ in this life, the more glory with Christ in the future. . . . The righteous shall be held in everlasting remembrance.)[12] A more spatial arrangement of the cell graffiti was made by the martyr Henry Walpole in his cell in the Tower. As reported by a subsequent prisoner, Fr. John Gerard:

> I discovered his little oratory where there had been a narrow window. . . . [T]here on either side he had chalked the names of all the orders of Angels. At the top, above the Cherubim and Seraphim, was the name of Mary, Mother of God; and then above it the name of Jesus; above that again the name of God written in Latin, Greek and Hebrew characters.

> It was a great comfort to me to find myself in a place sanctified by this great and holy martyr.[13]

A similar arrangement of occluded reference was devised for his place of imprisonment by the recusant squire Sir Thomas Tresham (1545–1605). He was reconciled to Catholicism in 1580 by the Jesuit missionary Robert Parsons (hence, I suspect, the prominent Jesuit badge on his confession of faith in stone, the Rushton Triangular Lodge), and thereafter he lived the harried life of a recusant member of the elite, subject to fines and expropriations of his property for as long as he refused to conform to the religion of the state. Although unswerving in his loyalty to Elizabeth, he was equally inflexible in his religious opinions. Thus, although he had periods at liberty at his houses in Northamptonshire, in the course of which he occupied himself in building his four symbolic buildings and rebuilding Rushton Hall to include an oppositionally Catholic oratory, he spent much of his adult life in imprisonment of various degrees of stringency. He died in 1605, leaving his last building, Lyveden New Build, unfinished, and his family declined thereafter, partly through the involvement of his son Francis on the margins of the Gunpowder Plot of that year.

No trace remains of the scheme of decoration that he undertook in his place of detainment at Ely in 1596–97, which involved the participation of a professional painter. Sir Thomas knew that his Catholic fellow prisoners had painted crucifixes in their rooms and that these had been washed out by their Protestant jailers. So he resolved on a numerological and emblematic scheme of great obscurity and complexity involving initial letters, monograms, and emblems "in laud of the Blessed Mother of God."[14] Among these symbolic representations, he included the device of the hen with her chickens, a common enough allegorical representation of the church as guardian of the faithful, but colored three of the chickens red and the rest white so that the casual observer might mistake them for a representation of Tresham's three male and nine female children.

A similar ambiguity of signification attends Tresham's most celebrated work, the Triangular Lodge at Rushton in Northamptonshire, which he began in the appropriately triune year of 1593, and for which a detailed correspondence with his mason survives (fig. 3). In this case there is a suggestion that the problem I raised at the beginning of this essay as to the dangers of making a confession of a proscribed faith in lasting stone may have been resolved

Fig. 3. Triangular Lodge, Rushton, Northamptonshire, England. Photo by author.

by employment of a Catholic mason for the fine, more symbolically charged carving. This structure employs every variation of three in dimension, symbol, and numerology to make its essential point: the praise of the Trinity is achieved through the recollection of the pivotal event in human history (the Crucifixion) through the sacrifice of the Mass. In this sense it is an action of personal location: it is a building that writes Tresham himself into this history of salvation, as he would have done whenever he was able to hear Mass by crossing himself in the name of the Trinity at the beginning and end of the liturgy.

Tresham's Triangular Lodge is one of the most remarkable buildings in England. It is unequivocally oppositional, in the deepest sense recusant. Its positioning is matter for further thought. It is placed almost invisibly on an obscure lane behind Tresham's house at Rushton. Regardless of convenience or practicality, it is in the shape of an equilateral triangle: the three sides stand for the Trinity, and each is thirty-three feet, three inches long.[15] Numerologies abound in the inscriptions: 1580 (the year of Tresham's conversion) and other, less explicable numbers, 3509, 3898. A continuous inscription on the frieze above the upper story is of thirty-three letters on each side. Each face of the lodge is dedicated to a different person of the Trinity by this frieze inscription.

For the Father the inscription on the southeast side reads, *Aperiatur terra et germinet salvatorem* (Let the earth open and bring forth a Savior [Isa. 35:8]); the north face, which is nearest to the little road that runs along the park wall, is dedicated to the Son in the apparently innocuous and rhetorical *Quis separabit nos a charitate Christi* (Who will separate us from the love of Christ? [Rom. 8:35]). But this becomes a specific protest at the moment when one observes that the doorway is in the shape of a keyhole: "Outside the Church of Peter there is no salvation." The southwest side is dedicated to the Holy Spirit in the words *Consideravi opera tua domine et expavi* (I have seen your works, O Lord, and been afraid [apparently adapting Ecclus. 7:14]). The gables are decorated with eucharistic emblems, the seven-branched candelabrum, the seven eyes of God, the pelican. The central chimney, apparently unsupported, alludes to the miraculous nature of the Mass, and its shaft has symbols of the Mass, IHS, the Lamb and cross, and the chalice.

Tresham's last building is the Garden Lodge at Lyveden near Oundle, generally known as Lyveden New Build. Progressing from the Triangular Lodge, its scheme is worked out on a base of fours and fives. The lodge is in the form of a Greek cross. There is a metope frieze above the ground floor and a frieze above the upper floor; the lower frieze contains a series of emblems of Catholic significance, referring particularly to the Passion and the Mater Dolorosa, presented as "hieroglyphic" as they were understood at the time, symbols of the passion of Christ between the metopes of the frieze, while the upper frieze matches these images with words: *Iesus mundi Salus—Gaude Mater Virgo Maria—Verbum autem Crucis pereuntibus quidem Stultitia est* [1 Cor. 1:18]—*Iesus, Beatus Venter qui te portavit—Maria Virgo Sponsa innupta—T. eam. alt.—Benedixit te Deus in aeternum Maria—Mihi autem absit gloriari nisi in Cruce Domini XP.* Most of these are straightforward scriptural quotations. The Corinthians passage develops a consciously recusant significance if the *second* half of the verse is brought into play: "For the preaching of the cross is to them that perish foolishness; but unto us which are saved it is the power of God." The most problematic of these inscriptions is characteristically the one in which Tresham inscribes himself, *T. eam alt.* We must remember that Tresham's oratory at Rushton Hall shows crucifixion on a Tau cross and plays with the T in its inscription. In this inscription at Lyveden, Tresham is mediating himself into the sacred history. T is therefore both the cross and Tresham. Given that most of the reference in this frieze at Lyveden is to the Virgin, *eam* presumably refers to her, so I would be happiest with reading *alt* as a verb—*altat,* from *altare*—so that the sense would be "Tresham and/or the cross exalts Her." On the Triangular Lodge is the punning inscription *Tres testimoniam dant* (There are three who bear witness / "Tres" bears witness). (Tresham signed himself "your Tres" in letters to his wife.) Tresham placed himself within the complex Trinitarian and eucharistic scheme of salvation. The master of the inscribed house has also inscribed himself at Lyveden into the system of symbolic inscriptions.

The work of the Packington family at Harvington Hall, Worcestershire, consists of a series of decorated rooms, from perhaps 1560–75, finely executed but consisting only of foliage, grotesque work, and arabesques. However, the room known as the large chapel has pomegranates, vines, and lilies among the foliage decorations on its walls, quietly eucharistic, quietly Marian. The exception to this reticence is the startling decoration of the "Little Chapel," most likely painted in 1600, at which time the house was certainly in recusant hands. The limewashed walls are painted with vast, stylized drops of blood and water forming vertical chains. The effect is haunting and extraordinary;

the reminiscence of the world of the Martyrs' Picture and the chapel of the English College at Rome is palpable.

At Norbury Manor in Derbyshire, there exists a room with scriptural quotations written in ink directly onto the oak paneling. The inscriptions are thought to be the work of Sir Anthony Fitzherbert and to date from about 1612.[16] The whole paneled room has inscriptions on every part, all quotations from the Vulgate, rendering the room a *locus meditationis* not unlike what Michel de Montaigne constructed for himself in his tower-study at the Chateau de Montaigne, with its beams inscribed with sober injunctions to virtue and endurance. Although most of the Norbury sententiae are unexceptional biblical quotations, several of them have a distinctly oppositional undertone. Near the door is written *Qui non intrat per ostium in ovile ovium . . . ille est fur et latro* (Whoever does not enter the sheepfold by the door is a thief and robber [John 10:1]). The clergy of the new church who do not enter through the true portal of the Catholic Church are thieves who betray the flock of God. On the right side of the fireplace is *Radix enim omnium malorum est cupiditas, quam quidam appetentes erraverunt a fide et inseruerunt se doloribus multis* (For the love of money is the root of all evil: those who covet it err from the faith and pierce themselves through with many arrows [1 Tim. 6:10]). In context this would seem to be a sentence of reproof to those (including Sir Anthony's troubled elder brother) who have conformed to the new dispensation. In a similar vein, the inscription on the south wall, *Nolite omni spiritui credere sed probate spiritus ex Deo sint* (Believe not every spirit but try the spirits whether they are of God [1 John 4:1]), has a double signification in an era where both sides of the conflict laid claim to truth in religion. By the door, near the drawing of the skull, are two sentences of consolation in present misfortune and of hope for a future state, not unlike the prison inscription of St. Philip Howard: "For here we have no continuing city, but we seek one to come" (Heb. 13:14) and "And the [celestial] city had no need of the sun, neither of the moon to shine in it, for the glory of God did lighten it and its light is the Lamb" (Rev. 21:23). Again we have an articulated space that is in some degree an action of positioning on the part of its owner and also a site full of double significations that reveal their full pattern only to the instructed reader.

As might be expected, several old houses in the intensely recusant county of Lancashire bear inscriptions of Catholic allegiance: among these is Samlesbury Hall, which belonged to the Southworth family from circa 1330 until 1679.[17] There the South Range upper oriels with their carved windowsills may originate in the building campaign of 1545; one has the sacred monogram IHS, and this marks the place where the chapel was originally sited. The significant point for our purpose here is that the family left this and other carvings in place, and perhaps copied them in later building campaigns, in the spirit of Catholic antiquarianism that asserted the antiquity and continuity of Catholicism as opposed to Protestant innovation.

A more complex system of signification attends the beautiful and remote farmhouse building at Hesketh End, off Judd Holmes Lane, near Chipping, in an area intensely Catholic to this day.[18] Inside the house itself (in the front first-floor room of the cross-wing) and built into the nineteenth-century farm steadings are stones inscribed with the sacred monogram and crosses. These suggest strongly that the house was recusant Catholic, and there is an oral tradition attaching to it locally as a Mass-house. There is also an inscribed date stone now built into the farm buildings: "Alstun hath inherited here IB 18 yer." The sacred monogram surmounts the cut-stone attic window. The really strange element at Hesketh End is a frieze of raised-sunk lettering two lines high, beginning on the cross-wing and continuing onto the return wall of the main wing, protected by a drip-stone. This is done with such care and expense (raised-sunk is inevitably more expensive than V-cut lettering) and protected so carefully that it was obviously of great importance to its deviser. There is an inscription reading "Richarde Alstun 53" over a blocked window. Pevsner gives the date for the major refitting (or rebuild) that produced the long inscription with its series of dates as 1582; the project was undertaken by Robert Alston, the son of the Richard commemorated in the 1553 inscription. There is also reference to a Richard Junior, a child aged five, in the main inscription. The main inscription is a complex locating of the Alstons, father and son, in English and religious history at the time of the rebuilding of the house. Robert Alston was twenty-five, Richard Junior was five; it was 5,553 years from the creation of the world and 524 from the Norman Conquest; it was the twenty-fifth year of Elizabeth's reign; Brutus founded London in 1108 BC; Caesar conquered England in 58 BC; the Saxons conquered England in 447 (thereafter "Episcopat IB"); the Danes conquered England in 1018; England was divided into shires or counties (no date given); the Battle of Flodden Field took place in 1513; England received the Faith in AD 179.

What does all this mean? It would be easy to dismiss it as no more than the idle jottings on the flyleaf of the history textbook were it not clear that considerable expense had been incurred in putting the chronology into a form in which it could survive the centuries. I would suggest that what is important here is an *omission* that would have struck any contemporary immediately. There is no mention of the Reformation, none of Henry VIII. All other significant dates, as they might have been understood in 1582, are present, from the foundation of civilization in Britain through the invasions to the Battle of Flodden Field, which may be thought of as victory over the most recent threat to English sovereignty. Elizabeth is unequivocally recognized as sovereign, as she was by the vast majority of English Catholics: there is none of the equivocal form of words found elsewhere among supporters of the claims of Mary Stuart. So what we have here is the Alston family locating themselves as loyal Catholics, as inheritors of the history of England, as true Englishmen ignoring the religious innovations of their time.[19] The omission is crucial; it bears the meaning of the inscription.

Alexander Seton, the church papist chancellor of Scotland through its most rabidly Calvinist era, left a discreet recusant building in Pinkie House, Mussleburgh, East Lothian.[20] Seton's 1613 painted gallery has a trompe l'oeil cupola and a series of feigned paintings representing emblem subjects mostly from the *Emblemata Horatiana* of Otto van Veen (Antwerp, 1607). There is a very good case for reading the iconography as a description of the mental world of a church papist. It continually stresses the need for modesty, caution, and prudence. There is no doubt of Seton's skill in emblematics: he had been educated by the Jesuits in Rome. He was described after his death as "a great humanist in prose and in poecie, Greek and Latine, well versed in the mathematicks and [having] great skill in architecture and herauldrie."[21]

In the case of Seton we are dealing with a prominent officer of state with a high public profile who had more than once been required to offer public professions of his Reformed faith by attending Presbyterian acts of worship as a condition of continuing to hold public office. This meant that any covert signs of his real doctrinal position would need to be oblique. Nevertheless, the inscriptions and emblems that he displayed around 1617 in this *villa suburbana* at Pinkie House contain one or two curious allusions. One of the more notable of these is in the monumental inscription originally carved on the house itself, proclaiming that Seton built his house as a "suburbana aedificia" that has nothing to do with warfare but is dedicated to the "decent pleasures of heart and mind." There is nothing controversial in this neo-Stoic modesty, but the inscription ends with a very curious prayer—invariably left unquoted by modern commentators who have cited it: *Deo optimo Maximo rerum omnium Authori Largitori Conservatori Iehovae Statori cujus nutu [?] beneficioque stant omnia certa Honor Omnis gloria Eulogia Kai Eucharistica* (To the greatest and best God, creator, dispenser and protector of all things, Jehovah Stator, whose will and benefit ensure us in the possession of all gifts, honor and glory, praise and thanks). Given its very curious appellations of the deity—Jehovah Stator is Livy's epithet for Jupiter as protector—it is very difficult to see what signals such a lapidary inscription would be sending to the informed reader. We have no independent witness as to how a fellow Catholic at this period would have interpreted those signals. Its syncretic tendency to hide any Catholic reference beneath a veil of classical allusion is of a piece, however, with the neo-Stoic emphasis that Michael Bath has argued as a doctrinally neutral maneuver motivating the emblems from Otto Vaenius and other sources that Seton painted in his long gallery.[22] The gallery itself offers one of the most consistent attempts in Scotland to reproduce an Italian painted room of the high Renaissance: each of the emblems painted in feigned frames, apparently hanging from the fictive architecture of the ceiling, is accompanied by a meditation in a fictive inscription tablet underneath. Thus the long room offers a complex set of points for meditation on the conduct of a public life amidst spiritual and temporal difficulties.[23]

We probably find better evidence of the way similar emblems were interpreted as communicating Catholic faith, not in Alexander Seton's emblematic decoration, but in the emblems associated with similar decorative objects such as the embroideries executed by Mary Queen of Scots, to which I referred earlier. The emblematic centerpiece to the Oxburgh "Marian Hanging," with its motto *Virescit vulnere virtus,* was cited as evidence of treason at the trial of the Duke of Norfolk. Emblems were also cited as evidence in other trials, including that of St. Philip Howard, Earl of Arundel, whose prison inscription I mentioned above.[24]

Further north in Scotland, "Provost Skene's House" in Guestrow, Aberdeen, contains a painted gallery (or, more likely, chapel) dating from the 1630s (fig. 4). Very little is known of the man, Matthew Lumsden, who commissioned this painted work on the top floor of an older house, although Michael Bath's most recent work adduces almost certain recusant Catholic associations: Lumsden fought against Charles I in the 1639 "Bishops' War," which would normally be read as a sign of at least firm Protestant convictions, but numerous members of his family were at various times in the midcentury prosecuted and imprisoned for hearing Mass. The painted scheme covers the

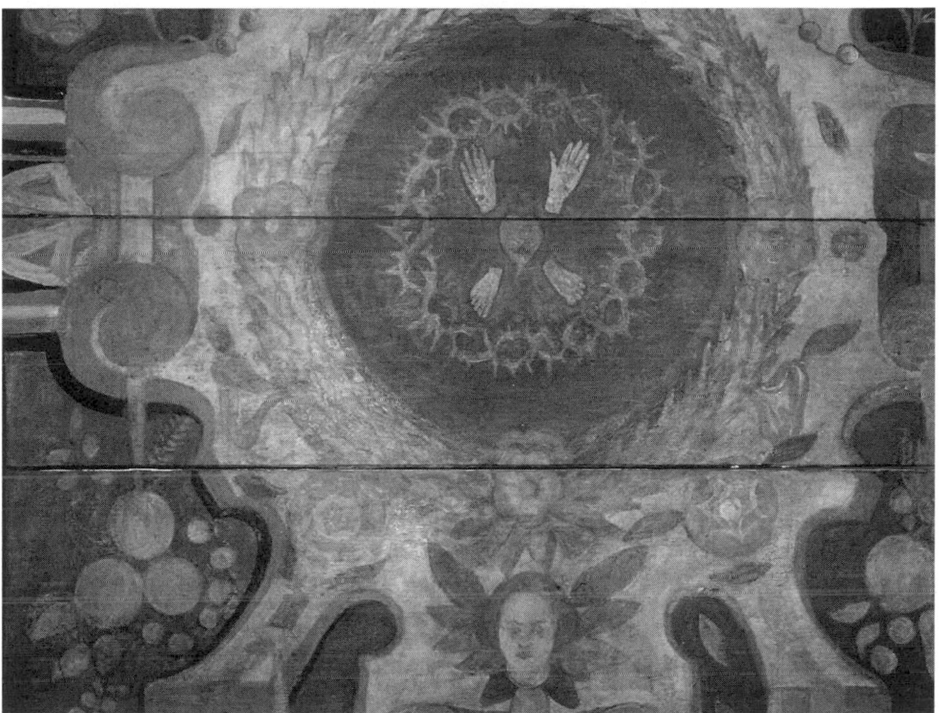

Fig. 4. Provost Skene's House, Aberdeen, Scotland, painted ceiling. Photo by author.

whole of the coved ceiling. The background is of a starry sky, seen behind strong architectural framing that surrounds roundels with badges and panels with biblical (or Rosary) scenes. Two of the roundels have the Jesuit IHS and the Five Wounds (heart at center, hands and feet radiant, crown of thorns encircling), the elements of the badge of the Pilgrimage of Grace, although arranged differently in this case. These two badges would seem too "Catholic" even for the most relaxed Aberdonian Lutheran, and it is certainly established by papers in the Jesuit archives in Rome that there was a Jesuit presence in Aberdeen almost throughout the penal times. The scenes do not now make a narrative (several are damaged), but Annunciation, Crucifixion, and Resurrection survive in the center of the ceiling. The use and history of the room are unknown, and the surrounding house was subsequently divided into tenements and the painted work obscured.[25]

It should be added briefly that two other Scottish seventeenth-century places would seem to have borne painted imagery of a distinctly Catholic tendency. The merchant's house in Burntisland, Fife (an otherwise notably Protestant town, with strong Dutch connections and a purpose-built, centrally planned church designed for preaching only), subsequently identified as "Mary Somerville's House," had a room with Sybils, an Agnus Dei, and a picture of Our Lady, but the condition of the painted wood is now too poor to make any further conjecture as to an original scheme.[26] Another at least crypto-Catholic scheme is at Largs in Ayrshire, where Sir Robert Montgomerie of Skelmorlie built a burial aisle, as was the Scottish custom, for himself and his family. His was begun to contain the body of the wife who had predeceased him (local legend has her killed in a feuding raid, and indeed her husband had spent the years of his youth prosecuting a notably untidy feud with the neighboring Cunninghams, but the inscription on her tomb implies the far more probable death in childbirth), and he specifically records on his own coffin-plate that he used to meditate by her coffin. The vault of the Skelmorlie Aisle (finished in the inauspicious Covenanting year of 1638) has an unexceptional northern late Renaissance mixture of images: emblems of the twelve tribes of Israel, quotations from the (Geneva) Bible, images of the seasons and of Old Testament incidents, personifications of the virtues. But there is also a thoroughly mysterious image of a female figure on a seashore, holding a flaming heart in a chalice, as though (and this is my own preliminary conjecture) representing religion fleeing abroad from the Reformers. The town in the background looks like St. Andrews, once the seat of the primate of Scotland. Very much more investigation (and probably archival luck) will be required before this complex scheme can be fully explained.[27]

At the fortified house of Hutton John in Cumbria, the recusant Andrew Hudleston added a stylistically retrograde range to an existing tower-house in 1662. The praeterite style may be conscious, a claiming of continuity with the past, the kind of Catholic antiquarianism known in the neighboring county of Lancashire. Hudleston's top-floor chapel and priest's quarters were swept away in remodelings undertaken by later, Protestant Hudlestons, but the exterior remains much as it was in the 1660s. There are windows in the shape of hearts at ground-floor level and on the top floor. Nicolaus Pevsner emphasizes that these are quite out of the ordinary and clearly symbolic and Catholic in a way that he connects directly to Sir Thomas Tresham's use of symbols on his buildings.[28] The chapel window is marked plainly by a heart-window surmounted by a cross and the inscription *In hoc signo vinces* (Under this banner / by this sign, you will conquer) (fig. 5).

Fig. 5. Hutton John, Cumbria, England, cross and inscription on gable. Photo by author.

The historical reference is to the vision of the first Christian emperor, Constantine, before the battle of the Miluvian Bridge. In his dream the cross is the banner under which he will obtain victory. Constantine was an emperor whose place of birth was claimed to have been northern England. (Constantine's vision of the cross is one of the scenes that was painted on the walls of the chapel of the Venerable English College in Rome and engraved in the *Ecclesiae Anglicanae trophaea* of 1582.) There is a more local application of the inscription, again an assertion of the antiquity of the Roman Church in England: the English saint-king St. Oswald was believed to have had a similar vision before the Cumbrian battle of Heavenfield. Andrew Hudleston's inscription is not only promising eventual victory and alluding to the heart-oriented Catholic devotional texts of the seventeenth century but also staking a claim to history by referring back to the first Christian emperor, to the early Christian kings of Britain (we must remember that there are imaginary portraits of these kings at St. Alban's College, Valladolid),[29] and to Catholic continuity ever since. It is quite likely that Hudleston is also alluding to the recently restored Charles II, who was sheltered as a fugitive at the end of the civil war by another branch of the Hudleston family, and it is not impossible that he is covertly referring to the rumors that Charles had already, however secretly, embraced Catholicism. Hutton John is not far removed geographically from the nearest recusant magnate at Greystoke, and there is other evidence of Catholic allegiance in this part of Cumberland.[30]

This would certainly be the case on the border of Yorkshire and Lancashire, in relatively remote country, near the present-day Stonyhurst College, where significant recusant monuments were added to the late-sixteenth-century Shireburne (or Sherburne) chapel on the north side of the (Anglican) Church of All Hallows at Mitton, West Yorkshire. These monuments, which commemorate members of the Shireburne family who died in 1667, 1689, and 1693, were all commissioned by Isabel Shireburne in the 1690s, payment being made to the sculptor William Stanton in 1699.[31] These are the last monuments in England (before the Gothic revival) to have recumbent effigies, with the legs of the male figures crossed like fourteenth-century knights. Again, there is a clear sense of a specifically recusant approach to time and change, another refusal of assent to the innovating present, an absolutely conscious imitation of the forms of the monuments to medieval Shireburns elsewhere in the chapel. As in the example that will follow, and as in the omissions from the chronology in the frieze at Hesketh End, the implicit refusal to accept innovation, the whole package of the state church with the new men who enforced attendance at it, or to recognize the legitimacy of enactments following the Henrician schism seems to be a pattern in northwestern recusant inscriptions and artifacts.

The last example from the seventeenth century demonstrates this in a charmingly simple way. It is of interest also in embodying a Latin distich presumably authored by a woman. On the wall of Aldcliffe Hall by Lancaster (now demolished), two unmarried sisters of the Dalton family placed the following defiant inscription that survives today in the Lancaster Museum: *Catholicae Virgines sumus / Mutare vel tempore spernimus, Ano Dni 1674* (We are Catholic virgins and scorn to change with the times),[32] thus neatly defining the allegiance of their house and also claiming a stake in that "struggle for history" to which I referred earlier.

In summary, Tresham's recusant spaces and their successors are encoded, for all their patent symbolic intentions: they declare their oppositional character only to an instructed (Catholic) observer, whereas they show the uninstructed spectator, at least initially, only a generalized and unexceptional devotion. "Quis separabit nos a charitate Christi?" is the innocent question apparently posed by the outer face of Tresham's Triangular Lodge, to which the answer is returned powerfully in encoded form: "The usurping heretics in power in England."

By way of epilogue, it might be possible to argue that Alexander Pope's first Twickenham grotto (not the refashioned "geological" grotto, which survives in part today)[33] was very much a work deriving from a seventeenth-century tradition of symbolic place, drawing on the Jesuit theorists René Rapin and Athanasius Kircher, and that it might be seen as an echo of the deliberately oppositional Catholic spaces of the previous century. As well as being the most celebrated poet of early Georgian England, Pope was one of Georgian England's most visible Catholic laymen. Despite his friendships with some of the most powerful of his contemporaries, he more than once suffered the minor penalties imposed by the penal laws.[34] His own life was permanently marked by the hasty and enforced sale of his father's house in Windsor Forest to comply with the laws against papists and Jacobites: he sometimes had to leave the (rented) house at Twickenham, which he had made famous with garden and grotto, if the royal court was nearby and thus he, as a papist, closer to the person of the sovereign than the penal laws permitted. The enforced sale of the only land and garden that his family had owned puts Pope's frequent eulogies of the settled man living on inherited land—imitated from the Roman poet Horace's commonplace praise of this as the ideal life—in a bitter, revisionary, recusant relation to his Latin original.[35] Indeed, Pope's *Rape of the Lock* can most sensibly be interpreted as an epic of the proscribed recusants and Jacobites of Hanoverian England, its central rhetorical figure of deflationary bathos a simple and accurate response to the symbolic powerlessness in every part of life to which the recusants of Pope's social circle were condemned by the penal laws: disarmed, debarred from public office, threatened in the succession of their lands and belongings from one generation to the next, fined, harassed, and debarred from official education and the ownership of property.

When we consider Pope's celebrated grotto (fig. 6), we find that it is a place as much retrospective as prospective in its meaning and arrangement. The image that we can see here is of the grotto as it was remodeled in the last few years of Pope's life: that is, as an imitation, however mannered, of the natural arrangement of rocks and minerals within a cave. Even in this naturalistic state, the stonework of the grotto still bears two carved slabs dating from the seventeenth century.[36] These show respectively the crown of thorns and the *Arma Christi,* that arrangement of the Five Wounds that constituted the badge of the last Catholic rising, the Pilgrimage of Grace, of which we saw a version at Provost Skene's house in Aberdeen. The *Arma Christi* are prominent over the entrance to the central corridor that leads into the grotto. These stones seem, at a reasoned guess, to be from the North, and definitely from the recusant North; we can presume that they are remnants from a house associated with the family of Pope's mother. So in this sense the grotto is associated with the Catholic tradition of houses such as Harvington, Stonor, Rushton, and Hutton John. It is also associated with one possibly Catholic, possibly sacred, grotto of the English eighteenth century that (as oral tradition alone maintains) commemorates the site of the finding of the relics of St. Kenelm at Winchcombe in Gloucestershire.

This is unproven. The little grotto is certainly on the site of part of Winchcombe Abbey, and the relics of the boy-saint Kenelm were certainly exhumed from the abbey site, close at hand, where they had been venerated. Another oral tradition says that the relics were placed in the grotto temporarily after being exhumed in the early nineteenth century. At the moment it is very difficult to judge: the available sources, including the entry in the government register of buildings of architectural interest, all appear to derive from the description of the little grotto in Barbara Jones's inventory of follies and grottoes.[37]

Fig. 6. Bleby House, Winchcombe, Gloucestershire, England, exterior of grotto. Photo by author.

This charming little structure is listed as being of very early-eighteenth-century date, antedating the construction of Pope's grotto or of the grottoes of any of his friends. Inside it was clearly originally covered entirely with oyster shells, snail shells, and reflective glass. A private communication suggests that oyster shells set into a panel in a wall were one covert sign of a recusant house, my informant quoting the story as told of Mapledurham.[38] If this is the case, and I have yet to find another source for it, then Pope may have had an awareness of the associations of these shells, although the juxtaposition of oyster and snail shells at Winchcombe might suggest an economical use of the things nearest to hand rather than any encoded reference. In any case the effect of the little grotto at Bleby House must have been enchanting. The grotto, and the elegant house in whose garden it stands, offer a number of puzzles. The house is now entirely Georgian in appearance but is of earlier origins, and a superlative early-seventeenth-century stone loggia (now built into the cellars) certainly suggests that this has been a house of consequence for some time. The story about the association of the little grotto with the relics of St. Kenelm is, at the moment, in the realm of unverified oral tradition, although certainly the garden of Bleby House now occupies a site that was once within the precincts of the Abbey of Winchcombe. The relics of St. Kenelm were certainly found in the former abbey grounds. There is no doubt that there was a recusant cult of St. Kenelm and other British saints, as the naming of the celebrated Kenelm Digby would suggest.

Another name that recurs in recusant circles is that of Winifred, the tutelar of St. Winifred's well in Flintshire, a perpetual site of pilgrimage (indeed another recusant space) throughout the penal times. Alison Shell has also discovered that at least one contemporary of Pope (Thomas Gent of York, a writer of elegant guidebooks) appears to have associated Pope with this recusant pilgrimage site in his *British Piety Display'd* (York, 1742) and implies that Pope encouraged him at an early stage of the composition of his guide to St. Winifred's well.[39]

The state of Pope's grotto as it was for most of his lifetime, and before the naturalistic rearrangement that we see, bore clearer relation to the world of the seventeenth-century virtuoso. Originally spars, shells, fossils, and precious minerals were arranged as in a virtuoso's cabinet, albeit one masquerading as an enchanted cave in a late Baroque romance. We are not far from the world of the Collegio Romano, from the Jesuit Athanasius Kircher's wonderful and prodigious stones. The original grotto reminds us even more of the world of the seventeenth-century Jesuit virtuoso in that it had insets of mirrors to catch reflections from the proximate river, as well as a most Kircherian device, a lens set into the door that transformed the grotto into a camera obscura.

I have paused for a concluding moment on Pope's garden to demonstrate that these recusant spaces do not end with the end of the seventeenth century and that much work remains to be done on the sites of the new generation of Jacobite recusant Catholics. The questions of place, meaning, and meditation that occupy Richeome and Hawkins are no less long-lived than are the influences of the confrontational iconographies of the chapels in Rome and Valladolid. Elements of symbolism and the architectural use of *imprese* and inscriptions to encode the recusant refusal of the innovating state church distinguish the works of Sir Thomas Tresham, Alexander Seton, and the Alston family at Hesketh End. From Catholic loyalist squire to church papist chancellor of Scotland to Catholic Lancashire yeoman, all are united in making their dwellings and rooms discreet expressions of their faith through the use of space, symbol, and inscription.

Notes

1. This little recusant oratory almost certainly relates to the family of John Woodhope, who responded to the interrogation at the Venerable English College in Rome in 1629; see *The Responsa Scholarum of the English College, Rome,* ed. Anthony Kenny (London: Catholic Record Society, 1962–63), 2:407 [no. 696, 1629]:

> Quod nomen meum vereum Iohannes Woodhope sit et patris Nicholaus Woodhope, et matris Elenora et quod natus, educatus et denique vixi in commitatu Herefordiae et in parochia Abye Dore. . . . [D]uobus fratris unus sit homo religiosus alter maximus natu sit crudelissimus haereticus, condotio parentum decem autquindecem libros per annum valeat, homo mediae sortis. Quod secundum Anglicanum morum syntaxi, poesis confuse operam dederim, adeo ut ista studia nam diu absolverim. Quod per totam aetatem in haeresi vixerim exceptis quatros vel quinque annis, in quibus conversus essem ad catholicam religione persuasatione catholicorum quibuscum parentes et sorores catholicam religionem colant.

2. Dom Bede Camm, *Forgotten Shrines; An Account of Some Old Catholic Halls and Families in England, and of Relics and Memorials of the English Martyrs* (St. Louis, MO: B. Herder, 1910), vii. Dom Bede is the first writer to make a substantial collection of descriptions of recusant houses. I should perhaps point out that of all the buildings discussed here, only Norbury Hall is in Camm's book.

3. Erasmus, *Convivium religiosum* (1522), discussed briefly in *The Oxford Companion to Gardens,* ed. Patrick Goode and Michael Lancaster (Oxford: Oxford University Press, 1986), 390. Another interesting example from the early sixteenth century is Gilles Corrozet, *Les blasons domestiques, contenant les decorations d'une maison honneste, et du menage estant en icelle* (Paris: Corrozet, 1539).

4. Much information on Valladolid is in Michael Williams, *St. Alban's College, Valladolid* (New York: St. Martin's Press, 1986); the ceremonial for the Vulnerata is discussed in Alison Shell, *Catholicism, Controversy and the English Literary Imagination, 1558–1660* (Cambridge: Cambridge University Press, 1999), 200–207. Further manuscript evidence for royal receptions at Valladolid is found in Madrid, BNE MS 6001 (visit of Philip II) and BNE MS 2492 (visit of Philip III). In the library of St. Alban's College, Valladolid, there is a copy of Camden's *Annales* without ownership mark (although with a charming *probatio pennae* on the flyleaf that reads, "We be three Lancashire lads"), which is thoroughly expurgated with obliteration of all royal titles applied to Elizabeth and with progressively more passionate marginalia presenting the Catholic perception of the history and topography of England. Whoever wielded the pen clearly hated Burleigh with a passion: his name never occurs, but the pen has all but scored through the paper. Speed's *History* is also annotated. I

was enabled to inspect these copies through the kindness of Dr. Javier Burrieza Sanchez, archivist of the college, and Andrew Nicoll, archivist of the Catholic Church in Scotland.

5. Venerable English College, Rome, Liber 1422.

6. Henry Hawkins, S.J., *Partheneia Sacra, or the mysterious and delicious garden of the Sacred Parthenes, set forth and enriched with pious devices and emblemes* (Rouen, 1633).

7. Louis Richeome, *Le peinture spirituelle* (Lyons, 1611). "Le sixieme livre . . . des Iardins" describes the gardens.

8. Santina M. Levey, *An Elizabethan Inheritance: The Hardwick Hall Textiles* (London: National Trust, 1998), 35, 68–73.

9. PRO, Kew, Sp 53/21, fols. 108r–v, [109r blank], 109v, French-language inventory, listing forty-nine devices, translation printed in *Calendar of State Papers (Scotland), 1547–1603,* vol. 9, *1586–88* (Glasgow, 1915), 502–4, "Devices of the Queen of Scots Bed," where it is dated October 1587.

10. National Library of Scotland, Hawthornden MSS, vol. 12, Fowler's papers and scrolls, fols. 50–52, inventory of forty-three "devyces"; NLS, Hawthornden MSS, vol. 12, Fowler's Papers and Scrolls, fol. 21, list of thirty-one devices headed "5 April 1603 after the King's departure I did observe these devyses upon the queens his mother's bed," signed by Fowler at the end.

11. Letter, dated July 1, 1619, from William Drummond of Hawthornden to Ben Jonson, printed in Drummond's *Works* (Edinburgh, 1711); see Michael Bath, *Renaissance Decorative Painting in Scotland* (Edinburgh: National Museums of Scotland, 2003), 34–35. Again I owe these precise citations of sources to Prof. Michael Bath, from work in progress on Mary Queen of Scots as emblematist.

12. Yeoman Warder B. A. Harrison, *A Guide to the Inscriptions in the Beauchamp Tower* (London: Tower of London, n.d.).

13. [John Gerard], *The Autobiography of an Elizabethan,* trans. Philip Caraman (London: Longmans, 1951), 104–5.

14. Historical Manuscripts Commission, *Report on Manuscripts in Various Collections,* vol. 3 (London: HMSO, 1904), xix–xxi and xliii–iv.

15. This is clearly the intention; in fact, precise modern measuring devices find that the walls are thirty-three feet and four inches long.

16. There are various antiquarian accounts of this room; a summary can be found in J. Tilley, *Old Halls, Manors and Families of Derbyshire,* 4 vols. (London, 1892–1902), 2:135.

17. Sir Nicolaus Pevsner, *The Buildings of England: North Lancashire* (Harmondsworth: Penguin, 1969), 216–17.

18. Ibid., 94. The house is now in very good hands, a young farming family taking exemplary care of it. Visits are only possible by prior appointment.

19. I know only one comparable artifact, and this is the stone, now at Craigston Castle, Aberdeenshire, taken from the Castle of Cromarty, where it had been in the hands of the writer Sir Thomas Urquhart; it dates the rebuilding of the castle according to a series of fantastical chronologies. The chronologies at Judd Holmes Lane would seem to bear some resemblance also to the version of English history later set forth by Richard Verstegan in his controversial *A Restitution of Decayed Intelligence* (Antwerp, 1605).

20. Seton's religious allegiance can be in no doubt, as Archivum Romanum Societatis Jesu MS Anglia 42, fol. 203r, testifies: "Quod idem Rex a Catholica Religione non omnio abhorreat indicia sunt clarissima. Regnae Scotiae Cancellarium, qui pro Regis officio fungitur, creavit Alexandrum Setonium piae memoriae Gregorii 13 alumnum. Hic in Seminario Romano studiviit Philosophiae et Theologiae, et quamvis suo magno malo, simulavit se cum haereticis consentire, rex tam probe scit eum esse Catholicam."

21. Bath, *Renaissance Decorative Painting*, 80, quoting Richard Maitland, *The History of the House of Seton, to 1559* (Glasgow: Maitland Club, 1829), 63.

22. Ibid., 79–103.

23. I am indebted to Anne Dillon (personal communication) for the thought that this scheme of emblems, with further related texts for meditation, and with its stoic and consolatory tenor, is closely related to the poetic and figurative compositions taught in Jesuit schools and that the whole also bears an apprehensible relation to the devised emblems and inscriptions on a unified theme that were displayed on prize days at Jesuit colleges.

24. Michael Bath (personal communication from a forthcoming book on Mary Queen of Scots and her embroideries) kindly amplifies this information:

> This same device was identified as one of the incriminating imprese cited as evidence at the trial of Philip Howard, Earl of Arundel, in 1589: "Then was produced an emblematical piece found in the earl's cabinet, which had on the one side a Hand bitten with a Serpent shaking the Serpent into the Fire, about which was written this Poesie, *Quis contra nos?*" and on the other side, "a Lion Rampant, with his chops all bloody, with this poesie, *Tamen Leo*" (Hargrave, *Complete Collection of State Trials*, 1776, Vol. I, col. 166). Mary uses this "Quis contra nos" emblem, amongst the other emblems which go back to Paradin, in the border to her "Las Pennas Passan" embroidery. The biblical "quis contra nos" motto is found elsewhere in Scotland at this period. Glasgow University Library holds a copy of the *Historia Animalium* of Conrad Gesner, shelfmark Bh5-b.1–3, which carries the owner's signature "Jo. Bellenden" beside the printer's mark and in the same hand is the date "4. Ma 1598," with the inscription "Si deus pro

nobis quis contra nos. Rom.8.31." This is not, however, the translator of Boece, who died in 1550, but probably Sir John Bellenden of Achinoul. I have no evidence that he was a crypto-Catholic, and more work needs to be done before we could say with any certainty that such a text carried any Catholic coding. The kind of testimony from fellow Catholics recognizing such an inflection in any of these emblems and inscriptions is unfortunately lacking.

25. Bath, *Renaissance Decorative Painting,* 123–27, has a very useful discussion of Skene's House. The very seriously damaged last scene on the ceiling has been plausibly identified as a Coronation of the Virgin.

26. Ibid.,124.

27. Ibid., 128–45. Bath makes it clear that Sir Robert was believed to be a Catholic; see especially 145.

28. Nicolaus Pevsner, *Cumberland and Westmorland* (Harmondsworth: Penguin, 1967), 141–42.

29. Another such saint-king, his armor decorated with the pelican in its piety, of late-seventeenth-century date and quite possibly of Spanish origin, is (without provenance) part of the picture collection of the University of Aberdeen. The most plausible conjecture as to its origins is that it may have formed part of the temporary fitting up of the Trinity Church in Aberdeen for Catholic worship under James VII and II.

30. Hutton John is a private house, never open to the public. There is nothing to see, of recusant interest, other than the inscribed stones recorded fully here. I have promised the owners to stress here their desire that their privacy be respected.

31. Nicolaus Pevsner and Enid Welsford, *The Buildings of England, Yorkshire, The West Riding* (Harmondsworth: Penguin, 1979), 369–70.

32. Sharon Lambert, *Monks, Martyrs and Mayors* (Lancaster: Lancaster University Press, n.d.).

33. A very full and informative discussion of the stages of the evolution of Pope's grotto can be found in Anthony Beccles Willson, *Alexander Pope's Grotto in Twickenham* (London: Garden History Society, 1998).

34. An excellent account of this is found in Paul Gabriner, "The Papist's House, the Papist's Horse," in *Centennial Hauntings: Pope, Byron and Eliot,* ed. C. C. Barfoot and Theo D'Haen (Atlanta, GA: Rodopi, 1990), 13–64. Also see Maynard Mack, *Alexander Pope: A Life* (New Haven: Yale University Press, 1985), esp. 336–39.

35. I will treat of these matters at length elsewhere, but preliminary investigation of imagery of shadow and light in Pope would seem to offer a frequent coded meaning that "shadowed" or "overshadowed" accompanies the Catholics, the *gens lucifugum.*

36. See Maynard Mack, *The Garden and the City* (London: Oxford University Press, 1969), 63–65. In one of his very rare oversights, Mack does not realize the cultural history of the Passion Shield in England.

37. This information and access to the grotto were given by the present owner, Duncan Michie, Esq. Please do not attempt to visit him without a written request, made well in advance. For the original printed assertion of the Catholic associations of the grotto, see Barbara Jones, *Follies and Grottoes* (London: Constable, 1974), 327.

38. John Seward, Esq., at Pluscarden Abbey, Moray, November 2002.

39. Pope's grotto had a rivulet and spring, at least in its earlier stage. St. Winifred's well is a much larger well-house and chapel. Shell's discovery was what seems a clear allusion to Pope in Gent's work tracing the history of St. Winifred's well in Flintshire in Wales, a place that never quite died out as a focus of recusant devotion, despite repeated attempts to suppress it. See Thomas Gent, *British piety display'd in the glorious life, suffering, and death of the blessed St Winefred . . . Part the fifth* (York: printed by the author Thomas Gent, 1742), 12.

Hail, *publick* FRIEND! Lov'd by fair *B-rl-ngton*,
Since I must call You by no other Name;
Behold St. *Win'frid*'s Life, which, when begun,
Kind, you approv'd—that set my Soul a-flame!

2

Women Catholics and Latin Culture

Jane Stevenson

The focus of this essay is on English Catholic culture, but it should not be forgotten that a number of significant Catholic women writers in other parts of Europe, some of whom were in religious orders, also used Latin. They include the humanist nun and Latin poet Suor Lorenza Strozzi[1] and Sóror Violante do Céu, who published her *Rhythmas varias* in Rouen in 1646 and "cultivated the sacred Latin muses."[2] Particularly when one is talking about individuals conversant with Latin, influence from outside the English-speaking tradition should never be discounted, but in any case early modern Catholic culture was not, and could not be, entirely English. Any Catholic education in England had to take place within the family, and women could not take up the religious life in England. Whereas in Catholic countries many upper-class girls were educated in convents, and some of them decided to stay there (or even became the victims of forced vocations), this was not the case in England. Englishwomen became nuns only because they had evolved a deeply held belief that they had a vocation for the religious life and were prepared to undergo considerable risk and difficulty to attain this state. Early modern Catholic Englishwomen could therefore be found all over the Catholic world but particularly in France, Spain, and the Spanish Netherlands (modern Belgium). Many of the women who went abroad for the sake of religion kept in touch with sisters or daughters at home: the Aston family of Tixall are particularly well attested in this respect. There might therefore be reason to think a priori that although the best-known early modern women scholars, such as the Cooke sisters and Lucy Hutchinson, were Puritans, elite Catholic women's education might be at least as language conscious as that of Anglicans or Nonconformists, and there is some evidence that this is the case.

We should not forget the usefulness of Latin in early modern Europe.[3] To begin with, a reading knowledge of Latin opened up the Bible to Catholics, which was important, since the Catholic Church resisted the vernacularization of the liturgy. Catholic translations of the New and Old Testaments came out in 1582 and 1602 respectively, and while there was less stress on lay Bible reading in Catholic than in Protestant communities, educated Catholics might well read their Bible. It is perfectly clear that some did so in Latin. The learned Jane Owen certainly read the Latin Bible, for she quotes it freely: "Gods sacred Word assureth you, that you may buy Heauen with Good Workes: *Venite possidete paratum vobis regnum; Esurivi enim, et dedistis manducare*, &c. Matth. 25."[4] "It may be said of you, as was said of Cornelius the Centurion, Act. 10 *Elleemosinae vestrae commmoratae sunt in conspectu Dei.*"[5] The Book of Hours was the "woman's book" par excellence;[6] and though English and bilingual editions were issued by Catholic presses in centers such as Antwerp and St Omer's, Latin texts were used by some women. Jane Dormer could read the Office of Our Lady in Latin before she was seven.[7] Mary Ward's first plan for her institute (1612) lays down that "[the sisters] shall daily recite piously and devoutly the greater canonical hours or the office of the Blessed Virgin, according to each one's ability"; ability in this context means Latinity.[8]

As Mary Ward suggests, women who went into religion had a particular need for Latin because they were required to sing the Office. The constitutions of the English Benedictine nuns of Cambrai and Paris specifically state that the Divine Office and profession ceremonies were sung in Latin by the quire nuns. In the late Middle Ages, nuns often had often done so uncomprehendingly. The early German humanist Conrad Celtis jeered: "They sing, and they do not understand what they ask in the sacred song, / Like a cow mooing in the middle of the marketplace."[9] However, this was not the practice in early modern convents. Quire nuns, who sang the Office, either arrived with some command of Latin or began to learn it. Witness Paula, née Elizabeth, Hubert: "His daughter came over, and was received here, but finding herself very weak, and not apt to learn Latin, she would not undertake any more than to be a white sister."[10] The various seventeenth-century convent annals, such as those published by the Catholic Record Society, make it absolutely clear that some nuns in each house were Latinate, though not all. For example: "In this year (1633) upon the 8th day of July died most blessedly our worthy Mother Prioress [Mary Wiseman]. She had her Latin tongue perfect, and hath left us many homilies and sermons of the holy fathers translated into English, which she did with great facility, whilst some small respite of health permitted her."[11] It is worth observing that the surviving library catalog of the Benedictine nuns of Cambrai (Cambrai, BN 901) contains two copies of Alvares's *Introduction to the Latin Tongue for Young Students*, 1684 and 1686, indicating that some of the women who came to the convent without Latin acquired it there.[12] A letter written in 1629 by Dom Augustine Baker on the nuns of Cambrai notes, "I wish I had Hilton's *Scala Perfectionis* in Latin. It would help the understanding of the English (and some of them understand Latin)."[13] The spiritual *Collections* made by and for the nuns of Paris and Cambrai as material for private meditation show an easy familiarity with Latin.[14]

Nuns had other uses for Latin besides the liturgy and pious reading. Dame Anne Neville, in the mid-seventeenth century, records the resolution of a dispute over authority: "Wee immediatly gave them the latin statutes to peruse, and poyntd out the place where it gives the community the choyce of tow Religious men to be present with the Bishope."[15] There could be no clearer demonstration of the way that knowledge of Latin could be power: it made a great difference to enclosed nuns if they could choose their own supervisors. It is worth remembering, furthermore, that widowed Catholic gentlewomen sometimes chose to become nuns in middle or old age. Therefore, if we imagine a pious English recusant family, such as the Astons, in which daughters as well as sons might decide to go abroad, there would always be a case for giving any daughter some Latin in case she found she needed it at some future point.[16] In the manor house of Braddocks, between Thaxted and Saffron Walden (Essex), Thomas and Jane Wiseman educated all eight of their children in Latin in the 1580s: "[T]he daughters as well as the sons were brought up to learning of the Latin tongue and Mr Wiseman, every Friday, would make an exhortation in Latin thereby to exercise them in that language as also to give them good instruction."[17] The four daughters all became nuns: two were Bridgettines in Portugal, and two were Augustinian canonesses in Louvain.

Third, Latin was important as a language of communication, the lingua franca of educated people.[18] When Mary Tudor married Felipe II, they were forced back onto Latin as their common language.[19] Few others can have needed it more than the original Galloping Girl, Mary Ward (b. 1585). She was taught Latin by her grandmother, Ursula Wright, by the time she was ten.[20] Her own writings are in English, Latin, Italian, Spanish, and French, and she perceived that other women shared the need. A hostile letter of 1621 from the English Catholic secular clergy represented her as a menace, partly because of the thoroughness with which she educated her followers: "[T]hose who come to her she instructed in Latin, trained them to hold exhortations publicly, engage in conversations with externs, manage families, etc. Preparing the most approved for [her] English Mission. . . . They profess the offices of the Apostolic function (i.e. of priests)."[21] The writings of Mary Ward's sister Barbara, who accompanied her to the Continent, break into odd phrases of Latin in a way that suggests the language was very familiar to her: "[W]hen proud thoughts assail me, *nihil sum:* when abject thoughts, *omnia possum;* when wilful thoughts: prompt obedience, *usque ad mortem.*"[22] It may not have been instruction in Latin in a simple sense that annoyed Mary Ward's enemies: few, if any, voices were raised against the notion that religious women should passively *comprehend* Latin. But Ward was teaching the active use of Latin, and, it would seem, rhetoric ("holding exhortations publicly"), and a significant strand in humanist education since the fifteenth century had deplored the teaching of rhetoric to women.[23] Juan Luis Vives, whose treatise "The Instruction of a Christian Woman," written for Mary Tudor in 1523, was influential in England, took this view: as Richard Hyrde's translation has it, "As for eloquence, I have no great care, nor a woman needeth it not . . . nor is it no shame for a woman to hold her peace. . . . [I]t neither becometh a woman to rule a school, nor to live amongst men, or speak abroad, and shake off her demureness and honesty."[24] There would certainly have been detractors minded to argue that Mary Ward was doing all these things and that they were blameworthy.

There are identifiable traditions of Latin education for women in a number of recusant families—not only that of St. Thomas More. On the accession of Elizabeth I, Jane Nudigate, Lady Dormer, took herself off to Flanders with her granddaughter Jane Dormer (b. 1538), who later became the Duchess of Feria. Lady Dormer settled in Louvain, where she lived for twelve years, till 1571, acting as a refuge and harbor for banished priests and

Catholic gentlemen.[25] When she died, her other granddaughter, Lady Hungerford, went out to Louvain, separating from her husband to do so, and took over the household, living on the Continent for thirty-two years. Lady Hungerford was almost certainly, like her cousin Jane, Latinate. She left a rather curious composition: "The Lady Hungerford's Meditacions upon the Beades," a meditation on the Rosary. Lady Hungerford evidently expanded the simple repetition of the basic Rosary by using this set of meditations on the Joyful Mysteries of the Virgin, themes suggested by each clause of the prayer. As it is presented in its original form, the center of the page is taken up by a large picture of a rosary, with the stanzas of the "Meditacion" arranged around it counterclockwise, beginning at twelve o'clock. Each stanza is also accompanied by a small picture, the whole forming a richly polysemic devotional focus.[26] She therefore clearly attached meaning to the Latin words of the Ave Maria.

The Lady Hungerfords Meditacions upon the Beades

IN NOMINE PATRIS
If my disciple thou wilt be
take up thy crosse and follow me:
The crosse that was most odious
is by my death made glorious.
AVE MARIA
With humble mynde I take my way,
unto the blessed virgin pure:
Upon my knees Ave to saye,
that she may helpe my sinnes to cure.
GRATIA PLENA
O Marie meeke haile full of grace
whom when Elizabeth did veu
She sayde ther was with her in place
the mother of her lord Jesu
DOMINUS TECUM
O lady deare our lorde with thee
whom shipheards first in manger finde
A starr from th'east did guyd kinges three
to visit him with devout mynde.

Benedicta tu in Mulieribus
Among women thou blessed be,
who skapte the swordes that th'infantes slew
Whiles Herod sought most cruelly,
with all to kill thy sonne Jesu.
Et Benedictus Fructus ventris tui
The fruit of thy wombe blessed be,
whom wrongfully to death they drew:
What greater crosse coulde come to thee,
than this thou bare with Christ Jesu.
Sancta Maria ora pro nobis
O holy mother praye for me,
whose sinnes deserve eternall payn
That after death my soule maye be,
where my sweete Jesu now doth raygn.
Marie bare Christ at yeres fifteen,
he lived in earthe thre and thirtie:
Fyfteen yeres after was she seen
assumpt to heaven at threskore three.

The female members of the household of St. Thomas More and their descendants are inevitably the key witnesses to Catholic women's Latin culture in early-sixteenth-century England. It is worth asking whether, as Mattingly has suggested, it was Henry VIII's queen, the humanistically educated Catherine of Aragon (daughter of Fernando and Isabel), who provided the model for the new style of educated woman.[27] She educated her own daughter Mary Tudor thoroughly: the latter spoke Latin, Italian, and French and could read her mother's letters in Spanish. The Mores' story has often been told, but what I want to emphasize here is the continuity of the tradition of women's education that it reveals. Margaret More's reputation is substantial, measured by a variety of solid achievements. Thomas Stapleton notes that he saw Greek and Latin prose and verse by Margaret More, and she is known to have written a treatise on the Four Last Things in friendly competition with her father, though only his unfinished treatment was published.[28] Margaret, in turn, conscientiously educated her own daughter Mary. Roger Ascham revealed in a letter of January 15, 1554, to Mary Clarke, née Roper, that Margaret about twenty years earlier had tried to persuade him to become a tutor in Greek and Latin to herself and Margaret's other children (and that, having failed to do so, she had found them an alternative teacher).[29] Mary Clarke, the daughter, later Mary Basset, translated her grandfather Sir Thomas More's *History of the Passion* from Latin to English, as well as making a Latin version of the first book of Eusebius's *Ecclesiastical History* with an English version of the first five books,[30] and she was considered one of the learned lights of the court of Queen Mary Tudor.[31] But the story does not end there: the More family continued to educate daughters in Latin into the seventeenth century. Dame Bridget More (b. 1609), who became prioress of the Convent of Our Blessed Lady in Paris, wrote a Latin letter that survives, requesting that her congregation be put under papal protection to prevent it from being encroached upon by French diocesan authorities.[32] Dame Gertrude More (1604–33), poet, mystic, and Benedictine nun of Cambrai, was a great-great-granddaughter of Sir Thomas More. She had some Latin. Her *Ideot's Devotions*, 1658, includes the prayer:

> I beseech you, all Saints, and thee especially, most benign
> Father St Benet, with knees bent and hands heaved up, that together
> with me ye crave of the Lord that He grant me a happy end.
> Maria mater gratiae,
> Mater misericordiae,
> To nos ab hoste protege
> Et hora mortis suscipe, Amen
> Nihil aliud teipsum, Domine
> Credo vivere bona Domini in terra viventium.

Another member of St. Thomas's household, More's foster-daughter Margaret Gigs, illustrates even more clearly the persistence of Latin culture in this group of families. She was particularly interested in algebra, and she married John Clement, a distinguished Grecian, who helped with the Aldine edition of Galen. "As the only Englishman who could wear the mantle of Linacre, his prestige in the humanist community was probably unsurpassed, and both he and his wife received the tribute of one of Leland's *Epithalamia*."[33] Later in her life, as an exile in Madrid for the sake of religion with four grown daughters to worry about, Margaret Clement, née Gigs, gave a well-received Latin oration before Felipe II of Spain, probably because she was seeking his patronage. Since he was generous to English and Irish exiles, she may well have received it, and if she did, her Latin learning was of direct use to her.[34] She tutored her four daughters in Latin and Greek.[35] Her daughter Helen, who married Thomas Prideaux*** and settled in Madrid, instructed her own daughter, Magdalena, in Latin and Greek.[36] Magdalena Copley, née Prideaux***, taught her daughters Mary and Helen Copley to read Latin, for when they eventually left Spain to enter the Flemish convent founded by their great-aunt Margaret Clement they took with them their copy of Virgil.[37] When they were interrogated at night, they hid their Catholic books in bed with them, leaving the Virgil out to be confiscated.[38] It is not necessarily fair in the circumstances to deduce that they were reluctant students of the classics, though of course this may have been the case. What is remarkable here is the clarity of the evidence for a mother-to-daughter family tradition of highly educated women over four generations.

Another point that is suggested by the More household is a tradition of Catholic humanist marriage, which has received less attention than contemporary developments in Protestant family life. Thomas More's Latin epigram on choosing a wife, published in 1516, argues that only an educated woman is a true friend and companion: "[I]t will be difficult to choose between her perfect power of expression and her thoughtful understanding of all kinds of affairs."[39] More's letter to Gonell makes clear his commitment to the ideal of virtue acquired through education, especially for women.[40] In his *Epigram*, More endows women with *virtus*—a notion involving intellectual, moral, and rhetorical strength—and not merely with *castitas*. He repeatedly connects *virtus* and learning and considers both desirable for women.[41] The two Margarets, More and Gigs, married men as educated as themselves and educated their daughters; their daughters in turn, educated their granddaughters. Latin culture was not simply a preparation for the convent but a feature of domestic life. It is worth stressing this point, since a significant strand in modern historiography associates Puritanism with "an exaltation of the marriage relationship, a demand for household religious education and discipline, and a slight but noteworthy elevation of the position of women within the household."[42] Yet devoted, companionate marriage based on intellectual affinity and shared interests was clearly also part of recusant culture in England; the Astons among others are witness to this.[43] Seventeenth-century England was an increasingly literate and book-using culture, and women of all confessions were beneficiaries.

There is also evidence that the educative role of the mother was part of recusant culture. Margaret Roper, née More, when her husband was sent to the Tower, was discovered by "certain sent from the king to search her house, upon a sudden running upon her, not puling and lamenting, but full busily teaching her children."[44] It is also worth noting that Mary Ward was taught Latin by her grandmother. At a royal level, Catherine of Aragon oversaw her daughter's education, as her own mother, Isobel of Castile, had done for her. There must certainly have been later Catholic Englishwomen who acted as educators and catechists in the family circle.[45] In Richard Smith's *Life of the most Honourable and Vertuous Lady, the La. Magdalen, Viscountesse Montague* (1627), an account of a Catholic noblewoman by a man who had been her priest, the author says that at the time of the Gunpowder Plot, when she feared to have a priest in the house, "dismissing the advertiser with a manly courage and full confidence in God, she sayd to her Confessor: Let us say the litanies, and commit this matter to God. As well at other times often, as when she lay in her extreme infirmity, she strictly commaunded her children, encouraged her servants, and importunately exhorted all persons . . . constantly to retaine the Catholike fayth. . . . [B]y her example and admonitions she reduced two of her neerest kinred into the lap of the church."[46] Catholic women may not have exercised explicitly catechetical functions within the family in quite the same way that devout Protestants did, but it is clear from an account such as this that it is taken for granted that a Catholic noblewoman would teach her children, household, and kin by both example and actual exhortation. Similarly, the life of the remarkable Dorothy Lawson, written by her chaplain, shows her presiding over a household in which Mass was said in the morning, evensong in the afternoon, and the Litany of the Saints, with all her servants present, between eight and nine at night. There were regular catechisms, "to whch the children of her neighbours were called with her own household, and herself never absent, delighting much to hear them examined and distributing medals and Agnus Deis to those that answered best."[47] Richard Woodcoke, in his *Godly and Learned answer to a lewd and unlearned pamphlet* (1608), complains of the ability of Catholic women to defend their faith by well-supported argument: "every child and audacious woman amongst them presuming to speak Fathers and Doctors as if their idolatrous priests and familiars did speake in them."[48] Such a testimony from an enemy suggests that some contemporaries judged standards of women's education in recusant households to be, if anything, higher than those of their Protestant neighbors.

It is obvious that in the seventeenth century, since Catholic children could seldom be educated outside the house at all, there was a need for household religious education and discipline in recusant circles as well as in Protestant ones: ideally, in gentry Catholic households, such education would be supplied by a domestic chaplain, but, as Lady Montague's story suggests, such men were not necessarily to be had. Elizabeth Grymeston of Grimston Garth, Yorkshire, was probably one such educating mother: her *Miscellanea, Meditations, Memoratives* (1604 et seq.) is a counseling tract for her son, partly in verse, printed after her death, without her family's consent (or so he says), by a confidential servant, William Smith. Her original letter of dedication "to her louing sonne Bernye Grymeston" makes an unselfconscious use of Latin tags that is comparable to the way Latin is used by an educated man of the period, or by a woman such as the Puritan Anne Bacon: "I resolud to breake the barren soile of my fruitlesse braine, to dictate something for thy direction; the rather for that as I am now a dead woman among the liuing, so stand I doubtfull of thy father's life; which albeit God hath preserud from eight seuerall sinister assaults, by which it hath beene sought; yet for that I see that *Quem saepè transit casus, aliquando inuenit*, I leaue thee this portable *veni mecum* for thy Counsellor in which thou maiest see the true portrature of thy mothers minde."[49] Elizabeth Grymeston was reading classical Latin: when she says, "I must confine my selfe to the limits of an epistle, *Quae non debet implere sinistram manum*" (which ought not to fill the left hand), she is quoting Seneca.[50] On the other hand, the tag *Haud citò progreditur ad maiora peccata, qui parua reformidat* (Someone who corrects peccadilloes does not quickly progress to major sins) sounds essentially Christian, though I have not identified the source text.

It is difficult to think about Latinate Stuart Catholic women without thinking of Elizabeth Cary (née Tanfield), Countess of Falkland (ca. 1585–1639): "Afterwards, by herself, without a teacher, and while still a child, she learned French, Spanish and Italian (which she always understood quite perfectly). She learned Latin in the same manner (without being taught) and understood it perfectly when she was young, translating the Epistles of Seneca from Latin to English. After having long discontinued it, she was much more imperfect in it, so when a little time before her death she translated some of Blosius out of Latin, she was fain to help herself somewhat with the Spanish translation."[51] Since she was both an autodidact and a convert, she is not central to this narrative, but it is highly interesting to find that her daughters, brought up as Catholics, were literary, and almost certainly Latin literate as well. Her daughter Dame Clementia Cary, a nun of Cambrai and subsequently of Paris under the abbacy of Dame Bridget More, sister of Dame Gertrude, gives evidence of her Latin culture with her chosen mottoes: *In nidulo meo moriar mundo ut vivam solus Deo* (May I die to the world in my little nest [my cell], that I may live only for God) and *Domine quamvis ad agendum nequeam, cellulam tamen meam servandam valeam* (O Lord, whatever I may fail to do, may I always manage to keep my cell).[52]

There is some further evidence to set beside the evidence of the Wiseman household and Elizabeth Grymeston's work to suggest that Latin culture was reasonably widespread among Catholic gentlewomen and not simply a peculiarity of court circles. Jane Owen, who has already been mentioned in the context of Bible study, is described on the title page of her *An Antidote against Purgatory or discourse, wherein it is shewed that good-workes, and almes-deeds, performed in the name of Christ, are a chiefe meanes for the preventing, or mitigating the torments of purgatory* both as "the honour of her sex for learning in England" and as "late of God-Stow in Oxfordshire."[53] Her work could hardly be more Catholic, given that it defends both justification by works and the doctrine of purgatory. This Jane Owen was certainly Latin literate: apart from her casual use of Latin tags, she translates extensively from Cardinal Bellarmine's *Liber de aeterna felicitate* and *De gemitu columbae*. She has been identified by Retha Warnicke with the contemporary Jane Owen who wrote Latin verse and was a relative of the epigrammatist John Owen. It certainly seems surprising that there should be two Jane Owens in or around Oxford, both Latin literate, at about the same time. But Jane was one of the commonest women's names, and Owen was common among people of Welsh origin, and John Owen the epigrammatist was so actively hostile to Catholicism that a rich Catholic uncle disinherited him and his works were placed on the *Index*.[54] Had the learned niece of John Owen been a Catholic, let alone as polemic a one as the author of *An Antidote*, it is hard to see how her learning could have attracted such epithets as *learned* and *wise* or verbs such as *reverence* from both Owen and his friend Hayman, who was also notably anti-Catholic. It might be possible to resolve the problem by suggesting that she converted late in life, but there is not the slightest indication in *An Antidote* that this might be so. In any case, the Catholic Jane Owen reveals in her *Antidote against Purgatory* both her own knowledge of Latin and her assumption that not all her readership would have the same knowledge: she intends, she says, "the best meanes to preuent, at least to asswage, and mitigate them [the most dreadful torments of purgatory]: *gratum opus agricolis*; a labour (I hope) pleasing to such, who are desirous to cultivate their owne Soules."[55]

In a remote Cumbrian church, St. Mary's, Sebergham, there is a monument to Thomas Denton of Warnell, a local magnate,[56] entirely in Latin, that includes two sets of verses: a rather elegant distich from "B. E.,"[57] identifiable from an English inscription on another slab, now destroyed, as Bernard Ellis,[58] and a less polished pair of elegiac couplets that seem to be introduced by the words *De me, A.D. uxor.* This suggests that Mrs. Denton was the author of the couplets, and the shape of the inscription seems to imply that she was part of a milieu in which Latin was used; that is, she and Ellis used this inscription as a sort of miniature *tumulus.* The second Mrs. Denton, who was responsible for this monument, was Anne Aislabie, from a Yorkshire family, and all that is otherwise known about her is that she was presented as a recusant on December 26, 1599. The English poem that also once formed part of this monument hints, in coded language, that Denton was a church papist, or even a recusant.[59]

De A. D.
Me Uxor .
Cumbria Warnellem Thomam Deplorat Ademptum
Denton qui Siquidem Deltaton Alter Erat
Nempe Pius Sapiens, Ex omni Parte Quadratus
Qualem vix Hodie Secula Nostra Ferunt

[By Me, AD, Wife
Cumbria mourns, deprived of Thomas Warnell
Denton, who was as if another Deltaton [a constellation]
Assuredly wise and pious, proper [squared-off] on all sides
Our Age can scarcely produce another such.]

Another moment of Catholic women's Latinity is suggestive of a variety of connotations for the use of that language; like the Sebergham inscription, it is epigraphic and from a remote part of the country. In 1674, two unmarried sisters, the Daltons, were living at Aldcliffe Hall in Lancashire; they placed a stone on their house that states:

Catholicae
virgines nos
sumus: Mutare
vel tempore
Spernimus
Ano Dni
1674[60]

> [We are Catholic virgins: We scorn to change with the times. Year of the Lord, 1674.]

They were firm defenders of their faith: Mr. Goolden, a missionary priest, was living with them by 1687 and died there in 1694. Sharon Lambe suggests that it is likely he ran a kind of junior seminary at Aldcliffe, preparing boys to enter the continental colleges. There is no way of telling whether it was Goolden or his hostesses, the Daltons, who were the writers of this inscription, but it is certainly possible that they did and that they might also have been involved in education. The idea of "scorning to change with the times" is found in other early modern English Catholic writings. Through the use of Latin, the Daltons are identified with an older world; they also ensure that despite the boldness of their challenge not everyone will be able to read it.

The last woman to be considered here is the only seventeenth-century Irishwoman from an "Old English" (i.e., Hiberno-Norman) family who is known to have written anything,[61] Eleanor Burnell. She did so in Latin.[62] Her family background was both aristocratic and strongly Catholic.[63] Her ancestor Robert Burnell was appointed Baron of the Exchequer in Ireland in 1402, and the family acquired the manor and lands of Balgriffin in the country of Dublin in the early fifteenth century. In 1535, John Burnell was attainted and executed at Tyburn for having been one of the principal supporters of Thomas Fitzgerald in his war against the Pale. His son Henry Burnell was thought able by Sir Henry Sidney in 1577, but "he thirsteth earnestly to see the English government withdrawn from hence." He was nonetheless appointed Justice of the Queen's Bench in 1589. During the persecution of recusants in 1605 he was put under house arrest, although he was very aged, for having participated in a deputation formed by the principal Roman Catholics of the Pale to petition for a remission of the religious disabilities imposed on them.[64]

Eleanor's father, son of the last man mentioned, also a Henry Burnell, is the author of *Landgartha. A Tragie-Comedy, as it was presented in the new Theater in Dublin, with good applause, being an Ancient story.* The two surviving poems, one in hexameters, one in elegiac couplets, are among the prefatory verses in her father's play, which was performed in the Werburgh Street Theatre in Dublin on St. Patrick's Day, 1640, the last play performed in Ireland before the civil war broke out.[65] The prologue of *Landgartha* is spoken by an Amazon with a battle-ax in her hand, and the prefatory epistle comments, "Bodily force too in a woman (were it but to defend its own Fort) is a perfection, though it cannot be expected but from a few of you." It suggests an attitude in Henry Burnell that might also account for his daughter's sophisticated education.[66] Nothing is known of how Eleanor Burnell fared in the tragedy that was 1640s Ireland. Her father became a member of the Irish confederation set up in 1642,[67] and Gilbert claims that he wrote other plays "which haveing never been published, are not now accessible,"[68] but at this point, the family disappears from historical record. Her verse strikes notes of both family pride and national, or rather, Old English chauvinism.

Patri suo Charissimo operis Encomium

Melpomene tua tela (parens) contexta Thalia est,[69]
  judicio quamvis non trutinanda meo est:[70]
Me tua sed certam solers facundia verax
  expertorum hominum & fama diurna facit,
Te nullis potuisse tuis errare, decorum
  omnimodo Scænis, sed tenuisse triplcx;
Nempe modum retinendo (docent ut scripta sagacis
  Flacci) personæ, temporis, atque loci.
Ad te à Iuvernis flexit victoria vatem
  partibus his cedunt Brutiginæque tibi.
Fama quidam tendet, quacunque auratus Apollo
  se tua: tu vives dum vehet amnis aquas.
Tu pater Aonio deducens vertice musas,
  gloria (non fallor) posteritatis eris.
Terra tuas certum est exhauriet extera laudes;
  clarescet scriptis insula nostra tuis

[Encomium on the work of her Beloved Father

Woven together on your loom, Father, Melpomene is also Thalia—
Though this ought not to be weighed in my scale!
However, your skilled, truthful eloquence
And the daily report of competent men
Make me certain that you cannot have erred in any of your undertakings
But have in all ways maintained threefold propriety on the stage:
Namely, by exercising restraint (as the writings of the sagacious Horace
  instruct)

With regard to person, time, and place.
Victory has turned away from the Irish toward you [in your
capacity as] a poet,
And the [English] descended from Brutus in these regions yield to you.
Your fame indeed will spread wherever golden Apollo. . . .[71]
you will live as long as the river [Liffey?] conveys its waters.
You, Father, bringing the Muses down from the Aonian mountaintop,
Are to be, unless I am mistaken, the glory of posterity.
It is certain that a foreign land will drink its fill of your praises;
Our island shall become famous thanks to your writings.]

Eleanor Burnell's poem thus serves as a reminder that even the definition of "English," particularly for a Catholic, was problematic in this period. As a descendant of the "Old English," she may well have shared Stanihurst's view that the English of Dublin preserved a purer English language and culture than the English of London. She looks over the water to an *extera terra*—a foreign land—probably England itself, in this case, but in so doing she stands for early modern Catholic women more generally, for whom *exterae terrae*, whether the kingdom of heaven or the kingdoms of the Catholic nations of Europe, were inescapable reference points in their cultural and social lives and were often approached through the medium of Latin.

Notes

1. Jane Stevenson, "The Latin Poetry of Suor Lorenza Strozzi," in *Women Writing Latin from Roman Antiquity to Early Modern Europe*, ed. Laurie Churchill, Phyllis R. Brown, and Jane E. Jeffrey, 3 vols. (New York: Routledge, 2002), 3:109–32.

2. Jacobus Quetif and Jacobus Echard, *Scriptores ordinis praedicatorum*, 2 vols. (Paris: Christophe Baillard and Nicolas Simart, 1721), 2:844–45; see also Aubrey Bell, *Portuguese Literature* (Oxford: Clarendon Press, 1922), 107.

3. Recently addressed by Francoise Waquet, *Latin, or the Empire of a Sign*, trans. John Howe (New York: Verso, 2000).

4. Jane Owen, *An Antidote against Purgatory*, pub. posthumously, probably on the Continent, in 1634 (St. Omer: English College Press, 1634; reprinted as English Recusant Literature 166 [Menston: Scolar Press, 1973]), *6.

5. Ibid., *6v.

6. Brian Richardson, *Printing, Writers and Readers in Renaissance Italy* (Cambridge: Cambridge University Press, 1999), 144–47, 146.

7. Henry Clifford, *The Life of Jane Dormer, Duchess of Feria*, ed. Joseph Stevenson (London: Burns and Oates, 1887), 59. Jane was lady-in-waiting to Mary Tudor, slept in Mary's bedchamber, read the office with her, kept her wearing jewels, and carved her meat. The Antwerp edition of Thomas More's *Dialogue of Comfort* (1573) was dedicated to Jane Dormer. Her Book of Hours survives in Madrid, Biblioteca naçional 174, dated 1585, "para la ilustrisima señora Doña Juana Dormer duquesa de Feria."

8. M. Emmanuel Orchard, I. B. V. M., ed., *Till God Will: Mary Ward through Her Writings* (London: Darton, Longman and Todd, 1985), 36.

9. Conrad Celtis, *Fünf Bücher Epigramme*, ed. Karl Hartfelder (Hildesheim: Olms, 1963), 4:85. The same point was made by Sir David Lindsay in his *Dialog Concerning the Monarche* (1553), ed. John Small, Early English Text Society, o.s., 11 (London: N. Trübner, 1865), 21: "Tharefore I think one gret dirisioun / to here thir Nunnis & Systeris nycht & day / syngand and sayand psalmes and orisoun, / nocht vnderstandyng quhat they syng or say, / bot lyke one stirlyng or ane Papingay."

10. Adam Hamilton, ed., *The Chronicle of the English Augustine Canonesses Regular of the Lateran at St Monica's in Louvain, 1625–1644*, 2 vols. (Edinburgh: Sands, 1906), 2:47.

11. Ibid., 104.

12. Dorothy Latz, ed., *"Glow-Worm Light": Writings of Seventeenth-Century English Recusant Women from Original Manuscripts* (Salzburg: Institut für Anglistik und Amerikanistik, 1989), 20, from the catalog of the nuns' library preserved at Cambrai, Bibliothèque municipale, 901.

13. Ibid., 27.

14. Ibid., 135–45.

15. Lady Abbess of St. Scholastica's Abbey, Teignmouth, ed., "Abbess Neville's Annal of Five Communities of English Benedictine Nuns in Flanders, 1598–1687," in *Miscellanea V*, Catholic Record Society 6 (London: Burns and Oates, 1909), 1–72, 28. Mary Neville (Dame Anne), b. 1605, daughter of Henry, Baron Abergavenny, was the abbess of a community that was founded from that of Ghent and settled at Pontoise (22).

16. Gertrude Thimelby, née Aston, after a happy but brief marriage, retired to the convent in Louvain where her sister-in-law Winefrid Thimelby was abbess. Jane Stevenson and Peter Davidson, eds., *Early Modern Women Poets* (London: Oxford University Press, 2001), 255.

17. C. S. Durrant, *A Link between Flemish Mystics and English Martyrs* (London: Burns and Oates, 1925), 422.

18. Peter Burke, *The Art of Conversation* (Cambridge: Polity Press, 1993), 34–65.

19. There is an important letter from Catherine of Aragon to Mary concerning two books, *De vita Christi* and Jerome's *Letters*. Garrett Mattingly, *Catherine of Aragon* (London: Jonathan Cape, 1942), 142–43. Her translation of the Prayer

of St. Thomas Aquinas, done when she was twelve, survives. Maria Dowling, *Humanism in the Age of Henry VIII* (Beckenham: Croom Helm, 1986), 228. She spoke Latin, Italian, and French and could read her mother's letters in Spanish. She undertook the translation of Erasmus's paraphrase of the Gospel of John at the urging of Katherine Parr, though she abandoned it due to ill health, and she communicated with Katherine in Latin (presumably as practice for them both). Vives wrote *De instructione feminae* as a syllabus for her, but her first tutor was Thomas Linacre. From 1525, when she was nominally princess of Wales with a court at Ludlow, she was taught by John Featherstone. In the year 1525 Ludovico Vives dedicated to her 213 *Symbola,* or short and intricate sentences, in few words, which we would commonly call mottoes, with paraphrasing on every one of them. The first was *Scopus vitae Christus,* the last was *Mente Deo defixus.* Henry Clifford, *Life of Jane Dormer,* 82.

20. Margaret Mary Littlehales, *Mary Ward: Pilgrim and Mystic* (Tunbridge Wells: Burns and Oates, 1998), 20.

21. Latz, *"Glow-Worm Light,"* 161.

22. Mother Mary Philip, *Companions of Mary Ward* (London: Burns, Oates and Washbourne, 1939), 46.

23. Margaret L. King, *Women of the Renaissance* (Chicago: University of Chicago Press, 1991), 194. The English edition of *The Instruction of a Christian Woman* was published in London by T. Berthelet in 1529. It is excerpted in Foster Watson, ed., *Vives and the Renascence Education of Women* (London: Edward Arnold, 1912), 54–55.

24 Juan Luis Vives, "The Instruction of a Christian Woman" (1523), trans. Richard Hyrde, in Watson, *Vives,* 54–55.

25. Lady Dormer herself was from a family that later had a strong reputation for learning. Vivien Larminie, *Wealth, Kinship and Culture: The Seventeenth Century Newdigates of Arbury and Their World* (Woodbridge: RHS/Boydell Press, 1995).

26. John Bucke, *Instructions for the use of the beades* (Louvain, 1589), foldout rear endpaper. While Lady Hungerford's authorship of these verses cannot be finally proved, it is strongly suggested by Bucke's note: "Lastlie I have added some rules to know from whence evell thoughes do proced eand meanes to avoyde them: with a figure or portrature of the beades, conteining your Ladyshippes usuall Meditacion upon them" (6). The diagram is printed by Patricia Crawford in *Women and Religion in England, 1500–1720* (New York: Routledge, 1993), 81.

27. Mattingly, *Catherine of Aragon,* 142–43.

28. Thomas Stapleton, *The Life and Illustrious Martyrdom of Sir Thomas More,* trans. Philip E. Hallett, ed. E. E. Reynolds (New York: Fordham University Press, 1966), 103–4, 106–17.

29. Roger Ascham, *The Whole Works,* ed. J. A. Giles, 3 vols. (London: Library of Old Authors, 1865), 1:166.

30. This is preserved in manuscript, London, British Library MS Harley 1860, dedicated during the reign of Edward VI to the future Queen Mary. This seems to be the actual MS presented to Mary, though it has lost its original binding of purple velvet. J. K. McConica, *English Humanists and Reformation Politics* (Oxford: Clarendon Press, 1965), 266.

31. Dowling, *Humanism,* 222.

32. Città del Vaticano, Barberini Lat. 8624, no. 35.

33. McConica, *English Humanists,* 270.

34. Juan Perez de Moya, *Varia historia de sanctos e illustres mugeres en todo genero de virtudes* (Madrid: Francisco Sanchez, 1583), 3:311v. Felipe II also showed other evidence of sympathy for learned women: he gave a life pension to the Portuguese Latinist Publia Hortensia de Castro, and Luisa Sigea sought his patronage.

35. This is confirmed by Elizabeth Shirley's "Life of Margaret Clement" (one of the daughters; MS held by the Priory of our Blessed Lady of Nazareth in Bruges, with a copy, St. Monica's MS Q29, in the Priory of Our Lady of Good Counsel, Sayers Common, West Sussex), which refers to her having learned "greek and Latten" from her mother (quoted by Durrant, *Link between Flemish Mystics,* 420).

36. de Moya, *Varia historia,* 3:311; Durrant, *Link between Flemish Mystics,* 420.

37. Retha M. Warnicke, *Women of the English Renaissance and Reformation* (Westport, CT: Greenwood Press, 1983), 47–48, 52.

38. Durrant, *Link between Flemish Mystics,* 421, based on Elizabeth Shirley, "Life of Margaret Clement," 1:114–5. There is a detailed biographic account of Bridget Copley in I. A. Mumayiz, "A Biographical Study of Robert Southwell" (PhD diss., Trinity College, Dublin, 1986), 1:36.

39. Petrus Scriverius, ed., *Dominico Baudii Amores* (Amsterdam: Ludovicus Elzevir, 1638), Thomas Morus, Anglus, "Qualis uxor deligenda, ad Candidum," 281–88, trans. in Pamela Joseph Benson, *The Invention of the Renaissance Woman: The Challenge of Female Independence in the Literature and Thought of Italy and England* (University Park: Pennsylvania State University Press, 1992), 158–59.

40. E. F. Rogers, ed., *Correspondence of Sir Thomas More* (Princeton: Princeton University Press, 1947), no. 63. Judith P. Jones and Sherianne Sellers Seibel, "Thomas More's Feminism: To Reform or Re-form," in *Quincentennial Essays on St. Thomas More,* ed. Michael J. Moore (Boone, NC: Appalachian State University Press, 1978), 67–77, 71.

41. Lee Cullen Khanna, "Images of Women in Thomas More's Poetry," in Moore, *Quincentennial Essays,* 78–88, 82–83.

42. Margo Todd, *Christian Humanism and the Puritan Social Order* (Cambridge: Cambridge University Press, 1987), 5. Frances E. Dolan, *Whores of Babylon: Catholicism, Gender, and Seventeenth-Century Print Culture* (Ithaca: Cornell University Press, 1999), by contrast, points to Catholic women's empowerment within the household (50–51).

43. See, for example, Gertrude Thimelby, née Aston's poem on her husband: "To Her Husband, on New Year's Day 1651," in Stevenson and Davidson, *Early Modern Women Poets*, 255–56.

44. Nicholas Harpsfield, *The Life and Death of Sir Thomas More . . . written in the tyme of Queene Marie*, ed. E.V. Hitchcock, Early English Text Society, o.s., 186 (London: Oxford University Press, 1932), 19, 75, 79; Todd, *Christian Humanism*, 108–9.

45. For example, if Ward's follower Winifred Wigmore could say the Little Office of Our Lady at the age of five, then her family were taking care with daughters' education (Philip, *Companions of Mary Ward*, 110). Note also that there were educating Catholic fathers other than St. Thomas More: the Earl of Arundel oversaw the Latin- and Greek-based humanist education of his daughters (Jane and Mary Fitzalan). See the new year's gifts for their father, BL MSS Royal 15 A ix and 12 A i–iv. There was a powerfully companionate relationship between the earl and his daughter Jane (Mary died at seventeen), as there had been between More and Margaret; see Sears Jayne and Francis R. Johnson, *The Lumley Library: The Catalogue of 1609* (London: Trustees of the British Museum, 1956).

46. Suzanne Trill, Kate Chegdzoy, and Melanie Osborne, eds., *Lay by Your Needles, Ladies, Take the Pen* (London: Arnold, 1997), 125–30, 128.

47. William Palmes, S.J., *The Life of Mrs Dorothy Lawson* (1646), 43.

48. sig. A3.

49. Elizabeth Grymeston, *Miscellanea, Meditations, Memoratives* (1604 et seq.), A3–B1, A3r–v.

50. Seneca *Epistolae* 5.45.xiii. A scroll was held in both hands, the portion being read in the right, the portion already read in the left. A letter is a single sheet held in the right hand; therefore, to say that "a letter should not fill the left hand" is to say that it should not be more than one page long.

51. Latz, *"Glow-Worm Light,"* 123 (excerpts from Dame Clementina Cary's life of her mother, Elizabeth Cary).

52. Rev. Mother Prioress of Colwich, O. S. B., ed., "The English Benedictine Nuns of the Convent of Our Blessed Lady of Good Hope, in Paris, now St Benedict's Priory, Colwich, Staffs," in *Miscellanea VII*, Catholic Record Society 9 (London: Catholic Record Society, 1911).

53. Owen, *Antidote against Purgatory*.

54. Leicester Bradner, *Musae Anglicanae: A History of Anglo-Latin Poetry* (New York: Modern Language Association of America, 1940), 89.

55. Owen, *Antidote against Purgatory*, *2v.

56. Warnell was a local estate, which had originated as an abbatial hunting preserve; see T. H. B. Graham, "Sebergham," *Transactions of the Cumberland and Westmorland Antiquarian and Archaeological Society*, n.s., 23 (1923): 49–55.

57. Printed in Nikolaus Pevsner, *The Buildings of England: Cumberland and Westmorland* (Harmondsworth: Penguin Books, 1967), 188.

58. William Nicolson, *Miscellany of the Diocese of Carlisle,* ed. R. S. Ferguson (London: George Bell and Sons, 1877), 10–11. The Denton monument also once included an English poem by John Ellis, also recorded by Nicolson; the complex as a whole is reminiscent of Lady Elizabeth Russell's monument for her husband and brother-in-law at Bisham, with inscriptions by both herself and others.

59. This is no longer *in situ* but is printed in Nicolson, *Miscellany.*

60. Sharon Lambe, *Monks, Martyrs and Mayors: The History of Lancaster's Roman Catholic Community and Cathedral, 1094–1991* (Lancaster: Lancaster University Press, n.d.). The stone is now in Lancaster City Museum.

61. There is little evidence for women's learning in early modern Ireland: Katherine Philips's friend "Philo-philippa" was Irish, was strongly feminist, and had an extensive classical education, revealed in the poem she published in 1667, which had given her an acquaintance with the stories of learned and/or heroic women of the past, such as Cornelia, mother of the Gracchi, but we do not know her name, let alone whether she accessed classical literature in Latin or in translation (Stevenson and Davidson, *Early Modern Women Poets,* 402–7).

62. Richard Stanihurst, who was also Old English, celebrated the learning of a good number of his compatriots, but all of them were male. See his "A Plain and Perfect Description of Ireland," in *Chronicles of England, Scotland and Ireland,* ed. R.[aphael] Holinshed (London: J. Harrison, 1577).

63. Her mother was Lady Frances Dillon, daughter of Sir James Dillon, the first Earl of Roscommon. My thanks to Jane Ohlmeyer for help with Irish prosopography.

64. John T. Gilbert, *A History of the City of Dublin* (Dublin, 1854–59), 3 vols., facsimile ed. (Shannon: Irish University Press, 1972), 1:296.

65. Henry Burnell, *Landgartha. A Tragie-Comedy, as it was presented in the new Theater in Dublin, with good applause, being an Ancient story, written by H. B.* (Dublin: n.p., 1641). Other writers of gratulatory verse are John Bermingham, Henry Burnell's cousin, and Philippus Patricius, in Latin. On the context, see Alan J. Fletcher, *Drama and the Performing Arts in Pre-Cromwellian Ireland* (Cambridge: D. S. Brewer, 2001), 450. It was not usual to perform plays during Lent, but the opening session of the Dublin Parliament had taken place the day before, and apparently court needs had been allowed to supersede both precedence and principle.

66. The choice of metaphor also suggests that he might perhaps have known François Billon, *Le fort inexpugnable de l'honneur du sexe femenin* (Paris: Jan D'Allyer, 1555).

67. Peter Kavanagh, *The Irish Theatre, Being a History of the Drama in Ireland from the Earliest Period up to the Present Day* (Tralee: Kerryman, 1946), 40–45.

68. Gilbert, *History of the City*, 1:41. One piece that may possibly be ascribed to him is *The Worlds Idol: Plutus, a Comedy, written in Greek by Aristophanes*, translated by H. H. B., together with his notes (London: W. G., 1659). The notes make no reference to Ireland but are learned and odd: they cite, among other sources, the Bible, Montaigne, Herodotus, Diodorus Siculus, Antiphanes, Xenophon, Dio Cassius, and Menander. It would be usual to find that the father of a Latinate daughter was more than usually learned.

69. Reading conjecturally *est* for *et*: my thanks to Dr. Janet Fairweather for advice.

70. The interpretation of lines 1–2 with their mixed metaphors is difficult. Burnell, who apparently implies that the work is tragicomic, or can simultaneously be seen as tragic and comic, compares her father's literary work with a loom. *Tua tela* has to be nominative, not ablative, because of the scansion, and it is improbable that *tela* should be construed as neuter plural "weapons" in view of the "weaving" connotations of *contexta*.

71. *Se tua* cannot possibly be right, but what the correct reading might be is unclear. A verb is required, possibly *sedet*.

3

"Rich Embrodered Churchstuffe"

The Vestments of Helena Wintour

Sophie Holroyd

In November 1668 Jesuit Father George Grey wrote to his provincial to say that he had been to see Helena Wintour, daughter of Gunpowder Plotter Robert, at her home at Badgecourt on the family's Worcestershire estates. The primary purpose of his visit had been to establish the extent of the bequests Wintour intended to make to the Jesuits in her will, but Grey also made particular mention of the way Wintour was spending her days: "She hath bene these many yeares, and is yet, piously employed in making rich embrodered Churchstuffe, which she designes for this particular Mission, or the intended College, not being willing it should be conveyed beyond Sea upon colour of safe custodie, least it should never returne againe. A parcell of curious worke I saw actually *in fieri* upon the frame; but I understand she hath severall whole suits ech of severall colours, to comply with the Rubrickes."[1] Considering how much recusant textile material was destroyed in the sixteenth and seventeenth centuries, it is extraordinary that Wintour's "rich embrodered churchstuffe" should have survived and that it can be attributed to her. Its survival is even more extraordinary given that on Wintour's death in 1670 the vestments were divided into two collections, both of which have come down to us more or less intact.

Comparatively little is known of Helena Wintour. She was born around 1600, which would have made her about five years old at the time of her father's execution for involvement in the Gunpowder Plot. Unusually, for the female members of the Plotters' families, she remained in England. She never married but lived a quiet life of prayer and charitable works on the Cooksey estates that had been recovered for the family at some point after they were forfeited to the crown in 1605.[2] Apart from a little correspondence, scant mention in the correspondence of others, and a few documents of public record, Wintour left no textual trace behind. But where text has been erased, Wintour's textiles speak for her. After a brief discussion of what little is known about vestments associated with the English recusants, this essay seeks to read Wintour's design concept, her choices of embroidered liturgy, symbolism, and iconography. It begins by suggesting that Wintour used the undertaking to practice a personal form of Jesuit-led meditation on the Virgin Mary. Then it uses Henry Hawkins's Jesuit emblem book *Partheneia Sacra* to read Wintour's floral and other imagery as Marian emblems. Finally, the essay suggests that, although Wintour's liturgical colors may "comply with the Rubrickes" in the design details and especially in the textual relationship of embroidered liturgy to Tridentine liturgy, Helena Wintour used her vestments as a space in which to emphasize certain aspects of her religious experience.

Invisible Stitches: The Catholic Recusants

A report to Worcestershire High Sheriff Sir Richard Walsh, dated December 4, 1605, records that in "a hollow place within a wall near unto the clock house" at Huddington, home of Helena Wintour's father Robert, searchers had found "a cross gilt with the picture of Christ, and other pictures upon it, a chalice of silver partly gilt, with a little plate or cover to the said chalice, and certain boxes of singing bread, and all other ornaments fit for a Popish priest to say Mass in."[3] Their haul of church vestments, of "ornaments" associated with recusant Catholicism, was one of many that the recusant population of England suffered during the later sixteenth and early seventeenth centuries. There remain a few scattered and tattered examples, such as an early-seventeenth-century vestment associated with St. Edmund Arrowsmith and an early-sixteenth-century vestment decorated with a medieval orphrey used by the Sheldons at Beoley.[4] Even vestments carried across to the Continent, or made there in the exiled religious houses to which many recusant women fled from religious persecution at home, were destroyed either in visitations or during the complicated continental peregrinations of the nuns, which mostly ended in the destruction of their houses during the French Revolution.[5] Any study of recusant vestments must piece together the surviving (mostly partisan) records of the making and use of vestments from official reports or from correspondence, diaries, autobiographies, and other written sources.[6] In this context, Helena Wintour's vestments as a surviving body are an outstanding exception.

In the early days of the Jesuit English mission, recusant houses were not furnished with the wherewithal to host secret Catholic masses. John Gerard recalled in his autobiography that in his early days as a missioner he found most houses unprovisioned: "At first I used to take round with me my own Mass equipment. It was simple but fitting and specially made so that it could be carried easily. . . . In this way I was able to say Mass in the morning wherever I happened to lodge. . . . My hosts could seldom provide the essentials for Mass and I therefore had to bring them myself." Later on in his narrative he describes these portable clothes: "Though light and easy to carry about, they were beautifully made from red silk embroidered with silver lace." But in testimony to the effectiveness of the mission and the efforts of the underground community to replace confiscated articles, he states that "after a few years there was no need to do this. In nearly every house I visited later I would find vestments and everything else laid out ready for me."[7]

Gerard himself nurtured this production. He showed one of his early hostesses, the mother of Henry Drury of Lawshill, "some fine vestments, which were a gift to [him], and in this way encouraged the good widow to make others like them." Her own chapel furnishings, he maintained, were "old and worn and anything but helpful to devotion."[8] This passing reference serves to indicate the importance of fine vestments not only in the Mass but also as an aid to worship. Vestments, in fact, constituted a devotional structure in themselves: medieval symbolism described by Thomas à Kempis in *Imitatio Christi* formalized vestments into a "living picture of the passion and death of our Lord."[9] The notion of a "living picture" was important; vestments not only had pictures of the events of Christ's life literally embroidered onto them but also occupied an essential place in the performance of Catholic liturgy: "The symbolic system of vesting expresses the putting on of Christ by the officiant. Thus the amice symbolises the helmet of salvation, and the alb, maniple, girdle and stole are symbolic of purity, contrition, continence and immortality. The chasuble symbolises obedience and also the burden of the priest's responsibility."[10]

Making vestments to aid devotion was itself a sign of devotion. An unnamed lady in Gerard's account "took to making beautiful vestments" on her conversion,[11] vestments that, it is implied, were understood to be a testament to her conversion. Sewing them played a part in the articulation, manifestation, and profession of her faith. That there was a "public" nature to such embroidery is underscored by the biographer of Anne Dacres, wife of Philip Howard, Earl of Arundel. He records that "church ornaments of her own making and contriving" were publicly discussed and "much admired" in the close community that was the Catholic circle "for their rich, rare and curiouse workmanship."[12] The result of the devotional application of such skill was in some cases the creation of rich treasures with the power to move and impress: when the justices burst into Elizabeth Vaux's house in July 1599 in search of popish priests, John Gerard had just set up his altar ready to celebrate Mass. "The magistrates saw the chapel door open, went in, and discovered a beautifully furnished altar with Mass vestments laid out beside it. Even these heretics were amazed at them."[13] Details of these works have unfortunately not been transmitted, but other records preserve lengthier descriptions of the kind of textiles worked and protected by Catholic recusants.

The well-known recusant Vaux family, despite the financial problems caused by recusancy fines, had a well-appointed chapel: "Our vestments were both plentiful and costly. We had two sets for each colour which the Church uses; one for ordinary use, the other for feast days: some of these latter were embroidered with gold and pearls, and figured by well-skilled hands."[14] Some idea of what these might have looked like is provided by the Lady Wintour white vestment, figured all over with gold and pearl-embroidered peasecods (see fig. 5 below). That these sets of vestments were often complete and extensive is shown by an undated inventory circa 1606, listing relics and vestments associated with the Vaux sisters Anne and Eleanor (Brooksby), sisters-in-law to the young widow Elizabeth Vaux: "For churchstuff a vestment of cloth of silver and embroidered cross upon it, stole and maniple of the same. Item a vestment of cloth of gold, stole and maniple. Item a cope of the same. Item two tunicles [dalmatics] of purple. Item a taffeta vestment with an embroidered Jesus. Item an altarcloth to that with letters about: these two things were Mr Page's the martyr."[15] The altar cloth might have been a similar style to those Wintour vestments that are also decorated with "letters about": prayers for intercession, monograms, and even words and phrases from the Mass (see figs. 10, 14, and 17 below).

The Vaux family also had in their possession older, family vestments, showing that the Reformation had up to this point failed to make a clean sweep of the church furnishings. In 1612, when Elizabeth and her son Lord Vaux were arraigned and found guilty of refusing to swear the Oath of Allegiance, the goods confiscated included "two crimson copes left by the ancestors of the house, worth £100."[16] The fate of most of this haul was probably typical: of "the rich altar furniture, plate and vestments" seized "in the King's name" on their arrest and brought to London together with Elizabeth, the textiles were all that was permanently lost; the rest of Lord Vaux's property was returned to him the following year.

If the recusants had any chance at all of saving their vestments, they had to conceal them, and in contrast to Gerard's early portable set, vestments were traditionally bulky and highly visible. Existing family chapels like that at Huddington were fitted with secret storage space. In one corner of the Packingtons' chapel at Harvington Hall in Worcestershire, for example, "massing stuff" was hidden under two floorboards.[17] Secret rooms, priest's holes, were built into the existing fabric of buildings. In the Winchester home of Lady Mary West, widow of Sir Owen West, searchers discovered in December 1583 "another place, more secret, vaulted underground," where they found "a chest bound with iron, wherein were all kinds of Massing apparel . . . needlework cloths upon velvet for the altar."[18] An inventory of material discovered during a raid on Samlesbury Hall in Lancashire listed "imprimis, one canabie to hange over the alter founde in a secrett vawlte over the dyninge chamber."[19]

Some justices swept down onto households so fast that the Catholics had no time to hide their equipment. While much was taken, the Jesuits record instances of miraculous lacunae in the searches. Father Garnet wrote of one occasion at the Vaux's house, where the pursuivant "was completely blind to the most obvious significance of what he had touched. . . . Before the very eyes of [a pursuivant] lay folded a dalmatic of great value, and yet, though he unfolded everything else he never even touched this."[20]

A sixteenth- or seventeenth-century patchwork dalmatic that has survived may provide an explanation for such an oversight: the geometric diamond patches are pieced together to form the subtle shape of a cross when the overall design is seen whole and unfolded from a distance. It is easy to imagine how a searcher might pass over this vestment if it were "camouflaged" as a domestic quilt and folded and placed with other household linen, as he looked for more sumptuous textiles, the cloth of gold and silver, the silks and the lace mentioned in other accounts.[21] Another seventeenth-century "pedlar's" chasuble held by the Bar Convent in York might have had a similar history: its simple strips of silk represent all the liturgical colors, white, green, purple and red, and its black linen lining meant that it could also be used reversed. But in the end the largest part of all vestments associated with the recusant Catholic community disappeared, and what remained was severed from its historical provenance.

The recusant practice of embroidering church textiles as it is understood from this brief introduction can certainly shed initial light on Helena Wintour's vestments, and Wintour's existing vestments may in some cases suggest how lost vestments might have looked. They demonstrate in any case that the English mission was still effective in influencing the production of vestments for domestic use half a century after Gerard's experiences. And as will be seen, supporting the fragmentary records with their implied assertions of the importance of vestments to recusant spirituality, Wintour's vestments can be shown to have had a central importance to her own worship, both meditative in her daily life and devotional in her daily offices.

"Rich Embrodered Churchstuffe": The Wintour Vestments

Although Wintour died intestate, she signed an instrument on the day of her death to bequeath "unto the said Society all the Vestments and other Alter ornaments therto belonging wherto I am at present possessed."[22] The bequest was immediately the subject of acrimonious dispute between the Society of Jesus and Wintour's heir Lady Mary Kemp Wintour, widow of Wintour's nephew George. According to Henry Chadwick's summary of the Jesuit records of events, the Jesuits, "wearied and alarmed by her importunities," handed her "two out of the four best sets of vestments."[23] The Jesuit sets are currently kept at Stonyhurst College in Clitheroe, Lancashire, and the Lady Wintour sets are currently held in a private collection.

The extant vestments correspond to Grey's description of "severall whole suits ech of severall colours, to comply with the Rubrickes." The Stonyhurst collection is made up of a set of white High Mass vestments comprising a cope (fig. 1), a deacon's dalmatic (fig. 2), a subdeacon's dalmatic, a chasuble (the so-called "Alleluia vestment," fig. 3) with a chalice veil, burse, stole, and maniple (not contemporary), and a set of red vestments comprising a chasuble (fig. 4) with matching chalice veil, burse, stole, and maniple. The Lady Wintour set comprises three sets of chasuble, stole, maniple, and veil in white (fig. 5), green (fig. 6), and black (fig. 7), with an additional white veil and burse. The embroidered slips have in most cases been reapplied onto newer backing fabric, except for the Lady Wintour white vestment, which appears to have retained its original ground. The High Mass vestments were created in the nineteenth century from embroidered slips taken from antependia, or altar frontals, made by Wintour. Brother Houghton, sacristan at Stonyhurst for fifty years and in office when the vestments came there from another Jesuit mission in 1854, left notes concerning the vestments. Of the Wintour Alleluia chasuble and dalmatics, he said that "the embroidery of these vestments and a cope also were brought here by Fr Johnson when he was Provincial. His reverence can tell the history. They were a red and white antependium and a white chasuble and they were all arranged as they are now."[24] The creation of the High Mass vestments from Helena Wintour's original textiles must be borne in mind when making a study of the iconography, but when the vestments were made up with the embroidery, the design concept was essentially conserved.

Wintour developed a striking vocabulary of design elements that she used consistently throughout her vestments. The floral symbols of Mary and Christ are uniting elements, as are their monograms, but the vestments also incorporate liturgical and other texts, as well as Wintour's personal and family arms, crest, and motto. The Jesuit motto AMDG (*Ad maiorem Dei gloriam*, "to the greater glory of God") recurs, as does the IHS monogram in rays of glory, a familiar Jesuit device. IG and XA monograms recall the Jesuit saints Ignatius of Loyola and Francis Xavier, and one of two embroidered dates, 1655 and 1656, may commemorate the centenary in 1656 of Ignatius of Loyola's death.

"A Garden *of al flowers": Meditations on the Virgin*

The documentary and iconographical link between Wintour and her vestments and the Society of Jesus provides a useful key to reading her chosen iconography, for Wintour's treatment of her design elements is strongly reminiscent of the Jesuit strategy to fuse emblem and meditation, developed from

Fig. 1. High Mass cope assembled from the embroidery of Helena Wintour, dated 1656. Courtesy of Stonyhurst College Library. Photos of Stonyhurst vestments by author.

Fig. 2. Deacon's dalmatic, assembled from the embroidery of Helena Wintour, mid-seventeenth century. Courtesy of Stonyhurst College Library.

Fig. 3. "Alleluia" white vestment, Helena Wintour, dated 1655. Courtesy of Stonyhurst College Library.

Fig. 4. Red vestment, Helena Wintour, mid-seventeenth century. Courtesy of Stonyhurst College Library.

Fig. 5. Lady Wintour white vestment, Helena Wintour, mid-seventeenth century. Courtesy of Private Collection. Photos of private collection vestments by author.

Fig. 6. Lady Wintour green vestment, Helena Wintour, mid-seventeenth century. Courtesy of Private Collection.

Fig. 7. Lady Wintour black vestment, Helena Wintour, mid-seventeenth century. Courtesy of Private Collection.

the *Spiritual Exercises* of Ignatius of Loyola.[25] The Ignatian method applies each of the senses in turn, perceived with heightened intensity, to create a vivid mental picture of the subject for meditation. The intensely visualized image is the first part of a tripartite meditative structure: the *compositio loci*, in which one sees "with the sight of the imagination the corporeal place where the thing is found which I want to contemplate," is followed by analysis and finally the *colloquium*, "as one friend speaks to another, or as a servant to his master; now asking some grace, now blaming oneself for some misdeed, now communicating one's affairs, and asking advice in them."[26] Although the Jesuits used the underlying tripartite structure provided by their founder's *Spiritual Exercises*, they did not consider themselves bound by it and, on the contrary, applied the method to their media in various ways. Herman Hugo's technique in *Pia desiderata* of 1642, for example, has been interpreted as representing the *compositio loci* by the tripartite emblem's *pictura*, the analysis by the explanatory poem, and the *colloquium* by the final epigram.[27]

Hugo's emblematic structure for meditation is paralleled in Wintour's vestments by her choice and treatment of design elements. Her use of polychromy to render floral surfaces with vividly imagined iridian intensity (fig. 8) is the equivalent in embroidery of the Ignatian heightened sense of vision *(compositio loci)*. The Marian or Christological monogram provides direction for interpretation and analysis (fig. 9), and the dialogue and petition of the *colloquium* are rendered by her personal and family arms, crest, and motto, and in particular by the plea for intercession on the Alleluia vestment, *orate pro me, Helena Wintovr* (fig. 10). The design and production of these vestments are the product, as Grey tells us, of years of work, of hours, days, and weeks spent designing the compositions, obtaining the embroidery materials, executing the slips, applying them to the backing fabric, and making up the vestments. It is entirely possible that the retired, contemplative Wintour meditated as part of her daily devotions upon the task she had undertaken and upon the individual emblematic elements, so meticulously detailed.

While the Jesuit application of emblems to meditation is in general a useful tool with which to bring Wintour's emblematic iconography into focus, a comparison with Henry Hawkins's 1633 emblem book *Partheneia Sacra* makes a more detailed reading possible.[28] Hawkins, dedicating his emblem book to "*the pleasure and deuotion especially of the* PARTHENIAN SODALITIE *of her Immaculate* CONCEPTION," uses the traditional conceit of the Virgin Mary as *hortus conclusus* as a framework on which to hang a seven-part structure for

Fig. 8. Iris detail of Lady Wintour green vestment.

Fig. 9. MAR monogram detail of red vestment.

Fig. 10. *Orate pro me Helena Wintovr* detail of "Alleluia" vestment.

meditation.[29] The emblematic elements of Hawkins's Marian garden, roses, lilies, fountains, and so on, are meditated upon in detail, and each of the seven sections (Symbol, Devise, Character, Morals, Essay, Discourse, Emblem, Poesie, and Apostrophe) reveals greater depths of Marian significance behind the figure. Such extended exploration of Marian garden emblems is unusual: works such as Sabine Chambers's 1619 *The Garden of Our B. Lady* confine the conceit of a garden to the introduction: "to giue you a full description of this Garden, and to tell you . . . what Roses, what Lyllies adorne it, were neuer to end; wherefore desiring you to be curious perusers of it your selues, & not to passe any thing vnnoted" (sig. 6r).[30] Instead of being emblematic, they constitute guided recitations of the rosary.

Hawkins's extended explanations of Marian garden emblems and his status as a Jesuit missioner make *Partheneia Sacra* a particularly useful tool for decoding botanical imagery on vestments that evince a strong Marian devotion and Jesuit influence. Wintour chooses the garden as her main design element, and it is a sign that may be read in many ways. On one level it signifies the embroiderer herself, for in creating her explosion of many-colored floral emblems Wintour represents the image of "the Hart consecrated to the love of Jesus," which according to Hawkins "is a flourishing garden."[31] And by setting her Christological monograms among floral iconography Wintour suggests the moment when Christ appeared to his disciples "in the forme and habit of a *Gardener*," tending the "*Garden* of their Soules" (sig. A1v). Wintour's garden also recalls the *hortus conclusus* of the Song of Solomon 4:12: the fringe or borders containing the embroidered slips act as the garden's boundary walls, containing and protecting their virtue entirely within, as Hawkins's "plat-forme of the garden" is laid out for the reader, "enclosed round, and compassed-in with a wal" (1).

But for Wintour, and for Hawkins, the garden in general and the *hortus conclusus* in particular are quintessentially emblems of the Virgin Mary and of her Immaculate Conception. Wintour's presentation of her floral emblems is analogous to that of Hawkins, who announces to the sodality readers his intention to "personate, and make her appeare to your viewes . . . in the habit . . . of a *Garden,* under the veyle of Symbols" (sig. A1r). Thus, in Wintour's garden, as in Hawkins's "emblem of the Rose," single blooms emblematic of the Virgin rise directly out of the ground: on the front and backs of the deacon's and subdeacon's dalmatics, these alternate between two Marian floral emblems, carnations and stylized marigolds bearing the Virgin's monogram, the crowned letters MAR (fig. 2). Flanking the flowers are vines heavy with bunches of grapes, emblematic of Christ. In emblematic terms the garden that is Mary is here envisaged as the fertile ground that nourished the Savior. But the overwhelming majority of the other flowers and fruits depicted in Wintour's embroidered garden are emblematic of Mary, and when a flower is emblematic of Christ, an alternative or simultaneous Marian reading is almost always possible. Unlike the revealed meaning of the monogrammed blooms on the dalmatics, most of the embroidered flowers must be meditated upon with diligence for their true significance to be revealed, for, like Hawkins, Wintour would not wish one "perfunctoriously to view her only, and passe her ouer with a slender glance of the eye" (sig. A1iv). Just as in an exercise of Ignatian meditation, the object viewed must be analyzed. With the *compositio loci* of the sensual embroidered garden before him, the beholder must picture himself entering it with the mind, "and with the wings of Contemplation . . . secretly view, reflect, review, survey, delight, contemplate, and enjoy the hidden and sublime perfections therein, and lastly obtaine, no doubt, anie reasonable suite at the hands of the SACRED PARTHENES" (4). Like a guide or example, the embroiderer lays out the steps of her own meditative process, culminating in her colloquial request for intercession: "*orate pro me Helena Wintovr.*"

Wintour and Hawkins share a common emblematic vocabulary, Hawkins's explicit, Wintour's implicit. The introductory tour round Hawkins's garden maps Wintour's embroidered surfaces and lays out the significance of their "Flowers of al Vertues" to clearer view: "the LILLIE of spotles and immaculate Chastitie, the ROSE of Shamfastnes and bashful Modestie . . . the Gilloflower ol *[sic]* Patience, the Marygold of Charitie . . . the SVNFLOWER of Contemplatiõ, the Tulip of Beautie and gracefulnes" (11). The shared emblematic vocabulary continues in the level of detail provided. Where Hawkins in his meditative essays expands the detail of his botanical descriptions, Wintour embroiders in silk and gold thread just such naturalistic and sensuous color effects. Thus the outline of her columbine (the "dove-flower," emblematic of the Holy Spirit and thus of the Annunciation) is picked out in gold thread (fig. 11), like Hawkins's "columbin" exquisitely "enameled with drops of gold" (10). Wintour pursues the same painstaking observation in depicting tulip leaves with minute and startling gradations of color as Hawkins, in his meditative exhortation to "[L]ooke and obserue it wel. How were it possible, one would think, so thin a leaf, bred and nourished in

Fig. 11. Columbine detail of Lady Wintour white vestment.

the same ayre, and proceeding from the same stem, should be golden in the bottome, violet without, saffron within, bordered on the edge with fine gold, and the prickle of the point blew as a goodlie Saphir?" (10).

In Wintour's depiction of roses at various stages of bloom (one, like Hawkins's rose, is "yet in its folds, and dares not hazard so much as to peepe forth; this heer puts forth the bud, and now half-open smiles withal, and showes forth a glimps of its purple, through a cliff *[sic]* of the green Case") we may read emblems both of the blushing, bashful virgin "when her glorious Paranimph discouered her Embassage to her in her secret closet" and of the exalted Queen of Heaven, "a glad spectacle vnto GOD," who is exhorted to "shew . . . thy face, for thy face is comelie" (8–9, 18, 23). And Wintour presents for us (to cite one last example) an embroidered equivalent of Hawkins's "Essay upon the Rose" (fig. 12), with "certain golden points, and little threds of Musk or Saffron, sticking into the hart of the *Rose*. But to speake of the fires of its Carnation, the snow of the white Satin, the fine Emralds, cut into little toungs round about . . . [would] fortify the hart . . . clear the cristal of the eyes . . . banish clowdes . . . coole our harts" (20–21). Wintour's full spectrum of glowing colors invites close scrutiny and analogous emblematic analysis.

The imagery that describes gardens and embroidery overlaps. As Hawkins's garden is "the Pallace of *Flora's* pomps, where is the wardrobe of her richest mantles, powdred with the starres of flowwers, and al embroadred with flowrie stones," so Wintour's vestments, embroidered with silks and precious metals and enriched with a wealth of pearls and semiprecious stones, recall the robes of the Virgin they depict (6). The sunflower or "Heliotropion" is "a verie Mart of silks, sarcenets, taffeties, and satins" (49). Its center is like "some finer cloth wrought with curious needle-work" (52). Reaching for the most vivid metaphors he can imagine, Hawkins describes lilies as seeming to be made "of white Satin, streaked without, and al embroadred within with gold" (9). The vestments themselves are a performative surface, a ceremonial textile integral to and symbolic of the performance of the Mass, and in this context Wintour's embroidered flowers sewn onto the silks are mirrored by Hawkins's elucidation of the garden as symbol and device: it is, he says, "a goodlie Amphitheatre of flowers, vpon whose leaues, delicious beauties stand, as on a stage, to be gazed on, and to play their parts, not to see so much, as to be seen" (5). The act of gazing in meditation is transformative, but in a simile in which he explains the process of emblematic signification Hawkins attributes a special effectiveness to the medium of iconographical textiles to

Fig. 12. Rose detail of Lady Wintour green vestment.

help signify something beyond imagining: "to behold, as in a Tapestrie, the Symbol turned into an *Embleme*, piously cõposed" (3).

Hawkins's text also sheds light on the elements of Wintour's garden that are not botanical. He anchors the jewels that ornament and enrich Wintour's embroidered surface in the iconography of the Virgin. Jewels reflect another aspect of the embroidered emblematic garden, and vice versa, since the Virgin-as-garden is "the Cabinet of flowrie gems, or gems of flowers" (6). Pearls are a particular feature of the Lady Wintour white vestment, and its wide vertical band of scrolling gold peapods filled with hundreds of pearls and enclosing large monograms of Christ and Mary in glories of rays is a striking and unique design (fig. 5). According to Marina Warner, the association of the Virgin with a pearl is rare but was debated in the mid-seventeenth century in connection with the search for the most effective way of representing the Immaculate Conception in visual terms. A pearl, "pure and imperishable," is also "glistening, white, and spherical, an exact epiphany of the moon," and represents Mary both in her aspect of Queen of the Heavens and in her aspect as *Stella maris*, Star of the Sea.[32] Despite these attributes, says Warner, "The suggestion was not acted upon, principally because there is no biblical foundation for associating the Virgin with a pearl."[33]

But Hawkins's text is one of the few that does develop the notion, devoting a whole section to a meditation on the emblematic representation of the Virgin as a pearl. He describes it as a polyvalent symbol, signifying that the Virgin is both "the *Pearl* itself" and the "*Mother* of the true *Oriental Pearl*, which descended from heauen" (190). Wintour's enclosure of the ray-surrounded monograms of both Christ and the Virgin in her pearl-covered embroidered design represents this same double significance, Mary-as-pearl and Mary-as-Mother-of-pearl: "the *Virgin-Mother-Pearl* itself, which opened her Virginal soule, at her mysterious *Annunciation* . . . to receive the new *Margarit*: that is, to conceaue that precious *Pearle, Christ Iesus,* in her womb. . . . The Celestial deaw of the *Holie-Ghost* descended into her, and so this infant-*Pearl* was diuinely begot in the virginal womb of the Virgin-mother-*Pearl*" (192).

Wintour's peapods are themselves an effective Marian emblem. She shows them opened to show their ordered pearly contents, in the same way as embroidered pomegranates on the same vestment are split open to reveal the seeds. The pomegranate (ancient symbol of fertility harnessed in the iconography of the Virgin, such as the Madonna of the Pomegranate in Naples), flanking the peapod band on the Lady Wintour white chasuble, is an element of Hawkins's garden. It is "an ordination of Vertues, and a wonderful sweetnes of Deuotion; for loe, Pomegranats haue their graines disposed in an admirable order, and are indeed most delicious fruits; to which kind of Apples the *Spouse* invites her *Spouse*" (15).

Other, nonbotanical features of Wintour's embroidered garden also occur as emblems in *Partheneia Sacra*. Like the pearl, Wintour's phoenix, hen, and dove are double symbols. The phoenix is the central image on the Lady Wintour white burse (fig. 13) and appears on the back of the subdeacon's dalmatic surmounted by an arch inscribed *Resvrgenti* (to the Resurrecting One). It was a symbol of Christ's resurrection from the early church onwards, although an unusual one.[34] On the eucharistic burse the phoenix emphasizes the Resurrection that transformed the supreme sacrifice of Christ's crucifixion into redemption, and indeed, on the antependium from which the dalmatic was made, it was one of a five-paneled sequence that included the pelican in her piety, symbol of Christ, who feeds his children with his blood. But Hawkins makes it clear that within Wintour's Marian-centered iconography the phoenix does double duty. For Hawkins the phoenix is the Virgin, for when God "framed the Incomparable *Virgin Marie*, and chose her to be his *Mother*, he made her so incomparable a *Phœnix*, not only to al, that euer were, or shal be, but euen to such, as he intended or was able to frame" (263). Hawkins emphasizes the doubleness of the symbol by juxtaposing his phoenix with images of wounds shared by Christ and his mother:

> *one* Virgin-Mother, *Phenix of her kind,*
> *And we her* Sonne *without a father find.*
> *The* Sonne's *and* Mothers *paines in one are mixt,*
> *His side, a Launce, her soule a Sword transfixt.*
> (266)

The image of the soul or heart transfixed with a sword occurs on every Marian monogram embroidered by Wintour (see, for example, fig. 9).[35]

The hen-and-chicks emblem now applied to the front of the deacon's dalmatic (fig. 2) has its origins in Matthew 23:37 and Luke 13:84, in Christ's simile "[H]ow often would I have gathered thy children together, even as a hen gathereth her chickens under her wings." Hawkins, however, includes the hen in his garden because she is "a truly gallant Symbol of the fruitful *Mother* of GOD" (179). In Hawkins's vision, it is the Virgin-as-hen who is

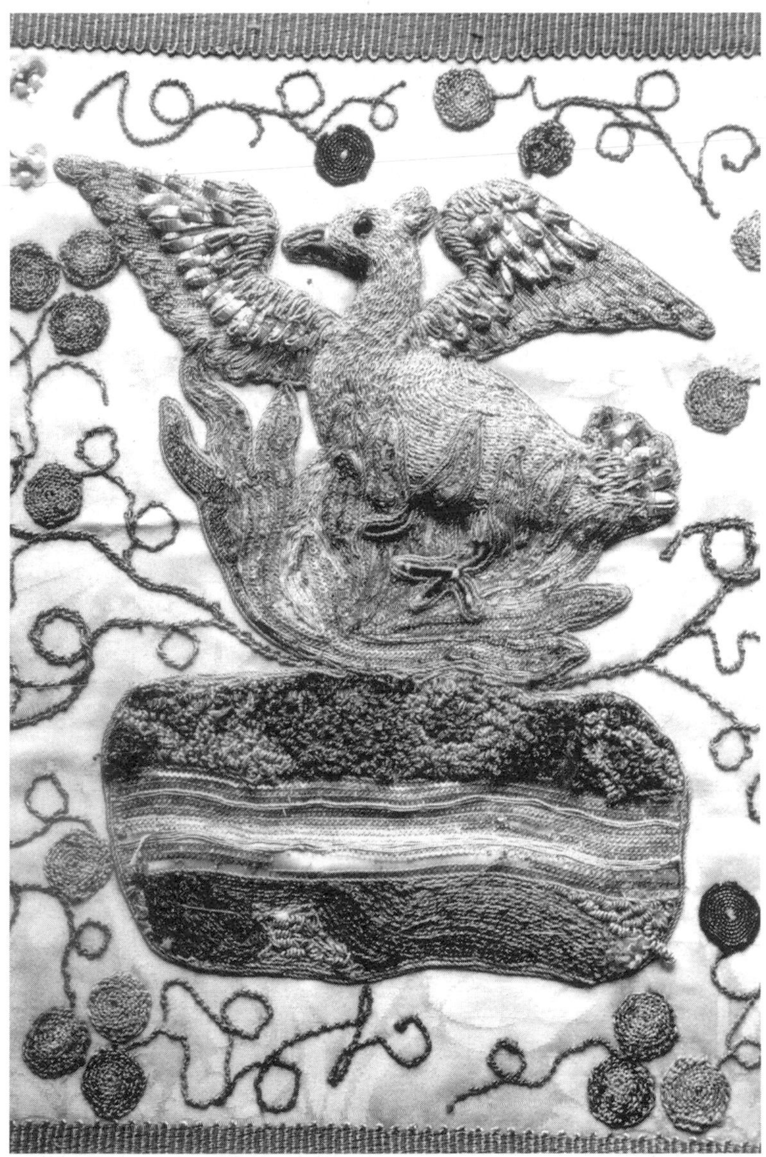

Fig. 13. Phoenix detail of burse, Helena Wintour, mid-seventeenth century. Courtesy of Private Collection.

the protector, who "wil rather euen dye in the place in defence of her brood, then by flying away leaue them in anie danger," and there is "*No mother, like the* Hen, *preserues her yong, / Protects, & shelters with her wings*" (179, 183). The hen is the symbol of the double fruitfulness of the Virgin: her natural fruitfulness as the mother of Jesus Christ and her spiritual or mystical fruitfulness. The notion of mystical fruitfulness applies the Gospel verses to Mary's relationship with the wider church and visualizes a "fecunditie" "which euen filles and embraceth the whole world, that inuocates and calles vpon the name of MARIE, and their common *Mother*" (179, 180). This symbol is particularly appropriate to the persecuted church appealing to the protection of their Lord.[36] Perhaps more significantly for the hen's appearance in the context of Helena Wintour's embroidery, Hawkins singles out the hen as the special signifier of the sodality: "But nothing demonstrates her spiritual fecunditie so much as the innumerable multitudes of Families of the *Sodalitie of her Immaculate Conception,* the true *Parthenian Children of our Sacred Parthenes* . . . which with al obseruance and due worship serue her as the *Mother* of GOD, and their common Parent: while they doubt not by her meanes to be led . . . and to obtaine Eternal saluation, if they serue her truly indeed, and but obserue the Rules of her said *Sodalities*" (180).

The dove is, of course, the principal symbol of the Holy Ghost and as such appears on the back of Wintour's red chasuble and on the front at the place where the arms and vertical element of the cross shape meet (fig. 4). A third dove is placed at the center of the matching red veil. More unusually, the dove is also a central design element on the Lady Wintour black vestment (fig. 7), intended for use on Good Friday and in the Masses and Offices of the Dead.[37] The placing of the embroidered doves in relation to the other elements of the designs is structurally significant and may provide the key to the dove's appearance on the black vestment.[38] On the chasubles all three doves are placed immediately above a large Marian monogram, producing a hierarchical, symbolic representation both of Mary's immaculacy and of the Annunciation. This notion is arresting and unanticipated on a vestment designed to be worn at Pentecost, on which embroidered tongues of flame and clouds of falling dew illustrate the descent of the Holy Spirit to the Apostles. The conjunction of dove and monogram suggest that this embroiderer envisages the descent of Pentecostal grace through Marian devotion, and a devotion to the Immaculate Conception and Annunciation in particular. On the front and back of the red chasuble grace is visualized as dew dropping from the wings of a dove onto the Marian monogram in a glory of rays.

Hawkins glosses dew at length in *Partheneia Sacra,* where its fall is synonymous with the Annunciation: "*Deawing,* that is, the *Incarnation.*" Thus Mary "is sayd to be *ful of Grace,* which is a kind of *Deaw*" (64, 63). Hawkins's emblem suggests that the Pentecostal descent of the Holy Spirit to the Apostles is understood by Wintour in terms of the descent of the Holy Spirit to Mary at the Annunciation, the grace of which descends further to Wintour herself and her family in emblematic showers of Marian dew falling upon Wintour's personal and family devices and heraldry at the base of the vestment. And indeed, Marian intercession is understood by Hawkins in the same terms as the Annunciation, as Mary "with her graces and fauors, as *Deawes* falling from heauen, perpetually doth nothing, but showre downe vpon her children and Deuotes" (68). On the back of the red chasuble Wintour's hope for Marian intercession is perhaps envisaged as being achieved through the mediation of the Society of Jesus, since between the Marian monogram and her initials she has inserted the Jesuit motto AMDG. Alternatively, Wintour's embroidery, "to the greater glory of God," may be her response to her trust in the Virgin's intercession. Wintour's red vestment is richly ornamented with diamonds, rubies, garnets, and hundreds of large pearls, and her jeweled drops of dew are rendered in a rainbow of variously colored silks and silver thread. She renders in embroidered terms Hawkins's conception of spiritual dew being closely linked with the idea of mystical pearls (68), an idea based on the fact that, seen from one side, a drop of dew "wil looke like an Orient-pearl, and being turnd some other way, becomes a glowing Carbuncle, then a Saphir, and after an Emerald, and so an Amethist" (66). Finally, Hawkins names dew as the origin of the garden: "[T]he *Deaw* it is which falling on our gardens empearls them with a thousand muskie gemmes: Heer it makes the Rose, there the Flowerdeluce; here the Tulips. . . . It is the *deaw,* that couers the rose with scarlet, that clothes the lillie with innocencie . . . which embroders the marygold with gold, and enriches al the flowers with gold, silk and pearls" (62–63). Dew first creates the flowers themselves and then, in an extension important for understanding Wintour's emblematic process, endows them with symbolic meaning by giving them color.

This reading of Wintour's Marian-oriented understanding of Pentecost is strengthened by the employment of the same juxtaposition of dove and monogram on the front of the black vestment, used on Good Friday, when the Feast of the Compassion of Our Lady is also celebrated. Here Wintour has emphasized the Marian role in the events of Christ's passion, organizing a series of monograms and ciphers below the dove to emphasize Christ's maternal

Fig. 14. IOS, MRA, AN, MAR, and IO monogram detail of Lady Wintour black vestment.

lineage: his mother Mary (MR, MRA, MAR), Mary's mother Anne (AN), her father Joachim (IO), and Christ's father Joseph (IOSPH, IOS) (fig. 14). The sixteenth-century Jesuit Marian devotees St. Ignatius (IG) and St. Francis Xavier (XA) are, on the back of the vestment, included in the monogrammed hierarchy. Hawkins's "Poesie on the Dove" provides an explanation for the dove's presence on the black vestment. The final couplet yokes the image of Virgin-as-dove to crucifixion: "But while her Sonne is shadowed on the Crosse, / The mourning Doue in blackes laments her losse."[39]

The notion of the Virgin as a "mourning Doue in blackes" is perhaps linked in the Jesuit or Jesuit-directed mind to the Madonna of Monserrat, one of the mysterious "Black Madonnas." Before this twelfth-century image Ignatius of Loyola in 1522 spent the night in prayer that led him to found the Society of Jesus. The Madonna of Monserrat holds the child Jesus, clasping a pine cone, on her lap. On Wintour's Alleluia vestment, slips of pine cone sprays anchor into the design a panel of Spanish embroidery showing a scene from Revelation (fig. 18). As Hawkins's "Poesie on the Phoenix" drew a reflec-

Fig. 15. Dove wing detail of red vestment.

tive comparison between the wounds of Christ and his mother, so here the experience of the grieving mother reflects her son's death, since "*they in colour sute, / and to the flower correspond's the fruit.*" In arranging the elements of her black vestment, Wintour has chosen to understand Good Friday through a distinctly Marian experience, coming to the crucifixion as a devotee of the grieving mother-as-dove. Likewise, the masses and offices of the dead are filtered through iconography that sees the Virgin as the source of intercession.

The embroidered silver doves are splendid centerpieces, demonstrations of Wintour's virtuosity as an embroiderer and testifying to the centrality of the dove to her theology. The upper wing feathers of the doves on the Pentecostal chasuble and veil are formed from overlapping tabs of silver ribbon depending from double rows of pearls, and the lower feathers are rendered with painstaking double rows of tiny seed-pearls highlighted by vertical bands of silver thread and silver sequins (fig. 15). The dove on the black vestment has colored silks worked into the metal threads of its breast to give the impression of a flashing rainbow—perhaps the most striking of all Wintour's embroidered images (fig. 16). Hawkins provides a key for this unusual "impressionistic"

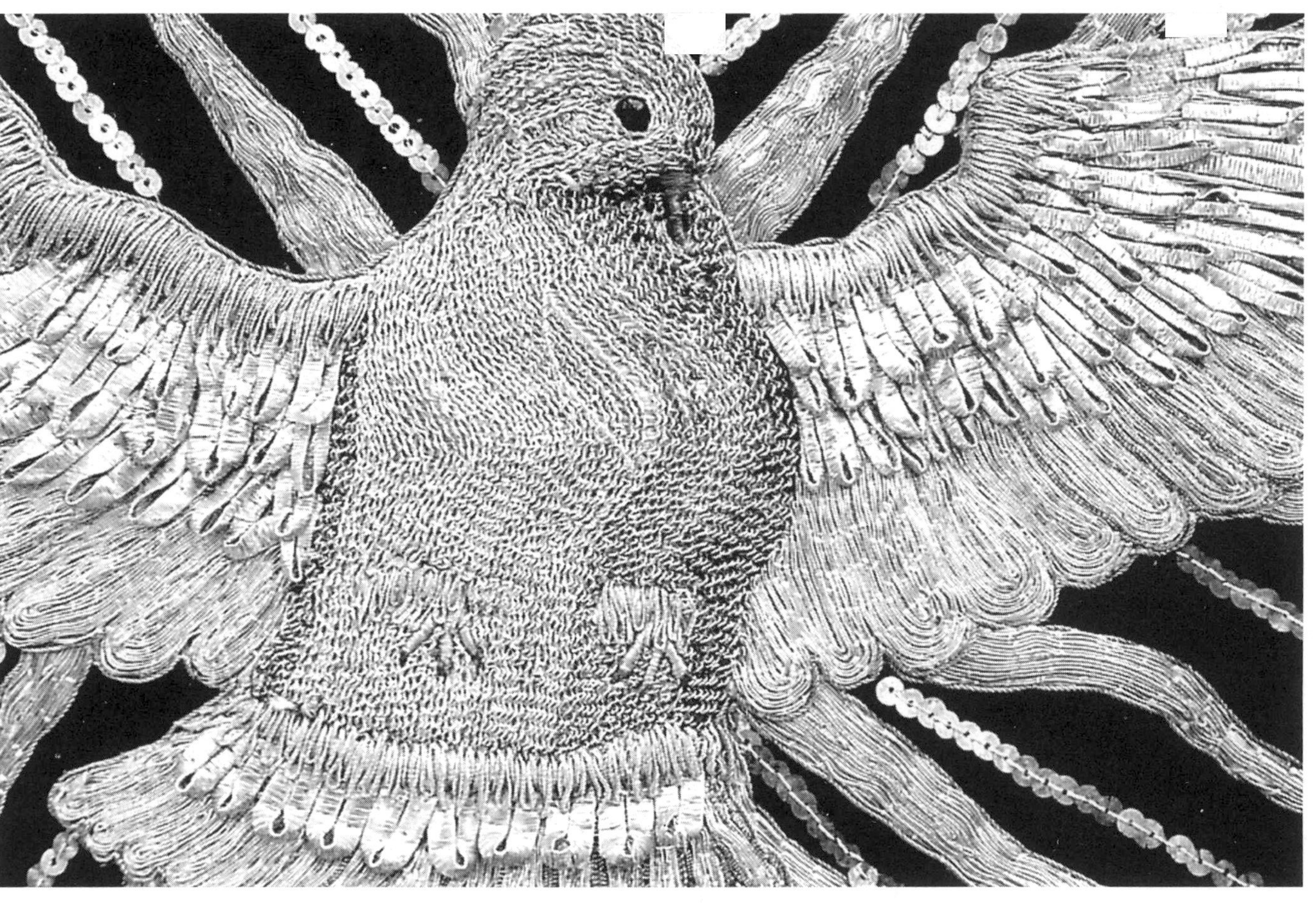

Fig. 16. Dove breast detail of black vestment.

feature that reinforces the reading for Wintour's dove as a Marian symbol in her Good Friday context. According to Hawkins, Mary-as-dove is exceptional in that "her neck being opposed to the Sun wil diuersify into a thousand coulours, more various then the Iris it-self, or that Bird of *Iuno* in al her pride; as scarlet, cerulean, flame-coulour, and yealding a flash, like the Carbuncle, with vermilion, ash-coulour, and manie others besides, which haue no name, but as you borrow them from other things" (201). Hawkins does not provide a theological interpretation for this natural curiosity beyond its denoting Mary's singularity. But on the mourning black of the Lady Wintour black vestment the rainbow-colored silks on the dove's breast stand out, a reminder both of the new covenant between God and his people and of Marian protection for her persecuted church in the darkest hour of the liturgical year.[40]

Partheneia Sacra, as Josephine Secker has noted, elucidates a "spirituality of retirement" for which the dove is the major emblematic vehicle.[41] The dove's habit of "digging . . . holes in the rock, and planting [its] litle pauillions there" makes the dove the pattern for the contemplative life of "Reading . . . Meditation . . . Contemplation" of Christ's life followed by the Virgin.[42] A shared position and a reflection on her retired and pious life may be indicated in Wintour's embroidery by the emphasis on the Virgin's immaculacy and Annunciation; the iconography of the Holy Spirit (such as the dove and rays of light) was particularly popular with nuns in the early seventeenth century.[43]

Hawkins's descriptions may or may not have served Helena Wintour, and she may or may not have followed his emblematic meditative process; no record of Wintour's reading matter has survived (although Hawkins spent his years as a missioner traveling in the West Midlands, where it is not impossible that he might have come into the circle of recusants in which Helena Wintour moved). But the parallel reading of printed and embroidered text has shed much light on Wintour's devotional practice, and the information so learned may usefully be borne in mind when making a closer study of the liturgical aspects of her embroidered texts.

Veni Sanctvs Spiritvs*: The Iconography of Personal Devotion*

The textual elements of Wintour's vestments are in themselves unusual. In exerting a choice over texts to embroider, including phrases from scriptural texts and nonscriptural hymns, from sequences and doxology, Wintour exerts a subtle influence over the interpretation of the Mass as it is performed. I want here to suggest that Wintour's choice of text is consistent with her choice of emblems, emphasizing a personal devotion to the Virgin Mary's Immaculate Conception and Annunciation, through which Wintour understands the Scriptures, the Offices, and the liturgical calendar.

It is unusual to see the early modern church and its ministers clothed in the liturgy. Monograms are familiar devices on church ornaments, including vestments and furnishings, as are heraldic representations of their donors, but Wintour's embroidered vestments emphasize the importance of the word, understood both literally, in terms of the spoken words of Scripture and liturgy, and spiritually as the Word made flesh. Her Jesuit priests, clothed in text, perform a literary and literal version of the raising of the Gospel to altar and congregation. These vestments are intended, not for an illiterate multitude, but for an intimate, literate minority, the educated recusant laity. Thus three biblical quotations in rings containing the Jesuit IHS monograms underscore the scriptural basis for the Jesuit devotion to the Holy Name and provide a textual gloss on the IHS monograms: on the front of the Alleluia vestment, *Sit nomen Domini benedictvm in eternvm* (Blessed be the name of the Lord forever), from Daniel 2:20; on the hood of the cope, *Datvm est nomen qvod est svper omne nomen* (God . . . hath . . . given him a name which is above every name), from Philippians 2:9; and on one of the Lady Wintour chalice veils, *Nomen dulce, nomen delectabile* (Sweet name, delectable name).[44]

Wintour's embroidered vestments narrate, symbolize, and perform the moment at which God becomes man and man relates to God through the mystery of the Sacrament. At the same time as the vestments play their integral role in the performance of the Sacrament and as the fertile Marian gardens on Wintour's dalmatics and the iconography of the Immaculate Conception and Annunciation on the red chasuble narrate the Word made flesh, the High Mass cope invites the Holy Spirit to descend with the words of the Golden Sequence, the Pentecostal gradual: *Veni Sanctvs Spiritvs, Veni pater pavpervm, Veni dator mvnervm, Veni lvmen cordivm* (Come Holy Spirit, Come thou Father of the poor, Come, thou Giver of gifts, Come, thou Light of hearts) (partially shown in fig. 17). The text in scrolls encloses flaming hearts for which Hawkins gives an emblematic gloss: the heart "enflamed with the love of Jesus shines al with light and flames."[45] We have seen how the red chasuble shares the Marian iconography of the Immaculate Conception and Annunciation with the rest of the vestments. But of course it also narrates,

Fig. 17. Orphrey detail of High Mass cope.

symbolizes, and performs a precise liturgical function with respect to the descent of the Holy Spirit in the same way as the High Mass cope.

Unexpectedly, the High Mass cope and the set of red vestments share their liturgical texts and iconography. Although she covers all the colors required by the rubrics in her collection of vestments, Wintour does not treat the events of the liturgical calendar in the same way. Textually, she emphasizes the descent of the Holy Ghost, imagined within her Marian iconography as referring to the Immaculate Conception, the Annunciation, and the Pentecostal events understood through the frame of Marian devotion. For example, she pares down the four sequences enshrined by Tridentine reform to just one, the Golden Sequence of Pentecost. The sequence is split between cope and red chasuble and is completed on the red veil with the exhortation *Veni Sancte Spiritvs, Reple tvorvm corda fidelivm* (Come Holy Spirit, fill the hearts of your faithful people). Helena Wintour's preference for the iconography of the Immaculate Conception, the Annunciation, and Pentecost extends throughout the liturgical year. Thus a silver dove appears on the Lady Wintour black vestment, the scrolling peapods and floral symbolism on the Lady Wintour white vestment emphasize the Virgin's own immaculacy and Christ's spotless incarnation, and the "LILLIE of spotles and immaculate Chastitie" ornaments the High Mass cope.

The text Wintour chose to illustrate the Easter liturgy is *Allelvia* (fig. 18). Omitted from the Masses and Offices in the nine weeks between Septuagesima and Easter, the Alleluia is the liturgical expression of joy and praise. It appears four times on the vestment, echoing the Roman usage of chanting the normal double Alleluia, a scriptural verse, and another Alleluia at Easter with an extra verse and another Alleluia added. Other liturgical texts might have been chosen. The panel of Spanish embroidery (integral to the design) depicts the vision of Revelation 5 in which a book is sealed with seven seals that "no man in heaven, nor in earth, neither under the earth, was able to open" (v. 3). A slain lamb standing "in the midst of the throne" is found worthy to break the seals and open the book, and a company of angels is heard "saying with a loud voice, Worthy is the Lamb that was slain to receive power, and riches, and wisdom, and strength, and honour, and glory, and blessing" (vv. 6, 12). Instead of this text, or the Paschal Sequence *Victimae paschali laudes,* the Alleluia has been chosen to anchor the vestment within the liturgy.

The simple, immediate Easter cry of joy is the textual expression of the uncontainable explosion of flowers bursting out of the confines of their strap-

Fig. 18. "Alleluia" detail of "Alleluia" vestment.

work panels. In the golden tulips of Wintour's embroidered Easter garden of resurrection, Christ's "bitter cup" is transformed into a living chalice. His love is represented by red and white carnations and roses. Scrolling vines and bunches of grapes symbolize not only Christ's redemptive blood and his victory over death but also his promise to his disciples in the parable of the vine. They celebrate the body of the newly established church, united in sacrament: "I am the vine, ye are the branches" (John 15:5). Pomegranates embroidered on the backs of the shoulder panels are split wide open to reveal their countless seeds, underscoring the creation of the Christian Church. And at the same time Wintour's iconography typically filters the Easter experience through Marian devotion: by placing a jewel-encrusted and crowned Marian monogram at the top of the front band above an IHS monogram in its glory of rays, Wintour glories in the apotheosis of the Mother of Christ through the resurrection of her Son. The Virgin's floral emblems reflect this apotheosis. No longer separate slips, the flowers appear to grow riotously from the same stems, drawn into a single design by the strapwork. They are all here: the lily of her chastity, the rose of her modesty and purification, the gillyflower of her patience, the marigold of her charity, and the tulip of her beauty and grace. And each virtue has been ornamented by the Easter miracle. The blood of Christ has drenched the embroidered golden lilies, and the white roses and carnations are each tinged with red, transforming the Virgin's garden into an emblem of the Resurrection.

The irrepressible riot of flowers and textual cry of joy on the Alleluia vestment are designed to provide the strongest possible contrast with the stripping of the altars on Maundy Thursday and the black vestments of Good Friday. As the Alleluia vestment illustrates a central moment in the Paschal liturgy, so the Lady Wintour black vestment illustrates the Good Friday Offices. Mass was not said on Good Friday and Holy Saturday. Instead, it was replaced with the Liturgy of the Word, the Veneration of the Cross, and the Reception of the Eucharist. Wintour responds to this spare liturgy by paring down her iconography to her series of Marian-related monograms, reflecting the Liturgy of the Word within the framework of the Feast of the Compassion of Our Lady. The conventional form of the cross on which the monograms are borne echoes the Veneration of the Cross. The final element of the Good Friday Office, the Reception of Communion, is dramatized by the presence of Wintour's embroidered silver dove.

Two other embroidered texts give indications of Helena Wintour's religious experience. Above and below the Golden Sequence on the left- and right-hand orphreys of the High Mass cope are phrases from the Te Deum, *Sanctvs, sanctvs, Dnvs Devs Sabaoth, Plena est orbis terra gloria tva* (Holy, holy, Lord God of Hosts, heaven and earth are full of your glory), and the Lesser Doxology, *Gloria Pri et Filio et Spiritv Sancto, sicvt erat in principio et nvnc et sempr* (Glory be to the Father, and to the Son, and to the Holy Ghost, as it was in the beginning, is now, and for ever shall be) (fig. 17). The scrolls containing the texts surround embroidered cherubim or seraphim, who continually cry the Sanctus, according to the Te Deum, and stand in for the missing text with their winged forms. The Sanctus itself is transposed to the bottom of the orphreys, in the place of donor heraldry, suggesting the adoration of the embroiderer. Both texts are contained in the breviary Offices (the lesser Gloria appended at the end of every psalm) and form an important part of the daily devotions recited alone or in small groups by the laity when a priest is not available to say Mass (indeed, the Greater Doxology that Wintour chose not to embroider, the Gloria in Excelsis, would have been more appropriate for the High Mass for which the cope was only subsequently created). The choice of texts embroidered on the original antependium may thus have served Wintour's private daily Offices. This notion is supported especially by the inclusion of the Te Deum, not part of the Mass itself.

Personal and family arms, crest and motto, Jesuit symbols and iconographical emphasis create a memorial that may be read clearly after three and a half centuries. Wintour's memorial is designed to be performed with each Mass. Her prayer for intercession, *ora pro me Helena Wintovr,* is directed as much to the Virgin as to the clergy who are clothed in the prayer and the laity who witness it. She "signs" her work with personal and family heraldry but also, perhaps, with floral iconography: a spray of honeysuckle at the base of the Lady Wintour green vestment where one would expect donor/maker heraldry to be found is conspicuous in its smaller scale and may be a modest reference to Wintour's enduring faith.[46]

While most of the unmarried women in the Gunpowder Plot families (including Helena's own sister Mary) left the country to seek refuge in the convents on the Continent, Helena Wintour remained in England, living the type of life that Hawkins advocated.[47] She remained unmarried, lived in retirement, and dedicated herself to prayer, self-sacrifice, works of charity, and support of the Catholic Church. In undertaking to embroider a cycle of vestments that uses as its central conceit the notion of the Virgin Mary as garden, Wintour emphasized a personal devotion to the Virgin Mary and to her Immaculate Conception and Annunciation. The iconography on the cope even envisages Wintour within the protection of the Marian garden, containing Wintour's personal heraldic devices within two arching floral compositions (fig. 19).

The Immaculate Conception was an issue of great contention in the sixteenth and seventeenth centuries. It was not enshrined in doctrine by the Council of Trent. Debate on the subject was banned by Pope Paul V in 1616, and indeed it was not declared dogma until Pope Pius IX's Bull of 1854.[48] Nonetheless the Immaculate Conception had its devoted followers. In Jesuit-led communities, in convents, and among those in the wider community who had taken private vows it was of vital significance and importance. It was reflected in the iconography they created and with which they surrounded themselves. The emphasis in Helena Wintour's embroidered *hortus conclusus* on the iconography of the Immaculate Conception, the ubiquity of pearls as

Fig. 19. Heraldic elements enclosed in garden, detail of High Mass cope.

both ornamental and structural device, the floral symbols of virginity and the Holy Spirit (lilies and columbines), the recurring dove and the rays of light surrounding her monograms, and the Jesuit-led doubleness of the phoenix and hen symbols are powerfully persuasive of a personal devotion to the Immaculate Conception and perhaps suggest that Wintour leaned toward, or had taken, private vows of the sort made by a member of a sodality dedicated to the Immaculate Conception.

Notes

I would like to thank the curators of both the Stonyhurst and the Lady Wintour sets of Helena Wintour's vestments for their many kindnesses and for allowing me access to examine and photograph the vestments. The staff at the Whitworth Gallery in Manchester also extended me much time on a visit to examine the Stonyhurst set while the vestments were briefly in their care.

1. Stonyhurst Archives, Stonyhurst College, Clitheroe, Lancashire, MSS A.I.22, no. 1.

2. T. G. Holt, S.J., "The Wintours, the Jesuits and Evenlench Farm, Tibberton: A Secret Trust," *Transactions of the Worcestershire Archaeological Society* 10 (1986): 71; H[enry] C[hadwick], "Helena Wintour and Her Vestments," *Stonyhurst Magazine* 29 (1948): 245.

3. Report, dated December 4, 1605, by William Walsh and Edward Newport to Sir Richard Walsh, Cecil MSS (Hatfield), vol. 191, no. 92, quoted in John Humphreys, *Studies in Worcester History: Being a Selection of Papers of Historical and Antiquarian Interest*, ed. E. A. B. Barnard (Birmingham: Cornish, 1938), 59.

4. The Arrowsmith vestment is now on display in the Museum of Lancashire and is illustrated at http://freespace.virgin.net/mick.gardner/vestment.htm. The Sheldon vestment is held by Downside Abbey.

5. A notable exception is the famous Syon Cope, preserved in the British Museum. The cope left the country with the Brigettine Syon nuns during the reign of Queen Elizabeth, and when the nuns returned from their enforced exile in Lisbon 250 years later the cope came too. Vestments and other church textiles were frequently given as dowries by nuns first taking the veil on the Continent: in 1678 one such dowry, "a flowred satteen suit of church stuffe; and all things compleat to itt; ritchly made up with gold and siluer lace," was presented to the Benedictines at Pontoise; see *Miscellanea X*, Publications of the Catholic Record Society 17 (Leeds: Whitehead, 1915), 257. Documents from the continental religious houses that record

faint traces of lost needlework are examined for information about needlework practices in exile in ch. 3 of S.J. Holroyd's "Embroidered Rhetoric: The Social, Religious and Political Functions of Elite Women's Needlework, c. 1560–1630" (PhD diss., University of Warwick, 2003).

6. The difficulties of researching in the area of recusant cultural production are summed up in the introduction to the proceedings of a conference held at Downside Abbey in June 2004: "Recusant Archives and Remains from the Three Kingdoms, 1560–1789: Catholics in Exile at Home and Abroad" (www.catholic-heritage.net/recusant/conference_proceedings.rtf): "By and large, the collections which originate from Catholicism under penalty are not research collections laid forth for the secular scholar, and indexed in ways to meet the needs of a secular scholar of culture or history. These are not collections specifically set up to serve the needs of the researcher, they are not the special collections rooms of university libraries. Most of the collections. . . are the accretions of particular institutions, specific houses, many of them colleges and religious houses, a few of them families. All have been subject to sudden dispersals and removals. At some time or another almost all of them have been subjected to arbitrary visitation and confiscation. They are organised on the whole in ways which reflect the enforced priorities of those who preserved them: accounts and title to property are always more likely to survive than are evidences of cultural production" (5). At the same conference, Eamon Duffy, in his introductory address, stressed the precariousness of the survival of "the Patrimony of the British and Irish Catholic Church" even now, stressing "the magnificence and fragility of that patrimony: its prodigious survival against the odds, but also its vulnerability at a time when religious houses are closing and amalgamating" (6).

7. John Gerard, *Autobiography of an Elizabethan*, 2nd ed., trans. Philip Caraman (New York: Longmans, Green, 1956), 40, 184, 40.

8. Ibid., 24.

9. Thomas à Kempis, *The Imitation of Christ* (New York: Oxford University Press, 1947), 4.5.3.

10. For an in-depth iconographical study of medieval vestments, see Penelope Earle Wallis, "The Iconography of English Embroidered Vestments c. 1250–c. 1500" (PhD diss., University of London, 1988).

11. Gerard, *Autobiography*, 190.

12. *The Lives of Philip Howard, Earl of Arundel . . . and of Anne Dacres, His Wife*, ed. Duke of Norfolk (London: Hurst and Blacket, 1857), 220.

13. Gerard, *Autobiography*, 152.

14. Ibid., 383.

15. Godfrey Anstruther, *Vaux of Harrowden: A Recusant Family* (Newport, MT: Johns, 1953), 386, citing State Papers 14/19, no. 2. The conservation of textiles associated with a martyr was typical (the St. Edmund Arrowsmith vestment, for example).

16. *Vaux Peerage Case before the House of Lords* (London: HMSO, 1836–37), 202, cited in Anstruther, *Vaux of Harrowden,* 406.

17. Michael Hodgetts, "The Priest-Holes at Harvington Hall," *Transactions of the Worcester Archaeological Society* 39 (1962): 5. The chapel still has its original wall paintings, dating to around 1600, of large red and white drops to symbolize the blood and water of the Passion. I am grateful to Jackie Thomas for this reference.

18. Michael Hodgetts, "Topographical Index, Part 1," *Recusant History* 16 (1982–83): 164.

19. Ibid., 168.

20. Stonyhurst, *Anglia,* 1:73, cited without further reference in Anstruther, *Vaux of Harrowden,* 190.

21 This vestment, known as the "Pedlar's Vestment," is held in the collection of All Saints Chapel, Wardour.

22. The bond confirming Wintour's intestacy is held together with the inventory of her goods and chattels in the Worcester Record Office, WRO wills series 008.7, May 9, 1671. Stonyhurst MSS A. I.22, no. 2 is an attested copy of the instrument that is referred to in other contemporary documents as her "will." It is reproduced in full in Chadwick, "Helena Wintour," 249–50.

23. Chadwick, "Helena Wintour," 247. The source of the information is a note dated April 5, 1854, written by Father Henry Campbell at Grafton (Stonyhurst MSS A. I.22). For reports of the dispute, see the unpublished catalog "Stonyhurst Vestments" prepared by T. G. Holt, S.J., 3–4, and Chadwick, "Helena Wintour," 245–47. For the history of the two collections after Wintour's death, see Holroyd, "Embroidered Rhetoric," 215–20.

24. Stonyhurst Archives, Brother Houghton's notebooks, 2:25.

25. The quotation in the title of this section is from Henry Hawkins, *Partheneia Sacra* (Rouen, 1633; reprint, Aldershot: Scolar Press, 1993), 79. Subsequent references to this edition are given in the text.

26. Ignatius of Loyola, *The Spiritual Exercises,* trans. Father Elder Mullan, S.J. (New York: P. J. Kennedy and Sons, 1914), 26, 27.

27. Karl Josef Höltgen in his introduction to the Scolar facsimile edition of *Partheneia Sacra,* 6. Höltgen also discusses Hawkins's development of the Ignatian structure into a new, seven-part form.

28. The son of Sir Thomas Hawkins of Nash Court, Kent, Henry Hawkins (1577–1646) entered the English College of the Society of Jesus in Rome four years after the death in January 1605 of his wife, Aphra Norton, after only eleven months of marriage. After studying with the society in Flanders, Hawkins returned to England as a missioner. For a more detailed personal and literary biography of Hawkins, see Höltgen's introduction to *Partheneia Sacra,* 1–12. Höltgen in his introduction and Rosemary Freeman in ch. 7 of *English Emblem Books* (London: Chatto and Windus,

1967) discuss both the Jesuit tradition of combining emblems with meditations and Hawkins's methods. Michael Bath devotes ch. 9 of *Speaking Pictures: English Emblem Books and Renaissance Culture* (New York: Longman, 1994) to Hawkins's "Symbolical Theology" (233–54), discussing in particular the relationship of *Partheneia Sacra* to the developing emblem tradition in terms of both its roots and its influence.

29. These sodalities, the members of which took private vows, were established for the purpose of perfecting personal virtue, for directing study and prayer, and for performing works of charity, self-sacrifice, and the conversion of souls to the Catholic faith. On sodalities, see Freeman, *English Emblem Books,* 180–81, and Philip McCosker, "Sodality of the Blessed Virgin Mary: Devotion or Institution?" *Stonyhurst Magazine* 50 (1997). Although members of sodalities were predominantly male, women were also granted membership: according to her biographer, Anne Dacres, Countess of Arundel, was "admitted into the Society or Confraternity of the Rosary, as also into the Sodality instituted in honour of the Immaculate Conception" (Duke of Norfolk, *Lives of Philip Howard,* 297–98).

30. Sabine Chambers, *The Garden of Our B. Lady,* ed. D. M. Rogers, English Recusant Literature 381 (1619; reprint, London: Scolar Press, 1978).

31. Stephanus Luzvic, *The Devout Hart,* trans. Henry Hawkins, English Recusant Literature 119 (Rouen: Cousturier, 1634; reprint, London: Scolar Press, 1975), 160.

32. Marina Warner, *Alone of All Her Sex: The Myth and Cult of the Virgin Mary,* enlarged ed. (London: Pan, 1985), 267.

33. Pearls had been employed as a symbol of the Virgin's purity much earlier, in the fifteenth century: see, for instance, "Fful pure in peerle / hire clothyng was," from the anonymous lyric "Undir a park" (London, British Library, MS Harley 2255, fols. 150v–151v, line 53). I am grateful to an anonymous reader for this reference.

34. F. L. Cross, ed., *Oxford Dictionary of the Christian Church* (New York: Oxford University Press, 1957), 1068.

35. The image of the pierced heart has its origin in Simeon's prophecy to Mary in the temple, that "a sword shall pierce through thy own soul also, that the thoughts of many hearts may be revealed" and is the symbol in Marian devotion of the Five Sorrowful Mysteries (Luke 2:35). Its presence adds weight to the notion that Wintour used her embroidery for meditation. The rose symbols of Marian mysteries, also central to meditative techniques, are all present on Wintour's vestments: the five petals of the white rose in Marian devotion signify the Five Joyful Mysteries of Mary (the Annunciation, the Visitation, the Nativity, the Presentation, the Finding of Christ in Temple); the five petals of the red rose are the Five Sorrowful Mysteries (the Prayer and Agony in the Garden, the Scourging at the Pillar, the Crowning with Thorns, the Carrying of the Cross, and the Crucifixion and Death of Christ); and the five petals of the gold rose are the Five Glorious Mysteries (the Resurrection, the Ascension, the Descent of the Holy Spirit to the Apostles, the Assumption, and the Coronation of the Virgin in Heaven and the Glory of the Saints).

36. The hen-and-chicks emblem was harnessed for this iconographical purpose by Sir Thomas Tresham, Helena Wintour's kinsman. The emblem is one of a number of devices used to ornament Tresham's architectural designs, according to a memorandum written July 15, 1597; see Historical Manuscripts Commission, *Report on Manuscripts in Various Collections*, vol. 3 (London: HMSO, 1904), xlv, 91.

37. The theory and practice of liturgical colors have varied enormously over time. The most complete study of available records is Sir William St. John Hope and E. G. Cuthbert F. Atchley's *English Liturgical Colours* (New York: Macmillan, 1918). It is generally agreed that the prevailing official stipulation was that red was the liturgical color for Passiontide and Good Friday (see, for example, Hope and Atchley, *English Liturgical Colours*, 162), but Hope and Atchley have shown many occurrences of black vestments in use for Good Friday. The tradition handed down with the Lady Wintour set is that the black vestment was for use on Good Friday.

38. The black vestment is believed to be in its original state, and the embroidery of the red chasuble was reapplied in the nineteenth century, conserving the original design. The similarities in the location of the dove with respect to the Marian monogram support this belief.

39. A marginal note by Hawkins quotes from Pierus Valerianus's *Hieroglyptica*: "Columbam nigram pingebat[ur] Aegiptu ad significanda[m] vidua[m] ca[ ]am et constantem: inquit Pierius" (Pierius says that the dove was painted black in Egypt to signify the [chaste?] and constant widow).

40. Freeman comments that Henry Peacham's *The Compleat Gentleman* glossed "divers colours together, as in . . . a pigeon's neck" (ed. G. S. Gordon [1634; reprint, Oxford: Clarendon Press, 1906], 155) and that this was a "conventional comparison" or "commonplace of description" (*English Emblem Books*, 190 n). Michael Bath does not agree that the image was common, suspecting that it was more "a technical image from contemporary discussion of the art of painting" (*Speaking Pictures*, 244).

41. Josephine Evetts Secker, "Henry Hawkins, S.J., 1577–1646: A Recusant Writer and Translator of the Early Seventeenth Century," *Recusant History* 11 (1971–72): 242.

42. Ibid., 199, 200–201.

43. See Geoffrey Scott's study "The Image of Augustine Baker," in *That Mysterious Man: Essays on Augustine Baker*, ed. Michael Woodward (Abergavenny: Three Peaks Press, 2001), 110. I am grateful to Father Scott for this reference and for his comments on an early version of this essay.

44. One source for this phrase is the Burnett Psalter, fols. 38r and 58r, in the Aberdeen University Library. The pages are illustrated at www.abdn.ac.uk/diss/historic/collects/bps/text/038r.htm and at www.abdn.ac.uk/diss/historic/collects/bps/text/058r.htm with a Latin transcription and English translation.

45. Luzvic, *Devout Hart*, 227.

46. Charlotte E. J. Mayhew gives this reading for the honeysuckle in an appendix of religious symbolism to "The Effects of Economic and Social Developments in the Seventeenth Century upon British Amateur Embroideries, with particular reference to the Collection in the National Museums of Scotland" (MA thesis, University of St. Andrews, 1998).

47. Mary Wintour joined the newly formed convent of St Monica's, Louvain, together with Francis Tresham's younger daughter Lucy (third cousin of Helena and Mary Wintour), and Dorothea Rookwood, half-sister of the Plotter Ambrose. Helena Wintour's third cousin once removed Joyce Vaux (daughter of Eliza and niece of Anne Vaux and Eleanor Brookesby) joined Mary Ward's Institute of the Blessed Virgin Mary with Dorothea Rookwood's sister Susanna. Helena Catesby became a nun in Flanders, as did Mary, Lady Percy, and Ambrose Rookwood's other half-sister Susanna. One woman connected to the Plot who did remain in England was Helena Wintour's second cousin twice removed Anne Vaux. She was the dedicatee of Leonard Lessius's *The Treasure of Vowed Chastity in Secular Persons*, trans. J.W. P [John Wilson Priest?] ([St. Omer's], 1621). She took secular vows and lived "to all intents and purposes as a nun" (Anstruther, *Vaux of Harrowden*, 189).

48. Warner, *Alone of All Her Sex*, 248, 247, 249.

4

A Cosmopolitan Court in a Confessional Age

Henrietta Maria Revisited

Caroline Hibbard

Queen Henrietta Maria's life and its impact on English politics provide a striking example of the international dimensions of early modern English Catholic culture, illustrating how difficult it is to discuss this culture in a purely English context. Arguably, her career served to emphasize and even exaggerate the "foreignness" of Catholicism, reopening the latent debate about Catholic loyalty and arousing unprecedented xenophobic expressions by the 1640s. She found herself described as an evil counselor and even as a traitor to the English people and as the focus for Catholic plotting against the English nation.[1] But although as a queen and a Frenchwoman Henrietta Maria had a very particular story, as a Catholic living in England her situation was not altogether unique or accidental. The survival of the Catholic faith in post-Reformation England depended on organization, financing, and to some extent clerical recruitment that was directed or generated from overseas. These facts of life made English Catholics perennially vulnerable to the charge that they were unpatriotic or even treasonous, even though the great majority of the lay Catholics were loyal subjects of the crown throughout the early modern period.[2] It is true that English lay Catholics were often (but not invariably) more "cosmopolitan" than their Protestant counterparts, but the international orientation of English Catholicism was far more than a matter of culture or attitude; it was institutionally their destiny.

By 1640, Henrietta Maria was already receiving the bad press that would accelerate during the civil war as she was demonized by the king's enemies. This brought about a precipitous and long-term decline in her reputation, which lingers in our sense that the political disaster she helped create was somehow an inevitable outcome of her personal character and background.[3] In this assumption, we adopt the perspective of her enemies, who defined the "culture wars" of their century as the struggle of the godly against Antichrist. Likewise, the evolution of English antipopery is now a familiar story: the character of the Henrician Reformation, more schismatic than "reformed," ensuring that the polemics of antipopery were deeply etched into national discourse, this polemic then reinforced by the Spanish marriage of Mary Tudor, later by the Armada, and finally by the Gunpowder Plot. In retrospect, this wider narrative has also acquired an aura of inevitability that obscures the energy devoted by three successive monarchs to ensuring that the de facto religious pluralism that they inherited did not destroy England's internal unity or external standing in the European world. In "revisiting" Henrietta Maria, it is worth trying to avoid the ex post facto perspective inherent in both these narratives and to look afresh at the queen's life before the Scottish crisis. Restoring contingency to the narrative will also reveal how, from 1638 onwards, the French-born queen came, ironically, to be identified with what might more plausibly be labeled a "Spanish" policy than a French one.

Some general reflections on cosmopolitan courts in this confessional age may help set the stage for this review. The religious schism of the Reformation caused enormous disruptions in both the domestic politics and the international relations of Europe, making a hash of careful geopolitical calculations of national interest, breaking traditional lines of communication, and cutting across the hierarchical organization of domestic society. This played out differently in each country, and not always to the permanent disadvantage of the prince; among the several peculiarities of the English situation was that an anointed monarch ruled over a state church with a highly Calvinistic theology.[4] And the culture and pretensions of anointed monarchs coexisted very uneasily with the predestinarian theology and apocalyptic outlook of Calvinism.

Externally, the Reformation had almost entirely negative effects on English foreign policy, reducing options, creating potential enemies, and complicating foreign alliances. For over a century, English monarchs can be seen struggling to free themselves from these constrictions in the international arena and to sustain English independence against the Catholic superpowers.[5] Elizabeth evaded part of this problem by refusing to marry, thus maintaining domestic stability by not introducing a sexual relationship with an emissary of Antichrist into the heart of the court; this (like so many of Elizabeth's policies) was not a permanent solution. England's safety as a small power lay in international alliances that would prevent the predominance of one Catholic power across the Channel, or—more alarming still—a united Catholic crusade against it.[6] Paradoxically, the countries best able to help and most likely to want to in the political conjuncture of the early seventeenth century were Catholic countries. It is interesting to speculate what might have been the effect of one of the two marriages suggested (before his premature death in 1612) for Prince Henry, the eldest son of James I. Tuscany and Savoy were both Catholic countries, although with less symbolic baggage than Spain.[7] A decade later the looming continental conflict between France and Spain had set them both in competition for the surviving English prince, whose value had risen as their enmity grew.

The French marriage of 1625 is then, from the English perspective, a prime example of the monarchy's attempts to escape from the limitations imposed by the Reformation on its freedom of maneuvering in the international arena.[8] France, after all, had been for at least thirty years the European great power to whom the English might best look for an ally with a nuanced view of religion—the land of *politiques* as well as Catholic crusades. An anecdote about the young queen suggests that she too, however orthodox her training, understood the religious ambiguities of French history: asked impertinently after her arrival if she could "abide" a Huguenot, she answered, "Why not? . . . Was not my father one?"[9] James I had spent seven years attempting to reach a settlement with Henry IV that would ensure the peace of Christendom,[10] and in the years after Henry's death, when Marie de Medici seemed to have entrenched a more *devot* domestic and foreign policy through the double marriage with Spain that she arranged in 1615, French Protestants looked to James as a source of potential support.[11] Another such balancing act by the English crown was the effort to retain ritual institutions that bridged the confessional gap. Notably, the Order of the Garter, to which Catholic princes and high nobility continued to be nominated, had modified its ceremonies by dropping the requiem Mass and the common communion.[12]

Prestigious dynastic alliances added to the renown of the court abroad, as did the magnificence of the court itself. At home, as the social, cultural and patronage center of the realm, the court by its splendor and by its maintenance of a decorous hierarchy helped to order domestic society.[13] The sumptuous display of material luxury—what we would call conspicuous consumption—usually had a restricted audience of courtiers and, especially, agents of foreign princes.[14] This pattern of courtly life was always open to criticism by English Calvinists, deeply uneasy as they were about the visual arts and all that resembled theater; in times of national crisis, there were calls for national fasting, humiliation, and repentance; but these came from Parliament or the London pulpits, and the early Stuart court rather resisted than took the lead in such events.[15]

If Calvinist observers were at best ambivalent about the secular splendor of the court, they were deeply and vocally suspicious of the religious practice there, which they regarded as near-popery, distorted by successive monarchs' desire to placate foreign Catholic princes.[16] The "unreformed" character of the liturgy and associated ceremony in the Chapel Royal from Elizabeth's accession onwards is certainly striking. If the liturgy of the 1559 Book of Common Prayer was, as critics alleged, but "half-reformed," that of the Chapel Royal was about quarter-reformed. After Edward VI, there were indeed sermons, sometimes lengthy, tolerated by Queen Elizabeth and appreciated by James I, but the service was otherwise profoundly conservative, with many features that would have been familiar to the court of Henry VII.[17] Catholic foreigners, when they had reason to enter the Chapel Royal or attend a service there, found a setting that looked familiar, although the language was not Latin but English. Like cathedrals, the Chapel Royal had become a sort of protected sanctuary for an essentially pre-Reformation order.[18] Diarmaid MacCulloch has remarked how irrelevant the cathedral liturgy was to a Protestant church and how it had "virtually no effect on the musical or devotional life of the parish churches beyond the walls of the cathedral closes";[19] much the same could be said of the Chapel Royal, save that its role at the center of national life gave it a shock value greater than that of the cathedrals.

The reasons for this liturgical conservatism seem to go beyond the monarchs' personal piety or concern for foreign sensibilities, into the "penumbra" of court ceremony surrounding the actual liturgy of the chapel and to some extent derived from it. Fiona Kisby has shown how much continuity there was in the ritual year and in important chapel practices—notably the very formal royal procession to the chapel—through and beyond the Reformation, and she points out that much of this chapel ritual is still visible in the reign of Queen Anne.[20] Moreover, there developed in sixteenth-century England, as in continental courts, what has been called the "sacralization of the prince," by which anointed monarchs, especially, appropriated gestures and symbols drawn from the traditional liturgy, both in their chapel ceremonial (use of the canopy in processions) and in secular ceremonies such as public dining.[21] While in Catholic countries the resemblance of the monarch's gestures to those of an officiating priest was another bond between prince and people, the audience in England was very different.

This disjunction was symptomatic of how little the Protestant Reformation had done for the English crown in consolidating elites and buttressing crown control over them, compared to the developments in the Catholic powers after the Catholic Reformation. Not only had the elite been split by the Reformation—this happened also in France—but the dominant segment found it difficult to unite under the crown in symbolic religious events. Unlike Spain or France, where Reformed Catholicism embedded the monarch in a powerfully refurbished liturgy,[22] few of the most powerful Protestant impulses of the English Reformation—"antipopery" aside—were associated with the ruler or dynasty from 1560 onwards. National shared ceremony in England was either secular/chivalric (royal entrees, joustings) or antipapal in emphasis (Accession Day, Guy Fawkes Day); it seldom had a positive religious character like that of the Te Deum sponsored by Henrietta Maria at her son's restoration in 1660.

The diminished role for English royalty in the public religious cult affected the queen as well as the king. There had been royal cults in pre-Reformation England, notably that of Edward the Confessor, to which both king and queen were especially attached. But the queens consort also drew heavily on association with the Queen of Heaven; they sponsored Marian devotions and were clothed publicly in Marian imagery that alluded to their role as intercessors, patrons, and progenitors.[23] In post-Reformation England, unlike France and Spain, the Marian structure and vocabulary were lost, and with these an important bridge between queens consort and their English subjects. It is a curiosity that Henrietta was greeted in the city of Winchester, through which she passed in the summer of 1625, in old-fashioned Marian terms; but both the Marian liturgies and confraternities that she sponsored at the court and her intercession for English Catholics were profoundly distasteful to most zealous Protestants.

The language in which the queen's critics expressed themselves allowed for few of the nuances or compromises required for the survival of monarchy in the complicated circumstances described above. A ferocious edge is already visible in attacks made on her soon after the marriage, in which she was compared to Jezebel and other idolaters, and the king was urged to repudiate her if he could not convert her "from the idols of her father's house."[24] Otherwise, God would turn against the king and the country. As Christopher Hill reminds us, "Good kings are rare in the Old Testament," bad kings were "usually those who spared idolaters," and God's judgment on evil kings was heavy.[25] But in the 1620s, both the number of such comments and the audience for them appears to have been relatively small. Following Old Testament warnings to their logical conclusions was too radical at this point for the bulk of a political nation that would take almost a decade after 1640 and the outbreak of civil war to decide that it could or must function without a king and a monarchy—a decision that, even then, was made by a small minority.

Nonetheless, what Patrick Collinson calls the "intensification of religiously inspired national feeling" posed, in the circumstances, a threat rather than a support to the monarchy.[26] The relationship between the English monarch and the religion of his or her subjects was always precarious in post-Reformation England. In their favored Old Testament references, the godly Protestants found moral messages for Israel the nation and Jerusalem its capital but rather fewer practical guidelines for the kings of Israel/England in their marriage and foreign policy. There did exist a Calvinist foreign policy option, embodying the apocalyptic vision of the Calvinist internationale, according to which Europe was engaged in the latter days of the "age-old struggle between the saints of Christ and the minions of Antichrist."[27] For a short while, as Professor Collinson has shown us, images of international Calvinist militancy clustered around the figure of Prince Henry, but they died with him in 1612 only to be reborn in parliamentarian literature in the 1640s.[28]

Financing an aggressive foreign policy would have required the crown to get the full collaboration of an English elite that was, by the 1620s, divided in religion and/or foreign policy orientation.[29] Among the elites, there was a spectrum from those endorsing peace, stability, and prosperity (which translated into a "pro-Spanish" stance) to those who embraced militant Calvinist apocalyptism. These aristocratic divisions, and the rather frightening confrontations between Charles I and his first parliaments, had the effect of paralyzing English policy until the departure of Buckingham, although in the early

1630s the possibility of a French alliance would reemerge. But in the end, the church militant was an image that was appropriated not by the state but by its enemies.

The arrival of the French queen in 1625 must be viewed against this complicated background of international fears and ambitions and domestic religious ambiguity. Although (as we have seen) there was an articulate segment of the English population to whom she was instantly suspect as Catholic and as a threat to be carefully observed from the outset, for a wider segment her "foreignness" was a more ambivalent quality, to be weighed against the obvious advantages of ensuring the succession. She was sent from France by a court that, although desperately anxious about her religious fidelity, thought the obstacle she would present to Spanish influence in England made this very risky enterprise worthwhile. It all turned out to be rather more complicated. We have the private letter written to her by her mother Marie de Medici—part of a genre of "advice to royal brides" such as was also given to Anne of Austria when she married into France in 1615. Although, as in every such marriage, she was advised that one of her main objectives was to nourish the political alliance that the marital one symbolized, she was also encouraged to embrace the needs and interests of her husband's subjects.[30] She was not (certainly not explicitly) expected to become a "mole" for her natal country; and indeed the loyalty that she (with other consorts) was expected to show to her marital realm was not a polite fiction. In 1625 the English ambassador in France reported that the French queen Anne, herself a Spaniard by birth, far from being upset about the recent failure of attempts to arrange a Spanish match for Prince Charles, was "French" enough to favor the Anglo-French match by which Charles would marry Henrietta Maria.[31] In her later life, despite all that had happened, Henrietta was not heard to utter a word of reproach against the English nation or people as such.

The internationalism of courts was taken for granted throughout Europe; there were few royalty whose nationality was unambiguous, since successful courts were by definition cosmopolitan. Henrietta's mother was Marie de Medici, whose father was Florentine and mother was Austrian; so Henrietta herself and her brother King Louis XIII were, at best, half French. Her two sisters, also married in their early teens, were consorts in Spain and Savoy. This cosmopolitan court culture—anticipated, often with pleasure, as the consorts brought their intellectual, cultural, and rich material baggage with them—was still the assumed world of Catholic Europe. Henrietta brought it with her, as she brought a revival of Marian devotion; although some who watched her arrival wanted nothing of it, others were willing to wait and watch and to look for a place for themselves at the new court. Principled estrangement from the court was not a tolerable option for most aristocrats, and in any case the end of Buckingham's turbulent career both distracted attention from the queen and provided in its *dénouement* a new opening for the ambition of his rivals. Until the duke's murder in August 1628, the young queen's role and influence on the king were scarcely important enough to attract much condemnation, but from that point until the opening of her new Somerset House chapel in December 1635 the implications and possibilities of her position become clearer, especially with the birth of the heir Prince Charles in May 1630.[32]

The first years of the royal marriage were famously tempestuous, and a year after Henrietta Maria's arrival the king sent a good number of her French attendants packing—especially the aristocrats—although she was left with a number of French women and their families who provided a kind of intimate (and generally unrecognized) core to the queen's household for the rest of her life. The ensuing war between England and France left her relatively isolated, but she deviated not a whit from her religious loyalties, and these years, which we can only glimpse darkly, seem to have tempered her. By 1629, with Buckingham dead, a royal baby on the way, the full attention and affection of her husband, and a nearly completed peace with France, her situation had dramatically changed. And she had escaped (permanently, as it turned out) any real "control" by the French government. The new ambassador Chateauneuf reported that she no longer cared to have a substantial French entourage, although she missed easy conversation in her language.[33]

Yet culturally she was fully French, surrounded by French families in her chamber and served by French clergy in her religious establishment—in 1630 French Capuchins replaced the earlier French Oratorians. She had been sent to England laden with the precious goods appropriate to a French royal household on the move, for which the term *trousseau* is inadequate, for every kind of precious object was involved—a proud display of the splendor of the French court. In addition to mountains of clothes, jewelry, and soft furnishings for her chambers, there was furniture—whole bedroom suites for the queen and a half dozen of her ladies—as well as complete equipment for her chapel and its twelve priests, coaches and harnessings, and silver and gold plate for table and chapel.[34]

This baggage was no sooner unpacked than it began to be augmented, at such a rate that by March 1628 her debts to various artisans and suppliers ("creditors and tradesmen") amounted to £30,000, almost £9,000 of this to goldsmiths and jewelers.[35] By then she had settled into a pattern of conspicuous consumption that was unshaken through the 1630s, and she must have provided a considerable stimulus to the luxury trades in London.[36] Mercers, woolen drapers, silkmen, and linen drapers established lasting connections with her household by 1630, and most could count on regular and very substantial purchases for a queen who had dozens of outfits made for her each year, tens of dozens of delicate shoes, and more pairs of gloves than there were days in the year (forty-eight a month) and who (judging from the furnishing receipts) frequently redecorated her bedroom and chambers.

Beyond this realm of the chambers, the queen was a lavish sponsor of architecture and garden building at the several royal palaces she controlled (she had more palaces, and more work done on them, than her husband did), and her interest in the visual arts was no discredit to the daughter of Europe's most lavish female patron of the arts.[37] Her production of masques and other entertainments at court is well known, but it is less recognized that both the secular entertainments and her Catholic chapel were supported by a separate musical establishment that was well financed and distinguished. The suppliers of her luxury goods were mainly English, the artisans largely although not exclusively French, and the musicians a very mixed lot. Few of the French artisans were brought across the Channel; rather, they emerged from the large international colony already resident in London and Westminster, who served a preexisting demand from court, aristocracy, and wealthy merchants.[38]

The queen's court, then, represented from her arrival a massive infusion of French fashions of all kinds into English elite society, regularly updated by the cross-Channel trips of her French chamber servants, who brought back goods and (we may speculate) fashion news, as well as other news, from the French court. Her court and the children's subsidiary courts set up in the 1630s also broadened avenues for place and patronage among the English (and Scottish) elite.[39] As we have seen, these were normal features of court life and were welcome to different segments of society for different reasons. Moreover, her court entertainments can be read as irenic efforts to bind courtiers across the religious divides, as Melinda Gough has argued.[40] And during the early and mid-1630s she would support a foreign policy attractive to Protestants.

But events beginning late in 1635 put a different face on the queen's activities, and distrust of her and her court deepened in the latter years of the decade. This began with the opening of her large new chapel at Somerset House in December 1635. This long-awaited building was provided with an elaborate forty-foot-high stage setting for the altar and exposition of the Sacrament designed in the latest Baroque fashion by the sculptor Dieussart. A pontifical High Mass was sung, and for three days the chapel was open to the London public.[41] It was a spectacular venue for the queen to show off her priests and musicians and their French version of Counter-Reformation Catholicism, and it launched her on a more tenacious encouragement of court Catholics and aggressive outreach to susceptible Protestants. The materiality of Catholic practice—those candles and processions that had been struck out of Protestant practice and the devotional items such as rosaries, pictures, and crosses that had been specifically prohibited in the Elizabethan treason legislation against the import of "superstitious" items from overseas—all this was now very visible in the heart of London.[42] Despite half-hearted attempts by the government to control access to the chapel, hundreds of English as well as foreign visitors attended the numerous services there, heard the public debates, and listened to the music; others outside the capital heard about all of this from newsletters and heard also about the conversions of court ladies in which the queen delighted. She had always wanted to be seen as the leading patron of English Catholics, a position the Spanish ambassador had traditionally enjoyed, and she still complained in 1637 that the English Catholics would not appreciate heaven itself if the Spanish had not procured it for them.[43] The late 1630s saw a competition among the Catholic ambassadors in London to provide religious services to English Catholics, a competition clearly stimulated by the hive of devotional activity at Somerset House. This new and brazen face of court Catholicism coincided with a shift in the queen's political orientation, which for a time in the mid-1630s had seemed bent on making good the promise of the original French alliance.

Developments in France since the queen's marriage had much altered the significance of her Frenchness. The Day of Dupes (November 1630), which saw Marie de Medici lose power and ultimately residence in France, had transformed the political scene for her daughter. Thereafter, Henrietta could never regard the policy of her brother's government, dominated now by Richelieu, as something to which she might give unstinted support.[44] For most of the next decade, her mother moved about in the territories of Richelieu's enemies, most often supported by Spain; many of Henrietta's friends were at one time or another involved in plots against Richelieu. When she communicated with the cardinal it was often to intercede for one of these aristocratic conspirators. It should not surprise us that successive French ambassadors found her unprepared to advance their projects, and their rather dismissive references to her as young and frivolous should be seen as the excuses for diplomatic failure that they were. She was interested enough in politics to intrigue with leading Protestant peers and the French ambassador Chateauneuf from 1629 to 1633 in the ways that Malcolm Smuts described for us long ago.[45]

And when France moved to outright war with Spain early in 1635, the queen appeared, for a time, as an unambiguously "French" political presence. Richelieu was trying to end his feud with the queen and get English support against Spain, and she fell in with this, lobbying councilors in support of a league with France that would have drawn England into the European conflict. Moreover, she did so in alliance with a group of English aristocrats—Holland, Northumberland, and Bedford among them—who were Protestant, even arguably "Puritan," and who wished England to move into an aggressive foreign policy modeled on the Elizabethan sea war with Spain.[46]

Besides aligning England with the one Catholic power that was willing to take on the Habsburg forces of Antichrist, this policy held out the added allure of possible office for these peers, which would have been closely connected with the prospect of a parliament (the king had been doing without one since 1629) that they would "deliver" for the king. It was probably never in the king's mind to go this far, but special ambassadors were exchanged, the hopeful Palatine princes visited, and a general air of high expectations lasted from 1635 to the middle of 1637.[47] The queen's motives in this endeavor are not fully clear; it is possible that she saw a rapprochement with Richelieu as an opportunity to get her mother readmitted to France.

As the pro-French initiative at court lost momentum in the summer of 1637, a different set of influences were taking hold of the queen's circle. George Con, who was the second and most effective of the papal emissaries to her court, was by then on the scene; he was close to agents of the Spanish courts (Madrid, Brussels) in London and was easily perceived as their ally. He encouraged the queen to build a *dévot* party at the court, to convert courtiers, and to conceive of all political problems from a Catholic perspective. Within a year, two potent intriguers against Richelieu—thus also friends of Spain—had descended on the court: the Duchess of Chevreuse and Marie de Medici herself, the latter surrounded by Italian and Spanish courtiers.

All these figures pressed the queen (and through her, the king) to interpret the Scottish political crisis that developed in 1638 as the entering stages of a campaign to extirpate Catholicism, a campaign that had to be combated with both domestic and international Catholic help. By the summer of 1640 the Earl of Strafford and other key (non-Catholic) figures at court were deep in negotiation with Spain for mutual assistance. This provided a factual basis to subsequent French propaganda aimed at wrenching English policy back away from a pro-Spanish tilt.

The French may well have done something to stir the pot in Scotland as the Covenanters organized in 1638–39 (the smoking gun has never been found), and they certainly were in close touch, even in collaboration, with the parliamentary opposition leaders of 1640–42. Thus they encouraged, among their English contacts, this hostile picture of a "Spaniolized" court Catholic party around the queen and were pleased to see the queen mother depart in mid-1641. The queen was still angling for help from France in 1642. Her elaborate bluffing, the flight to France starting in 1640 of various disgraced ministers, and the disclosure of the army plot involving French aid—all aroused popular comment and distrust. But among the parliamentary leaders it was understood by early 1641 that the French government had cast its lot with them.[48] Spain, however, continued even after the departure of the last papal agent and various foreign refugees in the summer of 1641 to evoke deep and widespread animosity. The outbreak of the Irish rebellion, led by soldiers who had been in Spanish employ, pushed that tide of sentiment ever further.

So we see in the Grand Remonstrance—the great justification of the parliamentary side late in 1641—the clear statement that Spain, not France, was the danger: "the interests and counsels of [France] being not so contrary to the good of religion and the prosperity of this kingdom as those of Spain."[49] The break with France in 1626 was to be regretted, as was the ensuing peace with Spain—so a lineup of "good papist, bad papist" was taken right back into the 1620s. In 1642 and 1643 the French ambassadors would act as an effective intermediary with Parliament on behalf of members of the queen's household, and ultimately of course the queen would take refuge in France (June 1644). But before then her political position had been irrevocably smeared—a great irony—as Spanish and therefore treacherous. By pursuing an eclectic, opportunistic "Catholic policy" as her program for confronting the king's discontented subjects, Henrietta had found herself labeled (for political purposes) as not French but Spanish. It was an effective strategy for her enemies to assimilate the newly perceived threat to the image of the old traditional enemy.

By the outbreak of the civil war, then, the queen had been identified as the principal enemy of the public good. If it was relatively easy to demonize her; it was a good deal more difficult for what was becoming "the opposition" to come to terms with the outlook of the king. And the parliamentarians of the 1640s were not the only ones who could not bridge the gap between a royal and a national understanding of loyalties and principles. Centuries later, looking at the king's behavior in 1645, S. R. Gardiner would utter a cry of frustration at the king's cosmopolitan outlook, his insistence on looking anywhere he thought he might get help to regain his authority: "Born of a Scottish father and a Danish mother, with a grandmother who was half French by birth and altogether French by breeding, with a French wife, with German nephews and a Dutch son-in-law, Charles had nothing in him in touch with that English national feeling . . . which no ruler of England can afford to despise."[50] This is the dilemma for cosmopolitan courts in a confessional age that Milton saw with a certain remorseless logic—the problem of monarchy is that kings mean queens: "of no less charge; in most likelihood outlandish [foreign] and papist."[51] But the queen, however papist and however outlandish (in both senses) her ideas about how to assist her husband in the gathering political crisis, played but a minor role in the origins of the crisis. Her activities created a menacing background against which English Protestants viewed the king's actions, but they were the king's actions and decisions, not hers, and they were not inevitable outcomes of the tensions between anointed monarchs and Calvinist subjects.[52]

Notes

1. Frances E. Dolan, *Whores of Babylon: Catholicism, Gender, and Seventeenth-Century Print Culture* (Ithaca: Cornell University Press, 1999), 118–36; Caroline Hibbard, *Charles I and the Popish Plot* (Chapel Hill: University of North Carolina Press, 1983), chs. 8 and 9. Michelle A. White, in *Henrietta Maria and the English Civil Wars* (Aldershot: Ashgate, 2006), has explored how Henrietta Maria figured in the parliamentary propaganda of the 1640s.

2. See C. M. Hibbard, "Early Stuart Catholicism: Revisions and Re-revisions," *Journal of Modern History* 52 (1980): 1–34, for this and the next paragraph.

3. On Henrietta's reputation, see Caroline Hibbard, the entry "Henrietta Maria" in the *Oxford Dictionary of National Biography* (Oxford: Oxford University Press, 2004), www.oxforddnb.com.

4. For English Calvinism and English Protestantism, see Patrick Collinson, "England and International Calvinism, 1558–1640," in *International Calvinism 1541–1715*, ed. Menna Prestwich (Oxford: Clarendon Press, 1985), 197–224.

5. Susan Doran, *England and Europe, 1485–1603*, 2nd ed. (New York: Longman, 1996), esp. ch. 8 and part 3 on how reactive Tudor policy had to be in the Elizabethan period, the degree of constant danger, and the threat of Catholic crusade.

6. A Franco-Spanish alliance against England was being actively promoted by Guidi di Bagno, the papal envoy to France, in 1627 and later. Letters from Bagno to Cardinal Francesco Barberini, Secretary of State, on this subject are in Vatican Library, Barberini Latini MS 8069, fols. 20 (May 28, 1627), 95 (August 13, 1627), 132–33 (August 27, 1627), 234–36 (October 22, 1627), and onwards.

7. Roy Strong, *Henry Prince of Wales and England's Lost Renaissance* (London: Thames and Hudson, 1986), 80–85.

8. Elizabeth had seriously entertained courtships from two successive French princes; see Susan Doran, *Monarchy and Matrimony: The Courtships of Elizabeth I* (London: Routledge, 1996), ch. 8.

9. Mead to Stuteville, June 17, 1625, in Henry Ellis, *Original Letters*, ser. 1, vol. 3 (London, 1825), 199.

10. Maurice Lee Jr., *James I and Henri IV: An Essay in English Foreign Policy, 1603–1610* (Urbana: University of Illinois Press, 1970).

11. W. B. Patterson, *King James VI and I and the Reunion of Christendom* (Cambridge: Cambridge University Press, 1997), ch. 5.

12. See Roy Strong, *The Cult of Elizabeth: Elizabethan Portraiture and Pageantry* (London: Thames and Hudson, 1977), ch. 6.

13. Caroline Hibbard, "The Theatre of Dynasty," in *The Stuart Court and Europe: Essays in Politics and Political Culture*, ed. R. Malcolm Smuts (Cambridge: Cambridge University Press, 1996), 156–76.

14. John Adamson, "Introduction: The Making of the Ancien Regime Court 1500–1700," in *The Princely Courts of Europe: Ritual Politics and Culture under the Ancien Regime, 1500–1750*, ed. John Adamson (London: Weidenfeld and Nicolson, 1999), 34–37. The fullest account of the English case is by R. M. Smuts, "Art and the Material Culture of Majesty in Early Stuart England," in Smuts, *Stuart Court and Europe*, 86–112.

15. Although see Collinson, "England and International Calvinism," 204–10, on national fasts and (limited) royal support for national collections.

16. See William Castle's critique of 1642, quoted by Irvonwy Morgan in *Prince Charles's Puritan Chaplain* (London: Allen and Unwin, 1957), 129. James I's renova-

tion of the chapels at St. James and Whitehall in the early 1620s was certainly carried out with an eye to the Spanish marriage negotiations; see Peter E. McCullough, *Sermons at Court: Politics and Religion in Elizabethan and Jacobean Preaching* (Cambridge: Cambridge University Press, 1998), 33–34.

17. McCullough, *Sermons at Court,* 26–27, on James I taking over the more elaborate ceremonial of the Elizabethan court when he moved south.

18. The relatively elaborate cathedral liturgy, reflecting episcopal conservatism regarding services that were only occasionally or sparsely attended by local laity, was intensified by pressure from Laud and his colleagues in the early seventeenth century and was sustained over the entire post-Reformation period by the role of the cathedrals as far and away the chief employers of professional musicians and thus training ground for court musical service. See Stanford Lehmberg, *Cathedrals under Siege* (University Park: Pennsylvania State University Press, 1996), chs. 1, 7, 8. A mounting tide of complaint against cathedrals, their chapters, and the bishops on the grounds of idle, frivolous, and unproductive living, negligence, and absenteeism bears witness to the distance, even hostility, between cathedrals and their surrounding communities and culminated in the campaign against them in the Long Parliament; see Lehmberg, *Cathedrals under Siege,* and Caroline M. Hibbard, "Episcopal Warriors in the British Wars of Religion," in *War and Government in Britain, 1598–1650,* ed. Mark Charles Fissel (Manchester: Manchester University Press, 1991), 164–92.

19. Diarmaid MacCulloch, *The Later Reformation* (London: Macmillan, 1990), 120.

20. Fiona Kisby, "'When the King Goeth a Procession': Chapel Ceremonies and Services, the Ritual Year, and Religious Reforms at the Early-Tudor Court, 1486–1547," *Journal of British Studies* 40 (2001): 44–75. She cites Robert Bucholz, "Nothing but Ceremony: Queen Anne and the Limitations of Royal Ritual," *Journal of British Studies* 30 (1991): 288–323.

21. Adamson, "Introduction," 28–31; for the developments in England, see, in the same volume, ch. 3 by Adamson, "The Tudor and Stuart Courts 1509–1714," esp. 101–5. For a literary approach to the sacralization of the English monarch, see Richard McCoy, *Alterations of State* (New York: Columbia University Press, 2002), esp. ch. 4, "Idolizing Kings: John Milton and Stuart Rule."

22. Adamson, "Introduction," 25–27, on the role of confraternities and Counter-Reformation religious orders, and 28 for the central cult of Corpus Christi. See also, in the same volume, 59–61 on the religious practice of the Spanish Habsburgs; 88–89 on religion at the court of the Valois and Bourbon kings of France; 173–74 and 179 on the Austrian Habsburgs; and 192–93 on the Wittelsbachs of Bavaria.

23. John Carmi Parsons, "Ritual and Symbol in the English Medieval Queenship to 1500," in *Women and Sovereignty,* ed. L. O. Fradenberg (Edinburgh: Edinburgh University Press, 1992), 60–77.

24. Christopher Hill, *The English Bible and the Seventeenth Century Revolution* (London: Penguin, 1994), 70, quoting Hugh Peter in a 1626 sermon; ibid., 69–72, on the evil of alien queens.

25. Ibid., 66, 52.

26. Patrick Collinson, *Birthpangs of Protestant England* (London: Macmillan, 1988), 9, and ch. 1 generally on the paradoxes of the "elect nation" in early-seventeenth-century England.

27. Bodo Nischan, "Confessionalism and Absolutism: The Case of Brandenburg," in *Calvinism in Europe, 1540–1620*, ed. Andrew Pettegree, Alastair Duke, and Gillian Lewis (Cambridge: Cambridge University Press, 1994), 186. His discussion of the Elector's 1613 conversion in the context of Calvinist apocalyptism is exemplary.

28. Collinson, *Birthpangs of Protestant England*, 130–31, and see ch. 5, "Wars of Religion," generally. Strong (*Henry Prince of Wales*, 136–37) describes Prince Henry's circle as Italianate and Francophile with "a passionate cult of Henri IV," which suggests a cultural blend that escapes the polarity of godly/Antichrist.

29. David Norbrook, *Poetry and Politics in the English Renaissance* (Oxford: Oxford University Press, 2002), ch. 9; and Simon Adams, "Spain or the Netherlands? The Dilemmas of Early Stuart Foreign Policy," in *Before the English Civil War: Essays on Early Stuart Politics and Governance*, ed. Howard Tomlinson (London: Macmillan, 1983), 79–101, are nuanced discussions of the problems England faced in the Thirty Years' War.

30. Cardinal de Richelieu, *Mémoires*, vol. 5 (Société de l'histoire de France, vol. 399, Paris, 1907–31 for 10 vols.), app. I, pp. 275–83, esp. 281.

31. Kensington (later Earl of Holland) to Buckingham, Paris, February 16, 1624, cited by Melinda Gough in "A Newly Discovered Performance by Henrietta Maria," *Huntington Library Quarterly* 65, nos. 3–4 (2002): 435–48. Anne of Austria was not always so "French"; she was involved in repeated indiscretions, a couple amounting to treason, in the late 1620s and 1630s.

32. See Caroline Hibbard, "Translating Royalty: Henrietta Maria and the Transition from Princess to Queen," *Court Historian* 5 (2000): 15–28, for this and the following paragraph.

33. Chateauneuf to Cardinal Richelieu, July 23, 1629, in Public Record Office [PRO] Baschet Transcripts 31/3/66, fol. 11.

34. Further details on this are in Caroline Hibbard, "Henrietta Maria in the 1630s: Perspectives on Consort Queens in *Ancien Regime* Courts," in *The 1630s: Interdisciplinary Approaches*, ed. Ian Atherton and Julie Sanders (Manchester: Manchester University Press, 2006), 92–110.

35. PRO, SC6 ChasI 1692.

36. This is suggested by the "Petition of many thousands of Courtiers, Citizens, Gentlemens and Trades-mens wives, inhabiting within the Cities of London

and Westminster, concerning the staying of the Queenes intended voyage into Holland" presented to the House of Lords on February 10, 1642; "all depending wholly for the sale of their commodities . . . upon the splendor and glory of the English court, and principally upon that of the Queen's Majesty," they fear that they will lose their livelihoods if she departs and beg Parliament to persuade her to stay.

37. See Hibbard, biography entry "Henrietta Maria."

38. The wider context of this luxury market is discussed by Linda Levy Peck, "Luxury and War: Reconsidering Luxury Consumption in Seventeenth-Century England," *Albion* 34 (2002): 1–23.

39. See Caroline Hibbard, "The Role of a Queen Consort: The Household and Court of Henrietta Maria, 1625–1642," in *Princes, Patronage and the Nobility: The Court at the Beginning of the Modern Age, c. 1450–1650,* ed. Ronald G. Asch and Adolf M. Birke (Oxford: Oxford University Press, 1991), 393–414.

40. Melinda Gough, "'Not as Myself': The Queen's Voice in Tempe Restored," *Modern Philology* 101 (August 2003): 48–67. For comparisons with the activities of Catherine de Medici, see also Erica Veevers, *Images of Love and Religion: Queen Henrietta Maria and Court Entertainments* (Cambridge: Cambridge University Press, 1989), ch. 6, esp. 191–202.

41. My article on this chapel and the Capuchins that served it is in preparation.

42. Legislation of 1571 (13 Eliz. I, c.2) against the bringing in of "any token or tokens, thing or things, called by the name of an *Agnus Dei,* or any crosses, pictures, beads or suchlike vain and superstitious things," in *Tudor Constitution: Documents and Commentary,* 2nd ed., ed. G. R. Elton (Cambridge: Cambridge University Press, 1982), 431.

43. Hibbard, *Charles I,* 61.

44. Great Britain, Public Record Office, *Calendar of State Papers and Manuscripts, Relating to English Affairs . . . in Venice . . . , 1603–75,* vols. 10–28 (London, 1864–1940), Calendar 1629–32, pp. 544–45 (letter of September 1631).

45. R. Malcolm Smuts, "Puritan Followers of Henrietta Maria in the 1630s," *English Historical Review* 93 (1978): 26–45. Chateauneuf was trying to unseat Richelieu, and the English figures had Portland in their sights.

46. Ibid., pp. 35–38.

47. Hibbard, *Charles I,* passim, for this and the narrative of the next three paragraphs.

48. The Triennial Act convinced the French government that they had nothing left to hope or fear from Charles I.

49. S. R. Gardiner, ed., *Constitutional Documents of the Puritan Revolution, 1628–1660,* (Oxford: Clarendon Press, 1889), 208.

50. S. R. Gardiner, *History of the Great Civil War, 1642–1649,* 4 vols. (1893; reprint, London: Longmans, Green, 1911), 2:202–3.

51. John Milton, "The Ready and Easy Way to Establish a Free Commonwealth," quoted in Dolan, *Whores of Babylon,* 123 n. 100.

52. Still the best assessment of Charles I's character as a king is in Conrad Russell, *The Causes of the English Civil War* (Oxford: Clarendon Press, 1990), ch. 8, "The Man Charles Stuart." Russell's suggestion that the king felt a deep sense of personal inadequacy is even more convincing as an explanation of his political inflexibility and incompetence in the context of our current understanding of sacralized monarchy.

5

Gender and Recusant Melancholia in Robert Southwell's *Mary Magdalene's Funeral Tears*

Gary Kuchar

In her 1994 work *The Renaissance Bible*, Debora Shuger demonstrates that the Renaissance tradition of Mary Magdalene narratives exemplifies the extent to which "the specter of female desire structures religious (and male) subjectivity."[1] What this provocative formulation really means is that Renaissance Magdalene narratives operate according to a conjunction of Ovidian eroticism, with its emphasis on abandoned, suffering women, and Aristotelian epistemology, in which the language of the soul is primarily imagistic rather than verbal. Through this conjunction of Ovidian and Aristotelian traditions, the personal nature of Magdalene's soul appears, in Shuger's words, as "the creation of frustrated eros."[2] In other words, the Renaissance Magdalene becomes aware of herself as a subject insofar as she lacks her object of desire. This process of coming into religious self-awareness vis-à-vis an eroticized experience of spiritual absence constitutes one of the most vital ways in which religious desire is predicated in late medieval and Renaissance devotional literature. It is not surprising, then, that the Magdalene figure provided an important model for the predication of ideal religious identities in Renaissance England, particularly, though not exclusively, within Catholic reading communities.[3]

While I concur with Shuger's general assessment of the subjective modes at stake in the English Renaissance tradition of *imitatio Magdalenia,* I would like to sharpen the interpretive focus in order to gain perspective on how Robert Southwell's 1591 version of this form of female religious subjectivity is an attempt to accommodate and at the same time intervene into the experience of being an Elizabethan recusant subject.[4] To accomplish this, I pursue two interrelated hypotheses regarding the socially symbolic aspects of Southwell's *Mary Magdalene's Funeral Tears.* First, I argue that Southwell's representation of Magdalene addresses and seeks to mitigate the recusant experience of religious/social paralysis—an experience that Southwell discusses more explicitly in his *Humble Supplication to her Majesty* (1591) and *An Epistle of Comfort* (1587–88) and implicitly throughout his devotional verse. I argue, in other words, that Magdalene's transition from her state of longing for Christ's physical body at his empty tomb to her spiritual relation with him after his resurrection operates as a model for the fashioning or more precisely interpellation[5] of the ideal recusant subject. This fashioning of the ideal Elizabethan Catholic occurs not only through the narrator's homiletic discourse in the *Epistle Dedicatorie* and conclusion, where such fashioning is relatively explicit, but also through Magdalene's transition from an inwardly divided, melancholic attachment to Christ's literal body to her recognition of a spiritual, and consequently more complete, relation with the resurrected Christ.[6] In terms of its sociosymbolic import, what is at stake in Magdalene's process of coming to know Christ within her heart rather than through physical proximity is the imaginative alleviation of the antagonisms and competing allegiances that characterize the lived experience of recusants. The practice of *imitatio Magdalenia* is thus politicized in Southwell's text: Magdalene's drama at Christ's empty tomb serves as a commentary on the recusant experience of social isolation and religious abandonment while providing a model example of how one should cope with such marginalization.

The second hypothesis I forward pertains to the way that Southwell negotiates—and in certain instances fails to negotiate—the potentially unsettling implications that arise from the extent to which female desire structures religious subjectivity within the Renaissance Magdalene tradition. The feminine and spiritually excessive nature of Magdalene inspires certain anxieties in Southwell's text regarding not only female desire but also the devotional power of women. Such anxieties have historically converged around Mary Magdalene and, in Southwell's case, were likely deepened by the unusually authoritative role that Elizabethan Catholic women played within the social and sacramental life of the recusant community.[7] As Megan Matchinske observes, "[R]ecusant mothers and wives gained considerable religious and familial leverage" in the Elizabethan period, "redefining the limits of both ecclesial and patriarchal control in conducting Catholic service, supervising priestly behavior, and acting as spiritual stand-ins for outwardly conforming husbands and sons."[8] Similarly, John Bossy argues that English Catholicism was based to a large extent on the power of aristocratic women, a power that was often wielded despite the resistance of their aristocratic husbands.[9]

Southwell himself speaks to the power recusant women had in the Catholic community in a letter dated January 12th 1587 when he observes that the "work of God is being pressed forward—often enough by delicate women who have taken on the courage of men."[10] As Christopher Devlin observes, Southwell's most important patroness, the Countess of Arundel, played a particularly influential role in the recusant community after the capture of her husband Philip Howard, making possible the first printing of his books; assisting other Catholics in need; and providing refuge for priests wanted by the authorities.[11] The sisters of Henry Vaux, another of Southwell's supporters, found themselves in a position similar to that of the Countess of Arundel, as they took up many of the responsibilities Henry shouldered before his capture.[12] As one might expect, the power these women wielded did not inspire unequivocal enthusiasm within the Catholic community. As Antonia Fraser has documented, there were tensions between the Vaux sisters and the important Catholic patriarch, Sir Thomas Tresham. These tensions reveal what we might otherwise suspect, that the power Catholic women possessed inspired ambivalence in at least some, if not most, male Catholic leaders.[13]

Given that the missionary priests were being housed and supported by women such as the Countess of Arundel and Anne Vaux, it is likely that they were less anxious about female power than the fathers, husbands, brothers, and uncles of such influential Catholic women. Nonetheless, missionaries such as Southwell register such anxiousness. Southwell's Jesuit colleague Henry Garnet, for instance, made sure that when he praised the Vaux sisters to his superior, the Jesuit General, he figured them as properly modest before praising them for bravery. In a letter to the Jesuit General, Garnet indicates that "though [Anne] has all a maiden's modesty and even shyness, yet in God's cause, and in the protection of His servants, *virgo* becomes *virago*."[14] This brief description of an influential Catholic woman is typical of how missionary writers sought to delineate the proper limits of female power, particularly in the context of homiletic works such as *Mary Magdalene's Funeral Tears*.[15] Thus, while scholars such as Francis E. Dolan[16] have demonstrated how the empowering of recusant women and the integral role played by feminine figures within the liturgical and theological life of Catholics gave rise to misogynistic anti-Catholic rhetoric in Protestant polemic, it is also important to pay attention to how the power of Catholic women inspired the sort of ambivalence within the English recusant community that we would presumably expect to see. Southwell's *Mary Magdalene's Funeral Tears* testifies to this ambivalence in both its thematic content and its formal, rhetorical structure.

Anxieties over female empowerment are visible in Southwell's *Mary Magdalene's Funeral Tears* in at least two ways. First, they are discernible in the text's oscillating emphasis between Mary's verboseness and her silence, between the emotionally persuasive power of her words and the spiritually compelling force of her tears. This opposition between words and tears—between Mary as an exemplar of a strong, thinking woman and as an icon of a silent, weeping convert—is charged with significance because it is conceptually tethered to the broader epistemological tensions between the excesses permitted by Christian devotion and the principles of temperance derived from Aristotelian ethics that structure the work homiletically. Second, then, anxieties over the intensity of Magdalene's passions are disclosed insofar as the tensions between Augustinian epistemology, which purports that God cannot be loved to excess, and Aristotelian ethics, which is based on principles of moderation, complicate, if not entirely unsettle, the text's homiletic aims. Indeed, while Magdalene is presented in the form of a devout Augustinian subject who experiences no limit to her capacity for spiritual desire, the text is homiletically framed in terms of an Aristotelian ethics of moderation that operates to curb both her physical excesses and her rhetorical persuasiveness. The tension between these two poles is registered in the way that Southwell's narrator both venerates and resists the power of fascination elicited by the Renaissance Magdalene; such tension discloses how he simultaneously honors and withdraws from the figure of this ideal female penitent.[17]

Magdalene and Recusant Marginalization

Exemplifying the pattern of a contemplative life along with the virtue of spiritual perseverance, Magdalene has been used, since the twelfth century onwards, to further the interests of marginalized Christian groups.[18] According to Susan Haskins, it is perhaps not too much to suggest that after the Council of Trent "Mary Magdalene might stand as the symbol of the Church Triumphant, a figure of the true Catholic Faith."[19] And although her legendary role as the *apostolorum apostola* developed through medieval hagiography and sermonizing largely disappeared in post-Tridentine Catholicism, the efficacy of her penitence remained an important part of Counter-Reformation culture—particularly its religious art.[20] Magdalene continues to appear in Counter-Reformation art and poetry as the *beata dilectrix Christi,* the blessed lover of Christ, as well as in her more traditional roles as convert and penitent.[21] By embodying the virtues of passionate devotion, perseverance, contemplative power, and articulateness, not to mention audacity, Magdalene makes an obvious, if not unproblematic, figure for emulation by early modern English Catholics in general and women in particular. Moreover, her experience at the empty tomb of Christ, which is the focus of Southwell's devotional homily, has obvious pertinence for a community in which, as Southwell described, there "is weeping almost unto death among wives who have no husbands, and families with no support."[22] Southwell's diagnosis of the English community is verified by John Gerard's account of his role in Elizabeth Vaux's household, a role that provides us with a view of the treatment Jesuits offered grieving recusants: "By degrees I healed my hostess's excessive sorrow. I told her our grief for the dead should be tempered. . . . So I gradually brought her round to turn her old sorrow into a sorrow of another and nobler kind, and then . . . to reflect that though her life hitherto had been a good and holy life, it could be made holier still by following as closely as possible the pattern of Our Lord's life and of His saints."[23] Southwell's *Mary Magdalene's Funeral Tears* depicts precisely this transition from a worldly to a spiritual sorrow, a transition from a weeping that originates in a love of self to a weeping that extends from the soul's attachment to God. As we shall see, though, representing this process is as rhetorically complex as it is ideologically fraught.

That Southwell's text encourages its recusant readers to see their own state of being spiritually and socially alienated mirrored in Magdalene's search for the absent Christ is alluded to in the *Epistle Dedicatorie* to Dorothy Arundel—daughter of Sir John Arundell of Lanherne and future Benedictine nun.[24] Appealing to the values of the Catholic gentry in particular, the opening epistle focuses on the nobility of resistance and strength embodied by Magdalene. In an effort to appeal to and reshape aristocratic sensibility, Southwell asserts that audacity "is the armor of strength, and the guide of glory, breaking the ice to the hardest exploits, and crowning valour with honourable victorie."[25] This honoring of Mary's audacity is central to the way in which the work as a whole presents Magdalene in a recalcitrant and resistant mood as she debates with the angels at Christ's empty tomb, justifying her tears and insisting throughout that she must speak with Christ himself. Indeed, while Southwell's Magdalene appears as a desperate, suicidal lover in the manner of the "weeper" tradition, the sense of dignity generated by her resistance to the angels at the tomb is consistent with the tradition of representing her as being of noble descent, as in Jacobus de Voragine's thirteenth-century digest, the *Legenda Aurea*, which depicts Mary as someone "of noble station, [who] came of royal lineage."[26] Keeping with the Magdalene tradition's tendency for ascribing multiple symbolic meanings to Mary, Southwell draws on different facets of the Magdalene figure to fashion a recusant subject who is spiritually noble in the face of spiritual alienation, a subject who is dignified even in the deepest thralls of religious torment.

The recusant context becomes apparent in the opening pages of the main narrative when Magdalene is confronted with Christ's empty tomb, and her feeling of being internally and externally paralyzed directly echoes Southwell's articulation of the catch-22 position experienced by Catholics in his *An Humble Supplication*. In his epistle to Elizabeth, Southwell complains that "[i]f we live at home as Catholiques, professing our owne, and refusing to profess a contrary religion, we can neither keep our places in the University, nor follow our studies in the Innes of Court, but we are imprisoned for Recusancy, impoverished, troubled and defamed. And yet if we leave all, and seeke free use of our Conscience and depart the Realme, taking such helpes as the Charity of other Cuntryes affordeth us, we are straight reckoned for *unnatural Subjects*."[27] Southwell here states the contradictory, even paralytic, nature of being a recusant, suggesting that Protestant authority has rendered the position of being Catholic abject and unnatural. When Southwell's Magdalene is first presented standing at Christ's empty tomb, she is caught in a similarly divided position. She is trapped, we are told, between "burning and bathing," "love and grief," her "poor eyes being troubled at once with two contrary offices, both to be clear in sight the better to seeke him, and yet cloudy with tears for missing the sight of him."[28] Magdalene articulates this same sense of division between two offices when she complains that "[i]f I stay here where he is not, I shall never finde him. If I would go further to seeke, I know not whether. To leave the Tombe is a death, and to stand helplesse by it an uncurable disease, so that all my comfort is now concluded in this, that I am left free to choose whether I will stay without helpe, or go without hope, that is in effect with what torment I will end my life."[29] The term "offices" that is used to contextualize Mary's complaint implies that the antagonisms which Magdalene faces are registered by a discontinuity between inward state and outward action. Her dilemma is visible externally to the extent that there are competing ceremonial or ritual "offices" that she must decide between; and it is internal to the extent that this decision rests upon the "office" or "function of an organ or faculty." In Magdalene's case this organ is the heart and the faculty is memory. This split between the inward conscience and the outward ceremonial that should be its expression is precisely the antagonism that characterizes the recusant's dilemma as Southwell describes it. And it is this antagonism that the work as a whole seeks to symbolically mitigate.

This form of radical self-division is the theme of Southwell's lyric poem "Marie Magdalene's complaint at Christ's death," in which Christ's absence is articulated as a form of spiritual death. Apostrophizing death, Magdalene declares that "my life from life is parted: / Death come take thy portion."[30] Here too, Magdalene's complaint voices a discernibly recusant feeling of alienation and spiritual entropy; an extended simile describing the effects of Christ's absence from the tomb serves as an oblique critique of Protestant eucharistic theology: "Where the truth once was, and is not, / Shaddowes are but vanitie: / Shewing want, that helpe they cannot: / Signes, not salves of miserie. / Paynted meat no hunger feedes, / Dying life each death exceeds."[31] Mary articulates her experience of Christ's absence from the tomb in a manner that parallels the absence of Christ's saving power in the Anglican Eucharist, as she expresses her desire for the actual presence of Christ's sacrificed flesh rather than the sacramentally powerless "signs" and merely "painted meat" of the Protestant rite. Southwell thus reminds his readers that the English Church renounced the belief that the Eucharist is a sacrifice of Christ's transubstantiated body which operates as a miraculous vehicle of grace, thereby providing the faithful receiver with the promise of eternal life through the cleansing of sins. In this respect, Mary's experience at the empty tomb serves as a relatively disguised commentary on the recusant experience of living without access to the transubstantiated presence of Christ's body in the consecrated host of the Catholic Mass. Offering an exemplary mode of response to Christ's absence, Southwell's Mary is presented as persevering in the face of spiritual death: "Though my life thou drav'st away, / Maugre thee my love shall stay" (41–42). By the time we reach this ending couplet, the abstraction "Death" has come to signify the English authorities who have removed

Christ's salvific presence from the Church, leaving Mary to sustain her "love" for and "life" in Christ while renouncing her attachment to earthly existence. Thus, while Christ's body is absent from the tomb she has come to embody his virtues through a saintly imitation of them, making those virtues visible to others.[32]

What must be overcome both in this lyric poem and in *Mary Magdalene's Funeral Tears* is the threat of a death that exceeds death, an oblivion of the spirit that constitutes the demise of Magdalene's very claim to being. In *An Humble Supplication*, Southwell describes this state of nonbeing as the effect of turning away from God, what he describes as a form of soul murder: "It is rather an *unnatural thing* to disobey the Author of nature for any Creature, in forsaking the Faith by which only we hope to be saved: And yet we must doe this, to the willfull murthering of our owne souls."[33] As we shall see, the narrator of *Funeral Tears* refers to this state of nonbeing, this death beyond death, as a "fatal oblivion"—a dissolution of memory and selfhood. To overcome this radical division within the self, Magdalene must unify the "two contrary offices" with which she is faced—thereby offering an exemplum for recusant readers to follow.

Magdalene's function as an example for recusant readers is further developed in *Funeral Tears* when the opposition of "contrary offices" that Magdalene confronts results in the same Petrarchan paradox Southwell uses elsewhere to convey the experience of recusant melancholia. In the *Supplication*, Southwell complains that "our Condition [as Catholics] be soe desolate, that we can neither be freed from outward misery, but by becoming inwardly more miserable."[34] It is exactly this paradoxical state that Magdalene faces when the narrator declares: "[D]rawing into her minde all pensive conceites, she museth and pineth in a consuming languor, taking comfort in nothing but in being comfortlesse."[35] There is nothing simple about this characteristically Southwellian paradox regarding recusant melancholia. Rather than a straightforward plea for sympathy, this paradox articulates the counterintuitive lesson that one becomes closest to Christ when one feels furthest from him. The idea here is that only in being abandoned and forsaken does one generate a genuine intimacy with Christ, who was himself forsaken and betrayed. More precisely, only when the experience of comfortlessness is itself exalted, made a sign of one's proximity to Christ, does one begin to assume the mode of being that Southwell is advocating. William Alabaster's "Upon Christ's Saying to Mary 'Why Weepest Thou?'"—a poem that directly echoes Southwell's Magdalene lyrics and *Funeral Tears*—summarizes, and might thus serve as a commentary on, the way the self-consuming force of Mary's weeping paradoxically discloses her proximity to Christ. Alabaster's poem, that is, encapsulates what Southwell's narrator calls "the wonderful effects of Marie's love":[36]

> I weep, yet weeping brings mere discontent,
> For as Christ's presence my tears seasoned,
> When through my tears his love I clearer read,
> So now his loss through them doth more augment.
> Yet let my tears once after him fast run
> To seek Christ out, and when my tears are done
> Mine eyes and heart shall after him pursue,
> Until his grace into mine eyes return,
> And beams reflect upon my rainbow's dew,
> And in my heart I feel his love to burn.[37]

In this peculiarly Petrarchan form of melancholia—one that both Southwell and Alabaster figure in terms of Mary's inward shift from a state of resisting her grief to a full-blown assumption of it—the experience of physically losing Christ coincides with spiritually gaining him. The verb "burn" signals how the process of deepening rather than defending against her sorrow leads Mary to experience Christ's spiritual presence as a form of physical absence, a state of pleasure in anguish. Before Southwell's Magdalene is able to attain this painful but rewarding spiritual state, she confronts the death that exceeds death—a state that brings into relief the particular importance of memory as a spiritual faculty for this herald of the Resurrection as well as for those working to continue the presence of the Catholic Church within a Protestant nation.

Indeed, when Mary is unable to locate Christ's body she experiences a psychic state that can be represented only as what the narrator calls a "fatal oblivion"—a loss of the other that is, as Augustine puts it, "more inward to me than my most inward part, higher than the highest element within me" (*interior intimo meo et superior summon meo*).[38] Because Christ is more herself than herself, the only thing that prevents the onset of this "fatal oblivion"—this forgetting of all forms of self-knowledge—is her capacity to articulate Christ's ongoing presence within her through, rather than despite, her melancholy. The status of being an "unnatural subject" is given unusually stark form here as Magdalene experiences the absence of Christ's body as the absence of all memory: "[I]f any thing did make her willing to live, it was only the unwillingnesse that his image should die with her, whose likeness love had limmed[39] in her heart, and treasured up in her sweetest memories. And had she not feared to breake the Table, and to break open the closet, to which she had entrusted this last relique of her lost happiness, the violence of grief would have melted her heart into inward bleeding teares, and blotted her remembrance with a fatall oblivion."[40] To recusants who may have had to go long stretches of time without receiving Mass, this ability to experience Christ's proximity through the work of memory would have been a particularly important virtue. In this way, the capacity for memory is honored here just as it is politicized. It is Mary's capacity to confess in both words and tears, "to break open the closet" of the heart in order to reveal Christ's true "likeness," that makes her worthy of emulation by recusants.

The Limits of Female Excess

As I have indicated, Magdalene's contemplative power—her ability to articulate Christ's presence through the force of her memory—becomes apparent only once she has faced the dark night of "fatal oblivion." This meditation on the relationship between grief and articulateness, along with its focus upon the dangers of remaining silent about one's grief, introduces a psychological dimension that is all but absent from Southwell's twelfth-century source text, the pseudo-Origenist work *An Homilie of Marye Magdalene*.[41] Where the pseudo-Origenist text translates the meaning of Mary's tears from sorrow to joy in homiletic rather than narrative terms, Southwell presents Magdalene's transition in the language of personal, spiritual maturation. Where the Origenist text is a narrative of incident, Southwell's is a narrative of character. In short, Southwell makes Mary's process of interpellation a more explicitly thematic and a more decisively psychological issue than it is in his twelfth-century source text. And bound up with the nature of her interpellation is the meaning of female grief, abandonment, and silence and the "excesses" therein.

The excessiveness of Magdalene's grief apparently troubled Southwell's nineteenth-century editors. In particular, the suicidal intensity of Magdalene's condition cited above appears to have been too much for his Victorian emendators to swallow. In the 1822 edition of the text, the word "bleeding" is excised and the word "fatal" has become "faithful."[42] This repressing of Mary's corporeality and the overall softening of the tragic force of her suffering are charged with significance to the extent that they call attention to anxieties that are already operative within the versions published in the 1590s. On the one hand, they repress the physical excesses inherent in Magdalene's grief—its expression through bloody tears—while, on the other hand, they emphasize her "faithful" but not ecstatic submissiveness to Christ. It is these same excesses that the homiletic structure of the text will limit in its imposition of an Aristotelian ethics of moderation on this verbally and passionately excessive herald of the Resurrection. Before the ethics of moderation is elaborated in the homiletic ending, however, Southwell's text resolves Magdalene's hyperbolic grief through the interpellating power of Christ's voice, which vivifies the "double funeral" of her soul:

> [W]hen shee heard thee call her in thy woonted manner, and with thy usual voice, her only name issuing from thy mouth, wrought so strange an alternation in her, as if she had been wholly newe made, when shee was only named. For whereas before the violence of hir grief had so benummbed her, that her bodie seemed but the hearse of her dead heart, and her heart the cophin of an unliving soul, and her whole presence but a representation of a double funerall of thine, and of her own: now with this one word [Mary] her senses are restored, her mind lightened, her heart quickened, and her soul revived.[43]

This is the real beginning of Mary's conversion from a state of suicidal grief to a spiritual relation with the resurrected Christ. God's calling of her name marks the moment of her *metanoia*—her widening of vision as a genuinely Christian subject who is aware of the Resurrection. The movement from "unliving soul" to a soul "quickened" and "revived" signals a shift in her spiritual comportment while also reframing the meaning of her excessive acts of grief earlier. Indeed, this passage marks the point at which Christ does the reforming that the angels at Mary's tomb were unable to do.[44]

While Southwell follows his source text in curbing Magdalene's excesses by describing them as a function of her limited understanding (she exists in a state of "holy error," as the pseudo-Origenist text puts it), his work places greater emphasis on the sacrifices Magdalene must make. The first important scene detailing the price of Mary's interpellation occurs when Christ declares much more than his traditional "touch me not." Having already birthed her through the power of naming, this rather wordy Christ begins to wean her. Dilating on John 20:17, Christ declares:

> It is nowe necessarie to weane thee from the comforte of my externall presence, that thou mayest learn to lodge me in the secrets of thy heart, and teache thy thoughtes to supplie the offices of outward senses. For in this visible shape I am not long to bee seen, being shortly to ascend unto my father: but what thy eye then seeth not, thy heart shall feele, and my silent parlee will find audience in thy inward eare. . . . Mary departeth from him like a hungrie infant pulled from a full teat, or a thirsty Hart chased from a sweet fountain. . . . Alas! said she, and cannot others be happy, without my unhappiness? or cannot their advantage be gained but through my loss?[45]

This passage furthers the resolution of the antagonisms between inward and outward offices articulated at the outset, marking an important moment in Magdalene's becoming free of the state of paralysis from which she has been suffering. From a homiletic standpoint, the text is working toward the idea that self-sacrifice is an expression of what Mary calls an "undivided love of Christ"[46]—a love that is presented as the means of fulfilling the apparent divisions between inward conscience and outward ceremonial which haunt Magdalene and her recusant reader. In the most basic of senses, the text is advocating that recusant readers alter their *internal* comportment toward their alienated condition rather than hoping for a change in the *external* circumstances causing the alienation itself. In this instance, following Magdalene as an exemplum means following her in internalizing the object that she identifies as the source of her claim to being—a process coincident with relinquishing the desire for his external presence. In this respect, the process of Magdalene's conversion from grief to joy functions as an allegory for the way that recusant conscience emerges as an interiorizing and exalting of one's suffering. The counterintuitive logic of this process is played out in Southwell's "The Prodigall childs soule wracke" when the speaker forgoes any hope of being released from the state of being "Enwrapped in the waves of wo," from which he can "no port for refuge go."[47] Instead of hoping to be freed from his position, Southwell's speaker "subdues" his desire for release as a means of attenuating his pain:

> I cried truce, I craved peace
> A league with death I would conclude,
> But vaine it was to sue release,
> Subdue I must or be subdude.[48]

While the speaker here dissolves his investment in his own desire as a means of inwardly releasing himself from an externally imposed state of paralysis, Magdalene is led to sacrifice her desire for Christ's literal presence as a means of attaining him spiritually, that is, internally. The process of her interpellation *is* this process of relinquishing desire for the comfort of Christ's literal presence. And like the mode of Christian interpellation described by Althusser, it has the structure of a forced choice: Subdue I must or be subdued.[49]

The literary models informing Mary's interpellation through Christ's "ravishing" voice are less scriptural than they are Ovidian. While Ovid's *Heroides* deeply informs the Renaissance Magdalene tradition, Southwell's Mary is unique insofar as she is presented as a Christianization, and an ambivalent one at that, of Ovidian figures of female speechlessness like Philomela and Lucrece. Indeed, what is striking about Southwell's representation of Magdalene's interpellation by Christ is its emphasis on her silence. In the twelfth-century text that Southwell is reworking, the narrator does not emphasize Mary's silence, nor does he introduce an opposition or tension between Mary's words and her tears. In Southwell's text, however, the nature of Mary's articulateness becomes a thematic problem. While Southwell follows the Origenist text's assertion of Magdalene's overwhelming desire to speak, a desire so profound she actually interrupts Christ, he then emphasizes her incapacity for speech. While this silence explicitly signals the emotionally and physically overwhelming state of union with Christ, thereby completing the resolution of her earlier state of fragmentation, it also implicitly limits Magdalene's authority as spiritual exemplum. The narrator's reference to her "unsyllabled breath" in the passage below reminds us that the recalcitrance she showed before the angels at Christ's tomb—a recalcitrance that is presented as being shortsighted if admirably audacious—was the function of an incomplete recognition of providential design. Her undivided love for Christ is thus tempered here by a recognition of fear. And this fear, not unimportantly, enforces silence:

> [R]avished with his voice, and impatient of delays, [she] taketh his talke out of his mouth, and to his first and yet onely word, answered but one other, calling him *Rabboni,* that is Maister. And then sodayne joy rousing all other passions, she could no more proceed in her own, than give him leave to go forward with his speech. Love would have spoken, but feare inforced silence. Hope frameth the words, but doubt melteth them in the passage: and when her inward conceits served [strived] to come out, her

> voice trembled, her tongue faltered, her breath failed. In fine tears issued in lieu of wordes, and deep sighes instead of long sentences; the [eye] supplying the mouths default, and the heart pressing out the unsyllabled breath at once, which the conflict of her disagreeing passions, would not suffer to be sorted into the several sounds of intelligible speeches.[50]

This passage continues the text's half-hearted endorsement of Magdalene's capacity for authoritative speech by emphasizing the point, made earlier, that her tears supplement and are, in fact, more articulate than her words: "Thy teares were interpreters of thy words, and thy innocent meaning was written in thy dolefull countenance."[51] This simultaneous endorsing and containing of Magdalene's persuasiveness—an ambivalence here registered in the word "innocent," which denotes purity and naïveté—is figured through an Ovidian thematics of female speechlessness. Conjoining the Counter-Reformational tradition of tear-literature with the Ovidian topos of female silence—which, as Lynn Enterline has shown, is not in any way straightforwardly antifeminist[52]—Southwell situates Magdalene's spiritual power in her capacity to weep rather than speak: "Mary—thy tears will obtain: they are too mighty orators to let any suit fail. . . . [H]ave they so persuasive a silence, and so conquering a complaint, that by yielding they overcome, and by entreating they command."[53] Here again, Magdalene's verbose recalcitrance before the angels at the tomb is qualified and recontextualized. Her capacity for speech is thematically subordinated by the articulateness of her silence.

What is at stake in Magdalene's silence is the specific mode of female (and recusant) subjectivity that Southwell is fashioning. Magdalene's silence—her experience of intimacy with Christ in a domain that is beyond language itself—discloses how ideal spiritual submissiveness is reached once complete satiation gives way again to total lack and the exquisite dolor of absence becomes its own impossible state of fullness. This point of excess, where the experience of physical absence is registered as a form of spiritual presence, and where pain bleeds into something beyond pleasure, demarcates a subjective mode in which one finds comfort in being comfortless and overcomes outward misery by becoming inwardly more miserable. The fulfillment of the *imitatio Magdalena* as Southwell presents it is achieved when desire for God becomes infinite rather than a finite expression of self-love. Southwell explains this distinction in his poem "On the Blessed Sacrament" when he asserts that "Selfelove cannot crave more then it fyndes, / Ambition to noe higher worth aspire, / The eagrest famyn of most hungry myndes / May fill, yea farre exceede their owne desire."[54] Love for God, on the other hand, as Southwell explains in the *Epistle Dedicatorie* of *Funeral Tears,* "could never exceed because the thing loved [is] of infinite pleasure."[55] Exemplifying this capacity for infinite desire, Magdalene embodies the incarnational paradox that an assumption of one's lack, one's awareness of radical incompleteness, is the paradoxical way toward being complete because it is the way toward (becoming like) Christ. Magdalene's "frustrated eros" is thus not only the means of coming into self-awareness; it is the very engine, the very substance of her saintliness. The experience of feeling absent from Christ is here made an integral part, rather than merely the occasion for, becoming like Magdalene. By making Mary's "frustrated eros" not merely the cause by which she comes to know herself as subject but the very means by which she paradoxically obtains her divine object, Southwell introduces a Petrarchan thematics of sublation from body to spirit, from mortal to immortal love, into his Ovidian and Counter-Reformation materials. The paradox of recusant melancholia as Southwell articulates it is Petrarchan in structure insofar as the absence of the physical object results in a deepened spiritual relation with it. By introducing this Petrarchan element into Mary's pursuit of Christ, Southwell engenders an *imitatio Magdalena* that is of particular relevance for recusants experiencing the absence of the church but not of God himself.

As I have suggested, however, this portrait of a female saint is not without its anxieties over female power. Southwell's text acknowledges the potentially overwhelming power of fascination and transformation that the Magdalene figure holds when the narrator asks if her image can "alter sex, change nature, and exceed all Art."[56] Throughout the text, Magdalene's power lies in the way that she exemplifies, and even takes to its limits, Augustine's epistemological licensing of excess. In *On Christian Doctrine* Augustine initiates a break from classical virtues of moderation when he declares that "there can never be too much love for God, nor too little of the impulses which impede it."[57] This principle becomes epistemologically justified insofar as the affections or passions are identified, not as an element of the sensitive appetite—the more animal part of the human creature—as in Aristotle, but rather as a function of the will. This epistemological shift is part and parcel with the change that Augustinian Christianity institutes regarding how one evaluates the nature of desire. Seeking to distinguish Christian asceticism from pagan forms of self-care, Augustine asserts that "in our discipline, the question is not *whether* the devout soul is angry, but why; not whether it is sad, but what causes its sadness; not whether it is afraid, but what is the object of its fear."[58] It is this aspect of Augustine's legacy that Nietzsche has in his sights when he declares with his own characteristic hyperbole: "Christianity wants to destroy, shatter, stun, intoxicate: there is only one thing it does not want: *measure,* and for this reason, it is in its deepest meaning barbaric, Asiatic, ignoble, un-Greek."[59] While Southwell's Magdalene embodies and even expresses these Augustinian principles of excess, his homiletic framework is organized by an Aristotelian ethics of moderation. The introduction of such a framework works to contain Magdalene's excesses—to demarcate, as it were, their proper ideological limits.

Indeed, it is precisely because Southwell is aware of the power of fascination that Magdalene's excesses possess that he not only licenses but also seeks to limit the transformative possibilities of Magdalene's passion. Underlying the representation of Mary's infinite desire and the capacity for recalcitrance that attends it is the question that many communities in Counter-Reformation Europe asked, namely, "How far can a woman's resistance of authority extend when it is in the name of the Catholic Church?"[60] In Southwell's text, this question is uneasily framed within an opposition between Aristotelian moderation and Augustinian excess—an opposition with important consequences for the structure of recusant subjectivity as Southwell imagines it. In the *Epistle Dedicatorie,* Southwell echoes Ignatius's warning about the dangers of excessive discipline and devotion, remarking that one should "teach his thoughts either to temper passion in the mean, or to give the bridle only where the excess cannot be faulty."[61] Such homiletic statements work to reinforce the accusation, made by both the narrator and the angels at Christ's empty tomb, that Mary's grief is excessive insofar as it is motivated by a misinterpretation of God's self-revelation. Mary is thus told that "thou deceivest thy self in thy own desires, and it well appeareth, that excess of grief, hath bred in thee a defect of due providence."[62] Such passages reinforce the ethically sophisticated (not to mention politically sensitive) point made in the *Epistle Dedicatorie* when Southwell asserts that "too much of the best is evill, and excesse in virtue, vice; so the passions let loose without limits, are imperfections, nothing being good that wanteth measure."[63] This counterintuitive sentiment discloses the extent to which the text is structured according to two distinct epistemological economies, one premised on a masculinized language of temperance and the other on a feminized language of excess. Most importantly, such statements work insofar as they introduce an ironic distance between the reader and Magdalene; for it is precisely this distance that Magdalene develops from her earlier state as a literalist, a lover of the body rather than the spirit. Such homiletic comments thus encourage one to identify with Magdalene's intense passion for Christ, but they warn that one should not do so too literally lest one's devotional commitments prove transgressive. The text as a whole thus teaches the lesson that Magdalene herself states regarding the subversive nature of following the law too literally: "[T]hrough too much preciseness in keeping the lawe, I have lost the lawmaker, and by being too scrupulous in observing his ceremonies, I am proved irreligious in loosing himselfe."[64] Southwell here pushes on the paradoxes already visible in the pseudo-Origenist text. In the earlier work the issue of preciseness is not evident, only the double-bind regarding the fact that had Magdalene stayed at the tomb she "wolde have obeied the lawe, / and have not kept him to whom the lawe it selfe is obediente."[65] Developing the paradoxes of Mary's "woeful case," Southwell's distinction focuses on Mary's comportment toward her perception of divine law rather than on the external oppositions between following and betraying the law. Things have thus turned inward, both in the course of Magdalene's literary history and in the development of Southwell's text itself. For the final lesson of Southwell's text is that a properly interpellated Catholic subject should be wary of the dangerously melancholic pleasures made available by an overly literal identification with images of religious perfection, particularly female ones that find their power in the experience of lack, frustration, and absence. Throughout the concluding homily and the work as a whole, Southwell wrestles with the potential for transgression inherent within the Magdalene figure—sometimes embracing it, sometimes eschewing it. The text's oscillations between excess and temperance, silence and speech, grief and joy, register the ways in which this work both licenses and seeks to police images of female power—a process with significant consequences for a recusant community so dependent upon women for its survival.[66]

Notes

1. Debora Shuger, *The Renaissance Bible: Scholarship, Sacrifice, and Subjectivity* (Berkeley: University of California Press, 1994), 191.

2. Ibid., 189.

3. For an example of a Protestant treatise on Magdalene, see the anonymous *Maryie Magdalenes Love* (London, 1595). For Protestant poetic treatments of her, see George Herbert's and Henry Vaughan's "Mary Magdalene" poems.

4. F.W. Brownlow, *Robert Southwell* (New York and London: Twayne, 1996), has gestured at the socially symbolic dimensions operative within the text, observing that Mary "is an English Catholic woman, and the violence that threatens her is that of contemporary England, just as the voices that cajole her to abandon her weeping have their parallel among those in England who were tempting the Catholics with the rewards of compromise and apostasy" (43). For other representations of Magdalene in early modern England, see *Complaynt of the Lover of Cryst Saynt Mary Magdaleyn* (London, 1520); *Maryie Magdalenes Love* (London, 1595); *Maries Exercise* (London, 1597); *Saint Mary Magdalenes Conversion* (London, 1603); *Mary Magdalens Lamentations for the Loss of her Master Jesus* (London, 1604); *S. Mary Magdalens Pilgrimage to Paradise* (London, 1617); *The Life and Death of Mary Magdalene* (London, 1620).

5. Although I adopt Louis Althusser's term for designating the process whereby an individual comes to recognize itself as a subject of authority, my analysis of the antagonisms inherent in Magdalene's interpellation make it clear that I diverge from his rather monolithic conception of the process. For a lucid critique of the totalizing nature of Althusser's model in "Ideology and the Ideological State Apparatus," which appears in *Lenin and Philosophy*, trans. Ben Brewster (New York: Monthly Review Press, 1971), 127–88, see Judith Butler's "'Conscience Doth Make Subjects of Us All': Althusser's *Subjection*," in *The Psychic Life of Power: Theories of Subjection* (Stanford: Stanford University Press, 1997), 106–31. For a competing reassessment of Althusser, see Slavoj Žižek, *The Sublime Object of Ideology* (New York: Verso, 1989), 43–53.

6. My reading differs from Shuger's on this point regarding the movement from body to spirit, from a literal to a sacramental relation to Christ. The physicality of Magdalene's religiosity notwithstanding, Shuger overstates the lack of dualism between corporeality and spirituality that structures Magdalene's relation with Christ when she asserts that in Southwell's text, as in other Renaissance Magdalene narratives, "there is no movement toward rising above the body, no transcendence" (*Renaissance Bible*, 175). This assessment runs the risk of blurring, if not collapsing, the different states Mary inhabits in the course of Southwell's text—her state before seeing the resurrected Christ and her state after. To overlook these varying states, one has to disregard Southwell's assertion in the opening *Epistle Dedicatorie* in which he describes his homiletic aim in terms of a sublation of physical to spiritual love: "passion, and especially this of love, is in these days the chief commander of men's actions, and the idol to which both tongues and pens do sacrifice their ill-bestowed labours; so there is nothing now more needful to be treated, than how to direct these humours into their due courses, and to draw this flood of affections into the right channel" (A3). This homiletic aim of turning from a physical to a spiritual object is reasserted by Christ when he declares to Mary that she must "be weaned from the comfort of my external presence that thou mayest learn to lodge in thee

the secrets of my heart" (74). Christ here exhorts Mary to adopt a spiritual attitude that is not accurately characterized as an "undifferentiated urgency" of both corporeal and spiritual longing—the terms Shuger uses to describe Mary's desire throughout the work (175). On the contrary, Christ is explaining the difference between a mature spiritual love that can admit physical absence and an immature love that requires literal proximity to his living body. Elsewhere this difference is configured in terms of Christ's mortal and resurrected bodies, a difference that relies upon a distinct opposition between the corporeal and spiritual (*Magdalene's Tears,* 73). Another way to approach this is to point out that Shuger's emphasis on the Ovidian and Aristotelian contexts obscures the Petrarchan dimensions of Southwell's representation of Magdalene—how Christ's physical absence paradoxically leads to a deepening of Magdalene's spiritual relation with him. I address the sacralization of Petrarchanism in Southwell's poetry in *Divine Subjection: The Rhetoric of Sacramental Devotion in Early Modern England* (Pittsburgh: Duquesne University Press, 2005), 76–91.

7. For a discussion of the responses that the Magdalene figure inspired in various communities and times, see Katherine Ludwig Jansen, *The Making of the Magdalen: Preaching and Popular Devotion in the Later Middle Ages* (Princeton: Princeton University Press, 2000), 247–306. For an example of the important role women played in the recusant community, see *An Elizabethan Recusant House, Comprising the Life of the Lady Magdalen, Viscountess Montague (1538–1608)*, ed. A. C. Southern (London: Sands, 1954).

8. Megan Matchinske, *Writing, Gender and State in Early Modern England* (Cambridge: Cambridge University Press, 1998), 55.

9. John Bossy, *English Catholic Community, 1570–1850* (New York: Oxford University Press, 1976), 153. Sarah L. Bastow, "'Worth Nothing, But Very Wilful': Catholic Recusant Women of Yorkshire, 1536–1642," *Recusant History* 25 (2001): 591–603, examines the domestic and devotional lives of recusant women in early modern Yorkshire, concluding that women "were frequently the main instigators and practitioners of . . . household Catholicism" (599). Bastow builds on Richard Rex's "Thomas Vavasour M.D.," *Recusant History* 20 (1989–90): 436–53, particularly its discussion of matriarchal Catholic households. Marie B. Rowlands, "Recusant Women 1560–1640," in *Women in English Society 1500–1800*, ed. Mary Prior (London: Methuen, 1985), 149–80, offers a general overview of English recusant women.

10. Cited in Christopher Devlin, *The Life of Robert Southwell: Poet and Martyr* (New York and London: Longmans, Green, 1956), 140.

11. Ibid., 199.

12. Ibid., 141.

13. Antonia Fraser, *The Gunpowder Plot: Terror and Faith in 1605* (London: Weidenfeld and Nicolson), 30–31, 66.

14. Cited in Godfrey Anstruther, *Vaux of Harrowden: A Recusant Family* (Newport, Monmouthshire: R. H. Johns, 1953), 189.

15. John Mush's "Life of Margaret Clitherow," in *The Catholics of York under Elizabeth*, ed. John Morris (London: Burns and Oates, 1891), and Henry Garnet's *A Treatise of Christian Renunciation* (London: Garnet's First Press, 1593) both deal with the question of female power in the Catholic community, though more in the context of marriage with a Protestant husband.

16. Francis E. Dolan, *Whores of Babylon: Catholicism, Gender, and Seventeenth-Century Print Culture* (Ithaca: Cornell University Press, 1999). See also Arthur F. Marotti, "Alienating Catholics in Early Modern England: Recusant Women, Jesuits and Ideological Fantasies," in *Catholicism and Anti-Catholicism in Early Modern English Texts* (New York: Macmillan, 1999), 1–34.

17. For a recent account of the highly conflictual and extremely malleable ways in which early modern writers appropriated Aristotle's principle of the mean into religious and other discourses, see Joshua Scodel, *Excess and the Mean in Early Modern English Literature* (Princeton: Princeton University Press, 2002).

18. Jansen, *Making of the Magdalen*, 37.

19. Susan Haskins, *Mary Magdalene: Myth and Metaphor* (New York: Harcourt Brace, 1993), 252.

20. Jansen, *Making of the Magdalen*, 335.

21. For a discussion of pictorial representations of Magdalene as blessed lover and penitent, see Haskins, *Mary Magdalene*, 256–67.

22. Cited in Devlin, *Life*, 138.

23. John Gerard, *The Autobiography of an Elizabethan*, trans. Philip Caraman (London: Longmans, 1951), 147.

24. Pierre Janelle indicates that Dorothy Arundel became a Benedictine nun in *Robert Southwell the Writer: A Study in Religious Inspiration* (New York: Mamaroneck, 1935; reprint, 1971), 59. So too does Brownlow, *Southwell*, 38.

25. Robert Southwell, *Mary Magdalene's Funeral Tears* (London: Printed by A[dam] I[slip] for G[abriel] C[awood], 1594), A4. All further citations of this work are from this edition unless otherwise noted. I modernize the title's spelling throughout.

26. Jacobus de Voragine, *The Golden Legend*, trans. Granger Ryan (London: Longmans, Green, 1941), 2:357. This view of Magdalene is presented in Caravaggio's *The Conversion of Mary Magdalene* (1600). In this distinctly Counter-Reformation depiction of Magdalene, she is seen wearing, as Haskins points out, a "magnificent gown of purple and white with red sleeves, her hair pinned up . . . clasping an orange blossom to her heart" (Haskins, *Mary Magdalene*, 257). For a discussion of Magdalene's impact on medieval women's devotion, see Susan Eberly, "Margery Kempe, St. Mary Magdalene, and Patterns of Contemplation," *Downside Review* 107 (1989): 209–23. For an account of other visual depictions of Magdalene, see Jane Dillenberger, "The Magdalen: Reflections on the Image of the Saint and Sinner in Chris-

tian Art," in *Women, Religion, and Social Change*, ed. Yvonne Yazbeck Haddad and Ellison Banks Findly (Albany: State University of New York Press, 1985), 115–46.

27. Robert Southwell, *An Humble Supplication To Her Majesty*, ed. R. C. Bald (Cambridge: Cambridge University Press, 1953), 3.

28. Southwell, *Funeral Tears*, 2–3.

29. Ibid., 19.

30. Robert Southwell, *The Poems of Robert Southwell, S.J.*, ed. James H. McDonald and Nancy Pollard Brown (Oxford: Clarendon Press, 1967), 45, line 1.

31. Ibid., lines 19–24.

32. Southwell's "Marie Magdalene's complaint at Christ's death" assumes the associations between Magdalene's conversion and the proper mode of receiving communion common to late medieval and Counter-Reformation Catholicism. St. Theresa voices this association when she records her meditations on Magdalene during the time in which her own soul was "awakened": "I was besides, very much devoted, to the glorious *S. Mary Magdalen*; and I thought much, and often, of her conversion; and especially whensoever I received the *B. Sacrament*. For, knowing, at that time, that our Lord was most certainly in my bosom, I placed myself at his feet, as conceiving, that my tears would not be dispised by him" (H2). *The life of the Holy Mother S. Teresa foundress of the reformation of the discalced Carmelites*, trans. Abraham Woodhead (London, 1671).

33. Southwell, *An Humble Supplication*, 3.

34. Ibid., 1.

35. Southwell, *Funeral Tears*, 17.

36. Ibid., 53.

37. William Alabaster, *The Sonnets of William Alabaster*, ed. G. M. Story and Helen Gardner ([London]: Oxford University Press, 1959), lines 5–14.

38. Augustine, *The Confessions of St. Augustine*, trans. Rex Warner (New York: New American Library, 1963), 44 (bk. 3, chap. 6, para. 11).

39. The 1594 edition that I am quoting has the word *limned* as "limitted." Every other edition I have consulted, including the original 1591 work, has *limned*, which makes more sense in this context.

40. Southwell, *Funeral Tears*, 6. The focus on the theme of memory in relation to Mary derives, in part, from Christ's words in Matt. 26:13: "Verily I say unto you, Wheresoever this gospel shall be preached in the whole world, there shall also this, that this woman hath done, be told for a memorial of her."

41. For discussions of Southwell's source, see Brownlow, *Southwell*, 35–37; Shuger, *Renaissance Bible*, 169. For a brief consideration of earlier English adaptations of the Pseudo-Origen work, see Rosemary Woolf, "English Imitations of the *Homelia Origenis De Maria Magdalena*," in *Chaucer and Middle English Studies in Honour of Rossell Hope Robbins*, ed. Beryl Rowland (London: George Allen and Unwin, 1974), 384–91.

42. Robert Southwell, *Mary Magdalen's funeral tears; The triumphs over death; and An epistle of comfort,* ed. W. Jos. Walter (London: Keating, 1822), 16.

43. Southwell, *Funeral Tears* (1594), 68.

44. This particular moment in the Gospel narrative of Christ's life is repeatedly represented in Elizabethan religious literature precisely because it marks the moment at which Magdalene lives out the difference between law and grace, between old and new dispensations, after Christ's physical death. At this liminal moment, Magdalene becomes the first "Christian" in the sense that she is the initial witness of Christ's Resurrection and thus the first to see him fulfill his messianic promise. The post-Reformation debates about the exact relation between law and gospel, between Old Testament judgment and New Testament mercy, are enacted at the level of subjective experience in this scene at the tomb and are thus repeatedly returned to as a way of thinking through the subjective states proper to Christian faith.

45. Southwell, *Funeral Tears,* 74.

46. Ibid., 27.

47. Southwell, *Poems,* 43, lines 6, 8.

48. Ibid., lines 33–36.

49. Southwell's most compelling expression of Catholic interpellation having the structure of a forced choice is his account of his entry into the Jesuit order described in a private letter:

> Through thy loving sweetness Christ, thou hast grasped to thyself my heart, and I must needs offer myself up a slave to thee. For thou hast vanquished me, o Lord Jesus, thou has vanquished me in a twofold fight. For when first I was assailed by thy holy inspirations, I resisted, as if the choosing me for one of thy Society brought more pleasure to thee than gain to myself. Thou sawest o Lord my infirmity, and with new engines shattering the ramparts of my heart, as I could flee nowhere to recover, being compelled, after a long struggle I gave myself up, and submitted myself to thy powerful hand.

Quoted in Pierre Janelle, *Robert Southwell the Writer: A Study in Religious Inspiration* (1935; reprint, New York: Mamaroneck, 1971), 13. I have slightly amended Janelle's translation. For a discussion of this passage, see my *Divine Subjection,* 41–46.

50. Southwell, *Funeral Tears,* 69–70.

51. Ibid., 59.

52. Enterline effectively argues that the theme of female speechlessness in Ovid functions more as a critique of patriarchy than as a symptom of it. See *The Rhetoric of the Body from Ovid to Shakespeare* (Cambridge: Cambridge University Press, 2000).

53. Southwell, *Funeral Tears,* 65.

54. Southwell, *Poems,* 26, lines 25–28.

55. Southwell, *Funeral Tears,* A5.

56. Ibid., 39.

57. Augustine, *On Christian Doctrine,* trans. D.W. Roberston Jr. (Indianapolis: Bobbs-Merrill, 1958), 226.

58. Augustine, *Concerning the City of God against the Pagans,* trans. Henry Bettenson (New York: Penguin, 1972), 349.

59. Nietzsche, *Human, All Too Human,* ed. Bernd Magnus, trans. Gary Handwerk (Stanford: Stanford University Press, 1995), 94.

60. The flip side of this question is the one that Protestant authorities in England asked: How far a woman who broke the law was responsible for her own actions? For a discussion of this question in the context of recusant women, see Rowlands, "Recusant Women 1560–1640."

61. Southwell, *Funeral Tears,* A8.

62. Ibid., 23.

63. Ibid., A4. Augustine articulates a similar point in the *Confessions* when he describes his tendency to be overly strict with himself regarding the pleasures of listening to church psalms: "I erre out of too precise a severity; yea very fierce am I sometimes in the desire of having the melody of all pleasant Musicke . . . banished both from mine owne eares and out of the whole Church too" (*Saint Augustines Confessions translated* [London: William Watts, 1631], 33).

64. Southwell, *Funeral Tears,* 22.

65. *An Homilie of Mary Magdalene* (London, 1565), B6.

66. Southwell's concern with the proper use of the passions is hardly unique within the context of English Catholic literature. Thomas Wright's 1601 treatise *The Passions of the Mind in General* directly engages many of the concerns regarding affect and desire implicit in Southwell's work.

6

Dame Barbara Constable

Catholic Antiquarian, Advisor, and Closet Missionary

Heather Wolfe

I shall never make an end if I should expresse all I could . . .

Barbara Constable, "Preface to the Reader," in
"Aduises For Confessors & Spirituall Directors" (1650)

I never was one of those that thought learninge and the exercise of pietie were incompatible.

Barbara Constable, "Preface to the Reader," in
"A breefe Treatise of learninge and preachinge" (1653)

In her forty-six years as an English Benedictine nun, Dame Barbara Constable (1617–84) wrote and compiled at least eleven original works and collections (average length, six hundred pages), transcribed twenty-five spiritual works, maintained her community's register of letters and instructions, and emended scribal copies of contemplative treatises after comparing them to the exemplars at her monastery, Our Lady of Consolation, Cambrai (founded 1623). None of her original writings were ever printed or copied, and few were ever circulated beyond their intended recipients: Constable's recusant family in the East Riding of Yorkshire and other English Benedictine monks and nuns. Yet this was a significant readership that had much to gain from her spiritual musings.

While it is not known if she held any official offices within the monastery, writing and transcription would have been considered her "work," one of her three main duties as a nun (work, prayer, and reading), as well as something to fill her free time. Of the surviving output of what has become known as the "Cambrai scriptorium," Constable's hand appears more frequently than that of any other monk or nun.[1] The survival of her transcriptions of the writings of Father Augustine Baker (1575–1641), spiritual director at Cambrai from 1624 to 1633, makes it possible to begin reconstructing the scribal practices that led to the preservation of his works. In turn, Baker was laboring to preserve and update the writings of medieval mystical writers such as Blosius, Hilton, Julian of Norwich, Rolle of Hampole, Suso, Tauler, and the author of the *Cloud of Unknowing*, and disseminate the writings of contemporary writers such as Barbanson (1581–1632), Benet of Canfield (1562–1611), and St. John of the Cross. In one of his treatises, Baker describes the need to recover these spiritual guides as follows: "they doe . . . tend or revive or continue the auncient most holy exercises of our order, & which brought it to that high large spreadinge & longe lastinge sanctity to which it arriued."[2] With the dissolution of the monasteries in England and the uncontrolled dispersal of their libraries a century earlier, many of these writings, essential for learning the ancient techniques for contemplative prayer, were in danger of being lost forever.

When English monasticism resurfaced on the Continent in the years following the Dissolution, a new generation of monks and nuns had minimal resources to give them a sense of spiritual continuity with their forefathers.[3] Antiquarians and historians such as John Bale, Matthew Parker, John Fox, and later Robert Cotton had purchased or salvaged medieval manuscripts from the dissolved monasteries in England, including registers, charters, chronicles, and lives of saints and martyrs. Protestants and Catholics alike realized the value of these manuscripts for, among other things, polemical ecclesiastical history—that is, establishing a religious ancestry that consisted either of a continual independent English church or England's continual link with Rome. The newly restored English Benedictine Congregation (est. 1619) was at the forefront of this recovery effort, and in 1622 Baker was charged with researching the records of the pre-Reformation Benedictine order in England to prove that the congregation had never been a dependency of Cluny or any other foreign congregation and that St. Gregory and St. Augustine, who converted

England, were indeed Benedictines.[4] The resulting work, *Apostolatus Benedictorum in Anglia*, based on extensive use of manuscripts in Robert Cotton's library, was published at Douai in 1626.[5] But the spiritual legacy had been largely neglected in the early stages of this recovery process.

Constable arrived at Cambrai a century after the Dissolution, five years after Baker's departure. One of the main purposes of the new English foundations on the Continent in the seventeenth century was to convert England back to Catholicism through prayer and the mission. In fact, nuns at Cambrai's daughter house, Our Lady of Good Hope, Paris, founded in 1651, made a promise at the time of their profession to devote their lives to England's conversion: "According to the vocation and holy institute of this Convent, I offer myself and all my actions for the Conversion of England, in union with our Fathers' labour of the Mission, and as they promise and swear to go and return as they are commanded, so will I live and die in this my offering in this Convent."[6] The nuns had a responsibility to provide the Catholics of England with an institutional memory. While they could not go on the mission in England like their male counterparts, they could, in relative freedom, contribute to the survival and flourishing of medieval English Catholic contemplative culture.

This essay demonstrates Constable's realization of the need to preserve, collect, and disseminate Baker's writings and the writings of the contemplative authors recommended by him, as well as her desire to provide and replenish resources for her family and her religious community so that they could engage in the spiritual readings and prayers of the "old religion," and her critical role in the output of a small-scale monastic scriptorium. She sought to correct the shortcomings of her contemporary monks and nuns in positions of authority by pointing them to examples from the past. Constable's original writings and compilations reveal as much her attempts to update and supply traditional monastic spiritual reading *(lectio divina)* and prayer for a broader audience as they do her struggle to justify her wide learning within a contemplative environment that stressed the exercise of the will over that of the understanding.[7]

The Constables of Everingham Park

Barbara Constable came from one of the leading recusant landowning families of the East Riding of Yorkshire, the Constables of Everingham Park. Her father, Sir Philip Constable, first baronet (1595–1664), and her mother, Anne

Roper (d. 1644), daughter of Sir William Roper of Eltham, Kent, had five children: Barbara (1617–84), Sir Marmaduke, second baronet (1619–80), Philip (1622–81), Thomas (d. 1712), and Catherine.[8] As in many Catholic families, the eldest son and heir married and remained in England, while three of the four remaining children joined English monastic communities on the Continent. Sir Marmaduke Constable married Anne Shirburne, daughter of the recusant Richard Shirburne (1586–1667) of Stonyhurst, Lancashire, in 1650 and assumed control of the family estates.[9] Barbara was professed at Our Lady of Consolation, Cambrai, in 1640. Educated at the Jesuit English College at St. Omer, Philip went on to reside at the English College in Rome from 1642 to 1645 before returning to England.[10] He then became a monk at St. Gregory's, Douai, in about 1660. Thomas (Augustine) was professed at St. Gregory's, Douai, in 1649.[11] Catherine married the recusant Edward Sheldon of Steeple Barton, Oxfordshire, in 1649 and remained devoutly Catholic.

The civil wars were not kind to the Constable family. Two of Sir Philip's brothers, Michael and Marmaduke, were killed fighting on the Royalist side. Sir Philip's estates were sequestered in 1642 and resequestered in 1650–51. Three-thousand-acre Everingham Park was looted and occupied; the similarly extensive Lincolnshire estates at West and Middle Rasen were rented to an army officer. In 1652, Sir Philip's name was included on the third Treason Act and his estates were forfeited to the Commonwealth, despite the concerted efforts of his cousin, the Puritan and regicide Sir William Constable of Flamborough.[12] But through some clever legal maneuvering Sir Philip was able to create the appearance of having sold his estates while still allowing his family to maintain control of them.[13] Recusancy fines, the long sequestration, and the payment of composition fines forced the Constable family to borrow heavily in London, and debts incurred during the civil wars were not discharged until at least 1679. In 1662, however, the situation had improved enough for Sir Philip Constable to invite relatives, friends, and tenants to a banquet at Everingham Hall from Christmas until Twelfth Night to celebrate saving their estates.[14]

The Popish Plot controversy brought new hardship to the family. Barbara Constable's nephew, Sir Philip Constable, later third baronet (1651–1706), was imprisoned for his faith in March 1678. The following year he was granted a pass to go to the Continent and upon his return was imprisoned again in July 1680 for refusing to take the Oath of Allegiance. He was released in 1683. At the same time, Sir Marmaduke, Barbara's brother, escaped abroad, dying in exile in Louvain in August 1680.

Barbara Constable was in Cambrai for the duration of the civil wars, and prior to her profession details of her life are spotty. Among the Constable papers now at the University of Hull, her name first appears in an account book for her father's West Rasen estate in 1634, when a halter was purchased for her horse.[15] Her father's early will (undated, but prior to her profession) leaves her £1500.[16] An inventory of household goods at Everingham Hall taken on August 11, 1637, lists the furnishings in the chambers of Sir Philip, her brother Marmaduke, and Barbara. Her chamber consisted of "a bedstead a fetherbed, a boulster, two pillowes, three blancketts, a red rugg, curtaines & vallance of red stuffe, a cupboard, & a trundle bedstead."[17]

Barbara Constable's deep interests in Roman Catholicism and in reading came at an early age. In "Gemitus Peccatorum," she explains that her mother dedicated her to the Virgin Mary as an infant. In "The Second part prosecuting the Excellency of M*ental* Prayer," she writes of her passion for reading: "I cannot but attribute much of my good (if I haue any in me) to the loue I haue alwais had euen from my Infancie to readinge, & I haue allwaies lookt vpon it as a great gift of god, & one of the prime meanes which he hath vsed to keepe me in the state of saluation."[18] An inventory of books taken in 1689 at Everingham Park suggests the range of printed books and manuscripts available to Constable, representing all subjects, including many Roman Catholic writings of a liturgical, devotional, and polemical nature.[19]

On August 31, 1638, Constable arrived at Our Lady of Consolation, Cambrai, with five other young women, including Lucy and Mary Cary, the two youngest daughters of Elizabeth Cary, Viscountess Dowager Falkland, and Catherine (Justina) Gascoigne, daughter of Sir Thomas Gascoigne of Barnbow Hall, Yorkshire, and niece of the abbess, Dame Catherine Gascoigne.[20] In 1640, Constable was professed. Her father's last will, dated February 20, 1664, leaves forty pounds to the English nuns at Cambrai and forty pounds each to the English nuns at Louvain, the English nuns at Brussels, and the English monks at Douai.[21]

Father Augustine Baker's Legacy to the English Benedictine Nuns of Cambrai and Paris

Baker's contribution to the spiritual welfare of the nuns of Cambrai and Paris cannot be underestimated. Before his arrival at Cambrai in 1624 as their spiritual advisor, the Cambrai nuns were probably influenced by the *Spiritual Exercises* of St. Ignatius of Loyola, a highly structured course of contemplation more suitable for lay Catholics than for enclosed nuns.[22] Baker immediately recognized that the nuns needed something more fitting to their state, a flexible method individually tailored to the needs of each nun. Thus in conferences with them he promoted a form of meditation and prayer that involved digesting and ruminating the written word to generate passively produced spontaneous prayer, proceeding at one's own pace through various stages: spiritual reading or meditation, active contemplation, and then passive contemplation, or mystic union.[23] At the nuns' request, he began writing treatises to assist them in their devotions. By the time he died in 1641, he had written over sixty treatises, and his audience extended beyond the twenty-nine nuns at Cambrai to include monks and laypeople as well. His instructions and spiritual "matter" were culled from a wide range of contemporary and medieval, English and continental, male and female authors.

Baker realized that many suitable Catholic mystic works were available only in Latin or old English. To narrow the gap between the contemplative practices of medieval monasticism and the needs of the many well-educated enclosed nuns at Cambrai, he encouraged the nuns to expand their manuscript and printed book collection and build a library to house it. To this end, he reestablished contact with Robert Cotton. In a letter dated June 3, 1629, Baker described his new job and living situation to Cotton and asked him for the donation of saints' lives and other devotional texts for Cambrai's library:

> Ever since my being w*i*th you I have lived in a cittie in thes forein partes, called Cambraie, assisting a convent of certein religious English women of the order of St Benet newlie erected. They are in number as yet but 29. They are inclosed and never seen by vs nor by anie other vnlesse it be rarelie vppon an extraordinarie occasion, but vppon no occasion maie they go furth, nor maie anie man or woman gette in vnto them. Yet I have my diet from them and vppon occasions conferre w*i*th them, but see not one another; and live in a house adioining to theirs. Their lives being contemplative the comon bookes of *th*e worlde are not for their purpose, and litle or nothing is in thes daies printed in English that is prop*er* for them. There were manie good English bookes in olde time whereof thoughe they have some, yet they want manie. And therevppon I am in their behallf becom*m*e an humble suitor vnto you, to bestowe on

> them such bookes as you please, either manuscript or printed being in English, conteining contemplation Saints lives or other devotions. Hampooles workes are proper for them. I wishe I had Hilltons scala perfectionis in latin; it woulde helpe the vnderstanding of the English (and some of them vnderstande latein) ~~or the English maie be made ^more^ intelligible by it~~ . . . This bearer will convey hether such bookes as it shall please you to single out and deliver to him.[24]

The request, which arrived shortly before Charles I's closure of Cotton's library, was apparently successful.[25] "A Catalogue of some printed bookes that I haue in this house" includes a telling note next to "Scale of Perfection" and "Pilgrimage of Perfect*ion*" [by William Bonde]: "Thes 2 being ours are as yet in Mr. Lewis his hands and are shortlie to come hether."[26] "Mr. Lewis" is most likely Morgan Lewis, master of the school at Abergavenny and the husband of Baker's niece, and could have served as the intermediary between Cotton and Baker.[27] Baker proceeded to write treatises on Hampole and Hilton, and Barbara Constable later transcribed them: "The Anchor of the Spirit . . . by S. Richard of Hampoll the Hermit and by me [Baker] made more intelligible" and "The Scale of Perfection."[28]

In "Concerning the Librarie of this howse," a treatise written shortly after Baker sent the letter to Cotton, he describes the importance of these medieval manuscripts and books and the need to preserve them:

> For as much as there is at this present (by the providence of god) a good and choice librarie in this howse consisting of bookes partlie manuscript and partlie of olde English print, which if they were lost or did perish, there is no hope nor meanes of coming againe by the like, therefore it is verie convenient and necessarie that some good course be taken for the preservation of those bookes, they being such as are proper for your estate that is contemplative, whome vulgar bookes or those that usuallie are sette furth now a daies can litle steed, being proper onlie for them that live in the worlde and leade active lives. . . . You have good olde English bookes that are never to be printed againe; you have Blossius his workes, Saint Gertruds Insinuations and other things, and are never liklie to be tra[n]slated againe. You have some other things of my translating and doeng such as they are; thes I saie once lost, there is no hope of anie such anew nor will money procure them againe.[29]

He advises that they make copies of these books, "whereof the originall shoulde euer remaine in the librarie . . . and the other that is the copie so written out, shoulde be it that usuallie shoulde be handled and used by others." The treatise also discusses the necessity of fire prevention, since "there is scarce anie anncient monasterie or nunnery but hath sometime or other ben consumed by fire," and the dangers of "dampishness."

A small group of nuns and monks diligently began transcribing his copious treatises as soon as he completed them, for their own monasteries, for other English Benedictine monasteries, and for lay Catholics back in England, and this tradition continued throughout the seventeenth century into the eighteenth. Baker successfully instilled in the nuns his sensitivity to textual bibliographical matters, library science, collecting, and copying. They fiercely defended his writings from accusations of "liberty" and "novelty" on multiple occasions, and the foundation of Cambrai's daughter house at Paris in 1651 was based on his teachings.[30]

Barbara Constable was the primary transcriber at Cambrai in the 1640s and 1650s, and her copies were transmitted to England and to other English Benedictine monasteries.[31] Her 1645 copy of the second part of Baker's "Treatise of the English Mission" has the ownership mark of Dom Andrew Whitfield, an English Benedictine monk from St. Gregory's who spent time on the mission.[32] Prior to becoming a monk, Thomas Constable received a copy of Baker's "Directions for Contemplation" (Books D. F. G. H.), "Coppied out for him by his dearest sister Barbara Constable anno 1645."[33] Her copy of Baker's "Confession," also completed in 1645, has the ownership mark of Thomas Roper, on her mother's side of family.[34] Other transcriptions did not travel as far. Baker's "First Part of Doubts," copied by Constable in 1652, has the ownership mark of Dame Magdalen Eure (d. 1662) of Cambrai,[35] while Lamspringe Abbey owned a copy in her hand of Baker's "Directions to shew how to make use of the Idiots Devotion," "The Order of Teaching," and "Summary of Perfection" (1653).[36] A collection of Baker treatises corrected partly by Constable and partly by Dame Elizabetha Augustina Cary at Cambrai belonged first to the Paris nuns and then, by 1657, to the English Benedictine monks of St. Edmund's, Paris.[37] Most likely other copies of Baker treatises made by Constable for members of the English Benedictine Congregation did not survive the French Republic's suppression of religious houses and expulsion of British subjects in 1793, when English monks and nuns were forcibly removed from their monasteries and their belongings seized.[38]

The earliest surviving transcription by Constable is dated 1644, the latest 1683. Of the roughly twenty-three surviving transcriptions in her hand, seventeen are Baker treatises, and four of these are the only surviving copies: Baker's "Apology," the second part of his "Treatise of the English Mission," and his treatises "Anchor of the Spirit" and "Scale of Perfection" ("translated into better English"). At least two other Baker treatises in the hands of English Benedictine monks contain her corrections, indicating that one of her responsibilities was comparing copies of Baker treatises at other monasteries to the exemplars at Cambrai—most likely copies of Baker's original autograph manuscripts with the autograph approbations by Fathers Leander Jones and Rudesind Barlow dating from 1629 and 1633, when Baker's works were under review by the English Benedictine Congregation.[39] Colophons to copies of Baker manuscripts in the hands of other scribes underscore the importance of proofreading as a form of authorization, much in the tradition of medieval scriptorial practice. Copies of his treatises made especially for the foundation at Paris contain notes such "compared with that I write it out of."[40] Dom Wilfrid Reeve at St. Edmund's, Paris, almost always provided a specific paper trail. For example, Baker's "Secretum II" was "Finished the 12th of May. 1678. Transcribed out of the Cambray Copy, wch had bin Compared wth the Originall. F.WR."[41] Since she lived at Cambrai, Constable played a critical role in the dissemination of authoritative copies of Baker's treatises. Their provenance indicates close manuscript ties between the English Benedictine monastic communities on the Continent, chiefly those at Cambrai, Paris, Douai, and Lamspringe, and are suggestive of the courier role played by monks going on the mission or providing support to the nuns, networks and horizontal exchanges that are largely invisible to us now.

Gathering and Framing, Order and Disorder, in Barbara Constable's Original Writings

Just as Baker gathered and framed material from a wide range of sources for the Cambrai nuns to use as "matter" for their meditation and prayer, Constable gathered and framed material for others to ruminate upon—confessors, spiritual directors, superiors, priests, preachers, missionaries, nuns, and seculars. Her rationale is best explained in a work on mental prayer dedicated to Dom Joseph Martin. In the preface to the reader, she says of the authors she cites: "tho: I perhaps make them speake ill English, they were buried amonge many other things concerninge other subjects which perhaps made them not so sufficiently taken notise of as they deserued."[42] In a collection of prayers dedicated to her sister Catherine, she explains that the devotions have been "collected out of diverse bookes as I met them for the most part not yet in our language."[43] In her dedication to Abbess Catherine Gascoigne, she similarly explains that she has "drawne these collections from amonge many other things which perhaps hindred them from beinge so well observed even by those they most concerned; as now they may beinge drawne apart from them and united together."[44] Constable had more time on her hands than her superiors, and more access to Catholic texts than her family in York. She was in a unique position to gather and translate material from a wide range of sources in order to provide personally tailored collections for lay Catholics and regulars, increasing the utility of heretofore obscure sources by arranging them thematically.

The range of authors she cites is unexpectedly broad, from many different time periods, countries, and religious orders. Authors include St. Ambrose, St. Anthony, St. Augustine, St. Bede, St. Benedict, St. Bernard, St. Bonaventure, St. Boniface, St. Catherine of Siena, St. Ciprian, St. Denis, St. Francis of Assisi, St. Gregory, St. Isidore of Damietta (i.e., Pelusium), St. Jerome, St. John the Apostle, St. John Chrysostom, St. Paul, John Gerson, and sixteenth- and seventeenth-century writers such as St. Francis de Sales, St. Francis Xavier, St. John of the Cross, Cardinal de Bérulle, St. Peter of Alcantara, the abbot of St. Cyran, the bishop of Grasse, the bishop of Lisieux, Cardinal Bellarmine, Pope Innocent, Brother John of St. Sampson, and Mr. Forest (Blessed John Forest). She moves fluidly from one author to the next, and her commentary is woven into the text so tightly that it is often hard to untangle her words from those of the authors she quotes.

Not surprisingly, Constable sometimes had difficulty handling her multiplicity of sources. While it was partly a convention of prefaces and dedications to apologize for the shortcomings of the ensuing work, there must have been an element of truth to her frequent confession that the extracts are not as well ordered as one could hope: "[T]hou are not to expect the order which perhaps another would have kept, by reason that I am faine to write them as I meete with them casuallie & haueinge but little time & lesse capacitie."[45] The schedule of an enclosed nun did not allow for unfettered time and access to the library, and there would have been a cap to the number of books she could have kept in her cell at any one time. However, despite her protestations otherwise, her capacity was greater than most of the nuns—she could read and translate Latin, and her ability to trawl through hundreds of books in Latin, French, and English in order to bring together and organize extracts based on a specific theme—the burdens of superiority, the responsibilities of confessors, the dangers of the mission, the importance of mental prayer, coping with desolation—was unique.

Dame Barbara Constable's Readers: Hypothetical and Real

Constable's original manuscript treatises and compilations were different from the collections assembled by other nuns at Cambrai and Paris. Surviving miscellanies from these two communities consist of fragments of devotional matter written on "loose papers" for personal use in one's cell. After a nun's death, her papers might be bound together or integrated into a collection of fragments in multiple hands for the edification of the community at large. Since "loose papers" were created for personal use, they rarely identified source materials, had no clear beginning or ending, and were usually undated and unsigned—in short, they were rarely intended to have a secondary audience.[46]

Constable, in contrast, always had a specific audience in mind, and the physical layout of her manuscripts reflects her intention to reach Catholics beyond the walls of her community. Her surviving writings fall into three general categories: writings for monks and nuns in positions of authority; Catholics experiencing desolation in prayer, including herself; and laypeople in need of basic texts and prayers. The physical layout of her manuscripts mimics printed books, replete with title pages, dedicatory letters, and prefaces to the readers. She uses red ink on her title pages and for Latin quotations. In most of her manuscripts she identifies herself as "S.B.C." on the title page and records her completion date on the last page. In this sense, Constable's manuscript writings were publications, providing her primary readers (the dedicatees) and secondary readers (addressed in the prefaces) with the necessary framework to contextualize them. Her dedications reveal their intended destination, and marks of provenance chart the radius of their dissemination.

A repeated theme in Constable's works dedicated to her superiors is the divine nature of their jobs, which, as mere mortals, they should assume with great reluctance and humility. Constable's concerns over the abuse of power may have stemmed from personal observation, but they also echo Baker's argument that one's best spiritual guide is oneself, since meddling with someone else's interior is something very few people are qualified to do. In "Gemitus Peccatorum," written in 1649, she presages the tenor of her later advice manuals with a frightening question: "What kind of spirituall guides are now a daies who doe tirannise ouer soules, worse by farre then heeretofore did the heathens ouer the christians?"[47]

To Father Benedict Stapleton, her confessor, she addresses a collection of advice for confessors and spiritual directors, warning him of "the greatnesse of the charge they take vpon them." In the preface to the readers, her tone is more urgent: "I may allso feare that some confessors and spirituall Directors may perhaps not so sufficientlie consider and know the greatnesse of the charge they take vpon them when they take care of one soule much more of many as some doe, nor how to comport themselues as they ought to do in so weightie an affaire, which hath often made me tremble and crie out. . . . I wish all those who too easilie ingage themselues in so weightie a matter did but consider it as I many times haue done, or that I were able to expresse what I conceaue of this matter." To Abbess Catherine Gascoigne she dedicates a work on superiors, hoping it will "comfort you to see the way of gouernment you hold to be confirmed by the examples of so many holy persons." To her general audience, however, Constable's advice is more admonitory. She writes of "the greate charge of superioritie," which is "a most dangerous and terrible thinge . . . wholy incompatible with humane abilities": "I haue much wondred yea and stand in greate amaze to see so many that haue but humane shoulders presse forwards so earnestlie (as it is to be feared some doe) and offer to vndertake so greate a burthen. . . . That euerie one is not fitte for it daylie experience doth sufficientlie shew."[48] She then specifies her secondary audience, readers that can appreciate her book only if it travels beyond the walls of her enclosed community: "It is not only written for women superiours though the person I haue perticularlie directed it to, be a woman, for many of the Collections will seeme more proper for men, and therefore lette both take what is proper for them."

In "Considerations for Preests," dedicated to Constable's brother, Thomas Augustine, who was about to be ordained, she cautions him about "the strickt obligation you haue to liue a more then ordinarie life." She observes that in the past priesthood was a responsibility eschewed by many saints, who esteemed themselves unworthy of it, while "it is a wonder to see persons in these lesse holy Ages so forward to vndertake it" and now "there are so many more ill ones then good ones."[49] Her opinion about the dearth of good leadership among monks "now adaies" is unrestrained, bordering on disgust. Within an enclosed community governed by hundreds of rules and precepts, closely observed by the community's confessor and chaplain,

Constable wrote with surprising freedom about the flaws she perceived within the English Benedictine hierarchy.

Spiritual aridity was experienced by regulars and laypeople alike. Because of Constable's personal experience with this problem, she was in a special position to offer encouragement to others. In "Gemitus Peccatorum or the Complaints of Sinners," Constable aspires to be a better nun, wondering "how any body can be merry, for methinkes I would allwaies weepe and lament; to pray is death to me, beinge not able to thinke of any thinge but distractions and vanity."[50] Despite its personal tone, Constable predicts that it will be read by others and expresses concern that it be read in the same spirit in which it was written: "I most humbly desire that it may neuer fall into the hands of those who readinge things out of curiosity know not how to glorify thee by them. . . . [T]hou knowest I had no other intention but to helpe my selfe in time of necessity, if any chance to get good by them lette them render thanks & praise to thee."[51] She empathizes with Dom Joseph Martin in the second part of her trilogy on mental prayer and desolation: "[T]here is not a harder passage to be stept ouer by those who exercise prayer then that of Desolation."[52] Constable and Martin had apparently corresponded on the subject of desolation, because she continues: "['I]t is tedious[,'] you say, [']I know not where I am nor what I doe,['] it is not your buisnes to see feele or know but to passe on, though you fall & stumble a thousand times & be euen forced to grope for y*ou*r way, for you will sooner come to the end by doeinge thus then by goeinge backwards & forwards as the most part of people now adayes doe in the way of prayer." Martin was a monk at St. Gregory's, Douai, where he lived for eleven years in solitude and silence, leaving the monastery only six times.[53] He died in England in 1662 or 1663 and most likely brought the book with him, for shortly afterward it came into the hands of a Protestant reader ("Tho*mas* Ginns 1708") who objected to some of the particularly Catholic parts in the margins of the manuscript. Did Constable anticipate the book making its way beyond the monastery of St. Gregory's, Douai, to England? We can only surmise from her reference in the preface to "all that reade this little treatise" that she did.[54]

Constable also served as a missionary of sorts, supplying general works to members of her family in England—masses, prayers for different festivals and times of day, and general spiritual advice. These manuscripts would have been delivered by priests going on the mission in York. To her eldest brother Sir Marmaduke, second baronet, she dedicated "A Spiritual Treatise, conteininge some advise for seculars composed by the unworthy Religious

Sister B.C. of Jesus of the holy Order of St. Benedict in the monastery of Our Lady of Consolation in Cambray of the English Congregation" (1663), which could be the book titled "A Spiritual Treatiss" in her nephew's library inventory of 1689 under the heading "New Manuscripts."[55] This treatise provides instructions on living a perfect spiritual life and examples that show "that secular persons have and now may be if they please as capable of the practise of the highest perfection as religious."[56]

Three volumes in Constable's hand contain her sister's ownership inscription ("Catherin Sheldon Booke"), and of these one is expressly dedicated to her, "A spirituall Incense Composed of diuers exercises of prayer, taken out of the liues of diuerse holy persons & Authors by the vnworthy Religious S^{r}.B.C. of Jesus of the most holy order of St Benet of the conuent of our Ladie of Comfort in Cambray. The 3^{d} Part."[57] Constable hoped that her sister "& all that shall make vse of it" would be edified on a daily basis by "the sweet odour of this celestiall exercise of prayer."[58] She endeavored to provide new material ("not yet in our language") arranged in an atypical "order & Method" so that it might prove refreshing for those grown weary by prayer.[59] In the preface to the reader she emphasizes the fact that many of the prayers are short, including "breefe & amorous sentences like sparkles of fire" that "inflame a soule but cause no tediousnes nor tire deuotion."[60] In addition to the ownership mark, the manuscript has two bookmarks consisting of strips of paper cut from a contemporary letter dated 1668. The other two manuscripts owned by Catharine Sheldon in Constable's hand are "Masses for some principall festiuities of the yeare translated out of the Missall. Good for the entertainment of those who vnderstand not the Latine" and another book of prayers, divided into six sections, beginning with "Morning prayers drawne out of the deuotions of the B. Fa: Bernard called the Poor Priest."[61]

There was clearly a demand for Roman Catholic material in England, both liturgical and devotional. Constable's brother, Dom Augustine (Thomas) Constable, provided the same sort of material for his niece-in-law, Anne (Radcliffe) Constable, wife of Sir Philip, third baronet, in March 1674: "The Garland of the blessed virgin Marie . . . translated out of an Auncient Coppie In lattine for the vse of ye Deuout faeminine sex by TC OSB." Replenishment was important, since manuscripts could literally be read to pieces. This copy of "The Garland" is actually in the hand of Philip, copied in December 1675. Also in this volume is another set of devotions copied in 1678, taken out of a book that "had [been] soe much used that itt was very hard to read in many places this . . . was the occasion off my writing them heare."[62]

Idleness, Learning, and Prayer: Barbara Constable's Spiritual Difficulties at Cambrai

The daily schedule of an enclosed nun could be grueling in its monotony, and as a result most nuns experienced spiritual aridity (also known as desolation or tepidity) at various points in their conventual life, when prayer seemed little more than an ungratifying and tedious chore. Sickness and physical infirmity could cause nuns to despair at their inability to perform their duties. At Cambrai, a nonfasting day consisted of the eight canonical hours of the Divine Office interspersed with two masses, beginning at 12:30 a.m. and ending at 6:30 p.m.: matins, lauds, prime, morning Mass, terce, conventual Mass, sext, none, evensong (vespers), and compline. The first meal was dinner, at 11:00 a.m., during which time there was "continuall reading and exact silence. All must serve and reade in their turnes (if they bee able), and can performe it with edification." In between were quarter-hour, half-hour, and hour-long periods of mental prayer in the choir, spiritual reading in the "work-house," recollection or preparation for offices in one's cell, recreation or free time, manual exercise, and work. Work (most likely embroidery) took place for forty-five minutes in the morning and an hour in the afternoon.[63] The nuns retired to their cells at 8:00 p.m.

Constable admits to periods of desolation in her spiritual life and expresses guilt about idle time spent in the infirmary. In "Gemitus Peccatorum," a series of personal prayers, she writes: "O my only joy, & true delight, to thee I speake & write, not as one who presumes to thinke herselfe worthy to doe it, but as one beinge banished farre from her beloved & true friend, cannot be at rest but indeavours to doe somethinge that may yeeld some comfort to her, sometimes writes, of him to him, & speaketh of & to him." She admits to her prayer being hampered by "distractions and vanity" and is frustrated by her fleeting ability to produce acts and aspirations—two of the stepping-stones to mystic union, the apex of mental prayer: "[O]nly now and then as it were far off I heare the sound of some verses of the psalmes, or some sayeings of the scripture, and sometimes some short aspirations which I had read heertofore in some bookes, beinge most commonly in latin, and which at the first sometimes I did not understand at all, but this passed so quick."[64] She excuses herself for writing, which she does not for "pride or ostentation sake but only to diverte my selfe and spende time which better and as I was obliged I had not abilitie enough to doe."[65] Her failure to fulfill her obligations as a member of the community weighs heavily on her conscience: "It is true . . . I am sickly. . . . [N]everthelesse me thinkes I see others a greate deale worse & yet they doe thee, & thy servants, much more service, & doe not faile in complyinge with their obligations, so much as I doe. I beseech thee not to take away these indispositions, but that I may behave my selfe as I ought."[66] In the dedicatory epistle to "Considerations or Reflexions vpon the Rule of the most glorious father St Benedict," she again draws attention to her inability to be a good nun and again expresses resolve to improve herself: "[H]avinge spent so much idle time in the monasterie where you commaund none shall be idle . . . alas miserable that I am what shall I say that have professed it this 16 yeares & solemnely promised to live accordinge to it [the Benedictine Rule], & yet am as much to beginne to practise it as a novice of an howres entrance. . . . [L]et me no longer live an idle tepid life as hitherto I confesse to have done."[67] This passage refers to chapter 48 of the Benedictine Rule, "Of the dayly hand labour," which states that "[i]dlenes is an enemy of the soule. . . . To the weake brethren, & tender of constitution, let such worke or art be inioyned as they maye be kept from idlenes, and yet not oppressed with soe much labour so as to be driuen awaye."[68] Constable's claims of idleness, positioned at the beginning of a six-hundred-page work, may strike one as disingenuous, but here she is speaking as much of spiritual idleness as she is of idleness in the workplace. The passages quoted above reflect a certain conventional humility and scrupulosity, but they also suggest something more particular to her individual situation—the almost guilty pleasure she took in writing her treatises.

One senses that her desolation was partly caused by discord between her love of reading and her sense that this passion impeded her prayer. Reading and writing, the only comforts to Constable during her periods of aridity and ill health, probably distracted her from her prayer, and prayer was her most important responsibility as a nun. The boldness with which she states her opinions about learning and reading is striking. While she attempted to temper the defensiveness of her comments by couching them in the opinions of other authors and by constructing the tension between learning and reading as applying to educated monks rather than enclosed nuns, the immediacy of her concerns is obvious. In his treatises, Baker repeatedly urged the nuns not to become carried away with reading and extolled the predisposition of their gender for the highest reaches of mental prayer because of the strength of their "will" and their lack of "understanding." He even expressed (in a treatise transcribed by Constable in 1645) a deeply held suspicion that learned women were "more vaine and phantasticall" than unlearned women and "soe in a greater impediment of attaining to the Divine Love" and that a woman's desire to learn was both impetuous and greedy.[69]

Constable's "A breefe Treatise of learninge and preachinge" is essentially a defense of the important relationship between learning and prayer, and she cites many ancient and authoritative authors to prove her thesis that "[l]earninge would never be such an impediment to the exercise of prayer and leadinge interne lives . . . as now adayes it is if it were practised with more moderation and mortification."[70] She espouses a model of responsible reading as a launch pad into prayer, since "that studie which is not directed to the sole glorie of god, is a short way to discend into hell; not preciselie because of the studie but because of the puffinge up and pride which it breedes."[71] Once again, she despairs at the ineptitude of modern religious: "[N]ow adaies people studie as if there were not a god."[72]

The first chapter of her treatise on mental prayer dedicated to Joseph Martin is titled "Of Readinge." The chapter begins with the zeal of a missionary: "Readinge . . . is a thinge that hath & doth the most conduce to the conuersion of soules . . . & many examples may be produced of diuerse persons both in former & later Ages that haue not thought of any thinge but the world & vanitie, who haue beene totally conuerted to a better life by readinge accidentally some good booke or other."[73] She closely echoes Baker's warning that one should not read "out of some curiositie or to driue awaie the time"[74] when she notes that reading has no spiritual benefit if it is done "only to kill time, or only out of a vaine Curiositie to know much."[75] However, she argues that there are certainly worse ways to kill time and that reading can actually protect one from truly dangerous thoughts: "Many haue so little to doe both in religion & out of religion, that if they doe not replenish their minds w*i*th such good things as are in spirituall bookes they must needs be full of vaine & idle images since the imagination is continually inuentinge, euerie one hath not the gift to pray much, what then shall they doe in the solitude of religion, but reade discreetly when they cannot pray."[76] Not only should one be able to read discreetly, but one should read from a variety of books to make "solitude & retirement nothinge so tedious as it is ordinarilie esteemed."[77] These solitary moments were a source of concern for Constable, who needed to distract herself from her distractions—the English Civil Wars, illness, financial troubles and disorder within the community, desolation, and concern about her family. The civil wars in England took their toll on the Cambrai nuns, claiming the lives of male relatives and cutting off the financial support they received from their families. In the 1640s the community had swelled to fifty nuns who were outgrowing their space, and at the General Chapter of 1649 (it met every four years) it was suggested that they disperse themselves among French monasteries to alleviate their poverty (they founded the daughter house at Paris instead). In the register of letters and chapter speeches in Constable's hand, Abbess Christina Brent, during her tenure as abbess from 1641 to 1645, speaks of the "patient suffring which we are like to haue much exercise of these sad times" and of the lack of discipline and propriety within the monastic walls: nuns were apt to "speake unhansomely," be late for Mass, "laugh and whisper to one another," and show "verie disgustfull lookes and dislikes."[78]

Constable's surviving transcriptions, translations, and compilations contribute to an understanding of the spiritual needs of both exiled English Catholics and lay Catholics in England. They also speak to her sense of mission to English recusants and her keen interest, following in Baker's footsteps, in utilizing examples from her religion's glorious past to help her contemporaries rise above the disorder and desolation of "now daies." She struggled to strike a balance between reading, writing, and mental prayer, justifying the place of learning within the contemplative life while acknowledging the potential for reading to interfere with mental prayer. It was a personal struggle turned into a public good, however, since she addressed her own shortcomings openly and went to great lengths to make the spiritual life easier for others than it was for her.

Appendix: A Chronological List of Original Works and Transcriptions in Dame Barbara Constable's Hand

1644

Augustine Baker, "The Scale of Perfection . . . translated into better English by the most reverend Father, Fr. Augustine Baker, religious of the holy Order of S. Benet, and by him called The School of Contemplation" (December 7, 1644) (ii + 345 pp.)
Downside Abbey, Baker MS 17

Augustine Baker, "A Treatise of the English Mission The first part" (iv + 413 pp.)
Downside Abbey, Baker MS 27

1645
Augustine Baker, "A Treatise of the English Mission The second part Composed by the very R^d^ father F Augustine Baker Preist & Monke of the holy order of St Bennit & of the English Congregation" ("Finis Transcribed 1645 march 20") (632 pp.)
Ownership mark: Dom Andrew Whitfield, d. 1688[79]
Ampleforth Abbey, MS SS119

Augustine Baker, "The Scale of Perfection the second Part composed by the same Author as did the first part. And Allso translated by the same translator as did the first and Called the schoole of Contemplation" (ii + 517 pp.)
Downside Abbey, Baker MS 18

Augustine Baker, "A Spiritual Treatise Intituled Confession by the Most R^d^ Father Fa: Austin Baker" ("1645 Finis") (xxiv + 459 pp.)
Ownership mark: Thomas Roper
Ampleforth Abbey, MS SS143

Augustine Baker, "Directions for Contemplation. Deuided into fower parts composed by the very R^d^: Father Fa: Austin Baker Monke of the holy order of St Benedict of the English Congregation & approued by the superiours of the same Congregation" ("Coppied out for him by his dearest sister Barbara Constable anno 1645") (x + 451 pp.)
Dedicated to: Thomas (Augustine) Constable
Ownership mark: Thomas Roper
Downside Abbey, Baker MS 2

1649
Augustine Baker, "The Idiots Devotion or the Desires of Love. Divided into sixteen parts or books, every part consisting of several exercises and every exercise of several points or matters" (June 6, 1649) (ii + 311 pp.)
Downside Abbey, Baker MS 36

Barbara Constable, "Gemitus Peccatorum or the Complaints of Sinners composed by a vertuous and religious Dame of the holy order of Saint Benedict liueing in the Monasterie of our Ladies of Comfort in Cambray. D: B: C:" (December 31, 1649) (510 pp.)
Stanbrook Abbey, "Gemitus Peccatorum" MS[80]

1650

Augustine Baker, "An Introduction or preparatiue to a treatise of the English Benedictine Mission. Composed by the verie R^d. Fa: Augustine Baker Preist & monke of the holie Order of St Benedict and of the English Congregation" (March 1, 1650) (306 pp.)

Downside Abbey, Baker MS 26

Barbara Constable, "Aduises For Confessors & Spirituall Directors for the most part taken out of the liues of late holy persons, by the most vnworthy Religious S.B.C." (November 20, 1650) (466 pp.)

Dedicated to: Father Benedict Stapleton, d. 1680[81]

Downside Abbey, MS 629

Barbara Constable, "Speculum Superiorum, Composed of diuerse Collections taken out of the liues & workes of holie persons, by the most vnworthy Religious S^r. Bar: Con: of Jesus" (December 2, 1650) (xviii + 502 pp.)

Dedicated to: Abbess Catherine Gascoigne

Colwich Abbey, MS H43

1652

Augustine Baker, "The first Part of Doubts. Composed by the most Rd Fa: Father Augustine Baker Preest & monke" ("1652 Finis March 18") (vi + 323 pp.)

Ownership mark: signed by D. Magdalen Eure, d. 1662 ("Str Magdalen Booke")

Ampleforth Abbey, MS SS69[82]

Barbara Constable, compiler, (1) Thomas Deschamps, "A method to confesse generally & perticularly for those who desire to serue god & frequent often the sacraments . . ." (title page + 194 unnumbered pages); (2) Gregory Mallet, "A Discourse of Contrition. Composed by the very Rd Fa: Father Gregorie Mallet Confessor of the English Benedictines of the holy order of St Benedict in Cambray of our Lady of Consolation" ("Finis. 1652 August 16") (title page + pp. 1–171); (3) Thomas Deschamps, "A little guide for those that desire to be spirituall. Composed by Mr Thomas deschamps Preest" (pp. 173–220); (4) "Eyght Poynts & an Abridgement of what is allready said wch euery faithfull soule may practise" (pp. 221–24); (5) "The day of a person that is free in his deuotions, & who hath no great temporall affaires.

Deuided into ten paces or stepps" (pp. 225–46); (6) "A consideration of the loue of god & charity wch may incite vs to loue him" (pp. 246–58); (7) "An exercise for those deuout soules that are purged from impurities & loue of themselues, & all created things" (pp. 259–81); (8) "An exercise for deuout soules who haue difficullty [sic.] to satisfy our lord by production of increated acts drawne from the same lord to satisfy himselfe" (pp. 282–303); (9) "Twelue abuses of a claustrall out of St Bernard" (p. 304) and "Twelue Abuses in the World" (pp. 305–6) ("Finis 1658 October 5th")
Stanbrook Abbey, Deschamps/Mallet MS

Ambrose Solomon of Angers, "The true life of the soule, Which euery good christian ought incessantly to breath if he will perfectlie aspire to heauen. Written by Bro: Ambrose Solimon of Angers Preest of the order of St Francis. Translated by Fa: G: M." (finished September 12, 1652) (424 pp.)
Downside Abbey, MS 74376

1653
Barbara Constable, (1) "Considerations for Preests: Composed of diuerse Collections gathered out of seuerall Authors by S.B.C. vnworthy Religious of the holy order of St Benet & of the English congregation"; (2) "A breefe Treatise of learninge & preachinge"; (3) "A discourse to Preachers"; (4) "For Missioners" (finished October 15, 1653) (vii + 248 pp.)
Dedicated to: Dom Augustine (Thomas) Constable
Downside Abbey, MS 552

Augustine Baker, (1) "Directions to shew how to make use of the exercises called idiots Devotion or the Desires of Love"; (2) "The Order of Teaching, or a Brief Calendar for the help of the memory of a spiritual instructor"; (3) "Summary of Perfection" (finished 1653) (iv + 389 pp.)
Ownership mark: Lambspring Abbey
Downside Abbey, Gillow Baker MS 1

1654
Vincent Latham, "A spirituall discourse composed by the most R^{d} Father Fa: ~~Augustine Baker~~ Vincent Latham Preest & monke of the holy order of St Benet & of the English Congregation" (finished December 13, 1654) (xii + 354 pp.)
Downside Abbey, MS 74375

1655
Barbara Constable, "Considerations or Reflexions vpon the Rule of the most glorious father St Benedict By a most vnworthy Religious of his order" (finished December 5, 1655) (vii + 531 pp.)
Dedicated to: St. Benedict
Downside Abbey, MS 627

1657
Barbara Constable, "A spirituall Incense Composed of diuers exercises of prayer, taken out of the liues of diuerse holy persons & Authors by the vnworthy Religious S^{r}.B.C. of Jesus of the most holy order of St Benet of the conuent of our Ladie of Comfort in Cambray. The 3^{d} Part" ("Finis 1657. May 13.") (920 pp.)
Dedicated to: Catherine Sheldon
Ownership mark: "Catherin Sheldon Booke"
Ampleforth Abbey, MS SS85c

Barbara Constable, "The Second part prosecuting the Excellency of M: Prayer Treating for ye most part of ye State of Desolation, of Extraordinary fauours visions &c Composed of Collections out of the workes & Liues of many H: Persons, & Transl. by ye vnworthy Religious S^{tr} B:C: of Jesvs. of ye most H: Order: of St: Bennet, & of ye English Congregation in Cambray" ("July 31. Finis 1657.") (595 pp.)
Dedicated to: Dom Joseph Martin (d. 1663)
Ownership mark: "Tho Ginns his Booke 1708"
Ampleforth Abbey, MS SS84

Constantin Barbanson, "The Secret Pathes of deuine loue Wherein true heauenly wisedome & the kingdome of god in our soules is hidden. Deuided into two Parts . . . Composed by the very R^{d}. F. Constantine Barbanson Capucin Preacher & Guardian of the Convent of Cullen. Translated by the very R^{d} F. Anselme Tuchet Monke of the holy order of S^{t}. Benet & of the English Congregation"[83] (finished November 12, 1657)
Ownership mark: Our Lady of Good Hope, Paris
Colwich Abbey, MS H20

1658
[for treatises copied in 1658, see first entry for 1652, items 3–9]

1659
Abbess Catherine Gascoigne, translator, "A Collection of some familiar answers vpon the conduct of soules in a Mistick life. Composed in french by S.C.L.S. a religious of Mont Martirs of the holy order of St Benit. Translated by our Rd Lady Abbesse" (finished October 18, 1659) (550 pp.)
Downside Abbey, MS 66812

1663
Barbara Constable, compiler, (1) "A letter of the venerable father Yuan concerning prayer"; (2) "St Dionysius the Areopagite," translated by Father Leander Norminton";[84] (3) "Of the nine degrees of Seraphick love"; (4) "Instructions for Prayer. Out of the delights of the spirit"; (5) "A meanes to raise our selues to the knowledg of the perfections of god" (finished March 27, 1663) (691 pp.)
Downside Abbey, MS 628

Barbara Constable, "A Spiritual Treatise, conteininge some advise for seculars composed by the unworthy Religious Sister B.C. of Jesus of the holy Order of St. Benedict in the monastery of Our Lady of Consolation in Cambray of the English Congregation" (finished June 16, 1663) (638 pp.)
Dedicated to: Sir Marmaduke Constable
Everingham Park (last known location)

1666
Barbara Constable, translator, "A Little Instruction to Teach a Secular Woman How One Should Live . . . translated out of an Old French Author Without a Name" (finished November 1666) (650 pp.)
Ownership mark: "Ann Constable, 1695"[85] on flyleaf
Everingham Park (last known location)

1668
Barbara Constable, compiler and translator, "This Booke Consists of Masses for some principall festiuities of the yeare translated out of the Missall. Good for the entertainment of those who vnderstand not the Latine" ("1668. Finis June 23") (745 pp.)
Ownership mark: "Catherin Sheldon Booke"
Ampleforth Abbey, MS SS85b

1681
Augustine Baker, "Discretion This Treatise declares the discretion that is to be vsed & held in the exercise of a spirituall life. Composed by the verie Rd Father Fa: Augustine Baker Preest & Monke of the most holie Order of St Benedict & of the English Congregation" ("June 10. Finis 1681") (xiii + 411 pp.)
Ampleforth Abbey, MS SS136

1683
Register of letters and instructions received by the community (finished October 7, 1683)
Lille, Archives departementales du Nord, MS 20H10

undated
Barbara Constable, compiler, (1) "Morning prayers drawne out of the deuotions of the B. Fa: Bernard called the Poor Priest"; (2) "Holy & christian prayers drawne out of the holy scripture & the Fathers of the church. To demaund of god the grace faithfullie to accomplish the dutics of christianitie"; (3) "An hundred & fifty prayers being the marrow of the Psalmes of Dauid, euerie prayer begging the grace that the psalme doth hold forth"; (4) "A sheafe of Myrrh & sweet Odors. Gathered out of fiftie Misteries of our lords passion"; (5) "An oblation to god of Children by their mothers so soon as they are borne, found to haue very good effects"; (6) "The Requiem Masse," including "The Preface for all Requiem & other ordinarie Masses w[ch] is to be found in the new Manuells" (655 pp.)
Ownership mark: "Catherin Sheldon Booke"
Ampleforth Abbey, MS SS85a

undated
Augustine Baker, (1) "The Anchor of the Spirit Consistinge in certeine verses that are heere expounded composed by the very Rd Father F Augustine Baker Preest & monke of the English Congregation of the holy order of St Benedict: To this is adioyned the Remedy against temptations written in old English by St Richard of Hampall the Eremit & by me made more intelligible" (240 pp.); (2) "The Apology of Father Baker for all his workes, wherein are certaine poynts worthy of consideration by such priuate persons as would censure these his writings" (105 pp.); (3) "A spirituall Alphabet For the vse of Beginners" (fragment only, 4 pp.)
Ampleforth Abbey, MS SS118

undated
Augustine Baker, "Certaine spiritual emblems or shorte sayeings, with their expositions for some of them. But for other of them, the soule will better know of her selfe, how to vnderstand and make best vse of them"
Downside Abbey, Baker MS 31

Notes

I am very grateful to Dame Margaret Truran of Stanbrook Abbey, Dame Benedict Rowell and the late Dame Cecilia Thorp of Colwich Abbey, Dom Philip Jebb and Dom Daniel Rees of Downside Abbey, Dom Anselm Cramer of Ampleforth Abbey, and Abbot Geoffrey Scott of Douai Abbey, for their generous assistance with the manuscripts described in this essay. Note on transcriptions: when abbreviated words are expanded, superscript letters are silently lowered and the added letters are italicized.

1. See Placid Spearritt, "The Survival of Medieval Spirituality among the Exiled English Black Monks," *American Benedictine Review* 25 (1974): 287–316, for an overview of the dissemination of Baker's treatises and a list of Baker manuscript treatises with short-titles. The article is reprinted (without the list) in *That Mysterious Man: Essays on Augustine Baker OSB, 1575–1641*, ed. Michael Woodward (Abergavenny: Three Peaks Press, 2001), 19–42. Spearritt estimates that roughly two hundred Baker-related manuscripts are extant. See also Justin McCann's "Descriptive Catalogue of MSS. in English and Foreign Libraries for the Works and Life of Father Augustine Baker," in *Memorials of Father Augustine Baker*, ed. Justin McCann and Hugh Connolly, Publications of the Catholic Record Society 33 (London: Catholic Record Society, 1933), 274–93.

2. Augustine Baker, "Apology," in Ampleforth Abbey, MS SS118, p. 100.

3. There were roughly 137 English nunneries at the time of the Dissolution. Between the years 1598 and 1670, twenty-two communities of English female religious were founded on the Continent. For lists of these communities and their foundation dates, see Eileen Power, *Medieval English Nunneries c. 1275 to 1535* (Cambridge: Cambridge University Press, 1922), 685–92, and Heather Wolfe, "The Scribal Hands and Dating of *Lady Falkland: Her Life*," *English Manuscript Studies 1100–1700* 9 (2000): 207.

4. The English Benedictine Congregation established continuity with the pre-Reformation English Benedictines through its last surviving member, Sigebert Buckley of Westminster Abbey.

5. Four volumes of Baker's autograph notes from this period of research are now at Jesus College, Oxford, MSS 75–78. A biography of Baker by Father Leander

Prichard describes his research and his chance meetings in Cotton's library with William Camden and James Ussher, with whom he entered into a disputation (McCann and Connolly, *Memorials*, 110–13).

6. "Constitutions," Colwich Abbey Archives, MS P2.

7. For a description of the early modern understanding of the different divisions of the soul, see Katharine Park, "The Organic Soul," in *The Cambridge History of Renaissance Philosophy*, ed. Charles B. Schmitt, Quentin Skinner, and Eckhard Kessler (Cambridge: Cambridge University Press, 1988), 466–67.

8. Another daughter, Anne, apparently died young.

9. They had at least three children, including Anne (b. 1655), who was professed at the English monastery at Louvain in 1672 (a 1670 letter from Mr. Bedingfield to Sir Marmaduke Constable discusses her impending vocation, University of Hull, Brynmor Jones Library [hereafter referred to as Hull], DDEV 68/42/127a). He had two sons: Phillip, who married Anne Radcliffe in 1672, and Marmaduke. His son Phillip's sister-in-law, Catherine Radcliffe, also became a nun (see an obligation signed by Philip Constable to pay his sister Catherine Radcliffe £20 at the time of her profession, Hull DDEV 68/135, May 25, 1675). Marmaduke traveled to the Continent at least three times between 1640 and 1660.

10. See Henry Foley, S.J., *Records of the English Province of the Society of Jesus*, vol. 3 (London: Burns and Oates, 1878), 207.

11. Thomas Constable was born at Eagle Castle in Lincolnshire and professed at St. Gregory's on August 22, 1649. He succeeded to the office of secretary to the president in 1657 and resigned 1659. Before, he had passed to mission in North Province. He was elected procurator and definitor of the Province of York at the Chapter of 1666 and was continued at the two following chapters (Athanasius Allanson, *Biography of the English Benedictines*, ed. Anselm Cramer [York: Ampleforth Abbey, 1999], 128).

12. Hull DDEV 68/248, p. 31, a parliamentary resolution dated July 15, 1651, to exclude Sir Philip Constable's estates from "the Bill for sale of severall Delinquents Estates. And his Landes not to bee sold."

13. For details about the sequestration of the Constable estates, see Peter Roebuck's "The Constables of Everingham: The Fortunes of a Catholic Royalist Family During the Civil War and Interregnum," *Recusant History* 9 (April 1967): 75–87, and *Yorkshire Baronets, 1640–1670: Families, Estates, and Fortunes* (Oxford: Oxford University Press, 1980), 154–61.

14. R. C. Wilton, "A List of Guests at Everingham Park, Christmas, 1662," in *Miscellanea*, Publications of the Catholic Record Society 27 (London: Catholic Record Society, 1927), 263.

15. A halter was purchased at Ragby Fair "for M[ist]ris Barbara's maire that was sold" on May 18, 1634 (Hull DDEV 56/1, p. 6, account book for the West Rasen household, 1633–34). According to the account book, the household at West Rasen

consisted of thirty-four individuals "resident constantly." According to Joseph Gillow, there is a painting of Barbara Constable, possibly by the parliamentarian portrait artist Robert Walker (1599–1658), at Burton Constable, seat of the Chichester-Constable branch of the family. For a reproduction, see Joseph Gillow, ed., "Records of the English Benedictine Nuns at Cambrai (now Stanbrook), 1620–1793," in *Miscellanea VIII,* Publications of the Catholic Record Society 13 (London: Catholic Record Society, 1913), facing p. 12. The secret chapel in the old hall at West Rasen is illustrated in the *London and Dublin Orthodox Journal,* September 8, 1838.

16. Hull DDEV 54/5.

17. Hull DDEV 66/8.

18. Barbara Constable, "Gemitus Peccatorum," Stanbrook Abbey, p. x, and "The Second part prosecuting the Excellency of M: Prayer Treating for y[e] most part of y[e] State of Desolation . . ." (1657), Ampleforth Abbey, MS SS84, p. 9.

19. Sir Philip Constable, "A Catalogue of Books 1689," Hull DDEV 68/4. The books belonged to Barbara Constable's nephew Sir Philip Constable, third baronet, who inherited Sir Philip, first baronet's books from his father, Sir Marmaduke, second baronet.

20. The antiquarian Ralph Sheldon's sister Catherine arrived at Cambrai in 1640, and his cousin married Barbara Constable's sister.

21. Hull DDEV 68/248, p. 72 ("The laste will and Testament of S[r] Phil Constable Barronett this 20th of Feb 1664").

22. Cambrai was founded in 1623. The nine original nuns would have encountered the Ignatian method in England, and been influenced by visiting priests and by three nuns (Dames Frances Gawen, Pudentiana Deacon, and Viviana Yaxley) from the English Benedictine community in Brussels, who had been sent to Cambrai to provide a model for monastic life, and whose spirituality had been formed by the *Exercises.*

23. Baker describes this method in many of his treatises, and it is summarized in Hugh Cressy's digest of Baker's works, *Sancta Sophia* (Douai, 1657). For a brief account of the successive stages of mental prayer, see Heather Wolfe, "Reading Bells and Loose Papers: Reading and Writing Practices of the English Benedictine Nuns of Cambrai and Paris," in *Early Modern Women's Manuscript Writing,* ed. Victoria Burke and Jonathan Gibson (Aldershot: Ashgate, 2004), 135–56.

24. Augustine Baker to Robert Cotton, June 3, 1629, British Library, Cotton Julius C. III, fol. 12. A facsimile appears in McCann and Connolly, *Memorials,* facing p. 281.

25. Cotton's library was closed on the pretense that Cotton had circulated a seditious paper, but in fact because the historical evidences within were perceived as a threat to the authority of the monarchy. He died in May 1631, before it reopened.

26. Augustine Baker, "A Catalogue of some printed bookes that I haue in this house," in an anthology of Baker treatises, Yale University, Beinecke Rare Book and Manuscript Library, MS Osborn b.268, p. 250.

27. Baker's reading list for the nuns includes "Hampolls workes in one volume," "Hampoll. A short Treatise of Temptations. It is among other things in a booke of olde English intituled a Booke of diuers Treatises, being in 4.° and hauing a black leather couer," and "Scale of Perfection. All. Especiallie I commende vnto you the matter of the Pilgrim, which is in the 2$^{d.}$ Booke the 21.22.23. and 24. chapters," both in Yale, MS Osborn b.268, pp. 247, 242, 238). For the identity of Mr. Lewis, see Jan Rhodes, "Some Writings of a Seventeenth-Century English Benedictine: Dom Augustine Baker O. S. B.," *Yale University Gazette*, April 1993, n. 18.

28. Augustine Baker, "The Anchor of the Spirit . . . by S. Richard of Hampoll the Hermit and by me [Baker] made more intelligible," in Ampleforth Abbey, MS SS118, and "The Scale of Perfection," Downside Abbey, Baker MSS 17–18, copied 1644–45.

29. Augustine Baker, "Concerning the Librarie of this howse," Colwich Abbey, MS H9.

30. The English Benedictine Congregation formally scrutinized Baker's writings in 1629, 1633 (at the request of the Cambrai community's vicar, Father Francis Hull), and 1655 (when Cressy was preparing to write an "epitome" of them). They came under suspicion for deemphasizing the role of confessors and chaplains and for containing unsanctioned "novel" material.

31. Dom Leander Prichard (chaplain at Cambrai 1661–69) and Dom Wilfrid Reeve were the most productive transcribers after Constable, making most of their copies in the 1660s and 1670s, respectively.

32. Augustine Baker, "A Treatise of the English Mission The second part Composed by the very Rd father F Augustine Baker Preist & Monke of the holy order of St Bennit & of the English Congregation," Ampleforth Abbey, MS SS119.

33. Augustine Baker, "Directions for Contemplation. Deuided into fower parts composed by the very Rd: Father Fa: Austin Baker Monke of the holy order of St Benedict of the English Congregation & approued by the superiours of the same Congregation," Downside Abbey, Baker MS 2.

34. Augustine Baker, "A Spiritual Treatise Intituled Confession by the Most Rd Father Fa: Austin Baker," Ampleforth Abbey, MS SS143.

35. Augustine Baker, "The first Part of Doubts. Composed by the most Rd Fa: Father Augustine Baker Preest & monke," Ampleforth Abbey, MS SS69.

36. All three of these are compiled in Downside Abbey, Gillow Baker MS 1.

37. Downside Abbey, Baker MS 29.

38. For a contemporary account of the seizure of their house and subsequent imprisonment of the Cambrini nuns, see Gillow, "Records . . . ," p. 21.

39. Constable corrected "Conversio Morum" (part of Downside Abbey, Baker MS 29) and "Contemplation D" (part of Ampleforth Abbey, MS SS49).

40. Colwich Abbey, MS H2.

41. For example, see Augustine Baker, "Secretum sive Mysticum, containing an exposition called The Cloud," pt. 2, Ampleforth Abbey, MS SS44, p. 158.

42. B. Constable, "Second part prosecuting. . . ." p. xiii.

43. Barbara Constable, "A spirituall Incense Composed of diuers exercises of prayer, taken out of the liues of diuerse holy persons & Authors by the vnworthy Religious Sr.B.C. of Jesus of the most holy order of St Benet of the conuent of our Ladie of Comfort in Cambray. The 3d Part," Ampleforth Abbey, MS SS85c, pp. ii–iii.

44. Barbara Constable, "Speculum Superiorum," (Colwich Abbey, MS H43), p. [iii].

45. Barbara Constable, "Aduises For Confessors & Spirituall Directors for the most part taken out of the liues of late holy persons, by the most vnworthy Religious S.B.C.," Downside Abbey, MS 629, p. xxi.

46. See Wolfe, "Reading Bells," 143–44.

47. B. Constable, "Gemitus Peccatorum," p. 98.

48. B. Constable, "Speculum Superiorum," pp. xi–xviii.

49. Barbara Constable, "Considerations for Preests: Composed of diuerse Collections gathered out of seuerall Authors by S.B.C. vnworthy Religious of the holy order of St Benet & of the English congregation," in Downside Abbey, MS 552, pp. vii–xi.

50. B. Constable, "Gemitus Peccatorum," pp. 335–36.

51. Ibid., 509–10. This MS was purchased in 1784 from a bookseller on New Bond Street. Father Benedict Rayment gave it to his sister, Dame Mary Ann Rayment, an English Benedictine nun at Winchester, in 1809. By 1812, it had been returned to the Constable family, who were the main benefactors of the Cambrai nuns when they returned to England after the French Revolution.

52. B. Constable, "Second part prosecuting . . . ," p. viii. In the dedication she states that part 1 is dedicated to her natural brother, and one can assume that part 3 is the manuscript dedicated to her sister Catherine Sheldon (B. Constable, "spirituall Incense").

53. According to a note written on p. [vi] of B. Constable, "Second part prosecuting . . ."

54. Ibid., pp. xiii, xvii.

55. P. Constable, "Catalogue of Books 1689." Barbara Constable probably saw her brother during his two trips to the Continent, in August 1655 and December 1657 (for passes to travel abroad, see Hull DDEV 68/248, pp. 61, 63).

56. Everingham Park MS. The dedication is printed in the Catholic Record Society's *Miscellanea VIII*, vol. 13 (1913), 10–12.

57. B. Constable, "spirituall Incense."

58. Ibid., [iv].

59. Ibid., [iii].

60. Ibid., [xiv].

61. These are Ampleforth Abbey MS SS85b and MS SS85a, respectively. All three manuscripts eventually found their way to Ireland, bearing the bookplate of the Fitzpatricks of Grantstown Manor. They were purchased by Dom Justin McCann from B. Halliday of Leicester and given to Ampleforth in July 1939.

62. Thomas Constable, comp., "A Booke of Holy Meditations Collected out of seuerall pious books and written by seuerall," Hull DDEV 67/10.

63. The schedule for the choir nuns is described in the Cambrai Constitutions, written in 1631 (Lille, Archives Départementales du Nord, MS 20H1).

64. B. Constable, "Gemitus Peccatorum," pp. 274, 336.

65. B. Constable, "Speculum Superiorium," p. [iii].

66. B. Constable, "Gemitus Peccatorum," p. 226.

67. Barbara Constable, "Considerations or Reflexions vpon the Rule of the most glorious father St Benedict," dedicatory letter to St. Benedict (Downside Abbey, MS 627, p. [iii]).

68. "The Second Booke of the Dialogves of S. Gregorie the Greate . . . Containinge the Life and Miracles of ovr Holie Father S. Benedict To which is adioned the Rule of the same Holie Patriarche" (1638), dedicatory letter to Anne Cary, who arrived at Cambrai in 1639. The nuns at Cambrai and Paris used this translation of the Benedictine rule, translated by Cuthbert Fursden, a Benedictine monk.

69. Augustine Baker, "Directions for Contemplation: Book D," in Colwich Abbey, MS H2, p. 176. Constable's transcription of "Directions" is Downside Abbey, Baker MS 2.

70. Barbara Constable, "A breefe Treatise of learninge and preachinge," in Downside Abbey, MS 552, p. 192.

71. Ibid., p. 180.

72. Ibid., p. 193.

73. B. Constable, "Second part prosecuting . . . ," p. 1.

74. Baker, "Directions for Contemplation: Book H," in Yale, Osborn MS b.268, p. 86.

75. B. Constable, "Second part prosecuting . . . ," p. 3.

76. Ibid., pp. 7–8.

77. Ibid., p. 38.

78. Register of letters and chapter speeches, Archives Departementales du Nord, Lille, MS 20H10, pp. 891–92. For a fuller description, see *Elizabeth Cary, Lady Falkland: Life and Letters,* ed. Heather Wolfe (Tempe, AZ: Medieval and Renaissance Texts and Studies, 2001), 54–58.

79. Professed at St. Gregory's on May 16, 1638. He spent time on the mission in the Ratcliffe family. In 1666, he was elected cathedral prior of Bath and definitor of the Province of York; he was elected definitor of the Regimen 1670. He died at St. Gregory's.

80. Title page not in her hand (hence "D.B.C." instead of "S.B.C.").

81. Of Carlton Hall, Yorkshire. He was educated at St. Gregory's and was professed on October 28, 1643. He taught theology and philosophy at the College of St. Vedast, where he received a Doctor of Divinity degree. At the 1653 Chapter, he was elected a definitor of the congregation. He was elected prior of St. Gregory's in 1657. He was appointed superior of the other Benedictines of the Royal Chapel of Henrietta Maria. At the 1666 Chapter, he was elected cathedral prior of Canterbury. In 1668, he was made definitor of the Regimen, and in 1669 he was made president.

82. Ampleforth Abbey, MS SS70, is the second part of Baker's "Doubts," signed "Str Magdalen E." and "Str Magdalen." Corrected by Constable, but not in her hand.

83. Same watermark as watermark of treatises 2–9 in a volume of treatises transcribed by Barbara Constable (Stanbrook Abbey, Deschamps/Mallet MS). Touchet was professed at St. Gregory's, Douai, on November 22, 1643. He appears to have died by 1689.

84. Leander Normington was professed soon after 1649 at St. Gregory's, Douai; he died in 1665.

85. Barbara Constable's niece, born 1655, daughter of Marmaduke and Anne Shirburne, became an Augustinian nun at St. Monica's in Louvain in 1672 (see n. 9).

7

"Now I ame a Catholique"

William Alabaster and the Early Modern Catholic Conversion Narrative

Molly Murray

Despite recent efforts to restore Catholic writing to the early modern canon, the conversion narrative continues to be understood as a predominantly Protestant genre.[1] The scholarly consensus has long held that the earliest forms of English life-writing arose from the Reformation's emphasis on individual self-scrutiny, given an extra push in the mid-seventeenth century by radical Protestant sects who encouraged their members to testify to the workings of the Holy Spirit within them.[2] For many literary critics, the value and interest of the so-called "Puritan conversion narrative" lie not only in the inwardness of its subject matter but also in the idiosyncrasies of its style. Patricia Caldwell has argued that early American Puritans were deeply uncomfortable with the "morphology of conversion," troubled by a nagging sense that they "could not reconcile the nature of saving grace with the orderly method of its production."[3] For Caldwell, the conversion narrative becomes most expressive when it makes "at least a momentary attempt to break out of the bonds of analysis and 'steps' and sequence," attempting to convey "more than could be rhetorically contained in a perfunctory arrangement" of incidents.[4] Other scholars of spiritual autobiography in early modern England have made more explicit their sense of an intimate connection between religious enthusiasm and literary invention. Owen Watkins notes the "persuasive vitality and intensity" in the autobiographical writings of the "vulgar prophets," which he sees as "attempts to expose the futility of all accepted forms of belief and worship," while Nigel Smith proposes that "some of the most strikingly fascinating uses of language in the seventeenth century may be found" on the antinomian fringes of midcentury Protestantism.[5] Such accounts have helped foster, or at least bolster, two related critical assumptions: that "greater freedom of worship . . . and new practices of worship" lead to new practices of literary self-expression and that Protestant dissatisfaction with "formalism" in religion produces (laudable) dissatisfaction with generic conventions in life-writing.[6]

The two parts of this essay will, respectively, challenge the two main claims I have just outlined. First, in responding to the common association of the conversion narrative with Protestant self-consciousness, I will consider a little-known body of early modern autobiographical narratives that present not just a turn from sin to salvation but a specific turn from Protestantism to Catholicism. As several historians have shown, post-Reformation England witnessed a surprisingly large number of religious conversions, *to* Catholicism as well as from it.[7] The first-person records of such denominational conversions, texts rarely if ever acknowledged by literary critics, differ dramatically from those life-writings produced within the Protestant churches.[8] Rather than a question about grace ("How can I know and how can I express my soul's relationship to God?") the church convert poses a question about form: "What kind of church is most likely to bring me closer to God?" These narratives of denominational conversion are resolutely nontranscendent, explicitly representing the "self" and the "soul" in historical and cultural contexts.[9] They show us that at least some writers of early modern conversion narratives did not rail against the schematized constraints of received ecclesiastical and narrative "morphology" but rather expressed their authorial and spiritual identities through engagement with these very constraints. In the second part of this essay, I will address the literary implications of this avowedly "formalist" conversion narrative more specifically and at greater length, focusing on the highly stylized and sophisticated religious autobiography composed in 1598 by the poet and Catholic convert William Alabaster.

The Responsa Scholarum *and the Form of Conversion*

Two bundles of unbound manuscripts, held in the library of the Venerable English College at Rome, provide an important and virtually unknown source for the study of early modern Catholic life-writing.[10] These bundles, known to English College archivists simply as *Scritture 37* and *38,* consist of several hundred first-person texts composed by men who arrived at the college to study between 1597 and 1685. More specifically, they are responses to a list of six questions, devised and administered by the Jesuit superiors of the college as a kind of diagnostic entrance exam (see appendix).[11] The questionnaire had obvious practical aims. The first two questions, for instance, would determine which of the students had wealth and social connections that could help the English missionary effort. Question 3 would allow instructors to place students at the appropriate level for lessons. Question 4, about mental and physical health, would identify those who might falter under the rigorous Jesuit training or the hazards of priesthood under penalty. Finally, questions about the students' religious backgrounds, by acknowledging the volatile state of denominational affiliation in England, would help ensure greater orthodoxy within the community. The vast majority of these men arrived at Rome having spent part of their lives as "heretics" (Protestants) or "schismatics" (nonpracticing Catholics), and the Jesuit authorities were well aware of the potential for dissent in such a heterogeneous community.[12] By having all prospective students describe their religious upbringing, the superiors could determine those who might need extra supervision, catechetical instruction, or vocational reassurance. With this requirement, however, the Jesuits also created a new forum for Catholic spiritual autobiography, separate from both the hagiographic triumphalism of missionary propaganda and the stridently polemic discourse of printed "motive" texts.[13]

Considering only those forty-six *responsa* written in the Elizabethan period, we discover a wide variety of personalities and attitudes toward the religious life, conveyed in a variety of prose styles. Many new students dispatch the questionnaire with a list of numbered responses phrased in rudimentary Latin, providing exactly the information requested and no more. Robert Caldwell, for instance, who entered the college in 1598 at the age of eighteen, offers barely one hundred words in response to all six questions. (His reply to question 3, in its entirety, reads: "I studied rhetoric for a while at Worcester with little progress.")[14] Others use the questionnaire as a kind of skeleton plot for an extensive and detailed life story. One such story comes from Henry Chaderton, who arrived at Rome in 1599 after converting to Catholicism at the relatively advanced age of forty-six. In lieu of a list of answers, Chaderton composed a lengthy autobiographical treatise in expert Latin. Not only is the account written in connected paragraphs rather than separated into numbered headings, but it also includes copious marginal notes to help readers follow the major developments in Chaderton's family history, childhood, education, embrace of the Catholic Church, and subsequent "*tribulationes.*"[15] Chaderton's detailed narrative, which takes up twenty-two printed pages in the edited edition of the *responsa,* suggests that some lay Catholics eagerly engaged in the work of autobiography, elaborating upon the minimal requirements of the entrance questionnaire in order to tell their individual stories.

The majority of the *responsa,* however, fall somewhere between the two stylistic extremes of Caldwell and Chaderton. Most students answer most questions quickly, dilating only in response to those questions that seem to have particular interest or relevance for them. The questions about family background, for instance, elicit a few lengthy genealogical digressions, especially from scions of noble Catholic houses. So John Copley, who entered the college in 1599, announces with evident pride that his father is the "Lord Thomas Copley, Baron Hoo and Wells," that his mother is a member of the noble Lutterell family, and that he is related by blood or marriage not only to Father Robert Southwell but also to a number of English Catholic aristocrats, whom he lists by name in what is by far the longest part of his text.[16] Even the questions about physical and mental health seem to have fired the imaginations of a few respondents. Thomas Hodgson, for instance, having been trained as a physician before entering the college, "describes, with a wealth of contemporary medical terms, how his stomach is weakened by an excess of cold and wet humours; how his head suffers from sympathetic pains; how his animal forces tend to sluggishness; how his distemper is offset and his superfluities voided by exercise or warm weather; how his loins are allergic to excessive heat and demand a doublet open at each side; how and why he has suffered twice from spermatorrhoea, thrice from fever, once from colic, and often from toothache and pains in the eyes."[17] Such an account, explicit to the point of absurdity, seems almost to parody the concept of "introspective" writing.

Other students took time to reflect on the state of their souls as well as their bodies or families. Of the forty-six Elizabethan *responsa,* thirty-seven were written by converts, a great many of whom respond to questions 4 and 5 with detailed accounts of circuitous paths to the seminary. Tom Webster reminds us that most English Protestants "regarded conversion as a process, a movement of several stages, election, vocation, humiliation, contrition, justification, adoption, sanctification, and glorification," so that their diaries record "the movements of the *ordo salutis*" over time.[18] In their responses to question 5, the Catholic converts at Rome are equally concerned with offering incremental narratives of their religious development. Rather than following the transcendent, spiritualizing pattern of the *ordo salutis,* however, they narrate their *denominational* progress in a world where one could have, like Robert Caldwall, heretical parents, a Catholic uncle, an "irreligious" brother, two schismatic sisters married to heretics, and one Catholic sister married to a schismatic.[19] Converts at the college, keenly aware of the differences among these designations, carefully document how and when they moved from one category to another. Thomas Hodgson, for instance, relates how he was initially a heretic and then was persuaded to embrace schism at the age of sixteen. Although "determined to put off his conversion until his career was sufficiently established," Hodgson finally could remain a schismatic no longer and one night "leapt from [his] bed, snatched [his] cloak, rushed to see Fr. Gerard, who was staying in the same house, and cried 'I have come to adore Him who was born for me in a stable: I want to be a Catholic.'"[20] William Tayler, nephew of a "very rich and very wicked Archpuritan of great fame," was accused of being a Catholic at Cambridge, "as was shown by his lonely wanderings, his friendship with known Papists, and his admiration for their way of life. Being at that time a schismatic, he denied being a Papist" until he converted with the help of a Welsh priest some years later.[21] Rather than a culminative moment of "inwardness," Hodgson, Tayler, and the other converts at the college represent conversion as a moment of revised outward affiliation, a separation of the regenerate self from "archpuritanism," "irreligion," and schism.

Just as these converts articulate the results of their conversions in specifically denominational terms, so they describe the experience of conversion itself as a result of specific outward influences. Rather than praising the ineffable power of God's grace in reforming their souls, these converts describe the concrete efforts made by family members, friends, and priests to bring them into the arms of the church. Thomas Newman was persuaded to become a Catholic by his "friend Mr. John Sweet."[22] Richard Fisher visited his Catholic brother imprisoned at Wisbech, who convinced Richard to join him in the Catholic Church.[23] Francis Young, in the words of the editorial summary, "could never be persuaded by his teachers that Protestantism was true Christianity; this was due partly to the example of his uncle, a Marian priest who had resigned his benefices and lay hidden in his father's house during his boyhood." Young's actual conversion took place when he left for Flanders "with like-minded companions."[24] In one of the only *responsa* composed in English, Nicholas Hart describes the difficulties of admitting his Catholic tendencies to his circle of high-spirited Protestant friends at the Inns of Court. "At the time I was in this perplexitie," he writes,

> there happened to be others in my chamber whoe weare talkinge of cominge over, to whom I made my desire knowne, but yet at the first I thought with myselfe not to acquaint anye, because I did presuppose that they would but laugh at me for utteringe perswadinge them selves that it was but some melacholye concyte and in like manner it would be passed over as soon as I uttered my mind unto them. I receyved great confort from them in that one in the Companye called by the name of mr. Strange, forthwyth promysed me to acquaint me with Fatther Garret [John Gerard, who eventually facilitated Hart's conversion].[25]

This account, like so many others in the collection, centers on the social dimension of an individual *psychomachia;* Hart describes his difficulties, and his eventual conversion, not in terms of the invisible vicissitudes of will (or grace), but rather as intimately related to his relationships with others.

Finally, the collection of *responsa scholarum* qualifies our understanding of the early modern conversion narrative in a number of important ways. First, and most obviously, its very existence disproves Paul Delany's contention that "Catholic laymen produced no religious autobiographies during the seventeenth century" and shows, moreover, that they did so significantly earlier than the accepted Protestant heyday of such writing.[26] Second, the *responsa* confirm Michael Questier's contention that many early modern Englishmen defined religious experience as a choice among churches on earth, a matter of engaging with the world rather than rejecting it entirely. This is not conversion as aversion, in other words, but conversion as adherence. In the varied voices of the *responsa,* we see that narratives of early modern religious experience were not necessarily records of the solitary soul in relation to God and Scripture but could be, instead, stories of the individual's negotiations with human institutions: confessional communities, families, political systems, nations, colleges, circles of friends. Finally, and perhaps most importantly, these texts suggest that expressive vitality in English religious autobiography was not necessarily the prerogative of antiformalists. While the students at the college unanimously follow the rubric of the questionnaire and accept the categories proposed for the analysis of their individual experiences, they nevertheless use these given forms to produce various and idiosyncratic life-writings. Turning now to the extended autobiography written by one of the students at the English College, William Alabaster, we can see this notion of conversion as an inventive engagement with cultural and ecclesiastical forms becoming both more complicated and more self-consciously literary.

William Alabaster's Textual Transformations

When William Alabaster arrived in Rome in 1598, he had already established a significant literary reputation in England. As early as 1592, the world of university drama had acclaimed his Senecan verse tragedy, *Roxana,* which Samuel Johnson would later declare second only to Milton's poetry in Renaissance Latinity.[27] In *Colin Clouts Come Home Againe,* Spenser singled out "*Alabaster* thoroughly taught / In all this skill, though knowen yet to few," on the basis of another poem: "that heroick song, / Which he hath of that mighty Princesse made[.]"[28] This "heroick song" was the *Elisaeis,* an epic intended to detail the progress of Elizabeth in her attempts to vanquish popery—and left unfinished (to Spenser's embarrassment, perhaps) when Alabaster converted to the very faith whose defeat it heralded.[29] His embrace of Catholicism would be relatively short-lived, however. After a period of exile on the Continent, and a subsequent period of anti-Jesuit Catholic loyalism in England, Alabaster recanted his Catholic conversion in 1611. He eventually became a royal chaplain to James I, although the "flat popery" of one of his sermons provoked Oliver Cromwell to deliver his maiden speech before the House of Commons.[30] Cromwell's accusation proved prescient; Alabaster again recanted soon after this episode and returned to the Catholic Church, beginning a renewed phase of ambiguous affiliation that ended only with his death in 1640.[31]

As one of the "serial converts" who exemplified the extreme confessional volatility of the early modern period, Alabaster earned the scorn of a number of critics, both in his own time and later, who questioned his theological sincerity and indeed his mental health.[32] He was, by his own admission, "proclaimed insane by the Anglican bishops," while his contemporary Ralph Winwood sarcastically dismissed him as an unstable figure, perennially preparing "*palinodiam canere.*"[33] Over a century later, Pierre Bayle devoted an entry in his *Dictionary* to Alabaster, mocking his initial Catholic conversion as a combination of naive aesthetics (he was swayed by "the Pomp and Splendor of the *Romish* Churches") and desperate ambition ("he . . . turned *Papist,* being satisfied, that he had no reason to expect better Preferment, at home").[34] Evidently, many found the antics of the "double or treble turncoat" incompatible with true religious conviction. In the remainder of this essay, I suggest that Alabaster's own writings about religious change are concerned not only with conviction but also with *convention*. His prose autobiography, written a year after his initial Catholic turn, represents conversion not only in terms of outward devotional and ecclesiastical forms (as we have already seen in the *responsa*) but also in terms of *literary* form. Alabaster insistently describes his religious turn as a matter of imitative reading and writing, experienced in the context of, and finally inscribed within, a tradition of other conversion narratives.

The first hint of this link between conversion and reading occurs in Alabaster's brief *responsum,* where he emphasizes the influence of a Catholic text on his religious development.[35] This was not unusual per se; many other students at the college mention books that aided their progress toward Catholic conviction. A representative example comes from Charles Yelverton, who recalls how "disagreements between heretics about the free will and the possibility of losing faith" led him to consult a Catholic "enchiridion of controversies," which settled his doubts on these subjects.[36] Yelverton, like most of the other students at the college, mentions his use of Catholic books as support for particularly difficult points of doctrine. Alabaster, by contrast, concentrates his description on the act of reading itself. "Chancing to cast my eye upon a certain book written by one Reginaldus, in defense of the Catholic cause," he writes, "I had not got through the preface when so great a flood of daylight broke in upon my soul, accompanied with so unusual an interior joy, that at that very moment a voice erupted from me: 'Now I am a Catholic.'"[37] This moment is as confusing as it is dramatic. Who, we might ask, was this "Reginaldus," and what was in his preface that enlightened Alabaster so fully and so quickly? Which elements of Catholic theology or ecclesiology did "Reginaldus" explain, and how did these convince Alabaster to abandon his promising career as a Protestant chaplain and poet?

Alabaster's longer prose narrative, produced soon after his arrival at Rome, provides surprising answers to these and other questions.[38] The composition of such a conversion narrative beyond the rubric of the *responsa* does not seem to have been standard practice at the English College, and the particular reasons behind this longer work have not been conclusively determined. We know, however, that the acting superior of the college, Robert Persons, began to translate Alabaster's text into Latin shortly after the English version was completed, a project that suggests a plan for its eventual print or manuscript publication.[39] Persons abandoned his translation in 1604, after Alabaster began to distance himself from the Jesuit mission in England.[40] In 1598, however, Persons might well have predicted an illustrious Jesuit career for Alabaster and might have wished to capitalize on his new protégé's literary gifts and prominence among Elizabethan courtiers, preachers, and poets. In the preface to his edition of the text, Dana Sutton speculates that Persons encouraged Alabaster's writing of a fuller autobiography with the explicit intention of circulating it beyond the college community.[41] The narrative of Alabaster's Catholic conversion would have become part of the "silent ministry" of Catholic texts, distributed to strengthen devotion among recusants who had limited access to spiritual advisors and confessors and also to effect more conversions among heretics and schismatics who had limited contact with missionary priests.[42]

This conversion narrative is not a narrativized version of Catholic propaganda, however, so much as a work of artful self-representation. In an earlier text entitled *Seven Motives*, now lost, Alabaster attempts to explain his embrace of Catholicism in entirely, conventionally doctrinal terms.[43] In the conversion narrative, by contrast, Alabaster elaborates on his *responsum* to describe more fully the attendant circumstances of his religious transformation. He begins his story by recounting his early activities in "the heate of heresie ambition and vanitie," when he not only composed the *Elisaeis* but also participated in the avant-garde ecumenism of the Essex circle.[44] He then explains how, as a Protestant chaplain among the heterodox company on Essex's Cadiz expedition in 1596, he became skilled in religious debate.[45] Alabaster boasts, in fact, that after returning from Cadiz he began to frequent London prisons in order to debate with Catholic priests there, confident in his ability to counter any Catholic argument with superior Protestant "reasonableness."[46] The mysterious text mentioned in the *responsum* came into his hands through one of his theological sparring partners, Father Thomas Wright.[47] Alabaster recalls that one night, after an inconclusive debate with Wright, the priest loaned him a book entitled *Refutation of Several Sundry Reprehensions* (Paris, 1583), a defense of the Douai-Rheims New Testament written by the Catholic controversialist William Rainolds (the "Reginaldus" of the *responsum*). He describes his reading in a passage that expands on the earlier account:

> I went to my lodging with this little booke of Mr William Reynaldes in my hand and sitting down after supper on my bedds side; to spend that ydle time, I begane to reede the preface therof, that treated very learnedly and lardgly out of the writinges of protestentes themselfes of their inconstant and deceatfull manner of proceedinges. I had not read for the space of a quarter of an howre (if I remember well) but as if those squames that fell from St Paules boddylye eyes . . . so was I lightned uppon the suddene, feeling my selfe so wonderfully and sencybly chaunged both in iudgment and affection as I remaned astonished at my trewe state. I fownde my minde wholie and perfectly Catholique in an instante, and so to be persuaded of all and everie poynt of Catholic religion together, as I beleved them all most undoubtedly and every point and parcell therof, though I knew not the reasons of all, nor made perhaps sure the arguments of the contrary parte. Nor did I desyer any perticuler resolution in any other question of controversie, for I saw most evidently in my inward iudgment, that all were trewe and nothing could be false which the Catholic Roman Church dyd propose to be beleeved. And feeling this in my selfe uppon the suddene with such inward light of evidens as I cold not contradict and with such force of affection as I cold not resist, I lept up from the place where I satt, and saide to myself, now I ame a Catholique, and then fell down upon my knees, and thanked God most hartely humbly and affecteously for so rare a benefitt. (118)

Alabaster adds details that give this episode a vivid verisimilitude: that Rainolds's book was "little,"[48] that he opened it "after supper sitting on [his] bedds syde," that he read for less than "a quarter of an howre," and that the "inward light of evidens" produced a dramatic physical reaction. Conspicuously absent, however, is any more detailed description of the *contents* of Rainolds's preface. Alabaster does not refer to sacraments, purgatory, papal infallibility, veneration of saints and martyrs, or the antiquity and visibility of the Catholic Church, topics that were the standard points of debate between Catholic and Protestant theologians and that Rainolds himself discusses at length.[49] A. D. Nock has proposed that religious conversion often resembles "a chemical process in which the addition of a catalytic agent produces a reaction for which all the elements are already present."[50] These "elements," in Alabaster's case, were a predilection for controversy and a familiarity with Catholic arguments. But what in Rainolds's text was the "catalytic agent"?

Alabaster offers two provocative suggestions. First, he implies that what Rainolds wrote in defense of Catholicism was in fact less important than how he expressed it. Alabaster marvels at how Rainolds "treated very learnedly and lardgly out of the writinges of protestentes themselfes"—in other words, deftly converting Protestant polemic claims into support for a Catholic position. Alabaster describes this "position," however, as an essentially stylistic critique, an objection to the Protestants' "inconstant and deceatfull manner of proceedinges." Similarly, Alabaster comments favorably on the manner of Rainolds's argumentation, rather than its matter, and goes on to define his own consequent epiphany in terms as ostentatious as they are vague: "Now," he announces, "I ame a Catholique." This statement itself seems also to rely on manner rather than matter for its effect; explanation is replaced by rhetorical gesture, by an expression of fervor that we are to accept as true because of the style in which it is expressed. Alabaster, in fact, insists that his conversion required no further thoughts of doctrine: "I fownde my minde wholie and perfectly Catholique in an instante," he insists, "nor did I desyer any perticuler resolution in any other question of controversie, for I saw most evidently in my inward iudgment, that all were trewe and nothing could be false which the Catholic Roman Church dyd propose to be beleeved." Rainolds's book, it seems, produced something more like literary inspiration than theological persuasion; Alabaster presents himself not as convinced but rather as *moved*.

Alabaster goes on to suggest that the effectiveness of Rainolds's book rests on ethical as well as stylistic grounds—not just how Rainolds argues, but who Rainolds is. He devotes several pages of his own autobiographical text, in fact, to narrating the "lyff and happy death" of the author whose book inspired it.[51] Such a focus on the exemplarity of the clergy was common in Catholic defenses of the priesthood. In his preface to the Douai-Rheims New Testament, for instance, Gregory Martin suggests that Catholics seek out priests of character and learning who can better explain the contents of Scripture to them.[52] Alabaster insists on Rainolds's exemplarity not just because of his character and learning, however, but also, and most importantly, because he is a Catholic *convert*. Rainolds is thus not only the successor of the two other converts Alabaster mentions, Paul and Tertullian, but also the precursor of Alabaster himself. The extensive account of Rainolds finally functions as a kind of a *mise en abîme* in the larger autobiographical text.[53] Like Alabaster, Rainolds had an early career as a fervent Protestant, even at times associating with "the familie of love and other new sects springing up."[54]

Like Alabaster, Rainolds "departed from a most prosperous and flourishing worldly state" when he left the church, exchanging this prosperity for "the state of Catholiques disgraced, empoverished and made odious to our Realme."[55] Alabaster describes Rainolds's similarly dramatic conversion to Catholicism, mentioning the popular (and most likely apocryphal) story that attributed it to the proselytizing of his brother John, a Catholic whom Rainolds simultaneously converted to Protestantism.[56] He focuses, however, on a moment of transformative reading: "[Rainolds] dyd so much detest Mr Jewels falshood in his wrytynge and was so angry with it," Alabaster asserts, that "for revenge he was wont to pull out the leafe where he founde it, and for that he could not passe over all the booke while he was in Ingland, he resolved to carrie it with hym . . . and styll to teare out leafes as he found treacherie."[57] Once he found himself carrying a book without pages, Rainolds realized that he had become a Catholic. Again, conversion has a textual trigger: if Alabaster's conversion occurred abruptly after he puts down Rainolds's book, Rainolds's conversion happens after he tears out every page in Jewel's book. In both cases, religious transformations result from intense readerly engagements. Rainolds is a "rare example indeede" for Alabaster, then, in his linked identities as convert, reader, and writer.[58]

Rainolds is not Alabaster's only model, however. In fact, Alabaster's text as a whole owes its most important debt to another, earlier conversion narrative: the *Confessions* of St. Augustine. The influence of Augustine on early modern Protestant thought and writing has been well established, especially by Perry Miller's classic essay on "the Augustinian strain of piety" in *The New England Mind*.[59] Louis Martz and, more recently, Michael Questier and Robert Dodaro have established that Catholics also used Augustine in early-seventeenth-century devotional and polemic writing, and indeed the *responsa scholarum* are peppered with mentions of the *Retractationes*, the epistles and tracts, and the pseudo-Augustinian *Meditations*.[60] None, however, mention the *Confessions*. Henry Chaderton, for instance, refers to "the works of St. Augustine, which [he] possessed complete except for the 6th volume," but mentions specifically only the sermons, the *De unitate ecclesiae*, and the work on purgatory. Although he was a convert himself, Chaderton seems not to have known, or at least not to have been much influenced by, Augustine's account of his own conversion.[61] Surveying the evidence, both Catholic and Protestant, Anne Ferry has categorically declared that "Augustine's *Confessions* were not known to sixteenth-century autobiographical writers, whose presentations of their experiences took very different forms."[62] Only slightly more cautiously, Paul Delany claims that early modern spiritual autobiographers were "remarkably little influenced by the *Confessions*," a claim for which he offers a speculative, generalizing explanation: "Conservatives in religion, who would have known Augustine's works, tended to write restrained autobiographies in which Augustinian fervour and self-accusation were carefully avoided. The Baptists and other enthusiastic sects were closer to the spirit of the *Confessions*, but his works were probably too scholarly and expensive for them, since he is very rarely mentioned in their writings."[63]

Alabaster's conversion narrative flatly contradicts such claims, reflecting the unmistakable influence of the *Confessions* in both form and "spirit." Like the *Confessions*, Alabaster's text consists of thirteen books, written as an extended second-person address: Augustine composes his book as a lengthy apologia to his God, while Alabaster dedicates his to an unnamed childhood friend.[64] Both texts begin by describing an early career of religious delusion, intellectual pride, social ambition, and sexual entanglement, all destined to be eradicated in the life of the humbled and literally chastened convert, the *novus homo*.[65] In Augustine's case, this early career involved petty crime, a lengthy affair with the mother of his illegitimate child, an effort to excel in secular literature, and adherence to the intellectually fraudulent Manichaean cult. Following this Augustinian paradigm, Alabaster elaborates on the terse acknowledgment of youthful heresy set down in his college *responsum*. He reminds his unnamed addressee of his matriculations at Westminster and Trinity, where he swore "an oathe [against the Catholic religion se]ven or [eight times, if I remember right, for which ble]st Jhesu forgeve [me]."[66] He describes his subsequent achievements in Protestant divinity and his desire for fame in both literary and theological arenas. Responding to the college questionnaire, Alabaster discreetly avoids any mention of the anti-Catholic epic *Elisaeis*. Here he admits that he began "[to write a wor]ke in Latyn verses [about the Queen and her re]ign [ag]ainst the Catholic Religion, and I presented to her the [first book, and I would have] presented the second, had not God in his mercy prevented me."[67] He admits, further, that he was "chaplaine for six yeares to the Right Honourable the Earl of Essex . . . and preached also at the Court and laide the plott to aspire in tyme to the highest dignities and honors, and for the upshott and seale of a sure protestant I was so nigh to have a wyfe that ther wanted nothing but the dispatche of that buisenes for which I have attendence at the Courte."[68] While this may well be a factual account, it nevertheless also seems fashioned after Augustine's account of his early career in Carthage, Rome, and Milan, "being seduced and seducing, being deceived and deceiving. . . pursu[ing] the empty glory of popularity" in verse competitions, and pursuing the empty consolations of occult philosophy among the followers of Faustus the Manichaean.[69]

Alabaster explicitly likens his own conversion to a story that "St. Augustine reconteth" in book 8 of the *Confessions*: how "the booke of St. *Antony* the monke his lyf" converted "two that lighted upon it."[70] This particular comparison might seem at first to elide the more obvious parallel between Alabaster's conversion and Augustine's own, but it also indicates one of the crucial formal similarities between the two conversion narratives. As we have seen, Alabaster includes within the larger story of his own religious change not only references to other conversions (Paul and Tertullian) but also an extended discussion of another convert whose text he was in the process of reading (Rainolds). So, too, Augustine weaves the story of his own conversion into a tissue of other second- and third-hand conversion narratives, all centered on textual encounters. He relates, for instance, the story of Victorinus, author of some Christian controversial works he has been skimming. Augustine learns from Simplicianus ("father to the then bishop Ambrose in the receiving of grace") that Victorinus is not just a Christian theologian but a Christian *convert*, whose conversion occurred after a dramatic moment of reading: "He read holy scripture, and all the Christian books with special care. After examining them, he said to Simplicianus . . . 'did you know that I am already a Christian'?"[71] Augustine follows Simplicianus's story of Victorinus with the story mentioned by Alabaster, an autobiographical digression narrated by another Christian convert, Ponticianus. Ponticianus tells Augustine how once he and his colleagues, wandering in the woods, came upon a house and "there found a book in which was written the Life of Antony. One of them began to read it. He was amazed and set on fire, and during his reading began to think of taking up this life."[72] Here, again, a skeptical man "chances" to read the story of another convert (a convert, moreover, who was himself converted by reading a text written by still another convert, St. Paul) and is, in turn, immediately converted by it.

Before narrating his own conversion, then, Augustine relates two conversion stories narrated by others: Simplicianus on Victorinus, and Ponticianus on himself. Each of these stories, in turn, contains a central allusion to another text (Victorinus reads Scripture, Ponticianus reads the biography of another convert).[73] Further, as a number of critics have shown, the intertextuality of the *Confessions* extends beyond such diegetic representations of reading and also involves more covert allusions to other literary metamorphoses in classical and scriptural writings.[74] The accumulation, indeed the superabundance, of such models ultimately makes Augustine's account of his own transformation in book 8 seem less surprising than formally inevitable. In that famous passage, Augustine describes how he withdrew one afternoon into an enclosed garden with his friend Alypius, carrying with him a copy of Scripture borrowed from a Christian mentor. Hearing a distant child's voice chanting *"tolle, lege,"* Augustine writes,

> I interpreted it solely as a divine command to me to open the book [of Scripture] and read the first chapter I might find. For I had heard how Antony happened to be present at the gospel reading, and took it as an admonition addressed to himself when the words were read: "Go, sell all you have, give to the poor, and you shall have treasure in heaven. . ." So I hurried back to the place where Alypius was sitting. There, I had put down the book of the apostle when I got up. I seized it, opened it, and in silence read the first passage on which my eyes lit: "Not in riots and drunken parties, not in eroticism and indecencies, not in strife and rivalry, but put on the Lord Jesus Christ and make no provision for the flesh in its lusts." I neither wished nor needed to read further. At once, with the last words of the sentence, it was as if a light of relief from all anxiety flooded into my heart. All the shadows of doubt were dispelled.[75]

Augustine the Manichaean reads the letters of the Christian convert Paul and is miraculously, instantaneously convinced of that which he had formerly doubted. But this very instantaneity has, of course, been foreshadowed by the conversions of Victorinus, Ponticianus, and Anthony before him. "In the text of the *Confessions,*" John Freccero writes, "conversion is always a literary event, a gloss on an anterior text."[76] More specifically, it is a literary event that *replaces* an anterior text, as the new convert tells his own narrative in what is at once a "gloss on" and a new instantiation of the existing narrative pattern. Inspired by a text that he ultimately "neither wish[es] nor need[s] to read further," the new convert will reenact, and then retell, the story with himself in the starring role.

Augustine is aware of this process of literary imitation and replacement; he proposes that his conversion, itself inspired by and modeled on other texts and other readers, can continue this exemplary work. Within the narrative, Augustine describes his successful efforts to convert his friend Alypius.[77] More importantly, however, Augustine presents the *Confessions* itself as a text that will serve the same crucially exemplary function for subsequent readers: "I am making this confession," he writes, "not only before [God] . . . but also in the ears of believing sons of men, sharers in my joy, conjoined with me in mortality, my fellow citizens and pilgrims, some who have gone before, some who follow after."[78] Those who would "follow after" include Sir Toby Matthew, whose conversion to Catholicism in the early seventeenth century led him to translate both the *Confessions* and other conversion narratives—his body of translations literally replacing the words of other converts with his own, creating a kind of conversion narrative by proxy.[79] Perhaps the most sensitive of Augustine's imitators in conversion and its narration, of course, is Petrarch, whose epistolary account of his epiphany on Mont Ventoux retells the central episode of the *Confessions*, complete with a moment of miraculous reading—a reading, in fact, *of* the *Confessions*.[80] Petrarch informs his addressee that he made his ascent out of "curiosity," inspired by reading Livy: in miniature, recreating an early career of sin and intellectual pride. At the summit of the mountain, "it occurred to me to look into the *Book of Confessions* of St. Augustine, a gift of your kindness. . . . I opened it and started to read at random." There he discovers a passage directly relevant to his errant novelty seeking: "And they go to admire the summits of mountains and the vast billows of the sea and the broadest rivers and the expanses of the ocean and the revolutions of the stars and they overlook themselves."[81] Petrarch acknowledges the similarity between this experience of reading and that of the author of the book he reads: "recalling how Augustine had supposed the same thing happening to him," and also that "something similar had already happened earlier to Antonius," Petrarch vows to change his life. Whether or not that vow is fulfilled, Petrarch engages in literary emulation by making it— as Jill Robbins puts it, Petrarch's "personal experience of conversion is also the conversion of and to the story."[82]

William Alabaster's relationship to Augustine—as reader, as writer, and as convert—is equally intimate. His description of his own Catholic conversion, reproduced above, bears an obvious resemblance to the central moment in book 8 of the *Confessions*: after an early career of false belief and intellectual pride, a man borrows a book from another, retires to a *locus amoenus* to read it, is miraculously brought to share the convictions of that book's author, and needs to read no further. That transformation, like Augustine's, echoes other conversion stories invoked in the text (Paul, Tertullian, Antony, Rainolds). Just as Augustine's conversion leads immediately to an effort to convert his friend Alypius, and eventually to his evangelical mission as Bishop of Hippo, so Alabaster describes how his conversion immediately inspired his efforts to convert his Protestant associates, particularly "my Lord and Master the Earle of Essex," and how it eventually led to a series of high-profile debates with divines including Lancelot Andrewes, John Overall, the bishop of Bath, the dean of Westminster, and the bishop of London. Finally, and most importantly, just as Augustine describes taking up the pen with the intention of converting others, Alabaster composes his conversion narrative—and the autobiographical sonnets written around the same time—as a way to "give the onset" to future readers, "to stir up others also that shold reed them to soew *[sic]* estimation of that which I felt in my self."[83] This effort to explain what he "felt in [him]self," however, does not produce an authorial pose of iconoclastic "authenticity" but rather an insistence on formal secondariness. If Alabaster wishes to convert his reader, he does so by proposing his own conversion as an event that is formally prefigured and thus endlessly imitable. Like Antony, Victorinus, Ponticianus, Augustine, Alypius, Rainolds, Petrarch, and finally Alabaster, the reader of this conversion narrative will undergo a transformation that is simultaneously "sudden" and emulative, not only inspired by prior stories of religious change but also anticipated by them.

In his invaluable study of denominational conversion in early modern England, Michael Questier notes that the church convert tends to "express his new perception of true religion by reference to [polemic] categories." He concludes that for this reason such accounts "did not contain the essence of conversion" but were simply politically or polemically motivated rationalizations, composed after the fact.[84] Such an analysis supposes, however, that there is such a thing as an "essence of conversion" separate from the forms in which it is experienced and the language in which it is described. This claim is complicated, if not implicitly disproved, by the *responsa scholarum*. These texts, while not meant for publication and not part of any polemic project, consistently represent conversion as an experience of *fitting in,* an experience intelligible and expressible only in terms of preexisting formal categories. In his longer conversion narrative, Alabaster not only insists upon the "coherence and connexion" of the Catholic Church itself but also, by emphasizing the formally determined aspects of religious change, proposes religious conversion as, in Robbins's words, a turn "to the story" as it has already been told.[85] His text is thus both the record of an individual life in late-sixteenth-century England and the latest instance of a "coherent and connected" tradition of spiritual metamorphosis and its narration beginning with "St. Augustine's Master," Paul.[86] By conflating forms of religious experience and forms of religious life-writing in this way, Alabaster finally offers his central, striking insight: that it is precisely this inevitably ex post facto quality of any conversion narrative that best conveys the "essence of conversion" itself.

Appendix: Capita, quibus ex Regularum praescriptis admittendi in hoc Collegium tenentur Respondere [Prescribed headings, to which those admitted into this college are made to respond]

1. Quodnam sit verum nomen suum et parentum? Quae aetas? Quis locus nativitatis et educationis? Ubi vixerit?
[What is [the student's] real name, and that of his parents? How old is he? Where was he born and educated? Where did he live?]

2. Quae sit status et conditio sua et parentum praecipuorumque amicorum? Si nobiles an plebii an mediae sortis? Divites an pauperes? Quosnam habeat fratres, sorores aut cognatos? Si haeretici an Catholici sint?
[What is his condition, and that of his parents and closest friends? Are they nobles, commoners, or of the middle sort? Rich or poor? What brothers, sisters, or relatives does he have? Are they Catholics or heretics?]

3. Quibus studiis, et ubi, operam dederit et quo progressu?
[What has he studied, and where, and with what progress?]

4. Qua valetudine utatur? Secunda, an adversa? Si animae aegritudinem vel sentiat, vel aliquando senserit, quae vel a litterarum studiis, vel a regularum observatione aliquem retardare posset?
[What kind of health does he enjoy, favorable or unfavorable? Does he now or has he ever felt any ailment of spirit that might inhibit his ability to study or to observe rules?]

5. Si in haeresi aliquando aut schismate vixerit? Quando, quibus praesidiis, cuius industria, fidem Catholicam amplexus sit, si aliquando fuerit haereticus? Quando ex Anglia discesserit? Cur Romam venerit, quidve ipsum induxerit ad hoc seminarium petendum? Si quid perpessus sit aliquando ob fidem Catholicam? Quid demum illi contigerit circa vocationem ad fidem Catholicam?
[Has he ever lived in heresy or schism? If he was ever a heretic, how and under what circumstances and with whose help did he embrace the Catholic faith? When did he leave England? Why did he come to Rome, and what led him to seek out this seminary? Has he ever suffered on account of his Catholic faith? What exactly were the circumstances of his calling to the Catholic faith?]

6. An propositum, et desiderium sentiat suscipiendi vitam ecclesiasticam? An decernat apud se constanter in virtute et literis operam ponere? An sentiat se paratum ad studendum iis rebus, et in ea classe, quam superiores assignabunt? An statuat submitterere se regulis, et disciplinae Collegii, et Superiorum directioni?
[Does he feel either the tendency or the desire to embrace the ecclesiastic life? Has he resolved to undertake the study of letters and good works with constancy? Does he feel prepared to study those subjects assigned by the superiors? Does he declare that he will submit to the rules and discipline of the college and the direction of the superiors?]

Notes

1. The breadth of the recent revival of interest in early modern Catholic literature can be seen in the essays collected in Arthur F. Marotti, ed., *Catholicism and Anti-Catholicism in Early Modern English Texts* (Basingstoke: Macmillan, 1999). Other noteworthy studies include Alison Shell, *Catholicism, Controversy and the English Literary Imagination* (Cambridge: Cambridge University Press, 1999); Ceri Sullivan, *Dismembered Rhetoric: English Recusant Writings, 1580–1603* (London: Associated University Presses, 1985); Frances Dolan, *Whores of Babylon: Catholicism, Gender, and Seventeenth-Century Print Culture* (Ithaca: Cornell University Press, 1999); and Alexandra Walsham, *Church Papists: Catholicism, Conformity and Confessional Polemic in Early Modern England* (London: Boydell Press, 1993). Such discussions of recusant polemic, hagiography, casuistry, martyrology, drama, and lyric have, in effect, paved the way for a reconsideration of Catholic autobiography, a genre of early modern Catholic writing that remains relatively overlooked by critics.

2. See William Haller, *The Rise of Puritanism* (New York: Columbia University Press, 1938); Owen Watkins, *The Puritan Experience: Studies in Spiritual Autobiography* (New York: Schocken, 1972); and Joan Webber, *The Eloquent "I": Style and Self in Seventeenth-Century Poetry* (Milwaukee: University of Wisconsin Press, 1968), 3–14. Although Paul Delany, *British Autobiography in the Seventeenth Century* (London: Routledge, 1969), 37, asserts that "members of all denominations contributed to the genre" of spiritual autobiography, he also asserts that "the natural autobiographical form for the Jesuit was *res gestae;* for the Calvinist, history of his soul." The fact that he dedicates only four pages of a 174-page book to Catholic autobiography reveals the value judgment implicit in that (questionable) distinction.

3. Patricia Caldwell, *The Puritan Conversion Narrative: The Beginnings of American Expression* (Cambridge: Cambridge University Press, 1983), 164. (The phrase "morphology of conversion" comes from Edmund Morgan, *Visible Saints: The History of a Puritan Idea* [Ithaca: Cornell University Press, 1963], 190.). Caldwell wishes to claim that this productive narrative trouble arises particularly in American Puritan writing (hence the second half of her title), but similar claims have been made for the work of English sectarians; see, for instance, Watkins, *Puritan Experience,* 209–10, and Tom Webster, "Writing to Redundancy: Approaches to Spiritual Journals and Early Modern Spirituality," *Historical Journal* 39 (1996): 35 n. 13.

4. Caldwell, *Puritan Conversion Narrative,* 166.

5. Watkins, *Puritan Experience,* 144–45. Among these "prophets" Watkins includes George Foster, Abiezer Coppe, Arise Evans, Joseph Salmon, Richard Coppin, Lawrence Clarkson, and Lodowick Muggleton. Nigel Smith, *Perfection Proclaimed: Language and Literature in English Radical Religion, 1640–1660* (Oxford: Clarendon Press, 1989), 15. Watkins finally qualifies his critical praise of radical expression somewhat, claiming that while "the prophets certainly produced work of more consistent literary interest than the other Puritan groups . . . they did so accidentally" (*Puritan Experience,* 233).

6. The phrase, omitting the crucial adjective *Protestant,* is from Nigel Smith's introduction to *Literature and Revolution in England, 1640–1660* (New Haven: Yale University Press, 1994). For a succinct discussion of Puritan attitudes toward "formalism," see J. C. Davis, "Against Formality: One Aspect of the English Revolution," *Transactions of the Royal Historical Society,* 6th ser., 3 (1993): 265–88.

7. See especially Michael Questier, *Conversion, Politics and Religion in England, 1580–1625* (Cambridge: Cambridge University Press, 1996). Questier's investigation of conversion complements some important general discussions of denominational instability in late-sixteenth-century England, particularly Eamon Duffy, *The Stripping of the Altars* (New Haven: Yale University Press, 1992); the essays in Christopher Haigh, ed., *The English Reformation Revised* (Cambridge: Cambridge University Press, 1987), and Haigh's own *English Reformations* (Oxford: Clarendon, 1993); John Bossy, *The English Catholic Community, 1570–1850* (London: Longman, 1975), 1–76;

and especially the works of Peter Lake, particularly *Moderate Puritans and the Elizabethan Church* (Cambridge: Cambridge University Press, 1982). See also Peter Milward, *Religious Controversies of the Elizabethan Age* (Lincoln: University of Nebraska Press, 1977).

8. An exception is Alison Shell's essay "Multiple Conversions and the Menippean Self: The Case of Richard Carpenter," in Marotti, *Catholicism and Anti-Catholicism*, 154–97. Shell is mainly interested, however, in Carpenter's idiosyncratic use of the conventions of Menippean satire and not in the more general literary implications of autobiographical narratives about church conversion. So, too, her sensitive discussion of conversion in *Catholicism, Controversy* (88–92) concentrates mainly on the nondenominational "conversion of the heart" figured in Catholic penitential poetry and not on the issue of outward confessional change.

9. Michael Mascuch, *Origins of the Individualist Self* (Cambridge: Polity Press, 1997), 13–24, begins his history of "individualist" life-writing with a cogent survey of theoretical ideas about the relationship of the autobiographical "subject" to cultural and discursive contexts.

10. Transcripts of the *responsa* are held among the Roman Transcripts in the Public Record Office in London, and a modern edition, *Responsa Scholarum of the English College, Rome, Part 1: 1598–1622*, and *Part 2: 1622–1685*, edited by Anthony Kenny, has been printed as volumes 54 and 55 of the Publications of the Catholic Record Society (London: Catholic Record Society, 1962–63). This edition reproduces the Latin *responsa* in their entirety, followed by shorter English summaries of their contents (rather than literal translations). In further quotations from the *responsa*, I shall provide the part and page number of the CRS publication as well as the college archive number.

11. For a description of Catholic education in exile, see Peter Guilday, *The English Catholic Refugees on the Continent, 1558–1795* (London: Longmans, 1914). Particular discussion of the English College can be found in A. C. F. Beales, *Education under Penalty: English Catholic Education from the Reformation to the Fall of James II* (London: Athlone Press, 1963), 49–72.

12. Several years earlier, members of the college had disagreed violently over the issue of England's war with Spain; many objected to the pro-Spanish position of the church, arguing that their Catholic identity did not obviate their political loyalty to Elizabeth. The questionnaire may, in fact, have been instituted by Robert Persons in response to this divisive dispute. See Michael Carrafiello, *Robert Parsons and English Catholicism* (London: Associated University Presses, 1998), 90–102, and, more generally, Arnold Pritchard, *Catholic Loyalism in Elizabethan England* (Chapel Hill: University of North Carolina Press, 1979).

13. Paul Delany focuses on the action-packed memoirs of two early modern fugitive priests, both originally intended for propagandistic purposes, and both translated and edited in this century by Philip Caraman: John Gerard, *Autobiography of a*

Hunted Priest (New York: Image Books, 1955), and William Weston, *The Autobiography of an Elizabethan* (London: Longmans, 1955). Michael Questier has surveyed the characteristics of "motive" texts, in which converts adduce particular points of doctrine as justification for their change of churches, in *Conversion, Politics*, 12–39.

14. *Responsa scholarum, part 1*, 10 (*Scrittura 37*, 345).

15. Ibid., 30–61 (*Scrittura 37*, 354).

16. Ibid., 19–22 (*Scrittura 37*, 351).

17. This is, obviously, a quotation from the editorial summary (Ibid., 94 [*Scrittura 37*, 368]).

18. Webster, "Writing to Redundancy," 43.

19. *Responsa scholarum, part 1*, 10 (*Scrittura 37*, 345).

20. Ibid., 94 (*Scrittura 37*, 368).

21. Ibid., 83 (editorial summary) (*Scrittura 37*, 365).

22. Ibid., 63 (*Scrittura 37*, 357).

23. Ibid., 17–18 (*Scrittura 37*, 349).

24. Ibid., 7–8 (*Scrittura 37*, 343).

25. Ibid., 28 (*Scrittura 37*, 353). Roughly a quarter of the students at the College credit Gerard with their conversions between 1598 and 1602.

26. Delany, *British Autobiography*, 46.

27. The play seems closely modeled on Luigi Groto's *La Dalida*. See John C. Coldeway, "William Alabaster's *Roxana*: Some Textual Considerations," in *Acta Conventus Neo-Latini Bononiensis*, ed. R. J. Schoeck (Binghamton: State University of New York Press, 1985), 413–19. Samuel Johnson, *Lives of the Poets*, ed. Arthur Waugh, 2 vols. (London: Oxford University Press, 1955–56), 1:65. A more outrageous endorsement comes from Thomas Fuller, who notes that the tragedy was once "so admirably acted in [Trinity] College, and so pathetically; a gentle-woman present thereat (Reader, I had it from an Author whose credit it is Sin with me to suspect) at the hearing of the last words thereof, *sequar; sequar*, so hideously pronounced, fell distracted and never fully recovered her senses." *History of the Worthies of England* (London, 1662), 70.

28. Edmund Spenser, *Colin Clouts Come Home Againe*, lines 400 ff., in *Shorter Poems of Edmund Spenser*, ed. William A. Oram et al. (New Haven: Yale University Press, 1989).

29. The single completed book of the *Elisaeis* has been translated and edited by Michael O'Connell, *The "Elisaeis" of William Alabaster*, Studies in Philology 76 (Chapel Hill: University of North Carolina Press, 1979).

30. S. C. Lomas, ed., *The Letters and Speeches of Oliver Cromwell, with Elucidations by Thomas Carlyle*, 3 vols. (London: Methuen, 1904), 1:57.

31. The best source for Alabaster's biography is Eleanor Jean Coutts, "The Life and Works of William Alabaster, 1568–1640" (PhD diss., University of Wis-

consin, 1956). See also the introduction to Helen Gardner and G. M. Story, ed., *The Sonnets of William Alabaster* (London: Oxford University Press, 1959), xi–xxiii, and Imogen Guiney, *Recusant Poets,* vol. 1 (London: Sheed and Ward, 1938), 339–45.

32. For some modern studies of serial converts, see Christopher Devlin, "An Unwilling Apostate: The Case of Anthony Tyrrell," *Month* 6 (1951): 346–58; Noel Malcolm, *De Dominis (1560–1624): Venetian, Anglican, Ecumenist and Relapsed Heretic* (London: Strickland and Scott, 1984) (cf. *Monsignor Fate'voi. Or: a Discovery of the Dalmatian Apostata, M. Antonius de Dominis* [1617]); Michael Questier, "Crypto-Catholicism, Anti-Calvinism and Conversion at the Jacobean Court: The Enigma of Benjamin Carier," *Journal of Ecclesiastical History* 47 (1996): 45–64; and again Shell, "Multiple Conversions."

33. Quoted in Coutts, "Life and Works," 4.

34. Pierre Bayle, *The Dictionary, Historical and Critical, of Mr. Peter Bayle,* vol. 1 (1734; reprint, London: Routledge, 1997), 174. The story of Alabaster's religious alterations would have had particular resonance for Bayle, a French Huguenot who had briefly converted to Catholicism before recanting and fleeing to Geneva. This section of Bayle's biography is discussed by Richard Popkin in his preface to the *Dictionary,* v.

35. *Responsa scholarum, part 1,* 1 (*Scrittura 37,* 341).

36. Ibid., 99–102 (*Scrittura 37,* 372).

37. Ibid., 2 (*Scrittura 37,* 341).

38. This manuscript remains in the English College, designated as V. E. C. *Liber* 1394. The typed transcription made by an English College archivist is reproduced in Clara Fazzari, ed., *Alabaster's Conversion (anno 1598)* (Firenze, 1983). An edited version of the text has more recently appeared in William Alabaster, *Unpublished Works by William Alabaster,* ed. Dana F. Sutton (Salzburg Studies in English Literature, Elizabethan and Renaissance Studies 126, 1997), 101–78. Sutton supplements the typescript, which has occasional lacunae due to the poor condition of the English manuscript, with his translation back from Persons's Latin (see below, n. 39), and with his own reconstructions of the syntax when there is no parallel in the incomplete Persons translation. I quote from Sutton's edition, with his editorial emendations in square brackets.

39. The manuscript of this partial translation, entitled *De Conversione Gul.mi Alabastri ad fidem Catholicam opusc.m P. Rob. Personii ex Anglico in Latinum idioma translatum,* is held in the English College as V. E. C. *Liber* 1395. See P. O. Kristeller, *Iter Italicum,* 565.

40. See Sutton's introduction to Alabaster, *Unpublished Works,* xx.

41. Ibid., xix–xx.

42. For the proselytizing work of Catholic texts, see Sullivan, *Dismembered Rhetoric,* 13–14; Nancy Pollard Brown, "Paperchase: The Dissemination of Catholic

Texts in Elizabethan England," *English Manuscript Studies 1100–1700* 1 (1989): 120–43; and H. Thurston, "Catholic Writers and Elizabethan Readers," *Month* 82 (1894): 457–76, and 83 (1895): 231–45.

43. Although no copies of this book are extant, the two printed refutations of it, Roger Fenton's *Answer to William Alablaster [sic] His Motives* (1599) and John Racster's *A Booke of the Seven Planets, Or, Seven Wandring Motives, of William Alablaster's Wit, Retrograded or Removed* (1598), include identical quotations from Alabaster's original text, allowing a tentative reconstruction of its contents.

44. In "Essex and Europe: Evidence from Confidential Instructions by the Earl of Essex 1595–96," *English Historical Review* 111 (1996): 380–81, Paul Hammer claims that although Essex "deliberately cultivated an international reputation as a supporter of toleration for English Catholics," the evidence suggests that he was firmly Protestant himself. For more on Essex's reputation as a proponent of toleration for Catholics, see A. J. Loomie, S.J., "A Catholic Petition to the Earl of Essex," *Recusant History* 7 (1963): 1–37.

45. The Cadiz voyage included not only Protestants of various stripes but Catholics and crypto-Catholics as well. See Paul Hammer, *The Polarisation of Elizabethan Politics: The Political Career of Robert Devereux, Second Earl of Essex, 1585–1597* (Cambridge: Cambridge University Press, 1999), 175.

46. Peter Lake and Michael Questier have shown that prisons were important centers of Catholic proselytizing. Peter Lake and Michael Questier, "Prisons, Priests, and People," in *England's Long Reformation, 1500–1800*, ed. Nicholas Tyacke (London: University College Press, 1998), 195–233.

47. Wright is best known as the author of *The Passions of the Mind in General* (1604), an idiosyncratic fusion of classical rhetorical theory and Ignatian meditative technique. See T. O. Sloan, "A Renaissance Controversialist on Rhetoric: Thomas Wright's *Passions of the Mind in Generall*," *Speech Monographs* 36 (1969): 38–54. Robert Caro has argued that Wright's rhetorical theory influenced Alabaster's English sonnets. Robert Caro, "William Alabaster: Rhetor, Meditator, Devotional Poet," *Recusant History* 19 (1988): 62–79 and 155–70. Wright was also allegedly responsible for the Catholic conversion of another poet, Ben Jonson. See T. A. Stroud, "Ben Jonson and Father Thomas Wright," *ELH* 14 (1947): 277–79; and J. P. Crowley, "'He took his religion by trust': The Matter of Ben Jonson's Conversion," *Renaissance and Reformation* 22 (1998): 53–70.

48. This is a characteristic moment of Alabastrian intellectual hubris; in fact, the book was nearly six hundred pages long.

49. Indeed, Rainolds begins to defend the doctrine of papal infallibility explicitly in the first paragraph of the preface. William Rainolds, *Refutation of Several Sundry Reprehensions* (Paris, 1583), sig. A2v.

50. A. D. Nock, *Conversion: The Old and the New in Religion from Alexander the Great to Augustine of Hippo* (Oxford: Clarendon Press, 1933), 266.

51. Alabaster, *Unpublished Works,* 115. Alabaster's chapter detailing the immediate circumstances of his own conversion is five pages long in the modern edition; his biography of Rainolds takes up three of those pages.

52. *New Testament* (Douai), sig A3r. Georges Tavard has shown how this idea was taken further by "fringe" Catholic theologians such as Thomas Stapleton, who maintained that tradition could be an independent source of religious truth. *Holy Writ or Holy Church* (London: Burns and Oates, 1959), 230.

53. Alabaster, *Unpublished Works,* 115.

54. Ibid.

55. Ibid., 117.

56. Alabaster also composed a Latin sonnet about this episode, translated by Hugh Holland and reprinted in Alabaster, *Unpublished Works,* 12–13:

Between two Bretheren Civil warres and worse
The nice poynt of Religion long did nurse.
For Reformation of the Faith he plyes;
That Faith should be reformed this denyes.
Reasons on both sides being apart propounded,
Both met alike, both fell confounded.
As hart could wish, each brother other takes,
As fates would have it, each his faith forsakes.
Without captiver both are captive led,
And to the victors camp the vanquished fled.
What fight is this, where conquered both are glad,
Yet either, to have conquered other, sad?

57. Alabaster, *Unpublished Works,* 116.

58. Ibid., 114.

59. Miller contends that Augustine "exerted the greatest single influence upon Puritan thought next to that of the Bible itself." Perry Miller, *The New England Mind: The Seventeenth Century* (Boston: Beacon Press, 1961), 4, and 3–34 passim. Owen Watkins notes that many mid-seventeenth-century Puritans looked to Augustine as a spiritual model; in 1641, for instance, the Puritan William Hinde wrote a life of another Puritan, John Bruen, constructed entirely as a series of comparisons between Bruen and Augustine (*Puritan Experience,* 59–61). Robert Bell argues for Augustine's influence on Bunyan, "Metamorphoses of Spiritual Autobiography," *ELH* 44 (1976): 108–26. For a historical survey of the reception of the *Confessions,* see Pierre Courcelle, *Les Confessions de Saint Augustin dans la tradition littéraire* (Paris: Études Augustiniennes, 1963).

60. Louis Martz notes the importance of the 1577 *Certaine select Prayers, gathered out of S. Augustines Meditations* in *The Poetry of Meditation* (New Haven: Yale

University Press, 1954). Robert Dodaro and Michael Questier consider two early Jacobean polemicists, one Catholic and one Protestant, who both use Augustine to support their doctrinal positions: Robert Dodaro and Michael Questier, "Strategies in Jacobean Polemic: The Use and Abuse of St. Augustine in English Theological Controversy," *Journal of Ecclesiastical History* 44 (1993): 432–49. Peter Milward, *Religious Controversies of the Elizabethan Period,* 1–8, has documented the use of Augustine and other patristics during the 1559 "Challenge" debate.

61. *Responsa scholarum, part 1,* 57 (*Scrittura 37,* 354).

62. Anne Ferry, *The "Inward" Language: Sonnets of Wyatt, Sidney, Shakespeare, Donne* (Chicago: University of Chicago Press, 1983), 39.

63. Delany, *British Autobiography,* 31–32.

64. Letters by exiled Catholic converts to friends and family in England were not uncommon in the period. See, for instance, Robert Markham's letter of February 1595 from Rome to his brother Sir Griffith Markham, a copy of which exists in the British Library (MS Lansdowne 96, fols. 81–82), or Nicholas Crynes, *The copy of a letter sent from an English gentleman, lately become a Catholike beyond the seas, to his Protestant friend in England. . .declaring his reasons for the change of his religion* (St. Omer, 1622). Sutton, in his introduction to Alabaster, *Unpublished Works,* xix, tentatively identifies the unnamed addressee of Alabaster's text as Hugh Holland, whose own conversion to Catholicism happened around the same time as Alabaster's.

65. Anne Hunsaker Hawkins, *Archetypes of Conversion: The Autobiographies of Augustine, Bunyan and Merton* (Lewisburg: Bucknell University Press, 1985), 17–19, 21, notes these characteristic components of the Augustinian narrative pattern.

66. Alabaster, *Unpublished Works,* 104. Robert Persons recalls taking the Oath of Supremacy in similar terms: "Itaque (proh! scelus!) bis iuramentum illud nequissimum iuvenis ambitiosus ne gradum ammiterem labiis pronunciavit, licet animo detestarer" (*Memoirs,* in *Miscellanea II,* Catholic Record Society 3 (London: Arden, 1906), 195.

67. Alabaster, *Unpublished Works,* 104.

68. Ibid., 104.

69. St. Augustine, *Confessions,* ed. and trans. Henry Chadwick (Oxford: Oxford University Press, 1991), book 5 passim.

70. Alabaster, *Unpublished Works,* 115.

71. Augustine, *Confessions,* 7.4.

72. Ibid., 8.15.

73. Brian Stock surveys this chain of readerly conversions in the *Confessions* as part of Augustine's larger theory of reading in chapter 3 of his *Augustine the Reader* (Cambridge, MA: Harvard University Press, 1996), 75–111.

74. Robert McMahon, "Autobiography as Text-Work: Augustine's Refiguring of Genesis 3 and Ovid's 'Narcissus' in His Conversion Account," *Exemplaria* 1 (1989): 337–66.

75. Augustine, *Confessions,* 8.29.

76. John Freccero, "The Fig Tree and the Laurel: Petrarch's Poetics," in *Literary Theory/Renaissance Texts,* ed. Patricia Parker and David Quint (Baltimore: Johns Hopkins University Press, 1986), 25.

77. Augustine, *Confessions,* 8.30.

78. Ibid., 10.6.

79. In addition to his English *Confessions* (1620), Matthew produced a translation of St. Teresa of Avila's *Vida,* retitled *The Flaming Hart* (Antwerp, 1642), which would influence the writing of another Catholic convert, Richard Crashaw. Matthew composed a kind of conversion narrative in 1640, as a letter to the Benedictine nun Mary Gage, since published as *A True Historical Relation of the Conversion of Sir Tobie Matthew* (London: Burns and Oates, 1904).

80. Courcelle, *Les Confessions de Saint Augustin,* 338, suggests that "toute la lettre de Pétrarque n'est qu'une longue citation textuelle, avec commentaire, des paragraphes augustiniens."

81. Petrarch, *Rerum familiarum libri I–VIII,* trans. Aldo Bernardo (Albany: State University of New York Press, 1975), 172–80, 178.

82. Jill Robbins, "Petrarch Reading Augustine: 'The Ascent of Mont Ventoux,'" *Philological Quarterly* 64 (1985): 533. Robbins nevertheless sees the imitation of Augustine as ultimately inconclusive. In this, she follows both Freccero, who sees Petrarch's exchanging "fig tree" for "laurel" as an abandoning of the Augustinian narrative of redemption for a purely literary self-referentiality, and Robert M. Durling, "The Ascent of Mont Ventoux and the Crisis of Allegory," *Italian Quarterly* 18 (1974): 7–28. See also Albert Ascoli's subtle discussion of Petrarchan ambiguity in "Petrarch's Middle Age: Memory, Imagination, History, and the 'Ascent of Mont Ventoux,'" *Stanford Italian Review* 10 (1989): 5–43.

83. Alabaster, *Unpublished Works,* 123. See also Shell, *Catholicism, Controversy,* 89.

84. Questier, *Conversion, Politics and Religion,* 37.

85. Alabaster, *Unpublished Works,* 128.

86. Ibid., 140.

8

Father John Gerard's Object Lessons

Relics and Devotional Objects in *Autobiography of a Hunted Priest*

Anne M. Myers

In his *Autobiography of a Hunted Priest*, probably written in 1609–10, Father John Gerard documents the difficult and often dangerous existence of Catholics in late Elizabethan England. Recording his experience as a Jesuit missionary, Gerard attends not only to the threats he and his Catholic friends faced but also to the specific practices by which they maintained the traditions of Catholic worship despite their precarious situation. Frequently, Gerard's interest in these survival tactics takes the form of a preoccupation with the persistence and preservation of relics and other objects central to Catholic devotion. Amid one description of his English Catholic acquaintances, Gerard pauses to list several relics he has received during his time in England. He writes: "I was given some very remarkable relics, and my friends had them finely set for me." He enumerates among them "a complete thorn of the holy crown of our Lord," "a forefinger of the martyr, Father Robert Sutton," "a silver head of St. Thomas of Canterbury" that "contains a piece of the saint's skull," and "a large part of St. Vita's arm."[1] The narrative function of such a list is not immediately clear. A collection of objects, after all, does nothing to advance Gerard's story. The context of this list, however, as well as its topical and thematic relationship to other points of Gerard's text, reveals why such objects are important. This essay will argue that from this concise list of relics and their accompanying descriptions we can derive two important foci of Gerard's *Autobiography*: to assert the continued survival of the Catholic community in England and to address the special threats faced by Reformation Catholics in general and by Jesuit missionaries in particular.

In Gerard's narrative, this list of relics follows an enumeration of heroic priests, converts, devout English Catholics, and young men whom Gerard eventually sent abroad for Jesuit training. This collection of remarkable individuals proves the strength of the English Catholic community, and for Gerard the collection of objects forms a logical continuation of this narrative thread. This continuity depends upon one unwritten—but, for Gerard, essential—assumption: that the community negotiates and creates the value of its own relics. This idea was not a recent development in the economy of relics. In his analysis of the medieval relic trade, Patrick Geary explains that the formation and persistence of a cult not only contributed to but created the status of saints and consequently their relics: "[C]anonization did not determine sainthood. If a dead person worked miracles that attracted an enthusiastic following, then that person was a saint with or without formal recognition. Conversely, without a cult, without a following, a person, regardless of the holiness of his or her life, would not be considered one of those special companions of God through whom he chose to act in the world."[2] In the *Autobiography* Gerard relies on a logical reversal of this principle: if a relic's value depends upon the presence of a believing community, then the very existence of a valued relic must in turn prove the existence of such a community. So, like the creation of converts and the proliferation of priests, these relics attest to the survival and resiliency of English Catholicism.

Geary lists the shared beliefs that underwrote the value of relics in medieval communities, and Reformation controversy, along with Gerard's text, affirms that these beliefs were still understood as the sources of a relic's value in the sixteenth and seventeenth centuries. Geary argues that the value of relics in late antiquity and the Middle Ages was based upon "three interrelated beliefs": first, that the human source of the relics "had been, during life and—more importantly—after death, a special friend of God"; second, "that the remains of such a saint were to be prized and treated in a special way"; and finally, "that the particular corpse or portion thereof was indeed the remains of that particular saint."[3] Since the value of a relic rested on the belief that it was authentic, those who possessed relics or potential relics (that had not yet been officially "elevated" by the community) were under constant pressure to prove that the relics were genuine by illustrating their "actual miraculous power": "This actual power was most important because communities often disagreed, even violently, over which one possessed the genuine relics of a particular saint. The determination of genuine claims ultimately rested on very pragmatic, functional evidence: If the relics worked, they were genuine. If they did not, they were not authentic."[4]

Protestant polemics acknowledge these beliefs by vehemently attacking them. As early as 1536, the First Henrician Injunctions note and dismiss the traditional miraculous powers of relics as part of what Keith Thomas calls "the whole apparatus of Catholic magic."[5] The injunctions admonish that worshipers "shall not set forth or extol any images, relics or miracles for any superstition or lucre, nor allure the people by enticements to the pilgrimage of any saint," for "they shall please God more by the true exercising of their bodily labour, travail, or occupation, and providing for their families, than if they went about on the said pilgrimages, and . . . it shall profit more their own soul's health, if they do bestow that upon the poor and needy, which they would have bestowed upon the said images or relics."[6] The Second Henrician Injunctions of 1538 enjoin readers: "[I]f you have heretofore declared to your parishioners anything to the extolling or setting forth of pilgrimages, feigned relics or images or any such superstition, you shall now openly, afore the same, recant and reprove the same, showing them, as the truth is, that you did the same upon no ground of Scripture, but as one being led and seduced by a common error and abuse crept into the Church, through the sufferance and avarice of those who felt profit by the same."[7] Likewise, parishioners are "not to repose their trust or affiance in any other works devised by men's fantasies beside Scripture; as in wandering to pilgrimages, offering of money, candles or tapers to images or relics, or kissing or licking the same."[8] In the Henrician Injunctions, relics and their supposed miracles are "feigned," the trappings of "superstition," the products of "avarice." They are neither genuine nor deserving of special treatment, especially not of attention and money that parishioners might profitably bestow elsewhere. Versions of these items appear in government injunctions and articles throughout the Edwardian and Elizabethan periods. As Keith Thomas summarizes, "Steps were . . . taken to eliminate any prayers which seemed to imply that supernatural power lay anywhere other than with God. Relics were no longer adored for their supposedly miraculous properties; and the idea of praying to the saints was regarded as reprehensible."[9] Writing in 1624, the Protestant Richard Montagu denounces both belief in the power of relics and the ways they are traditionally "prized and treated": "You may keepe, if you will, and lock up, if you please, in your Cabinet, or Casket, or where you will, Saint *Campions* thumb, Saint *Garnets* strawe, Saint *Lioilaies* hayre. . . . I know no Protestant will steale them from you." He continues, "Indeede, wee holde, and assuredly belieue, that Saint *Campions* thumb, Saint *Garnets* strawe, Saint *Storyes* halter neuer did, nor shall raise up any dead man."[10] Montagu reveals his disdain not only for the relics themselves—they are worthless objects undeserving of special treatment—but for their human sources. Montagu leaves little doubt as to whether he considers Saint Campion and his fellows special friends of God. Protestant detractors also argued that the majority of "relics" in circulation were not "indeed the remains of [a] particular saint." Eamon Duffy quotes Latimer's assertion that these objects were "pigs bones instead of saints' relics"[11] and records Nicholas Shaxton's concern that "[i]gnorant people were being deluded by false relics."[12]

Gerard unquestionably maintains all of the beliefs that his Protestant detractors attempt to strike down, but aside from an obvious disagreement about whether relics are valuable at all, Gerard's text does not respond to theirs. The first and third of the beliefs Geary lists establish the bases for a relic's value and so form logical targets for Protestant devaluations of relics. Gerard's list of relics, by contrast, shows his special concern with the second belief: that the relic is to be "prized and treated in a special way." He is interested in the outward behavior that provides visible evidence of belief. Because a relic's worth indicates the faith of community, the important question for Gerard is not whether a relic is real but whether it is valued. His history of Christ's thorn reveals his emphasis. Of this first and most ancient of the relics on his list, Gerard writes: "[It is] a complete thorn of the holy crown of our Lord which Mary, Queen of Scots, had brought with her from France (where the whole crown is kept) and had given to the Earl of Northumberland, who was later martyred. While he lived, the Earl used to carry it round his neck in a golden cross, and when he came to execution he gave it to his daughter, who gave it to me" (49). This history provides several examples of how the thorn is "prized and treated." Mary carries Christ's thorn with her from France. The earl stores the relic in gold, keeps it on his person, and hands it down to his daughter at the moment of his martyrdom. Gerard also considers it a precious gift whose history is worth recording. The authenticity of the saint cannot really be questioned here, but demonstration of the thorn's authenticity is conspicuously absent from the account. While Gerard apparently believes the relic is genuine, he makes no move toward proving its provenance to the reader.

On the one hand, the relic does function for Gerard in its traditional role as a connection to the power of Christ. Geary says of the saints: "Their corpses were seen as the *pignora,* literally, the security deposits left by the saints upon their deaths as guarantees of their continuing interest in the earthly community."[13] On the other hand, I would argue that Gerard's particular emphases emerge in response to the specific pressures of the Catholic persecution in England. Gerard recognizes that what is at stake in Reformation England is not the continuing interest of the saints in the earthly community but the continuing interest of the earthly community in relics and the saints. By embedding contemporary Catholics in his description of the relic, Gerard suggests that people who believe in and care for relics are as important and valuable as the relics themselves. The relic becomes the narrative occasion for recording the continued existence of these individuals whose actions prove and enable the persistence of English Catholicism. Through these individuals Gerard connects the veneration of relics to other acts of religious resistance. Gerard associates the relic with Mary, Queen of Scots, and the Earl of Northumberland, two prominent martyrs to the Catholic faith.[14] In addition, the earl's daughters have been given special significance as successful resisters of Protestant oppression earlier in the *Autobiography.*

Gerard, then, is not even addressing the points upon which Protestant antagonists most vigorously insist. Instead, he is writing for a specifically Catholic audience. Gerard wrote the *Autobiography* in Latin while he was living in Louvain and, as his translator says, "helping to train the English novices of the Society of Jesus for the mission he had just left" (xvii). In his own preface, Gerard says that at the orders of his superiors "I am setting down in a simple and faithful narrative all that happened to me, under God's providence, during the eighteen years I worked on the English mission." He protests that "what I achieved was insignificant" but that "He chose to do it through me, because I was a member—an unworthy one, I admit—of that body which has received from Jesus its head a remarkable outpouring of His Spirit for the healing of souls in this last era of a declining and gasping world" (xxiv). Gerard here evokes a desperation that he assumes his audience shares; from a Catholic point of view, England must really have seemed "a declining and gasping world." And it is to this desperation, rather than to Protestant polemics, that Gerard responds. He asserts that English Catholicism is not moribund but vital. The body of the *Autobiography* modifies our understanding of Gerard's prefatory remarks; his bleak description may apply to the moral degeneration of England itself, but it certainly does not apply to the Catholic community that continues to thrive there. In fact, for Gerard, faith is more clearly perceived against a backdrop of danger and persecution; acts of resistance strengthen and revitalize it.

The second of Gerard's "remarkable relics" literalizes the regenerative power of recusant faith. Gerard describes: "a silver head of Saint Thomas of Canterbury, and his mitre studded with precious stones," which contains a piece of the saint's skull. The skull itself "is about the breadth of two gold crowns and is thought to be the piece that was chipped off when he was so wickedly slain. The silver head was old and had lost some stones: but the gentleman in whose house I was staying had it repaired and finely ornamented. For this reason the Superior afterwards let him keep it in trust for the Society in his private chapel" (50). Gerard shows little interest in the pre-Reformation history of a relic that, if authentic, is about four hundred years old, nor does he express anxiety about whether it is genuine. His concern is not with the authenticity of the relic but with the relic's capacity to illustrate the authenticity of his host's faith. Gerard lavishes on the silver head a narrative attention that mirrors the pains his host takes in restoring it. Although Gerard says that the head "is small and of no great value in itself" (50), the detail of his description belies this statement. The head is "silver," "studded with precious stones," and "finely ornamented." The materials, however, are valuable only because of the way they are used. Their visual richness reflects the reverence with which the piece of skull is treated, showing that Protestant injunctions have destroyed neither the relic nor the host's belief in its value. In fact, both are set off to greater advantage: the reliquary shines the more brightly for its new stones, the host's faith for its immunity to Protestant persecution. Thus the account of the relic also offers an account of Gerard's host: a man who harbors priests, restores a reliquary, venerates relics, and keeps a private chapel in his house. His successful preservation of Catholic tradition makes him as worthy of record as the relic itself.

In these accounts of the skull and the thorn, Gerard deploys another narrative tactic through which he insists upon the resistance and survival of the Catholic community: the recording of circulation. Gerard's list of the relic's owners supplies it with a pedigree that consists not only of its source but of its circulation. An interest in the paths and methods by which such objects are circulated pervades Gerard's text. If the value of a relic indicates the survival of a community that values it, the circulation of a relic both creates and performs the religious and personal relationships among members of that community. In addition, belief in the value of relics and devotional objects functions like a language that identifies its speakers as members of the Catholic community. Protestants may understand the language, but their refusal to use it threatens to render it defunct. As long as Gerard has others to whom he can circulate the illicit objects of Catholic devotion, Catholicism is not a dead language in England.

The history of Saint Vita's bone, the fourth relic on the list, shows that in the absence of a publicly visible community the circulation of relics becomes an alternate way of documenting common faith. Gerard is given "a large piece of Saint Vita's arm," of which he writes:

> The relic came to me in this way. The parson of the place where the whole body (or at least a great part of it) was preserved and venerated in the old days found that he was always restive at night and could get no sleep. This went on for a long time. Then one day the thought struck him that this trouble came from his not paying proper and due respect to the bones which he had in his keeping. He felt he ought to give them to Catholics who were their rightful owners. This he did and slept well ever afterwards. A good priest told me this story and he gave me a large bone, which a devout Catholic is keeping on behalf of the society. (50)

Gerard contrasts the way that the bones were "preserved and venerated in the old days"—that is, in the communal site of a church—with the way they are necessarily preserved and venerated in his own time. Since they can no longer provide a publicly acknowledged focus for community worship, they are distributed among private individuals. Here the imagined integrity of Saint Vita's body replaces the visible integrity of the Catholic Church; the church, like the body, is fragmented into its individual members and displaced from central sites of worship. But while the distribution of the relics requires the fragmentation of the "whole body" of Saint Vita, the bones remain a symbolic, if not physical, connection to one another because of their common source.

The attention Gerard bestows on his relics demonstrates his claim that they are indeed "remarkable." They are rare, in some cases ancient, and—for those who believe they are genuine—irreproducible. For Gerard, however, relics may be substituted with Catholic objects that are more available, as long as they belong to the language of Catholic belief. While confined in the Tower of London, Gerard develops a system for circulating letters, as well as small crosses and rosaries fashioned from orange peels, to his friends in the Clink. These objects, specific to Catholic worship and history, work very much like relics in defining the members of the community and attesting to its survival. John S. Roberts's discussion in "The Rosary in Elizabethan England" argues that the rosary was associated especially with English Catholicism, making its circulation among English recusants a particularly appropriate reflection of their survival. He writes, "The Rosary was unquestionably the English devotion par excellence during the Middle Ages. In medieval England devotion to Mary was particularly fervent; in fact, England was piously called 'Our Lady's Dowry.'"[15] Hence the recusants extend an unbroken line of Catholic tradition by, as Roberts says, "re-enforcing a devotion that was already well established in the spiritual life of Englishmen."[16] In the context of Roberts's discussion, Gerard's orange-peel creations signify the vitality and survival of his religious community.

While rosaries and crosses functioned as a kind of spiritual currency, in Gerard's account they also serve a practical purpose as vehicles for the paper in which Gerard wraps them. On each wrapper, Gerard writes two simultaneous letters, one in charcoal and one in orange juice that remains invisible until exposed to heat. He describes his system: "In the pencilled letter I confined myself to spiritual topics, but in the white spaces between the lines I gave detailed instructions to friends of mine outside" (118). Gerard pays little attention to the content of either of these messages, foregrounding instead the methods by which the letters were circulated. His brief references to their content confirm this emphasis: "I wrote to my friends in orange juice, telling them to reply in the same way if they received the note, but not to say much at first, and to give the warder a little money, promising them something each time he brought them a rosary or a cross and a short written message from me assuring them that I was well" (118). The letters themselves discuss the manner of their circulation. In fact, Gerard specifically instructs his friends that the first letters should not "say much" and confines his own message to the simple statement that he "was well." The information itself is less important than the personal connection forged by its exchange.

Significantly, Gerard's interest in methods of circulation surpasses his interest in what is actually being circulated. Geary notes that in the Middle Ages circulation enhanced the value of a relic by proving its desirability: "[A]cquiring the relic gave it value because it was worth acquiring, and this acquisition . . . was itself evidence that the relics were genuine. Circulation thus created the commodity being circulated" (214). As Gerard details his methods of circulating items from the Tower, though, it becomes clear that in this case his valuation of circulation differs from that described by Geary. In both instances, circulation is a powerful mechanism, almost a commodity in itself. Gerard, however, responds to the challenges presented by his historical moment; he is less anxious about the desire to acquire and circulate the information than he is about the ability to do so. Furthermore, neither the orange peels nor the information itself seems to survive. Compared to most relics, orange peels are ephemeral. And for the most part, the specific information being circulated in the letters is absent from Gerard's account. By means of the *Autobiography*, proof of the objects' circulation outlives the objects themselves. Geary suggests that in a medieval community an object's circulation could be even more important than its identity. For Gerard, an object's circulation is so important that there is almost no object left.

Clearly, in this instance, the value of circulation does not lie in its capacity to create value for another object. It lies instead in the methods and mechanics by which it is accomplished. As Gerard describes his coded orange juice writing, the technique itself becomes a kind of Catholic object, circulated among Gerard and his friends by the letters and from Gerard to his readers by his account. The secret writing alludes specifically to its Catholic readers' shared history of persecution. The recipients of Gerard's letters will know what to do with them because they too are members of a community in which secrecy is vital. Their participation in a shared past defines the members of the community in the same way that their shared belief does. Gerard writes, "My friends received the rosary wrapped in paper. They knew that, given the chance, I would have written something in orange juice as I used to do when I was with them, and immediately they went to a room upstairs and putting the paper by the fire, read what I had written" (118). He connects their knowledge of the secret writing directly to their past relationships with him, so that to use this secret language becomes a continuation of that relationship. The system of secret names Gerard uses in his letters also reflects their purpose in cementing relationships: "I never wrote down their names in my letters, not even when I was at liberty, but I used other names that were recognized by the people I addressed. I called one 'my son' another 'my friend' or 'my nephew' and their wives 'sister,' 'daughter'" (119). Obviously, Gerard wishes to avoid incriminating his friends if the letters are intercepted, but his use of family terms rather than pseudonyms or some other code reinforces his personal ties to the recipients.

Even the chemical properties of orange juice enhance Gerard's ability to ensure that his readers will be a carefully controlled and closed community. He knows that only his intended recipients read his letters. Gerard explains that he writes the letters in orange juice rather than lemon juice because lemon juice "comes out just as well with water or heat. If the paper is taken out and dried, the writing disappears but it can be read a second time when it is moistened or heated again." Orange juice, by contrast, "cannot be read with water. . . . Heat brings it out, but it stays out. So a letter in orange juice cannot be delivered without the recipient knowing whether or not it has been read" (119). The code limits the membership of the community not only because it is in orange juice but also because it is in writing. Gerard's certainty about the readership of even his charcoal letters is conveniently increased by his realization that his warder, whom he pays to deliver them, cannot read. Perhaps unintentionally, Gerard reminds us that the social boundaries of his recusant community are as strict as its religious ones. The warder's illiteracy separates him from almost every Catholic Gerard mentions in the *Autobiography*, just as his willingness to take greater and greater risks for their ever-increasing bribes highlights the disparity between their financial resources and his own. Gerard's initial failure even to consider the possibility that his warder cannot read may indicate the insularity of his social experience. The recipients of his letters, his Catholic hosts, his converts, the communicants to whom he administers the Spiritual Exercises, and presumably his Jesuit readers are all members, not only of the recusant community, but of the upper class.

The case of John Arden demonstrates the two kinds of literacy required for inclusion in the recusant community. Arden, a Catholic gentleman confined to the Tower at the same time as Gerard, is able to read Gerard's charcoal message (as the warder cannot), but until he learns to read the orange juice code, face-to-face communication and shared religious ceremony are impossible. Gerard laments that "[d]uring my confinement in the Tower I was allowed no visitors and it was impossible therefore to deal directly with souls. I was able to do something, however, by correspondence, but only in the case of people I could trust not to reveal my secret arrangements for writing and receiving letters" (122). The secrecy that makes the code effective also limits its applications. Gerard can direct and confirm the spiritual lives only of those whose religious conviction and loyalty are already well established. With John Arden, however, it is not certainty of conviction—Arden has endured a long imprisonment for his faith—but comprehension of the code that is lacking. Unable "to deal directly with souls," Gerard specifically laments that he cannot say Mass by himself. Eventually Gerard realizes that he can see Arden's window from his cell and hopes that he might bribe his warder to allow them to visit. At first, however, Arden does not understand Gerard's secret communication. Although Gerard mimes to him how to hold the letter up to the fire to expose the writing, Arden misses the point: "My letter was taken and delivered, but the gentleman wrote nothing back as I had asked him to do. The next day, when he came out on the roof, he thanked me by signs, holding up in his hands the cross I had sent him" (129). Once again, the cross serves as an occasion for communication and the formation of personal ties; Gerard's purpose in sending such packets is not the distribution of his orange-peel handiwork. Through a more detailed pantomime, Gerard finally succeeds in conveying to Arden how to read the letter. In Arden's reply, Gerard says, "he said that the first time he thought I wanted him to burn the paper, because I had scribbled a few words in pencil on it, and he had done this" (129). Shared knowledge of the code, in addition to more extravagant bribing of the warder, allows the two men to meet and celebrate Mass. Gerard also uses his contact with Arden to extend his network of circulation by having Arden's wife conceal the items necessary for celebrating Mass in the clean laundry she brings her husband.

Like relics and shrines, Catholic priests were displaced from central sites of worship and had to be distributed among the members of the community for safekeeping. Gerard also uses patterns of circulation to reassert the centrality of the Jesuit priest in Catholic life. The letters from the Tower make Gerard a command center for both spiritual advice and tactical maneuvering. The relics on Gerard's list are passed through the hands of priests and distributed among the Catholic community by permission of the superior. In addition, in the story of William Wiseman, Gerard uses the particular route by which a Catholic object is circulated to insist upon his role as a spiritual director. Imprisoned "for three or four months," during which "neither his wife nor any friends were allowed near him," Wiseman writes a "notable work" entitled *A Triple Farewell to the World or Three Deaths in Different States of the Soul* (87). In some respects, Wiseman's circulation of the book resembles Gerard's circulation of letters from the Tower; the book is intended to maintain Wiseman's connection with a carefully defined community of readers. Wiseman "made it clear that the books were not for the general public: he had in mind first his own household, his wife, and his children, and, in the second place, his friends and relatives" (89). Gerard, however, distinguishes this particular network of circulation with an important detail: "as he completed each part he sent it to me to look over and correct any mistakes in doctrine" (89). Wiseman, a layman, writes a book of spiritual advice to other laypeople, but the pattern of its circulation makes Gerard a kind of authoritative central filter through which the book's content must pass. This story is also distinctive for Gerard's uncharacteristic attention to the content of the book, perhaps because its subject matter clearly reinforces the importance of the relationship forged by its circulation. Gerard outlines each part of the book in detail; its purpose is to impress upon the reader the necessity of accepting a Jesuit as one's spiritual director. He summarizes: "[H]e described the ideal spiritual guide in such detail that no doubt was left in the reader's mind that he meant a Jesuit, or, failing a Jesuit, a priest who was friendly to the Jesuits and sought their advice in his own difficulties" (88). Wiseman's practice of circulating the book through Gerard exemplifies and maintains the spiritual relationship between layperson and priest that the book itself extols.

Gerard cannot so elaborately describe the mechanisms through which illicit information, illicit objects, and even illicit priests are circulated among the Catholic community without acknowledging the constant and very real dangers that Jesuit missionaries face. Once again, a relic from Gerard's list helps illustrate his response to the special concerns of his Jesuit audience. Tucked between the accounts of Christ's thorn and St. Thomas's skull, the reader finds Gerard's history of Father Sutton's forefinger, which, according to the translator's note, was actually Sutton's thumb. The story demonstrates the same interest in veneration and circulation as the stories that frame it. This particular relic, though, presents a separate set of problems and pressures. Gerard writes:

> Two of these relics are old ones and were rescued from the pillage of a monastery. . . . The third is a forefinger of the martyr, Father Robert Sutton, the brother of the priest I mentioned on the first page of this

> book. By a wonderful providence of God this finger, together with the thumb, was preserved from decay, although the whole arm had been pinned up to be eaten by birds. When some Catholics came to remove it secretly (it had been exposed for a whole year) they found nothing but bones. The only parts still covered with flesh and skin were the thumb and finger which had been anointed with sacred oil at ordination and had been sanctified by the touch of the Blessed Sacrament. His brother, another good priest, kept the thumb in his possession and presented me with the forefinger. (49–50)

Here Gerard displays his customary concerns by documenting both the Catholics who rescued the relic in secret and the priest who preserved it and passed part of it on. Immediately, however, he separates this relic from the other three. This relic is not an "old one." The martyr in question is not Christ, or Thomas à Becket, or St. Vita, all of whom, whatever religious zeal they may inspire, died in past eras. Instead, Gerard possesses part of the violently fragmented body of a contemporary whose calling and history are remarkably similar to his own. Robert Sutton was martyred in 1587,[17] just one year before Gerard returned to England as a Jesuit missionary, and although Gerard probably did not know Sutton, he was tutored by one of Sutton's brothers, William. Like so many of Gerard's Catholic objects, the forefinger is doubly legible; it points at once toward the danger of Gerard's own situation and toward a historically established tradition of martyrdom. By relating the martyr to a figure in his own autobiography, Gerard jolts us from the sweeping scope of world history to the narrow, intimate scope of his personal story. At the same time, by including Sutton on a list of relic sources that includes Christ, Thomas à Becket, and Saint Vita, Gerard writes the violence of Elizabethan England directly into the history of Christian sainthood and martyrology. Notably, Sutton's digit is the only item on Gerard's list explicitly connected with a miracle, a detail that suggests Gerard's desire to assure the reader that Sutton really belongs in such illustrious company. To establish this contemporary priest among the ranks of traditional martyrs and saints, Gerard attempts to prove that Sutton really was, in Geary's words, "a special friend of God." These two possible readings of the finger can be logically extended to an iteration of the *Autobiography*'s message: English Catholicism is indestructible. Sutton's execution exterminates a priest, but it generates a martyr and a relic. The very blow that is intended to destroy Catholic tradition succeeds only in reinvigorating it.

The account of Sutton's forefinger suggests a practical, almost therapeutic purpose for the relic that it could not have served in medieval England when Catholicism was the dominant religion. Although contemplating the remains of a long-dead saint may have inspired compassion, English recusants must have identified uncomfortably with the victims of contemporary executions. Geary indicates that such a sense of close identification with the victim was not always part of the relic's devotional operation. He explains that after the mid-eighth century "[t]he most important donor of relics was, of course, the pope, who had at his disposal the vast treasury of the Roman catacombs, containing the remains of the early Roman martyrs."[18] In addition, relics did not necessarily have to be the result of a holy person's violent death: "With the toleration and support of Christianity in the Roman Empire beginning in the early fourth century, the production of martyrs ended. . . . Almost all the holy persons of the following centuries were those who lived heroic lives as friends of God rather than died heroic deaths."[19] Sutton's digit can offer Gerard neither the calming contemplation of a peaceful end nor the comfort of a few hundred years' distance. Sutton's execution looms not only as a grisly memory of the very recent past but as a constant possibility for Gerard's own future. To compare Gerard and Sutton is inevitable, and while the logical comparison of the conclusion may disturb even the modern reader, it must have been extremely disconcerting to the Jesuits, perhaps potential missionaries, reading Gerard's text. Precisely at moments when such connections become unavoidable, Catholic objects become the points of transfer between the history of an individual and the broader history of Catholic tradition that includes martyrs and saints, beginning with Christ himself.

By according the victims of contemporary executions the status and power of martyrs, Gerard makes his personal connections to them the source of comfort rather than of disconcerting identification. Using relics and devotional objects, Gerard reinforces his connections to these figures rather than seeking to distance himself from them. In the Tower of London, Gerard's imprisonment in the late Father Henry Walpole's cell provides a striking instance of comparison between Gerard and a contemporary victim of state violence. Gerard writes:

> The next morning I walked round my cell. In its dim light I found the name of the blessed Father Henry Walpole cut with a chisel on the wall. Then, close to it, I discovered his little oratory, where there had been a narrow window. . . . [T]here on either side he had chalked the names of

> all the orders of Angels. At the top, above the Cherubim and Seraphim, was the name of Jesus; above that again the name of God written in Latin, Greek, and Hebrew characters. It was a great comfort to me to find myself in a place sanctified by this great and holy martyr, and in the room where he had been tortured so many times—fourteen in all, as I have heard. (104–5)

Here the material presence of Walpole's writing allows Gerard to move from Walpole the Elizabethan priest and now-dead prisoner to Walpole the martyr. Gerard evokes Walpole as a living prisoner, cutting his name with a chisel and chalking the names of the orders of angels. He thus invites the reader to imagine both himself, reading the wall, and Walpole, writing on it, in the same space. As it links Gerard and his predecessor, the writing places Gerard on the same path that led Walpole to the executioner's block.

Despite the threat that this connection implies, the writing that conjures up the specter of Walpole as a prisoner becomes a sacred object that allows Gerard to transform the cell into a shrine "sanctified" by Walpole the "great and holy martyr." Just as Gerard uses Sutton's forefinger as a way of bringing Sutton's execution into the martyr tradition, he uses Walpole's writing to insert Walpole into the same tradition. Geary writes of earlier saints and holy men: "Even after his physical death, the power of the holy man remained in the places where he had lived and died."[20] As evidence of Walpole's presence, the writing transforms the space, and its power to do so in turn proves Walpole's own holiness and power. Transferred from Walpole's cell, Gerard voluntarily returns to it as often as possible to pray. When he is led from his cell to be examined concerning the whereabouts of Father Henry Garnet and subsequently tortured, he tells his jailer, "I am ready . . . but just let me say an *Our Father* and *Hail Mary* downstairs" (106). At the moment he faces the same torture that Walpole suffered, he seeks to connect himself to Walpole rather than to separate their fates. Making Walpole a martyr transforms this connection from a reminder of Gerard's own imminent suffering into a "great comfort."

Telling the story retrospectively, Gerard cannot fail to realize the obvious parallels he encourages the reader to draw between himself and Walpole. Some of Walpole's writings, passed on to Gerard, reify this relationship. Before Walpole was executed at York, "he wrote out in his own hand an account of a discussion he had with some ministers there. Part of it was given to me later with some meditations on the passion of Christ which he wrote in prison before his own passion." Like Sutton's forefinger and the orange juice letters from the Tower, this writing contains two messages, one of which was legible only to one familiar with recent Catholic history. Gerard's use of the verb *wrote* here reflects the two registers on which the letter functions. It refers both to the physical act of recording words on paper—Gerard specifies that the account is "in his own hand"—and the intellectual act of composing ideas: "an account of a discussion." Because Walpole had been tortured and had nearly lost the use of his hands (a fate that awaited Gerard himself): "I was hardly able to read what he had written, not only because he wrote in haste, but because his hand could barely form the letters. It looked like the writing of a schoolboy, not that of a scholar or gentleman" (105). While the writing is not the actual by-product of an execution, as Sutton's forefinger is, its physical qualities provide evidence of the violence done to Walpole's body. In the letter, Gerard reads of Walpole scarred and degraded by torture. Because Gerard knew firsthand the method of Walpole's torture—he fashioned his orange-peel crosses and rosaries as rehabilitating "finger exercises" (117)—the writing communicated to him a specific series of events that its content did not. Yet if Gerard read of Walpole's physical fate in the appearance of the writing, he used its content to interpret that fate spiritually, connecting Walpole's suffering to that of Christ, a point driven home by the repetition of the word *passion*.

Gerard's detailed knowledge of Walpole's life enabled him to understand the story told by the "schoolboy" quality of the writing, but it also allowed him to supply his readers with a fuller account of Walpole's intellectual and moral qualities—a story the writing does not tell: "Yet he was a courtier before Campion's execution and while he was still a layman wrote some beautiful English verses in his honour, telling how the martyr's blood had brought warmth into his life and many others' too, inspiring them to follow the more perfect way of Christ's counsels" (105). The most disturbing implications of Walpole's writing become the occasion for a narrative shift from Walpole's death to his life, from the writing as a physical manifestation of violence to an artifact revered for its spiritual associations. Gerard's semantics at this point reflect the change. *Wrote* here refers only to composition; there can be little doubt that the verses are "beautiful" because of the aesthetic qualities and religious content of the poetry rather than the handwriting. Gerard again gestures toward the martyr tradition by connecting Walpole to Campion, whose execution also takes on a double valence. His "blood" is simultaneously a physical and a spiritual substance. It marks the violent physical death that made him a martyr but also imparts spiritual "warmth" and vitality to the Catholic community.

If Gerard's readers were mainly Jesuits and Jesuit novices, his desire to respond to the dangers faced by priests makes sense. But hosts, converts, and Catholic abettors of any sort also faced financial punishment, imprisonment, and death. Gerard acknowledges this danger by reminding his readers that if execution was not a fate reserved for priests alone, neither was glorious martyrdom. In addition to paying homage to the martyred priests, Gerard includes the martyrdom accounts of two laypeople. In each case, Gerard translates his personal connection to the martyr into concrete objects that allow him, and by extension his readers, to derive comfort rather than fear from their own identification with the victims. While Gerard never refers to these objects as relics, he does accord them reliclike status by framing them with the story of the martyr's sentencing and death. Gerard's method in these accounts is chronological but not entirely logical. The narration of the martyr's death is interrupted by Gerard's description of the objects. Although these objects are not fragmented body parts and do not themselves carry any evidence of the martyr's execution or torture, Gerard embeds them in the context of the violent event, as though they were products of the execution itself.

Gerard's story about the martyr John Rigby, one of his own converts, contains a particularly uneasy note resulting from Gerard's awareness that Rigby not only was sentenced to death for a conversion that Gerard himself helped to effect but also was insufficiently instructed in how to withstand examination. Gerard writes: "He had been told that it was always sinful not to confess the Catholic faith and he may not have known that it was lawful to throw the burden of proof on the prosecution, as Catholics who are wise to it do" (80). Gerard begins the story of Rigby's death with his miracle-studded sentencing: "He heard the sentence with great joy, and while it was being pronounced, the chains in which he stood bound before the court, came loose and fell from his legs. The gaoler replaced them, but (I think I am right) they fell a second time" (80). He then interrupts the story of Rigby's martyrdom with a detailed description of the objects left him by the martyr. The first is a letter from Rigby "full of thanks for my making him a Catholic and helping him (it was ever so slightly) to that state of soul which he hoped would soon be made perfect by God." The second is one of the martyr's own belongings, which becomes, if not a relic, a kind of reliquary: "He sent me also his purse which I still have and use to this day in the martyr's honour—I carry my reliquary in it." Without transition, Gerard returns to the story of Rigby's death, telling how the martyr was "drawn to execution on the hurdle" (81). Gerard's narration follows a similar pattern in the story of Anne Line, a widow who helped Gerard manage one of the houses he established in London. Again the description of certain objects obtrudes into the story of her death: "Back in prison she sent, a short time before her execution, a letter to Father Page, the priest who had escaped at the time she was caught. I have the letter with me now." She also leaves Gerard "a large finely wrought cross of gold" (85) and her bed.

Far from deemphasizing his connection to these martyrs or attempting to avoid an uncomfortable sense of identification, Gerard uses objects to insist upon the closeness of these relationships. Gerard takes the letter from Rigby as an opportunity to iterate his role in converting Rigby to the Catholic faith. Although the letter from Mistress Line was originally written to Father Page, Gerard inserts, "Three times she mentioned me in the letter, referring to me as her Father" (85). Gerard invests these objects with the traditional curative and protective qualities of the relic. A connection to Rigby is a connection to God: "Thus this holy man went to heaven where I trust he intercedes for his unworthy Father in Christ" (81). Although Mistress Line bequeaths Gerard her bed, he is able to obtain only her coverlet, which, Gerard says, "I used afterwards whenever I was in London and felt safer under its protection" (85). Geary asserts that such powers had long been attributed to relics: "[R]elics *were* the saints, continuing to live among men. They were available sources of supernatural power for good or ill, and close contact with them or possession of them was a means of participating in that power."[21] Keith Thomas adds, "Holy relics became wonder-working fetishes, believed to have the power to cure illness and protect against danger."[22] Gerard used these objects to prove his close connection to the martyr, then attributed to the object the traditional qualities and powers of the relic. In this way, he transformed his relationships with these martyrs into a source of protection and comfort rather than a reminder of the threat inherent in the very existence of a contemporary relic.

Geary discusses the practice of enclosing *authenticae,* or records of a relic's history, in reliquaries and tombs.[23] Returning to Gerard's list of four relics—Christ's thorn, Sutton's forefinger, St. Thomas's skull, and St. Vita's bone—we might read his brief descriptions as a type of *authenticae* for the sacred objects he contains and preserves in the lines of his text. Rather than striving for "positive recognition of the relics' authenticity,"[24] though, Gerard's *authenticae* record not only the preservation of sacred objects but the preservation of a community. In this list alone, a potential Jesuit missionary might read brief histories not only of the relics but of recusant faith in Reformation England. He might deduce what would await him on his arrival in England: a vital and interconnected Catholic community in need of Jesuit guidance, as well as the possibility of a glorious martyrdom. Gerard writes that when he landed in England in November 1588, the Earl of Leicester "had sworn that by the end of the year there would be no Catholic left in the country" (8). The rest of his *Autobiography* sets out to prove the impossibility of such a project. For Gerard, English Catholics are not the anachronistic remnants of a dying community, and the Jesuit martyrs have not died in the service of a futile cause. Instead, he exhorts his readers to undertake a mission "for the greater glory of God and the good of many souls" (9). In the *Autobiography* the preservation, veneration, and circulation of Catholic objects are actions that point beyond themselves to the people that perform them. And because Gerard can use the treatment of objects as an index of a community's faith, he can also assert, through a list of four relics, that a Jesuit landing in England, far from facing certain failure, can anticipate a plentiful supply of devout and receptive Catholic souls.

Notes

1. John Gerard, *The Autobiography of a Hunted Priest*, trans. Philip Caraman (New York: Pellegrini and Cudahy, 1952), 49–50. Subsequent page citations are given parenthetically in the text.

2. Patrick J. Geary, *Living with the Dead in the Middle Ages* (Ithaca: Cornell University Press, 1994), 202.

3. Ibid., 201.

4. Ibid., 205.

5. Keith Thomas, *Religion and the Decline of Magic* (New York: Charles Scribner's Sons, 1971), 53.

6. "The First Henrician Injunctions, 1536," in *Documents of the English Reformation*, ed. Gerald Bray (Minneapolis: Fortress Press, 1994), 176.

7. "The Second Henrician Injunctions, 1538," in Bray, *Documents*, 181.

8. Ibid., 180.

9. Thomas, *Religion*, 62.

10. Richard Montagu, *A New Gagg for the New Gospell? No: A New Gagg for an Old Goose* (1624; reprint, Norwood, NJ: Walter J. Johnson, 1975), 231.

11. Eamon Duffy, *The Stripping of the Altars: Traditional Religion in England, 1400–1580* (New Haven: Yale University Press, 1992), 390.

12. Ibid., 414.

13. Geary, *Living with the Dead,* 202.

14. According to the translator's footnote, Thomas Percy, the Earl of Northumberland, was beheaded at York in 1572 (Gerard, *Autobiography,* 39 n.).

15. John S. Roberts, "The Rosary in Elizabethan England," *Month* 218 (1964): 192.

16. Ibid., 192.

17. According to the "The Modern Official List of Martyrs" published by the Catholic Record Society, *Unpublished Documents Relating to the English Martyrs,* vol. 1, *1584–1603,* ed. John Hungerford Pollen (London: J. Whitehead and Son, 1908), 10.

18. Geary, *Living with the Dead,* 209.

19. Ibid., 201.

20. Ibid., 165.

21. Ibid., 202.

22. Thomas, *Religion,* 26.

23. Geary, *Living with the Dead,* 203–4.

24. Ibid., 204.

9

The English Colleges and the English Nation

Allen, Persons, Verstegan, and Diasporic Nationalism

Mark Netzloff

Discussing English Catholic culture in the context of English nationhood would seem to bring together diametrically opposed categories, a perception that has only been reinforced by recent critical work on the early modern English nation. Richard Helgerson's *Forms of Nationhood*, for instance, analyzes English Catholic culture solely in terms of the Elizabethan period's memory of Marian Catholicism, thereby relegating this community to the English nation's past.[1] In a corollary argument, Linda Colley's *Britons* emphasizes Catholic culture's foreign provenance, situating it primarily as an external threat that roused nationalist sentiment in the eighteenth century.[2] As these groundbreaking studies so valuably reveal, anti-Catholicism played a crucial role in the formation of English national identity. Nonetheless, by focusing solely on anti-Catholic texts, as well as omitting any reference to recusant or expatriate writers, both Helgerson and Colley reiterate the exclusion of English Catholic culture from representations of the national community. As Alison Shell has noted, "[A]bsent from these discussions has been a consideration, or even a consciousness, of the other side: how English Catholics' experience of diaspora, combined with the necessity to re-evangelize a nation from overseas, shaped their ideas of nationhood."[3] Qualifying Shell's insightful point, however, my own argument is concerned less with recuperating an alternative or oppositional English Catholic "side" than with emphasizing the multiple and competing narratives of English nationhood that vied for authority in the early modern period. Catholics, too, participated in this struggle to define the nation, demonstrating how early modern English nationhood can be more productively conceptualized as a locus of identification ("Englishness"), one that was open to contestation and reimagining, rather than as a stable or monolithic entity ("*the* English nation") that could be dominated by any particular community.[4]

As Helgerson argues, one of the distinctive features of early modern English nationhood was a sense of the nation's territorial integrity, an emphasis upon the land itself as a consummate embodiment of Englishness.[5] Taken in these terms, the bond between the English nation and many early modern Catholics would seem to have been irrevocably severed. Their experience, instead, was one of diaspora, of continental migration and exile, a position marked by distance from an English homeland as well as opposition to the nation's dominant Protestant culture. Following the Elizabethan settlement, English Catholics, unable to complete degrees at Oxford and Cambridge, often chose to study at the seminaries formed by English Catholic exiles on the Continent.[6] The first English College, begun by William Allen at Douai (1568), was quickly joined by others: Owen Lewis, a Welsh canon lawyer, founded the English College in Rome (1576), while Robert Persons established several institutions, including seminaries at Valladolid (1589) and Seville (1592), as well as a preseminary school at St. Omer (1593).[7] The colleges were initially constituted on the basis of an academic program rather than an activist one; however, in the wake of Pius V's papal bull *Regnans in Excelsis* (1570)—which excommunicated Elizabeth I and implicitly called on English Catholics to depose their monarch—one of their primary tasks became the training of missionary priests for their return to England, efforts that accelerated under Allen and Persons's leadership of the English mission (beginning in 1580). Rather than severing ties to the English nation, diasporic English Catholics appropriated—and at other times contested—paradigms of English nationhood, and the seminaries occupied a unique position as extranational institutions attempting to intervene in English political life and the public sphere.[8] English authorities, however, interpreted this diasporic activism as a violation of national integrity, a threat to the nation's cultural boundaries as well as to the state's sovereignty.

Despite their political significance, the English Colleges have received only marginal attention in critical discussions of early modern English Catholic culture. In his introduction to *The English Catholic Community, 1570–1850*, John Bossy justifies his exclusion of Catholic expatriates from his study, arguing that exile placed this group in a separate tradition, as part of "Catholicisms of the continent," rather than in any relation to English history; he therefore mentions the English Catholic diaspora only as "it contributed directly to the history of the community in England."[9] Bossy rightly underscores the distinctiveness of early modern Catholic communities—whether those residing in England, Wales, Scotland, or Ireland, or those living in diaspora on the Continent or in the colonies. Nonetheless, he fails to consider the porous boundaries and pervasive interconnections between these communities and, as a result, reinforces a sense of English exceptionalism (albeit English *Catholic* exceptionalism). Caroline Hibbard, in a suggestive departure from Bossy's analysis, has stressed the need for historians and literary critics to devote greater attention to the international character of English Catholicism.[10] This essay takes up Hibbard's proposal, exploring the ways that Catholic polemical texts written from the position of continental diaspora offered their own formulations of English identity. In contrast to Helgerson's and Colley's implicit alignment of Protestantism with English nationhood, and in contradiction of Bossy's framework of an insular English Catholic experience, I argue that the writing of the English nation was also generated by its Catholic margins, and, moreover, that it was the experience of diaspora that enabled—rather than precluded—Catholic participation in constructions of nationhood.

This essay examines the distinct forms of national identity articulated by three key figures of the English Catholic diaspora: William Allen, Robert Persons, and Richard Verstegan. In his defense of the English Colleges, Allen reclaims the status of seminarians as loyal English subjects in exile, asserting a discourse of rights to defend their seeking refuge on the Continent. Endorsing a more activist stance than Allen, Persons's account of the English Colleges at Seville and Valladolid counters insular expressions of English identity by representing the seminaries as the inheritors of transcultural links with European nations. In contrast to the writings of Allen and Persons, my final example, Verstegan's antiquarian text *A Restitution of Decayed Intelligence in*

Antiquities, posits an essentialist model of cultural identity, counterbalancing the English Catholic community's own history of diaspora with a racialized embodiment of nationhood.

John Bossy and J. C. H. Aveling have characterized the English Colleges as conservative, traditional academic institutions that nonetheless progressively, and perhaps inadvertently, became the centers of activist political thought during the early years of the English mission.[11] However, this gradualist narrative does not give sufficient credit to the innovativeness, as well as surprising modernity, of the arguments raised by polemicists of the Catholic diaspora. In my analysis of selected texts by Allen, Persons, and Verstegan, I wish to mark a transition in the ways that these diasporic writers imagined national identity, a movement from a transnational, cosmopolitan activism, one that Benedict Anderson has recently described as an identity deriving from an "unbound seriality," to a national consciousness based on a "bound seriality." In the former paradigm, communal identity is distinguished by its "universal grounding," an awareness of connection to the struggles of other communities that takes into account the multiple determinants through which identity is constructed. By contrast, the latter case, of "bound seriality," is predicated by an "identitarian conception of ethnicity," an assertion of a monolithic, racial core to a community's identity, one that is held to remain unchanged despite circumstances of migration and diaspora.[12]

Underlying their inherent differences, however, these two poles of national identification share a common feature: both are often formulated by diasporic groups displaced from their original or imagined cultural location, a phenomenon that Anderson terms "long-distance nationalism."[13] While contemporary globalization has made this phenomenon more pervasive, Anderson notes the longer history of diasporic nationalism; his analysis begins, in fact, with the example of Mary Rowlandson and late-seventeenth-century settlers in New England, demonstrating how the early modern period can inform our own era of globalization. For early modern English Catholics, geographic dislocation from the English nation was compounded by an ideological rift from its dominant Protestant culture, yet it was precisely these forms of distance that enabled them to imagine England as a nation: "[E]xile," as John Dalberg-Acton remarked, "is the nursery of nationality."[14] However, the circumstances of travel and diaspora irrevocably altered the cultural position of English Catholic exiles, producing a hybridized identity that is reflected in descriptions of the Catholic expatriate community, from Anthony Munday's

English Roman Life to James Wadsworth's *English Spanish Pilgrime*.[15] Due to the syncretic qualities of their cultural identity, seminarians and other Catholic exiles assumed an anomalous position, one at odds with the homogeneity that increasingly defined expressions of English nationhood, including even the forms of Englishness posited by English Catholics themselves. Thus the hyphenated components of this identity—English *and* Roman, English *and* Spanish—attest to the overlapping, serialized, but also conflicting bonds that shape the articulation of national identities.

The experience of many Catholics in early modern England was characterized by travel, as well as internal displacement, for the active persecution of Catholic priests necessitated an existence of incognito migration from safe house to protective country estate. Early modern Catholic culture was thus inextricably linked with travel, a "traveling culture," to use James Clifford's terminology.[16] As Julian Yates notes in his analysis of the itinerant paths taken by missionary priests, "[T]o be a Catholic was to have a particular relationship to space, to England and its borders," quite often one that was "a tale of travel, of flight, return and concealment."[17] Appropriately, many statutes enforced against English Catholics were also intended to regulate internal and overseas travel. Catholics were listed alongside other suspect itinerant groups and targeted in antivagrant legislation, efforts that attempted to control the movement of Catholics within the realm,[18] while statutes limiting unlicensed foreign travel were often directed against seminarians and missionary priests as well as the importation of Catholic texts and paraphernalia.[19] The English Colleges were similarly associated with emerging networks of European travel: William Allen describes how many Englishmen had converted to Catholicism and enrolled in the colleges while touring the Continent, a claim that Lewis Owen, in his exposé of the English Colleges, cites as evidence of the ways that the seminaries preyed upon vulnerable English travelers.[20] Owen also refers to how missionary priests would mask their identities by disguising themselves as fashionable travelers, thereby blurring even further the distinctions between Catholics and other English travelers.[21]

As a consequence of English priests' missionary work, the travels of the English Catholic diaspora extended far beyond Europe as well. As Aveling notes, although the colleges ordained as many as eight hundred priests by 1603, a large number of seminarians never returned to England: some students died during their course of study, and others were deemed unfit, while a sizable proportion of English students were enlisted in other missionary efforts.[22] In an example that attests to a triangular network linking Catholics in England and Europe with those in the American colonies, John Vincent, an English priest stationed at St. Antony village in Brazil, wrote on June 21, 1593, to his friend Richard Gibbon, a Jesuit priest at the English College at Madrid, requesting books dealing with the persecution of Catholics in England.[23] Vincent's letter reflects the global reach of English Catholic culture. Yet even though English Catholics were dispersed in areas ranging from England to Spain to Brazil, this diaspora was bound together by a group identity; after all, Vincent was essentially asking for news from "home." The fact that this information could only be channeled indirectly—and through the English Colleges—demonstrates how these institutions provided a conduit for news and intelligence, in addition to serving as a center for the printing and dissemination of polemical literature.[24] Vincent's letter, in fact, requests that Gibbons send some of this published material to Brazil so that Vincent can circulate evidence of Protestant abuses against Catholics in England.[25]

The effect of travel on national allegiance and identity was one of the main concerns of a series of three royal proclamations issued between 1580 and 1582. These documents, which codified the status of the English Colleges as outlawed, alien institutions, correlated the Catholic diaspora with England's vulnerability to foreign invasion. The first proclamation (July 15, 1580) was prompted by reports of a Catholic conspiracy to invade England and restore Catholicism under Mary Stuart. Initially, this document imposes an ambiguous distinction between "such rebels and traitors as do live in foreign parts" and other exiles and seminarians, who "refusing to live here in their natural country . . . have wandered from place to place, and from one prince's court to another" (2:469).[26] Travel becomes metonymically linked with treason: to wander outside the English nation carries with it the risk of transgressing "natural" boundaries of allegiance, of being transformed from traveler to expatriate rebel. Yet the errant mobility of travelers, seminary students, and other temporary exiles also distinguishes this group from those who are settled, geographically and ideologically, in their resolve against England. A subsequent proclamation (January 10, 1581) therefore attempted to reclaim those "good and faithful subjects" who, through their travel and educations abroad, "have been thereby perverted" from "natural duties" to church and nation (2:482). One key stipulation called for families and guardians to provide authorities with the names of any family members living abroad, further mandating that they recall their children home within the space of four months. While intending to organize the national community as an aggregate of loyal households, this effort established a censuslike surveillance over Catholic families: those who did not come forward to be enumerated voluntarily, the proclamation stipulated, would be subject to unspecified penalties. However, the ultimate failure of these legislative efforts was illustrated by a third proclamation (April 1, 1582), which demanded that seminarians return within three months, an ultimatum issued a full year after the lapse of the previous deadline. Composed in the wake of Edmund Campion's execution the previous December, the proclamation testifies to the increasingly hard-line position adopted by the English state in response to the efforts of the English mission. Consequently, it evidences a greater concern for the travel of seminary priests within England than for the geographic mobility of subjects abroad. Significantly, though, the proclamation collapses distinctions between seminary priests in England and Catholic expatriates, condemning both as "traitors."[27]

This series of royal proclamations prompted William Allen to compose *An apologie and trve declaration of the institution and endeuours of the two English Colleges* (1581), a text that embraced the association of Catholic exiles with the "errors" of travel: whereas Elizabeth's proclamation of January 1581 had cast seminary priests as "vagrant counterfeit persons" (2:489), Allen redeems this characterization by noting a similar description of the apostles as "vagarants" *[sic]* in Corinthians 1:4 (sigs. L6v–L7).[28] Allen situates error, instead, with the physical and spiritual complacency of those who remain in England, a resistance to geographic travel that signals an underlying disinclination to engage in necessary spiritual "travail." Citing Augustine, he describes the pursuit of salvation as "the iustest cause to trauail" (sig. C7v), a point echoed in John Donne's "Satire III": "To stand inquiring right, is not to stray" (line 78).[29] As mentioned earlier, Allen even grants English travelers a key role in the founding of the English Colleges, noting that some of the earliest students were travelers who had experienced conversion during brief visits to the seminaries, events of "great and inexpected ioy" that would not have occurred if they "had taried in the English Vniuersities, or therwise had folowed the maner of our Countrie" (sig. D1). Despite his general praise of travel, however, Allen also reinforces the association of travelers with gossip and unlicensed news, a position that ironically reiterates Elizabethan anti-Catholic legislation: while Elizabeth's proclamations had targeted the "seditious" circulation of letters and pamphlets published on the Continent, he attributes negative reports of the English Colleges to "lewd trauailers" who "make vp a fardel of malicious slaunders and detractions of Popes and Princes, and vtter such seemly wares in their seditious sermons" (sigs. N2v–N3).[30]

In referring to an English "manner" supposedly abandoned by Catholic exiles, Allen is defining English identity in reference to custom and law, not in terms of an ethnically based cultural identity. Englishness, then, is constituted through adherence to English law, a loyalism that persists even in the context of exile and diaspora.[31] Taking issue with the July 1580 proclamation's assertion that seminarians have "fled into forraine partes and refuse to liue in our natural Countrie" (sig. A6), Allen dissevers loyalty to "publike authoritie" (sig. A5v) and "affection" to nation from geographic location; in his terms, exile enables dissent, not treason: "[W]e are not fugitiues," he declares, emphasizing that seminarians did not flee arrest in England or depart out of political protest but left only to preserve matters of conscience relating to religion (sig. B4v). In addition, given the recurring changes of state religion in recent English history, he anticipates an imminent Catholic restoration, after which time the clergy trained by the English Colleges will provide a necessary service to the state (sig. C4v). Allen dislodges theological debate from its association with political subversion, challenging Anglican officials to "a disputation" (sig. I1v) and calling for the free circulation of prohibited Catholic texts (sig. H2v).[32] He even forges a strategic alliance with nonconformists and other opponents of the Oath of Supremacy, offering these groups refuge in the English Colleges (sig. C7). Defending a right of conscience, Allen limits the power of the state to political matters: as he concludes, "there can be no iurisdiction ouer English mens soules" (sig. F4). Due to Elizabethan England's anomalous lack of religious toleration, which distinguished the nation from many regions of Europe as well as the Ottoman Empire and Persia (sig. A8v), the English Colleges provided a surrogate public sphere within the context of diaspora, a form of "action from a distance" necessitated by political realities.[33]

Although Allen has conventionally been viewed as a fairly conservative thinker, and more of a traditionalist than Robert Persons, his *Apologie* nonetheless shows his active engagement with contemporary politics, as with his defense of liberty of conscience and advocacy of an open national forum for theological debate.[34] His text also presciently recognizes the implications stemming from the emergence of a population of stateless, "displaced persons," or *Heimetlosen*, whom Hannah Arendt regards as emblematic of the upheavals of modernity. For Arendt, the right of asylum is the most fundamental and longest-standing obligation underlying international relations, a right she traces to classical precedents as well as the medieval principle of *Quid est in territorio est de territorio*. However, as twentieth-century European states increasingly refused to acknowledge the right of refuge, thereby producing a population of stateless minorities, the foundation of the state was transformed from one constituted as "an instrument of the law" to one serving, instead, as "an instrument of the nation."[35] Arendt's analysis of the social place of refugees has implications that resonate in periods prior to the twentieth century, and her critical framework helps situate the early modern English Catholic diaspora in a broader historical context in which the purview of citizenship became increasingly confined to the nation. In his defense of the English Colleges, Allen constructs Englishness on the basis of deterritorialized principles of law and social justice, forms of community not contingent upon the standard markers of nationhood: unconditional submission to the state, geographic residence, or ethnic origin.

Allen calls attention to the long history of English transcultural links with the Continent, especially Rome, noting the historical precedents in which the English have availed themselves of the right of refuge "in such like cases of distresse" (sig. B8v). However, in describing an "English Roman life," Allen emphasizes less the distinctiveness of English expatriate culture than Rome's central and traditional role as the exemplary site of sanctuary: Rome, he notes, has always served as "the citie of refuge and recourse of al Christians out of al Nations" (sig. C1). In his defense of English Catholics' right of refuge on the Continent, Allen counters the matrix of the nation with the cosmopolitan model of the "open city." Writing at a historical moment when the English state was constructing an unprecedented legal apparatus to ensure the exclusion of a sizable minority population, he legitimates the expatriate status of the Catholic diaspora by citing a paradigm—the city of refuge—that exemplifies the use of law as an instrument of social justice rather than repression.[36]

Whereas Allen treats the historical precedents and political implications of the Catholic diaspora, Robert Persons considers more fully the cultural effects of migration on English Catholic identity. Diverging from Allen's rights-based argument, Persons places a greater emphasis on questions of identity, thereby recognizing Catholic exiles' increasing distinctiveness from both their home and host nations. In his account of the English Colleges in two of his texts—*Newes from Spayne and Holland* (1593) and *A relation of the king of Spaines receiving in Valliodolid [sic]* (1592)—Persons depicts the seminaries as a community whose identity straddles English and European cultures. By associating these institutions with forms of cosmopolitanism and cultural hybridity, he provides a cultural model to offset the insularity that increasingly characterized English nationhood. Persons defends the activism of the colleges by stressing that their connections to Europe and the Spanish court actually preserve earlier transcultural traditions. His *Newes from Spayne and Holland* notes that the patron of the English College at Seville, Don Rodrigo de Castro y Quiñones, the archbishop and cardinal of Seville, was a descendant of the Dukes of Lancaster and therefore a figure embodying the legacies of medieval links between England and the Continent (sig. A6).[37] In addition, he acknowledges the growth of the seminaries out of preexisting English commercial ties to continental Europe, pointing out how the English Church of St. George in San Lucar (Sanlúcar de Barrameda), founded by English merchants, had recently been converted into a clerical residence (sig. A5). For Persons, the English Colleges do not subvert English traditions, as authorities would have it, but instead preserve and maintain them. As a point of contrast, he depicts the founding of the Church of England as an event that only weakened the nation by severing its alliances with the Continent. As he notes sarcastically, if England had become Lutheran, at least it would have had ties to German states (sig. D2v). The Protestant construction of the English nation, following Persons's argument, was ultimately based upon a debilitating foundation of isolationism and exceptionalism.

Both of Persons's texts describe entertainments provided by the English Colleges for visiting dignitaries from their host culture: *Newes from Spayne and Holland* chronicles Archbishop Castro's visit to the College at Seville, while *Relation of the king* discusses King Philip II's royal visit to St. Alban's College in August 1592.[38] The Seville entertainment takes place on the Feast of St. Thomas of Canterbury, an event that not only commemorates medieval Catholic England but also offers Becket as a model of political resistance to state power.[39] Persons extends this implication in *Relation of the king* by noting the presence of a descendant of another political martyr, Sir Thomas More, an unnamed figure who delivers a welcoming speech to King Philip.[40] The historical memory of Becket is further invoked in an emblem displayed by the students at Seville: entitled "the representation of the two persecutions by the two King Henryes of Ingland" (*Newes,* sig. B6v), this triptych juxtaposes images of Henry II, Henry VIII, and Elizabeth I, contrasting the penitent Henry II following Becket's murder with the unrepentant Henry VIII, "very fatt and furious" (sig. B7). In its third portrait, Elizabeth, described as the descendant of both Henries, is offered the motto, "*E duobus elige,* choose which you wil of thes two" (sig. B7v): "wishing her rather to follow the example of king Henry the second, that repented his sinnes, then king Henry the eight that died in the same" (sig. B8). In lieu of a single providential design underlying English national history, the entertainment foregrounds the multiple and competing narratives provided by the past, rendering the writing of a national future as a casuistical decision placed in the hands of political actors such as Queen Elizabeth.

Although Persons emphasizes how the seminaries preserve English Catholicism, as well as maintain traditional links with the Continent, his description of the college entertainments also marks the effects of migration and diaspora on English Catholic identity. In a sense, Persons moves from an elaboration of the *roots* of English Catholicism to a formulation of its *routes,* thereby acknowledging the ways that English Catholic culture had been transformed by its travels. The centerpiece of both entertainments is a series of speeches offered to the visiting dignitaries, presentations that are not delivered solely in the expected medium of Latin, or even the vernaculars of English or Spanish, but given, instead, in an impressive range of languages: Hebrew, Greek, Latin, English, Welsh, Scottish, French, Italian, Spanish, and Flemish. Persons notes the appropriateness of the fact that a community "dispersed in diuers contries and nations" should therefore "vtter in diuers languages" both in their sermons and in their published texts (*Relation of the king,* sigs. C1–C1v). In part, the multilingual training of the seminarians was necessary, due to the cultural range of their subsequent work as missionary priests. Yet this depiction also counters a recurring image of English travelers that highlighted their linguistic deficiencies, as in Shakespeare's *The Merchant of Venice* (1596), with Portia's characterization of her English suitor Lord Falconbridge, who, through his inability to converse in any language but English, is likened to a "dumb show" (1.2.73).[41] The pervasiveness of this stereotype is revealed by Persons's own noted surprise at the scholars' linguistic prowess, which, he comments, he would not have believed "if I had not seene and h[e]ard this my selfe" (*Newes,* sig. A8).

This multilingual performance also complicates the cultural positioning of the English Colleges. In his influential account of the history of nationalism, *Imagined Communities,* Benedict Anderson argues that the religious community, founded upon a unifying language such as Latin, was challenged and superseded by the territorial nation and a concomitant proliferation of writings in the vernacular.[42] However, the English Colleges do not conform to this paradigm of linguistic nationalism: Latin and English coexist and overlap in the seminarians' missionary work and publications, and English is not the sole, or even dominant, vernacular language. The equal status given to the Welsh language in Persons's text is a significant choice, as I will discuss later, given the relegation of Celtic cultures to a marginal position in the English mission. In contrast to many of his contemporaries, Persons recognizes the cultural diversity inherent in missionary efforts, noting the intention of Welsh students to return to preach in Wales (*Relation of the king,* sig. C5) and referring to the use of the Welsh language in published Catholic texts, including a grammar and a catechism (sig. C5).[43]

Extending Persons's analysis of the cultural effects of travel and exile on the identity of the Catholic expatriate community, Richard Verstegan draws on the experience of diaspora in an effort to locate the distinctive, immutable features of English identity.[44] Verstegan, an Antwerp-based English Catholic printer, polemicist, intelligence agent, and antiquarian, was one of the first writers to attribute Saxon and Germanic origins to the English nation. His antiquarian text *A Restitution of Decayed Intelligence in Antiquities* (1605) has been noted for its role in conferring a racial foundation to English identity.[45] The fact that it was a Catholic exile who helped perpetuate a Germanic myth of English identity would initially seem anomalous, if not inexplicable, but the racial essentialism underlying Verstegan's model of cultural identity is more intelligible when seen as a product of the English Catholic diaspora, part of a broader effort to counter the destabilizing effects of travel and migration on forms of community.

Verstegan's biography reflects the forms of displacement typifying the position of early modern English Catholics. Verstegan's grandfather and his family, Dutch refugees from the region of Guelderland, had settled in London sometime around 1500.[46] Verstegan published his first text, *The Post of the World* (1576), a guide for European travel translated from German, under the pseudonym Richard Rowlands, an anglicization of the middle name of his grandfather. Testifying to the unstable, hybrid cultural position he occupied, many accounts are unsure which name—Rowlands or Verstegan—was the writer's birth name and which was his alias.[47] His early years in England confirm his status as a fugitive subject: after having left Christ Church, Oxford, without taking a degree, a common practice for early modern Catholics, he was forced to flee England in 1582 to evade arrest for running a secret Catholic press in London.[48] A resident of Antwerp for the remainder of his life, Verstegan's departure for the Continent exemplifies how English Catholics' links with Europe were reinforced through migration and exile. Nevertheless, in spite of his family's Dutch origin, and his decades-long residence in the Spanish Netherlands, Verstegan insistently stresses his own Englishness. As he declares in his prefatory epistle to *A Restitution*, "[Y]et can I accompt my self of no other but of the English nation" (sigs. ++1–1v). The defensiveness of the initial word *yet* in this statement attests to how identification with the English nation offers Verstegan a stable foundation to offset the complexities of culture, language, and religion that define his own subject position. By rendering English culture as predominantly Saxon, and thus inherently Germanic, he attempts to subsume his own forms of difference within a historically grounded sameness.[49]

By tracing the Saxon influences on English culture in *A Restitution*, Verstegan counters images accentuating the insularity of English identity. He therefore rebuts narratives of cultural origin, such as the Brutus myth, and belittles efforts to derive English culture from an autochthonous source such as the Britons.[50] As Donna B. Hamilton remarks, "[H]e demonstrated that to be English was to be Saxon and Catholic and European,"[51] an unbound seriality that acknowledges the multiple affiliations that contribute to identity formation. Cultural identity, for Verstegan, is a product of historical change, one that derives, in particular, from historical patterns of migration and diaspora.[52] He supports this argument by opening his text with two key examples drawn from the furthest reaches of biblical prehistory: the migration of the sons of Noah and the dispersal of nations following the confusion of tongues at Babel (sigs. A1v, A3).[53] However, contradicting his earlier historical framework, Verstegan subsequently differentiates Germanic culture on the basis of three criteria of cultural purity: continual possession of its country, resistance to Roman conquest, and the "unmixed" character of the German language and people (sigs. F1v–F2). Moving away from a model of unbound seriality (English, but also Saxon, Catholic, and European), Verstegan extricates the Saxon origins of English culture from a broader, transnational history, positing an essential core to cultural identity—a bound seriality—that remains immutable, defying temporal change or spatial dislocation. For example, he counters the view of the English as a "mixed nation" by emphasizing the Germanic origin of invaders such as the Danes and Normans (sig. Aa2) and also minimizes the impact of the Norman invasion on English racial heritage, arguing that the cultural identity of this small group, whose influence was limited to the aristocracy, eventually disappeared altogether through assimilation and intermarriage with the English-Saxon population (sigs. Aa1–Aa2).

Verstegan's emphasis on the Saxon origins of English identity, and the racialism underlying this model, is intended to offer historical precedents for the activist politics of the Catholic diaspora. The preservation of Saxon culture following the imposition of Norman authority offers hope for the comparable durability of English Catholicism under Protestant rule. Tellingly, though, Verstegan does not fully articulate a rhetoric of a "Norman yoke" and therefore does not openly or directly endorse a policy of resistance. After all, he dedicates his text to King James, indicating his desire for a Catholic restoration through conversion rather than invasion. This pursuit of the king's favor reflects the agenda of a pro-Scottish faction among Catholic exiles, a group that had aspired to bring about James's conversion in the 1590s and was lobbying the monarch once more, albeit for the reduced goal of religious toleration, in the first years of his joint reign.[54] Verstegan's opening dedication to the king, which reminds James of his Saxon descent (sig. +2), would initially seem to reiterate the anti-Scottish rhetoric that followed James's accession to the English throne, reinforcing the perception of the Stuarts as irredeemably foreign. However, as Verstegan is careful to explain in his later discussion of the Norman invasion, the purity of the Saxon royal line was actually preserved through intermarriage with the Scottish dynasty, a fact that renders England's Scottish king more Saxon—and, ultimately, more English—than the English themselves (sigs. Z2v–Z3).[55] By anglicizing the Stuart dynasty, Verstegan differentiates the shared Saxon culture of the English and Scots from the British origins of the Welsh and Irish. Although he intends to provide a historical precedent for Anglo-Scottish union, he predicates this cultural alliance by differentiating a Saxon core culture from a British periphery. Not only does this framework of internal colonialism define cultural and national identity in terms of ethnicity rather than religion, but it also derogates regions with large Catholic populations, thereby undermining the possibility of pan-British Catholic unity.[56] As Christopher Highley has noted, "[T]he diverse expatriate communities cohered tenaciously along national and ethnic rather than confessional lines."[57]

The historical distinction Verstegan draws between English and British cultures was also maintained in the English seminaries on the Continent. The composite identity of these institutions—most often referred to as the *English*

Colleges—testifies to the creation of a homogenous national identification within the context of exile. A key example of this process is provided by Anthony Munday's *The English Roman Life* (1582) and its account of the rebellion of the English students at the college in Rome against their Welsh rector, Morys Clynog. Munday casts Clynog's preferment of Welsh students, as well as the successful efforts of the English students to replace him with Jesuit direction, exclusively in national terms. In establishing the college, Munday explains, the pope had mistakenly assumed the underlying similitude of English and Welsh students, "in that they came all out of one country."[58] Yet when the college's English students threaten to leave the seminary, prompting the intercession of the pontiff, Pope Gregory XIII ultimately sides with the English scholars, declaring that he has "made the Hospital for Englishmen, . . . and not for the Welshmen" (93). In a private audience with the group, he declares his admiration for the English students, whom he views as having forsaken their nation and forsworn allegiance to a heretical monarch (92). Because the Welsh lacked national sovereignty and were displaced within their own country, this statement insinuates that the Welsh scholars' own exile entailed less of a sacrifice. Like Pope Gregory, Munday elides the role of Welsh expatriates in the English College in Rome, although it was a Welshman, Owen Lewis, who had founded the seminary and appointed Clynog as rector in 1576, only three years prior to the events described in *The English Roman Life*. Munday also fails to recognize how Jesuit control actually served to radicalize the politics of the seminary, whose primary function thereafter was training students for the English mission. In fact, the English students had asked the Jesuits to intervene in order to help quell reports of internal dissent at the college, fearing that this information could reveal their names and thereby prevent their return to England as missionary priests.[59]

More than a century after Munday's account of "the national quarrel," this conflict between English and Welsh scholars was likened to earlier battles between the Saxons and Britons, a testament to the preservation, if not intensification, of the divisions marked by Verstegan and Munday.[60] The immediate aftermath of this episode also saw an increased level of ethnic identification among Welsh exiles, whose antipathy to English domination, coupled with their distance from home, motivated them to reassert the distinctiveness of their cultural identity and history. For example, Owen Lewis responded to the stirs in Rome in a letter to John Leslie, bishop of Ross and ambassador of Mary Stuart, imploring his Scottish colleague, "My lord, let us stick together, for we are the old and true inhabiters of the Isle of Britanny; these others be but usurpers and mere possessors."[61] In Lewis's formulation, the seminaries provided a refuge for "British" communities—Welsh and Scottish—displaced primarily not as an immediate result of the Reformation but as an effect of a longer history of internal colonialism.[62] Defending the English College as a Welsh enclave offered a chance to reestablish Welsh cultural autonomy within the environment of the continental seminary, thereby preserving the integrity of the Welsh as the aboriginal inhabitants of Britain. Other accounts of the Anglo-Welsh feud viewed cultural identity and history through the lens of class, stressing the antiquity of the Welsh nation as a way to elevate the status of Welsh students above that of their English counterparts. John Nicholls's *Iohn Niccols pilgrimage* (1581), for instance, depicts an argument between Welsh and English scholars in which national tensions are articulated through class-based insults: "I am a Gentleman quoth the one: thou art a rascall, quoth the other. The Welshman beginneth to fret and fume, and saith, albeit I came to Rome with broken & rent apparrell, yet I am borne of as good blood as thou art."[63] Here the Welsh student defends his ethnic and class positions by differentiating his diminished economic status from the legitimacy conferred by his "blood."

Contrary to the intentions of Lewis and others, the political activism of the Catholic diaspora, especially the English mission, increasingly came to be defined as an English project, one consisting primarily of missionary ventures in England—not Wales, Scotland, or Ireland—that was also dominated by English priests.[64] Allen, in his *Apologie,* had attempted to foreground the cosmopolitanism of English missionary projects, situating the English mission alongside other efforts in the East and West Indies. Ultimately, though, he too was forced to concede the nationalist sentiment motivating many seminary priests, who preferred to return to England rather than travel to other destinations. Likewise, Allen had to explain the incongruous absence of non-English priests in the mission, forcing him to argue, unconvincingly, that the number of English volunteers had rendered any additional recruits unnecessary.[65] Whereas Allen had clung to the cosmopolitan aspirations of the English mission, Verstegan's *Restitution* constructs a historical narrative that buttresses its nationalist implications, noting the role of English-Saxons in earlier missionary efforts on the Continent (sig. T2).[66] For Verstegan, the English mission offers the possibility to complete a historical circle by reversing the pattern of migration, bringing priests from the Continent to reconvert

England. However, both historical instances—Saxon missionary efforts and the English mission—are defined exclusively as English projects.[67] This anglicization of missionary activities marginalized European contexts and connections, a privileging of English Catholicism's English roots over its European routes.

The diasporic nationalism expressed by Verstegan ultimately proved to have far more historical influence than the cosmopolitanism advocated by Allen and Persons, an ascendency reflected in the later history of the English Colleges. When many of the seminaries and convents were dissolved at the time of the French Revolution, most of them subsequently relocated to England, where a few continue to this day, including Allen's Douai seminary, now Ushaw College, Durham, as well as Stonyhurst College, Lancashire, first established by Persons at St. Omer.[68] The fact that the seminarians received such a welcome reception upon their return marks a positive development, confirming as it does the diminished currency of anti-Catholic rhetoric in the early nineteenth century.[69] Nevertheless, the idea that the English Colleges "returned" or were "repatriated" to England bears further scrutiny: after all, not only does this framework elide their institutional history on the Continent, a period of more than two centuries, but it also overlooks the fact that the seminaries were indeed founded in Europe and therefore had no prior existence in England. The repatriation of the colleges demonstrates the historical consolidation of national identities over confessional, transcultural forms of affiliation; in a sense, Englishness trumped Catholicism, and the affective ties of nationhood proved more durable than religious divisions. This return to England also helped put an end to the activist politics of the Catholic diaspora, and afterwards the colleges settled into an academic and pastoral role far removed from the political engagement of Allen and Persons. The advances of repatriation, along with Catholic Emancipation in 1829, effectively foreclosed oppositional positions for the English Catholic community.

The English Colleges, like other European monastic institutions, had also fallen prey to the increasingly centralized authority of post-Enlightenment, secularized European nation-states.[70] In derogating the seminaries as vestiges of an antiquated, medieval past, these reform-minded Continental rulers—monarchs and republicans alike—could cast themselves, by contrast, as the agents of revolution, progress, and modernity. In some ways, such efforts entailed an appropriation of the political thought of the early modern English Catholic diaspora, a process that elided the modernity of their ideas in order to displace them, intellectually as well as geographically, as a community of lasting historical significance.

Notes

1. Richard Helgerson, *Forms of Nationhood: The Elizabethan Writing of England* (Chicago: University of Chicago Press, 1992), 249–68; see esp. 256–59 for a relevant discussion of the Protestant Marian exiles. Despite her sensitive attention to the bearing of post-Reformation religious culture on English nationhood, Claire McEachern similarly considers English Catholicism solely in terms of anti-Catholic polemic and iconography; see *The Poetics of English Nationhood, 1590–1612* (Cambridge: Cambridge University Press, 1996), esp. 34–82, 93–100. McEachern does note, however, that "those voices perhaps most eloquent and formative in their defense of popular sovereignty were those often quite 'other' to Tudor-Stuart orthodoxy: those of the Counter-Reformation" (9).

2. Linda Colley, *Britons: Forging the Nation, 1707–1837* (New Haven: Yale University Press, 1992), esp. 5–7, 23, 53; as Colley adds, the development of English, or British, national identity "cannot, in fact, be understood without reference to both European and world history" (9). On anti-Catholicism and English nationhood, also see Carol Z. Weiner, "The Beleaguered Isle: A Study of Elizabethan and Jacobean Anti-Catholicism," *Past and Present* 51 (1971): 27–62. For further discussion of the association of English Catholicism with the foreign, see Frances E. Dolan, *Whores of Babylon: Catholicism, Gender, and Seventeenth-Century Print Culture* (Ithaca: Cornell University Press, 1999), 16–44.

3. Alison Shell, *Catholicism, Controversy, and the English Literary Imagination, 1558–1660* (Cambridge: Cambridge University Press, 1999), 109.

4. As McEachern cogently argues, debates about the early modern English nation overlook that "no more fully realized nation ever exists": that is, the nation always represents an ideal of identification, not an actual referent. As she concludes, "A fiction of social unity can exist without a literal social unity; and it may well thrive on its absence" (*Poetics of English Nationhood*, 19–20).

5. Helgerson, *Forms of Nationhood*, 107–47.

6. Even though the majority of Catholics remained in England, there was a sizable expatriate community, one whose importance far surpassed their demographic numbers: while the population of students at the English Colleges (ca. 1600) has been estimated as more than four hundred, this figure does not include those stationed abroad as missionary priests or otherwise employed by the church (A. C. F. Beales, *Education under Penalty: English Catholic Education from the Reformation to the Fall of*

James II, 1547–1689 [London: Athlone Press, 1963], 128). Catholics remained on the Continent in other professional capacities as well, from mercenary service to positions in foreign courts; for a discussion of these groups, see especially John Walter Stoye, *English Travellers Abroad, 1604–1667* (New York: Octagon Books, 1968), and Edward Chaney, *The Evolution of the Grand Tour: Anglo-Italian Cultural Relations since the Renaissance* (London: Frank Cass, 1998).

7. There were thirty-five seminaries founded between 1568 and 1669 (Beales, *Education under Penalty*, 273–74), as well as twenty-two convents established in roughly the same period, 1594–1678 (Claire Walker, *Gender and Politics in Early Modern Europe: English Convents in France and the Low Countries* [New York: Palgrave, 2003], 17).

8. For Peter Lake and Michael Questier, the English mission was activist—rather than parochial—in its aims as well as its methods and consequently succeeded in drawing the English state into public debate ("Puritans, Papists, and the 'Public Sphere' in Early Modern England: The Edmund Campion Affair in Context," *Journal of Modern History* 72 [2000]: 587–627). Michael L. Carrafiello accentuates the political character of the mission even more strongly in "English Catholicism and the Jesuit Mission of 1580–1581," *Historical Journal* 37 (1994): 761–74. By contrast, Christopher Haigh emphasizes the limited goals and impact of the mission; see especially "From Monopoly to Minority: Catholicism in Early Modern England," *Transactions of the Royal Historical Society* 31 (1981): 129–47, and "The Continuity of Catholicism in the English Reformation," *Past and Present* 93 (1981): 37–69.

9. John Bossy, *The English Catholic Community 1570–1850* (New York: Oxford University Press, 1976), 6–7. Bossy does analyze the English Catholic diaspora in other articles, however, including "Rome and the Elizabethan Catholics: A Question of Geography," *Historical Journal* 7 (1964): 135–42, and "Catholicity and Nationality in the Northern Counter-Reformation," in *Religion and National Identity*, ed. Stuart Mews (Oxford: Blackwell, 1982), esp. 286.

10. Caroline Hibbard, "Early Stuart Catholicism: Revisions and Re-revisions," *Journal of Modern History* 52 (1980): 6, 22, 32. On a related note, Thomas H. Clancy, S.J., traces the role of Catholic exiles in transmitting continental political thought to England in *Papist Pamphleteers: The Allen-Persons Party and the Political Thought of the Counter-Reformation in England, 1572–1615* (Chicago: Loyola University Press, 1964).

11. See Bossy, *English Catholic Community*, 26, and J. C. H. Aveling, *The Handle and the Axe: The Catholic Recusants in England from Reformation to Emancipation* (London: Blond and Briggs, 1976), 50.

12. Benedict Anderson, "Nationalism, Identity, and the World-in-Motion: On the Logics of Seriality," in *Cosmopolitics: Thinking and Feeling beyond the Nation*, ed. Pheng Cheah and Bruce Robbins (Minneapolis: University of Minnesota Press, 1998), 117–33.

13. Anderson, "Exodus," *Critical Inquiry* 20 (1994): 326–27.

14. Quoted in ibid., 315.

15. Among James Wadsworth's texts, see *The English Spanish Pilgrime* (London, 1629), *Fvrther Observations of the English Spanish Pilgrime, concerning Spaine* (London, 1630), and *The Memoires of Mr. James Wadswort [sic], a Jesuit that recanted* (London, 1679).

16. James Clifford, *Routes: Travel and Translation in the Late Twentieth Century* (Cambridge, MA: Harvard University Press, 1997), 17–46.

17. Julian Yates, "Parasitic Geographies: Manifesting Catholic Identity in Early Modern England," in *Catholicism and Anti-Catholicism in Early Modern English Texts,* ed. Arthur F. Marotti (New York: Palgrave, 1999), 63–84.

18. On vagrancy and Catholic priests, see A. L. Beier, *Masterless Men: The Vagrancy Problem in England, 1560–1640* (London: Methuen, 1985), 139–42. However, many seminary priests resisted the association with vagrants provoked by an itinerant life, and they more often maintained fixed residences in gentry homes, a practice that relegated Catholicism to what Haigh describes as a "seigneurially structured" position ("From Monopoly to Minority," 130). As Robert Southwell wrote to a peripatetic colleague: "We are all, I acknowledge, pilgrims, but not vagrants: our life is uncertain, but not our road" (quoted in Haigh, "From Monopoly to Minority," 139).

19. As Beale notes, the 1571 Act "against fugitives over the sea" was the first statute to mandate licenses for overseas travel, a stipulation that allowed the state to regulate the duration and destination of travel as well as keep records on those leaving the realm (*Education under Penalty,* 38). Among later examples, see James F. Larkin and Paul L. Hughes, eds., *Stuart Royal Proclamations,* vol. 1, *Royal Proclamations of King James I, 1603–1625* (Oxford: Clarendon Press, 1973), 184–85, 329–36. For further discussion of the regulation of travel, see Mark Netzloff, *England's Internal Colonies: Class, Capital, and the Literature of Early Modern English Colonialism* (New York: Palgrave, 2003), 74–76.

20. William Allen, *An apologie and trve declaration of the institution and endeuours of the two English Colleges* (Mounts [Reims], 1581), sig. D.

21. Lewis Owen, *The rvnning register: recording a trve relation of the state of the English Colledges, Seminaries and Cloysters in all forraine parts* (London, 1626), sig. L3v. Further associating the English Colleges with networks of international travel and commerce, Owen accused Jesuits of parasitically profiting from the hazards of travel by outfitting transatlantic ships with prayer boxes, which desperate mariners would fill during storms and other moments of crisis (sig. K2v).

22. Aveling, *Handle and the Axe,* 63.

23. *Calendar of State Papers, Domestic,* vol. 3, *1591–94* (1867; reprint, Nendeln, Liechtenstein: Kraus Reprint, 1967), 353–55.

24. This communication was often transmitted by Richard Verstegan, who has been described as "the single most important English Catholic agent in the Low

Countries" (Richard W. Clement, "Richard Verstegan's Reinvention of Anglo-Saxon England: A Contribution from the Continent," in *Reinventing the Middle Ages and the Renaissance*, ed. William F. Gentrup [Turnhout: Brepols, 1998], 25; also see Beales, *Education under Penalty*, 68).

25. Vincent may have been requesting Verstegan's *Theatrvm Crudelitatum haereticorum nostri temporis* (Antwerp, 1587). As a counterpoint to Verstegan's text, Theodor de Bry's monumental twelve-volume *America* (1590–1623) transposed Verstegan's images of Protestant abuses against Catholics in England, Ireland, France, and the Low Countries to a depiction of Spanish atrocities in the New World.

26. Paul L. Hughes and James F. Larkin, eds., *Tudor Royal Proclamations*, vol. 2, *The Later Tudors (1553–1587)* (New Haven: Yale University Press, 1969). All citations to this work will be given parenthetically in the text.

27. This classification was legally codified by the "Act against Jesuits and Seminary Priests" (27 Eliz. I, c.2) (1585).

28. Hughes and Larkin, *Tudor Royal Proclamations*, 2:483. The April 1582 royal proclamation had similarly questioned whether those apprehended for vagrancy—"vagrant counterfeit persons"—were disguised seminary priests (2:489). All citations to Allen's *Apologie* are given parenthetically in the text.

29. John Donne, *The Complete English Poems*, ed. A. J. Smith (London: Penguin, 1971).

30. On official efforts to control the printing and dissemination of Catholic texts, see Hughes and Larkin, *Tudor Royal Proclamations*, 2:469, 490.

31. On the question of Catholic loyalism in the early modern period, see especially Peter Holmes, *Resistance and Compromise: The Political Thought of the Elizabethan Catholics* (Cambridge: Cambridge University Press, 1982), and Arnold Pritchard, *Catholic Loyalism in Elizabethan England* (Chapel Hill: University of North Carolina Press, 1979).

32. The call for public debate was a recurring feature of the English mission: on this issue, see Thomas S. McCoog, S.J., "'Playing the Champion': The Role of Disputation in the Jesuit Mission," in *The Reckoned Expense: Edmund Campion and the Early English Jesuits*, ed. Thomas S. McCoog (Woodbridge: Boydell Press, 1996), 119–39, as well as Lake and Questier, "Puritans, Papists," esp. 600–627.

33. For a related discussion, see Anthony Giddens, *The Consequences of Modernity* (Stanford: Stanford University Press, 1990), 21–29, 55–78.

34. For such views of Allen, see Aveling, *Handle and the Axe*, 54, and Bossy, *English Catholic Community*, 26.

35. Hannah Arendt, *The Origins of Totalitarianism* (1951; reprint, New York: Harcourt, Brace and World, 1966), 280, 275.

36. Jacques Derrida examines the historical implications of the city of refuge in "On Cosmopolitanism," in *On Cosmopolitanism and Forgiveness*, trans. Mark Dooley and Michael Hughes (New York: Routledge, 2001), 1–24.

37. Persons returns to this idea in *A conference about the next succession to the crowne of Ingland* (Antwerp, 1595), defending the claim to the English throne of Philip II and his daughter, the Infanta Isabella Clara Eugenia, based on their Lancastrian descent; for discussion, see Michael L. Carrafiello, *Robert Parsons and English Catholicism, 1580–1610* (London: Associated University Presses, 1998), 48–51.

38. A subsequent royal visit, by Philip III and Queen Margaret in 1600, is described in Antonio Ortiz, *A relation of the solemnetie wherewith the Catholike princes K. Phillip the III. and Quene Margaret were receyued in the Inglish Colledge of Valladolid* (Antwerp, 1601). For background on Persons's founding of the seminaries in Spain, see Francis Edwards, S.J., *Robert Persons: The Biography of an Elizabethan Jesuit, 1546–1610* (St. Louis: Institute of Jesuit Sources, 1995), 136–55, and Michael E. Williams, *St. Alban's College Valladolid: Four Centuries of Catholic Presence in Spain* (New York: St. Martin's Press, 1986), 1–33.

39. Robert Persons, *Newes from Spayne and Holland* (1593), sig. A7v. Further citations to this source are given parenthetically in the text. Persons therefore describes the English Catholics executed during Elizabeth I's reign as having preserved Becket's legacy (*Newes*, sig. B5v).

40. Robert Persons, *A relation of the king of Spaines receiving in Valliodolid* (1592), sig. C1v. Persons also defines English identity in relation to classical and biblical precedents of exile, citing the example of St. Alban, the first exile and martyr of England, after whom the college at Valladolid was named (*Relation of the king*, sig. A2v).

41. *The Riverside Shakespeare*, ed. G. Blakemore Evans et al. (Boston: Houghton Mifflin, 1997).

42. Benedict Anderson, *Imagined Communities: Reflections on the Origin and Spread of Nationalism* (1983; reprint, London: Verso, 1991), 12–19, 38–41.

43. As Haigh notes, Persons "was well aware of the needs of Wales and the North" ("From Monopoly to Minority," 147). Most likely, Persons is alluding to Gruffydd Robert's (Griffith Roberts's) *Y drych cristianogawl* (1587), the first Welsh-language text printed in Wales, and *Athrawaeth Gristnogawl* (1568), written by Morys Clynog (Maurice Clenocke), the Welsh rector of the English College at Rome; see Andrew Breeze, "Welsh and Cornish at Valladolid, 1591–1600," *Bulletin of the Board of Celtic Studies* 37 (1990): 108–11, and Shell, *Catholicism, Controversy*, 13. Ortiz's account of Philip III's visit to Valladolid in 1600 also mentions a speech delivered in Cornish (sigs. D4–D4v).

44. Bossy discusses Verstegan's influence on Persons in "Catholicity and Nationality," 292–93.

45. Hugh A. MacDougall, *Racial Myth in English History* (Hanover: University Press of New England, 1982), 47–48. Anthony G. Petti examines Verstegan's works in several articles, including "A Bibliography of the Writings of Richard Verstegan (c. 1550–1641)," *Recusant History* 7 (1963): 82–103. Among recent analyses of

Verstegan, see Donna B. Hamilton's articles "Richard Verstegan's *A Restitution of Decayed Intelligence* (1605): A Catholic Antiquarian Replies to John Foxe, Thomas Cooper, and Jean Bodin," *Prose Studies* 22 (1999): 1–38, "Catholic Use of Anglo-Saxon Precedents, 1565–1625," *Recusant History* 26 (2003): 537–55, and "Richard Verstegan and the Catholic Resistance: The Encoding of Antiquarianism and Love," in *Theatre and Religion: Lancastrian Shakespeare*, ed. Richard Dutton et al. (Manchester: Manchester University Press, 2003), 87–104. Also see Christopher Highley, "Richard Verstegan's Book of Martyrs," in *John Foxe and His World*, ed. Christopher Highley and John N. King (Burlington: Ashgate, 2002), 183–97, along with two essays from the same collection: Benedict Scott Robinson's "John Foxe and the Anglo-Saxons" (66–72) and Richard Williams's "'Libels and payntinges': Elizabethan Catholics and the International Campaign of Visual Propaganda" (198–215).

46. Richard Rowlands [Richard Verstegan], *The Post of the World* (London, 1576).

47. For example, Verstegan is listed under the name Richard Rowlands in *The Oxford Dictionary of National Biography* (Oxford: Oxford University Press, 2004), www.oxforddnb.com.

48. Graham Parry, *The Trophies of Time: English Antiquarians of the Seventeenth Century* (Oxford: Oxford University Press, 1995), 50.

49. However, Verstegan's subsequent career belied his earlier efforts to anglicize his identity, for he began to publish increasingly in Dutch, finally ceasing to write in English altogether after 1623 (Clement, "Richard Verstegan's Reinvention," 35). While possibly reflecting his gradual assimilation to Dutch culture, this transition also marks Verstegan's progressive rejection of a cosmopolitan position of unbound seriality. My analysis emphasizes that his transcultural position—as a writer who published in four languages (English, Latin, Dutch, and French) and was fluent in five others—was always offset, if not even contradicted, by the underlying desire for cultural homogeneity that pervades his work.

50. Verstegan presents the Britons as the ancestors of the Welsh, attesting to a racialized distinction between English and Welsh identities (*Restitution*, sigs. +4v, D4). He also acknowledges the possibility of a historical figure named Brutus but argues that he was more likely a Gaul general who had migrated from the Continent (sig. M3v).

51. Hamilton, "Catholic Use," 545.

52. Verstegan notes that even geological bodies are subject to forces of migration and, in an early version of the theory of continental drift, asserts that England was once physically part of the continent of Europe (*Restitution*, sigs. L4v–O4v). For an extended consideration of this issue, see Michael Windross, "Language, Earth and Water in Richard Verstegan's *Restitution of Decayed Intelligence* (1605) and *Nederlantsche Antiquiteyten* (1613)," *Dutch Crossing* 24 (2000): 67–95.

53. Colin Kidd analyzes early modern uses of these scriptural events in *British Identities before Nationalism: Ethnicity and Nationhood in the Atlantic World, 1600–1800* (Cambridge: Cambridge University Press, 1999); for his discussion of Verstegan, see 61–63, 77, 86–87, 111, 194, 218–23. McEachern also examines the topos of the Tower of Babel in *Poetics of English Nationhood*, 111–20.

54. Demonstrating the complicated national politics of the expatriate community, the pro-Scottish faction was led by Hugh Owen, one of the leading Welsh figures among Catholic exiles; for discussion of Owen, see Albert J. Loomie, *The Spanish Elizabethans: The English Exiles at the Court of Philip II* (New York: Fordham University Press, 1963), 52–93. On Persons's own "Scottish strategy" for the conversion of James VI, see Carrafiello, *Robert Parsons*, 24–31.

55. Verstegan notes that Margaret, sister to the Saxon King Edgar, had fled the Norman invasion by migrating to the Scottish court, where she married the Scottish king, Malcolm III (sig. Z2v). She thus offered a historical precedent for James VI and I's own joint title over England and Scotland, a claim deriving from the marriage of another English princess named Margaret, Henry VIII's sister, to a Scottish king, James IV.

56. Despite his more inclusive sense of the English mission's reach (see n. 43 above), Persons consciously organized his colleges on the basis of students' nationality, trying to avoid the type of conflict that had arisen in Rome. At Valladolid, for example, he "refused to consider an amalgamation with the Irish students," effectively expelling the latter group, who went on to establish the Irish College at Salamanca (Thomas Morrissey, "The Irish Student Diaspora in the Sixteenth Century and the Early Years of the Irish College at Salamanca," *Recusant History* 14 [1978]: 246).

57. Christopher Highley, "'The Lost British Lamb': English Catholic Exiles and the Problem of Britain," in *British Identities and English Renaissance Literature*, ed. David J. Baker and Willy Maley (Cambridge: Cambridge University Press, 2002), 40.

58. Anthony Munday, *The English Roman Life*, ed. Philip J. Ayres (Oxford: Clarendon Press, 1980), 79. For a recent discussion of Munday, see Donna B. Hamilton, *Anthony Munday and the Catholics, 1560–1633* (Burlington: Ashgate, 2005).

59. However, Jesuit control did not establish "English" authority over the college; although the English students had petitioned for an English rector, Clynog's successor was actually an Italian, Alfonso Agazzari (Munday, *English Roman Life*, 91 n.). Similarly, St. Alban's College in Valladolid was most often led by a Spanish rector in this period (Williams, *St. Alban's College, Valladolid*, 261–63).

60. See Charles Dodd, *The History of the English College at Doway* (London, 1713), sig. C3, and Thomas Hunter, S.J., *A Modest Defence of the Clergy and Religious, in a Discourse directed to R. C. Chaplain of an English Regiment, About his History of Doway College* (London, 1714), sig. D7.

61. *Letters and Memorials of William Cardinal Allen,* 82, quoted in Bossy, "Catholicity and Nationality," 294. The difficulties that Leslie faced in establishing a Scottish College on the Continent were evidenced by its frequent relocation, from Paris (1580–90) and Douai (1593–95 and from 1608 onward) to Louvain (1595–1608) (Beales, *Education under Penalty,* 269).

62. On internal colonialism, see Netzloff, *England's Internal Colonies,* esp. 1–15, 135–210.

63. John Nicholls, *Iohn Niccols pilgrimage, whrein is displaied the liues of the proude popes, ambitious cardinals, lecherous Bishops, fat bellied Monkes, and hypocriticall Iesuites* (London, 1581), sig. O6. Because the student body consisted of nearly an equal number of commoners and gentry in this period, class position—like national origin—was a crucial factor in the seminaries; see Bossy, *English Catholic Community,* 415.

64. According to Beales, the national quarrel at Rome led many colleges to resist admitting Welsh students, thereby limiting Welsh contributions to the mission even further (*Education under Penalty,* 45). Even though 218 Welsh students were enrolled in the English Colleges from 1568 to 1642, few of these priests returned to minister in Wales (Breeze, "Welsh and Cornish," 110; Haigh, "From Monopoly to Minority," 133, 135). As a point of comparison, Englishwomen similarly dominated English cloisters on the Continent, constituting over 93 percent of the total population, with relatively few nuns coming from Ireland (1.8 percent), Scotland (0.5 percent), or Wales (0.7 percent) (Walker, *Gender and Politics,* 39).

65. Allen, *Apologie,* sigs. K8–L1v, L5.

66. Persons similarly invoked the memory of earlier Saxon missions in his work, and he proposed reviving these efforts by drawing on the English Colleges to staff missionary efforts in northern Europe (Bossy, "Catholicity and Nationality," 293).

67. By contrast, in Allen's historical narrative, the initial conversion of the Britons was accomplished by the church in Rome, a cosmopolitan venture that served as a precedent for the English Colleges' reconversion of England (*Apologie,* sigs. C, K7).

68. For a list of institutions, see Edward Petre, *Notices of the English Colleges and Convents Established on the Continent after the Dissolution of Religious Houses in England,* ed. F. C. Husenbeth (Norwich: Bacon and Kinnebrook, 1849).

69. For analysis of the political contexts of Catholic Emancipation, see Colley, *Britons,* 324–34.

70. On this point, see Derek Beales, *Prosperity and Plunder: European Catholic Monasteries in the Age of Revolution, 1650–1815* (Cambridge: Cambridge University Press, 2003).

10

The Lives of Women Saints of Our Contrie of England

Gender and Nationalism in Recusant Hagiography

Catherine Sanok

The advent of English nationalism is often attributed to a specifically Protestant understanding of self and state, as the almost inevitable consequence of the country's liberation from the homogenizing influence of Rome. But several of the discourses associated with an emerging national identity have antecedents in late medieval traditions as well as adherents among early modern Catholic writers, who—like their Protestant countrymen—were interested in developing myths of national identity to establish the authority of their own religious practice. So, for example, the antiquarian project associated with figures like William Camden and Robert Cotton was also pursued by Catholic writers and in particular by Catholic hagiographers, who figured England in terms of its ancient religious history in legendaries devoted to native saints.[1] Nicholas Roscarrock—who produced an encyclopedic Catholic collection of native saints' lives (ca. 1610–20)[2]—borrowed books from Camden and clearly understood his work as both a contribution to a shared scholarly project and a defense of a specifically Catholic nationalism.[3] Roscarrock's work was never published, but other Catholic legendaries of native saints were available in printed editions: Roscarrock used John Wilson's *English*

Martyrologe, published at St. Omer in 1608 (with subsequent printings in 1640 and 1672), a legendary of ancient native saints to which Wilson appended a list of Catholics martyred in England since the reign of Henry VIII. Jerome Porter's *Flowers of the Lives of Our English Saincts,* which like Roscarrock's collection highlights its scholarly method through careful citation and comparison of sources, followed in 1632. In their very form, these collections insist on a close relationship between national and Catholic identity, against continuing attempts to represent them as antithetical in Stuart England.[4]

In this essay, I explore a special subset of this tradition, the nationalist legendaries devoted exclusively to female saints, in order to investigate the intersection of gender and nationalism they posit. Such legendaries are unusual: the single medieval precedent for an all-female collection of saints' lives in England is Osbern Bokenham's fifteenth-century *Legends of Holy Women.*[5] But at least three such legendaries circulated in the early seventeenth century. The first is a manuscript legendary, now in the Cambridge University Library (CUL 4457, formerly Phillips 13676), which recounts the lives of Anglo-Saxon saints like Etheldreda, Sexburge, Ethelburge, Hilda, and Edith, as well as the British Helen and Wenefred. It includes non-native saints as well, particularly those who had strong cults in pre-Reformation England, like Catherine of Alexandria and Margaret of Antioch. The second is Robert Buckland's lost but influential *Vitae sanctae mulierum Angliae,* probably also a manuscript work, but one that circulated relatively widely, as is attested by its citation in contemporary Catholic works produced in England and abroad.[6] The third is the focus of this essay, *The Lives of Women Saints of Our Contrie of England,* which may be a translation of Buckland's Latin legendary.[7] This collection comprises thirty-six legends of saints—mostly virgins and abbesses—from England's distant past: a few British saints, including Helena, Keyna, and Ursula, and Anglo-Saxon saints like Edburge, Ethelburge, Eanswide and Ebbe, Werburge, Walburge, and Wulfhilde, most of whom would have been as unfamiliar to seventeenth-century readers as they are to us.[8] The *Lives of Women Saints of Our Contrie of England* is the only one of these all-female legendaries available in a modern edition: it was published by Carl Horstmann for the Early English Text Society in 1886. Although my argument here addresses only this collection, all three of these legendaries use gender as an organizing category as they associate Englishness and Catholicism through the lives of native saints.

These legendaries testify to the surprising utility of feminine devotion for recusant writers interested in Englishness. It is surprising because, as

Frances Dolan and Arthur Marotti have demonstrated, gender was also a key category in anti-Catholic polemic. As Dolan shows in *Whores of Babylon*, Catholicism was represented as feminine in a range of Protestant discourses and demonized through misogynist stereotypes.[9] The association of Catholicism with the feminine was confirmed in the early modern social imagination by the presence of Catholic queens in Stuart England.[10] Recusancy laws further contributed to the feminization of religious difference: women were subject to less onerous penalties for recusancy, producing what Alexandra Walsham has called a division of confessional labor in Catholic households. The male head of house—for whom the professional and financial consequences of recusancy were higher—would attend parish services, while his wife refused.[11] These social factors may well have lent weight to the misogynist discourses examined by Dolan, who suggests that the muted place of martyred Catholic women in Catholic polemic reflects the substantial difficulty of recuperating the feminine as positive in recusant discourses.[12] These legendaries of native saints, then, are extraordinary for attempting precisely that: echoing the gender of Catholic devotion in Protestant discourses, some early modern recusant writers constructed a distinctly Catholic nationalism through narratives of female saints. These texts suggest one way that an understanding of religious models of identity and community can complement the important recent work done on secular, especially classical, models of early modern national consciousness.[13] Although the recusant legendaries I discuss here are admittedly peripheral to the dominant discourses of English identity formulated in the period, they highlight the place of the feminine in early modern constructions of Englishness, often occluded in masculine myths of national identity.

Mothers and Monumental Virgins

The recusant legendaries may help us to complicate and extend more broadly our understanding not only of early modern discourses but also of the intersection of gender and nationalism. If nationalism is Janus-faced, looking both to the past and to the future as it defines a political and ethnic community,[14] most work on nationalism as a gendered discourse has focused on the forward-looking perspective, especially on women's role as mothers in "reproducing" the nation.[15] This conceit surfaces in the *Lives of Women Saints of Our Contrie of England* too, although—as we will see—it is a minor exception to the legendary's overwhelming interest in defining England, and English

Christianity, through holy virgins. The first legend in the collection uses the maternal body to negotiate the relationship between England and the Roman Empire: it concerns Saint Helena, identified here, as in medieval legend, as the British mother of Constantine, the first Christian emperor.[16] The hagiographer carefully maps ancient Britain onto contemporary England at the opening of the legend: the story is set in "Britannie," parenthetically glossed "now England." A Roman general, and later emperor, Constantius Clorus, is sent to Roman Britain to "order some troubles," and while there he marries the British prince's daughter, Helena. Although he divorces her when he becomes emperor because she is "no Romane, but an externe and a Barbarian, by nation and the Romanes estimation" (30), he chooses their son Constantine as his successor. Rejected at first as barbarian, that is, the British Helena is ultimately revealed to transmit to her son not only her own ethnic identity but the rule of the Roman Empire as well. The legend, moreover, credits Constantine's generosity toward Christians and later his conversion to his mother's piety and instruction: Helena provides Constantine at once with a British identity and a Christian one. The Christianization of the empire is attendant on a British point of origin, a powerful narrative argument that the Roman context of Catholicism is not antithetical to a sense of national identity. The Helena legend thus neatly connects the text's nationalist agenda and its commitment to a universal Roman church.[17] In response to Protestant polarizations of an English and Roman church, the legendary begins with a story that imagines the Roman Empire at the moment of its Christianization as encompassed by—rather than encompassing—national identity through the maternal body and maternal example of Helena.

The other saints who figure the maternal reproduction of native identity and religious practice are Sexburge and her daughter Ermenlinde, who together with Ermenlinde's virgin daughter Werburge provide a saintly genealogy that also figures the progressive Christianization of England. Sexburge is responsible first for ridding the country of idolatry and later for establishing a line of holy women. She has one virgin daughter, Erkengodes, and another, Ermelinde, who also brings the people "to the knowledge and favour of Christ" through her "zeale and religious industrie" (58). Ermelinde's religious work, like that of her mother, is also procreative: her daughter Werburge becomes a professed virgin, and together they enter Ely Abbey, where Ermelinde's aunt Audrie served as abbess. A marginal note drawing attention to this genealogy reads, "O what a glorious societie, the grandmother and mother and neece, all religious together and Saints: and the Abbesse Aunt and a Sainte" (59). The text emphasizes the reproduction of sanctity within the context of an Anglo-Saxon aristocratic family, which represents in turn the larger national community. The repetition of Christian practice and identity in each generation itself figures the implications of the women's contributions to the conversion of the English. Like nobility itself, Catholicism is represented here as an inherited identity, intimately connected with the social and political structure and history of England itself.[18]

These four legends are the only ones in the *Lives of Women Saints of Our Contrie of England* that correspond to the recent critical emphasis on cultural fictions of "reproducing" the nation. The legendary's very limited use of this fiction is a consequence not only of the signal importance given to sexual purity in the lives of female saints but also of the substitution of literal mothers with a figurative one: the church itself. Citing Cyprian, the hagiographer insists that virgins "are the floure of the Churches seede, the honor and ornament of spirituall grace, the moste towardlie impes, the intire and incorrupt worke of praise and honor, the image of God, resembling our lordes holines (who was a virgin) and the moste worthie portion of Christ flocke: By them and in them dooth the glorious fertilitie of our mother the Church greatlie reioyce, and aboundantlie flourish: and howe much the more in number virgins augment and multiplie, so much the more dooth our mothers comfort increase" (11–12).

Women in the legendary who have virgin daughters point to the allegorical mother, the church, who is identified here as responsible for the reproduction of virgins and so of the nation itself, represented by their "entire and incorrupt" bodies.[19] Thus, aside from the few examples given above, the *Lives of Women Saints of Our Contrie of England* is concerned exclusively with virgins, an emphasis highlighted by the introductory chapters that preface the collection. After two initial chapters, on why God provides Christian countries with saints and why Irish and Scottish saints are included in this collection, the hagiographer offers an extended discussion of virginity, with chapters on the dignity of virgins, their behavior, their attire, injunctions to them to avoid attending marriages, and discussions of their manners and demeanor, taken out of Cyprian and Jerome (11–21). This emphasis requires us to turn away from modern accounts of the intersection between women and nationalism that focus on representations of reproduction and genealogy. Indeed, the legendary's own attention to the significant changes in the nation's ethnic and cultural makeup separating British from Anglo-Saxon and then post-Conquest England—the difference, that is, noted in the Helena legend between ancient Britain and contemporary England—challenges a reproductive or genealogical model of national identity.

Instead, the *Live of Women Saints of Our Contrie of England* locates national identity in a moment of origin and its reiteration or performance in contemporary devotional practice, and it uses virginal saints to figure both the originary and the iterable aspects of national identity. First, the virgin's body is posited as the material basis for national identity: the site of her death—often in defense of her chastity—is frequently marked by that event, with, for example, a spring whose uncommonly fresh waters figure both the purity of the saint's body and its continuing presence. More interesting, the female saint is presented as the exemplary basis for ethical and devotional behavior in the present: contemporary readers, that is, are encouraged to perform the native religious identity that she represents. These two aspects of national identity are intimately connected: the saint's enduring physical presence provides a warrant for taking her as an ethical example. But they are also potentially at odds. Either through its material residue or through the manifestation of its sacred status in the landscape, the virgin's body marks and guarantees the continuity of English Christian identity from its ancient British or Anglo-Saxon past to the present day. The text's presentation of the saint's exemplarity, in contrast, suggests the discontinuity of past and present, a discontinuity figured by gender. While the sacred past is represented by female saints in the *Lives of Women Saints or Our Contrie of England*, its ethical program is addressed primarily to a male audience. Enjoining men to imitate the heroic devotion of Anglo-Saxon virgins, the recusant legendary genders the difference between ancient English sanctity and contemporary English practice, between the sacred past and the social present.

In this, the Catholic legendary anticipates certain aspects of Julia Kristeva's argument about gender and nationalism in her essay "Women's Time."[20] The title refers primarily to time as structured by cycles of reproduction, which Kristeva understands as an alternative to, rather than an instrument of, nationalism, since it links women through a supranational category of identity.[21] But she is also interested in "monumental time," a static, originary, mythical time, which she notes is also often associated with the feminine. "Monumental time" provides an even more direct challenge to the "cursive" (i.e., progressive and linear) time of modern nationalist discourse. This opposition between monumental and linear time, between ancient origin and contemporary progress, is central to recent critical theories of nationalism, most influentially Homi Bhabha's discussion in "DissemiNation," which cites Kristeva's essay. Bhabha, however, dismisses the significance or symbolic work of gender in nationalist discourse. Implying that Kristeva's paradigm allows for a coherent model of national identity, Bhabha doubts that the tension between the past and present of national identity can be contained by the "gendered sign."[22] This rejection may respond to the apparently essentialist generalizations that inform some of Kristeva's argument. But it also overlooks the important heuristic she offers for understanding the gendered nature of time in nationalist discourse.

I introduce Kristeva and Bhabha here not only because I think their work can help us understand the cultural work of recusant collections of native saints' lives but also because the *Lives of Women Saints of Our Contrie of England* can in turn help us reopen the question they raise about gender and nationalism. The Catholic legendary offers a double, and inconsistent, argument in response to the dominant historiographic conceit of Protestant nationalist discourses: that history is organized around moments of rupture. On the one hand, it insists on the continuity of English national identity in the continuing physical presence of ancient virgin saints. On the other, it acknowledges the discontinuities of history but suggests that they can be overcome through the exemplary relation linking past and present, as contemporary audiences imitate the ancient devotion of native saints. This double answer is produced through and under the sign of gender: the monumental past is figured by female virgins and martyrs, while the present is gendered masculine through the text's ethical address. Bhabha, that is, might be right that gender cannot resolve the temporal split that threatens the coherence of a national ideal, but only by adopting Kristeva's attention to gender can we fully understand how that ideal can be organized around the fantasy of a past that is continuous with, but categorically different from, the present.

Gender, History, Exemplarity

The historicity of Protestant martyrs—defined against the legendary status of saints venerated in the Middle Ages and the ritual commemoration of them in the atemporal structure of the liturgy—was crucial to the way early modern polemicists defined an English national church. Foxe's enormously influential *Acts and Monuments* conflates the categories of martyrdom and historicity, at once defining the true church through those who have died for it and representing martyrdom itself as a mark of historical rupture and historical progress. For Foxe, that is, martyrdom produces historical periodization, separating the medieval past from the Protestant future.[23] Protestant martyrology is a form of historiography, not only because it aims to record factual events, but also because martyrdom generates history—a narrative of progress and transformation leading to the true church, and so also to England as a Protestant nation.

There is an analogous emphasis on history as the organizing framework for sacred event and religious identity in the recusant *Lives of Women Saints of Our Contrie of England*, a trace of the influence of Protestant martyrologies on the structure and program of the text. That the Catholic legendary is interested in historical, as well as moral, lessons is evident in its organization, which is chronological rather than liturgical.[24] The order of the legends thus outlines the history of English Christianity, figured through the lives and exemplary deaths of female saints. The collection begins, as we have seen, with Helen, who died around 326, and closes with the thirteenth-century Mechtilde. But while the *Lives of Women Saints of Our Contrie of England* follows Protestant discourses in emphasizing martyrdom as a historical event, a singular occurrence in linear history, it also insists that its significance could—and must—be continually reiterated through imitation of the saint. Indeed, its construction of English identity hinges on this idea of reiteration or *imitatio*, the exemplary structure through which contemporary behavior is identified as a repetition of the past. This structure guarantees cultural continuity: ethical imitation assumes that behavior and the social context in which it is performed remain—in broad outline at least—constant. In recusant legendaries like this one, *imitatio* denies the historical boundary constructed in Protestant discourse by offering an ideal model of an ancient English devotion to be imitated or performed by early modern Catholics.

In the medieval tradition from which the recusant legends borrow, the exemplary relationship between saint and audience depends largely—though not exclusively—on their shared sex: women saints are considered especially apt ethical models for female audiences, as hagiographers and other moral writers frequently insist. Some late medieval hagiographers used this expectation and the marked nature of the feminine to explore the idea of cultural continuity implied by imitation. The most pronounced example is Henry Bradshaw's late-fifteenth-century *Life of St. Werburge*, which offers the saint—a seventh-century Anglo-Saxon virgin and abbess—as a model for contemporary lay women, who are told to imitate the saint's humility, her modest clothing, and her devout prayers. The cultural continuity represented through Bradshaw's emphasis on Werburge's exemplarity is given physical expression in the saint's virginal body, which remains miraculously incorrupt for centuries after her death. It decays only with the Danish invasions (a miracle that protects it from infidel hands), and its residue, no longer figuring the integrity of Werburge's own identity, from this point guarantees instead the integrity and continuity of English identity. The shrine in which it had been preserved continues to protect Chester, the border town that protects England, from invasion by "innumerable barbarike nacions"—the Welsh, Picts, Scots, Danes, and others.[75] The dual focus of Bradshaw's legend, then, is on the ethical and physical continuity of Werburge and the nation she represents. Contemporary devotional practice in imitation of the saint, like her continuing physical presence, produces and reflects the historical continuity of English religious practice and national identity.

Bradshaw wrote the *Life of St. Werburge* at the end of the turbulent fifteenth century, during which English identity and the English nation were threatened by dynastic crises and civil war. His legend argues for cultural continuity on the grounds of the exemplary relationship linking contemporary women to an Anglo-Saxon saint. In imitating Werburge, late medieval women performed the mythical English identity the saint represented, even in everyday activities like dressing humbly or repeating a prayer attributed to the saint. Such ordinary ethical and devotional practices are not inherently English, of course, but Bradshaw represents them as such by identifying them as an imitation of the virginal Werburge, symbol and embodiment of Englishness itself. The nationalist implications of the story of this regional saint were clear to Richard Pynson, the king's printer, who published Bradshaw's poem in 1521 as part of a wider program of printing legends of native saints, creating a canon that was itself an important resource for Protestant and recusant antiquarian projects.

Like Bradshaw's poem, the *Lives of Women Saints of Our Contrie of England* understands Englishness as a category that must be reproduced in the practices of contemporary audiences, but it alters the gendered ethical address familiar from the medieval tradition. As we will see, the text speaks primarily to a masculine audience whose apostacy or church papacy is to be shamed by the stories of holy women who were eager to die for the faith. The legendary, that is, represents England's monumental past as "women's time" and its social present as masculine. In contrast to Bradshaw's fifteenth-century fantasy of a seamless history of English Christianity, uniting a seventh-century abbess and late medieval laywomen through shared devotional practice, the recusant legendary at once acknowledges and seeks to overcome the historical rupture of the Reformation by making men responsible for the ethical imitation of a mythical English devotion embodied by female saints.

In the first chapter of the text's long introduction, the hagiographer offers a careful explanation of the agenda and exemplary function of saints' lives that identifies the primary audience of the text as masculine. God uses the genre, he writes, "to open the eyes and awake the drousines of his slacke people," inspiring them with examples of extraordinary virtue. He mentions the virtue of princes who sacrifice wealth and honor to serve God, but women who do so offer an even more remarkable example:

> [W]hen they shall beholde fraile women to have taken up so weightie and greate Crosses, and to have carried them so cheerfullie albeit deyntilie bredd and brought up, and invited by the world to excellent advancements glorie and delightes; yet neglecting them all to follow Christ; how many may be confounded that for onelie mammocks and scrappes in comparison, neglect to serve god or forgoe his service? How many men may blush at their more than womannish weaknes, that can scarce beare any Crosse or verie small ones, when tender ladies have taken such strength and courage throughe love of their lord, to carrie so mightie burdens? Who may not be ashamed at the name of a man, that can not come nighe, or at least dare not endevour to contend in strength and labour with a weake woman? (3)

The hagiographer later makes the argument of this passage explicit with the emphatic statement, "I would to god men would imitate the laudable lives of women, and that wrinkled olde age would bestow what youth hath voluntarilie offered unto god" (10), a wish he attributes also to St. Jerome in his praise of Paula and Eustochium.[26] Male readers assume the ethical burden of hagiography, the weakness of their faith rebuked by examples of virtuous women, who, in turn, represent the monumental past against which action in the present is measured. The argument depends on a familiar misogynist assumption of women's physical and moral inferiority: the exorbitant value of feminine sanctity is linked to the assumption that women's virtue is itself extraordinary given their inherent weakness. Thus the compiler announces of women saints, "More potent also are they for their sex and number, who the weaker they were by nature, so much more admirable to excell the perfecter sex by grace" (9–10). Women's general deficit in ethical stature paradoxically affords it surplus value and guarantees its exemplarity, even as it confirms that men are more responsible for ethical imitation of the example set by female saints.

A trace of the misogynist theory of feminine inferiority is evident, as well, in the hagiographer's citation of Cyprian, who argued that virgins are exempt not only from the Edenic curse that women will labor in childbirth but also from social hierarchies that subordinate women to men. Cyprian promises virgins: "[N]either is a mortall man your maister, but your maister and head is Christ, as he is of men also: you are now equall with them in freedome" (13). Their virginity exempts them, that is, not only from the physical punishment that marks their sex, but also from the social and political formations that are otherwise considered proper to them as women. This points to the theoretical basis for the gendered paradigm of the legendary: eluding the limitations of her own body, the virgin establishes a monumental ideal that exempts her from the social order, while the ethical categories that the virgin so far exceeds are, conversely, gendered male.

Significantly, the virgin's body—as the exemplary basis of ethical action—is also the material basis for the legendary's nationalist agenda. For the hagiographer, the land itself is haunted by the spectral presence of these bodies, whose enduring physicality links past and present in an imagined community of national identity. Their legends are "so much the more forceiblie mooving, in that they have moste beene bredd in this land, where we our selves have beene borne, walked on this earth, on which we walke, filled this ayer which we draw with their renowned fame, sanctified it with their holie acts, blessed it with their merits, magnified it with their miracles, and enriched it with their sacred bones and bodies" (9).

The nationalist community of ancient saints and contemporary audiences is rooted in *place,* in the very ground and air, which provides continuity despite the disjunctions of political and religious change. The soil of England, enriched with the bones and bodies of martyrs, provides the physical foundation for nationalism and nationalist Catholicism. It is, moreover, the site of a mimetic relationship between ancient saints and contemporary readers, who walk on the same earth on which they walked and breathe the same air they breathed. The simple and inevitable repetition of such daily activities points to the more strenuous ethical imitation enjoined by the hagiographer: martyrdom for one's faith. But it also—more significantly—represents contemporary practice as a reiteration of the past, assuring the continuity of English Catholic identity in the most basic human activities.[27]

The legends that follow this introduction emphasize this material basis for ethical imitation. The body of the virgin witnesses her sanctity through its enduring presence. In the account of St. Withburg, the saint's miraculously intact body—it remains incorrupt for 354 years after her death—testifies "aboundantlie" to the purity of her soul in the absence of any textual record of her virtue ("written monuments and records fayling," 79).[28] The physical trace of the virgin's body is, in other legends, mapped onto the landscape itself: Inthware, for example, who was—the hagiographer notes, "an Englishe woman, as by her owne name is conjecured" (79)—is murdered by her brother because he falsely believes that she is a "harlott." "But god testified her holines and chastitie," the hagiographer insists, "presentlie with a strange miracle: For she having her head cutt of, did afterward with her owne handes, take up her head and carried it to the Church, whence she came: and withall in the same place, where she was killed there sprong a lyuelie fountayne" (80). The legend at once responds to anti-Catholic representations of devotion as a cover for illicit sexuality—of the sort Dolan describes in *Whores of Babylon*[29]—with the miraculous demonstration of Inthware's chastity and suggests that topographical features of England, its lively springs, are a physical trace of ancient Christian devotion in England. The life of Wenefride emphasizes related themes: she dedicates her virginity to Christ, proving the spiritual as well as bodily fertility of her parents, and rendering her own body inviolable. Like Inthware, she is beheaded—in this case by a pagan suitor whom she refuses—and a fountain, "which to this day continueth" (90), springs up in the place of her death. Wenefride, unlike Inthware, is resurrected by the prayers of her parents and parish church. Still the sweet-smelling moss at the fountain and its curative powers manifest the saint's continuing presence at the site of her violent (if temporary) death.

I would like to mention briefly one other legend that establishes the continuing presence of the saint, but on the Continent rather than in England: the legend of Ursula and the eleven thousand virgins who accompany her. Traditionally, Ursula is a British princess, desired by an English (i.e., Anglo-Saxon) prince. Although she is a Christian and he is a pagan, she agrees to marry him because he will otherwise destroy her father's kingdom. She requests time to go to Rome first, however, and demands eleven thousand virgins from his land as companions, all of whom she converts. The company is martyred on the return voyage when a storm forces them to land at Cologne. The *Lives of Women Saints of Our Contrie of England* changes this story, by way of Geoffrey of Monmouth's *History of the Kings of Britain*, in telling ways. Conanus, here a British king rather than an English one, leaves his land, along with the Roman legion, to settle on the Continent. Believing that "this new kingdome would not be stable and firme for long continuance, unlesse they had wives of their owne nation" (37), Conanus sends to Britain for Ursula and a company of virgins.[30] Although the narrative—in the person of Conanus—first proposes that marriage (and, implicitly, women's role as mothers) will ensure the continuity of this community, it is ultimately martyrdom that does so. There are three key changes to the traditional legend: the erasure of the ethnic difference between Conanus and Ursula, the displacement of Conanus from Britain to the Continent, and the omission of both the fact that he is pagan and the coercive nature of his marriage proposal. In the recusant legendary, he is a native of Britain exiled to the Continent by political circumstance; the continuity and identity of the British community he rules are confirmed by the arrival, and then the sacred deaths, of Ursula and her virgins. The legend argues for the continuity of national identity even for communities—like Catholics who had fled abroad—no longer in England. Indeed, the bodies of the martyrs so decisively transform the land that it will not admit any others: where they are buried, the legend concludes, "The ground or earth of that Church will receiue no other bodie, no not the corps of yong infants newlie baptized, but as it were vomiting them up againe in the night, they will be cast up aboue grounde, and not be conteyned within it, as hath often beene tried" (39). The ground walked on there, too, is the ground of a specifically English Catholic Church.

The recusant legendary, then, imagines the continuity of English Catholic identity in both a topography configured by Christian martyrs and the imitation of their exemplary ideal that takes place in that space. In the rhetoric of the recusant legendary, as we have seen, this continuity is to be accomplished primarily by men, to whom the collection is addressed. The gendering of past and present registers a breach between them. The mythical past that the legendary holds out as an ideal is, for its seventeenth-century Catholic audience, categorically "other," an otherness manifest in the gendered difference between ancient and modern devotion, between female saints and the male audience who are to take them as an example. But the idea of exemplarity itself promises to mend that difference, as contemporary audiences imitate or perform the English Christianity embodied by the country's ancient martyrs. In its explicit account of the distinction between the sacred past and the social present—between, that is, the national identity embodied by ancient British and Anglo-Saxon "women saints" and the contemporary devotion to which it enjoins a male audience—the *Lives of Women Saints of Our Contrie of England* both expresses and seeks to overcome a historical rupture through the category of gender.

The contradictions of this double agenda are vividly demonstrated by the awkwardness of presenting female saints, emphatically feminized through narratives of sexual pursuit and the miraculous intactness of the virgin's body, as ethical models for early modern Catholic men.[31] As other Catholic hagiographers like Wilson, Porter, and Roscarrock developed the tradition of legendaries devoted to native saints, they turned frequently to another all-female legendary, Buckland's *Vitae sanctae mulierum Angliae*, as a source, but they folded the legends of female saints into encyclopedic collections, eschewing the opposition between a feminine past and a masculine present developed in the all-female legendaries.[32] If the *Lives of Women Saints of Our Contrie of England* uses gender at once to represent and erase the difference between the past and present of English Catholicism, other recusant writers seem to recognize that it both excludes contemporary women from the performance of national religious identity and offers a narrow, largely irrelevant, example of that identity for contemporary men to imitate. It ultimately threatens, that is, to relegate English Catholicism to the past by rendering its active contemporary expression, by both women and men, impossible.

Notes

1. J. T. Rhodes provides a useful survey of this tradition, as well as other kinds of recusant hagiography circulating in the early modern period, in "English Books of Martyrs and Saints of the Late Sixteenth and Early Seventeenth Centuries," *Recusant History* 22 (1994): 7–25.

2. Cambridge University Library Additional 3041. Parts of the text have been edited by Nicholas Orme, *Nicholas Roscarrock's Lives of the Saints: Cornwall and Devon* (Exeter: Devon and Cornwall Record Society, 1992).

3. On Roscarrock's work and his relationship with Camden, see A. L. Rowse, "Nicholas Roscarrock and His Lives of the Saints," in *Studies in Social History: A Tribute to G. M. Trevelyan*, ed. J. H. Plumb (London: Longmans, Green, 1955), 3–31. On cross-confessional collaboration, see Antony Milton, "A Qualified Intolerance: The Limits and Ambiguities of Early Stuart Anti-Catholicism," in *Catholicism and Anti-Catholicism in Early Modern English Texts*, ed. Arthur Marotti (New York: St. Martin's Press, 1999), 85–115.

4. In this essay, I follow these texts in referring to England and Englishness as the focus and form of the political identity they construct. But this tradition does not clearly or consistently distinguish an idea of English identity from an idea of British identity. So while the first title page of Porter's collection limits its reference to English saints, a second page gives "The Flowers of the Lives of the Most Renowned Saincts of the Three Kingdoms England, Scotland, and Ireland." As the difference between the two suggests, this work, and the tradition as a whole, frequently uses England as a synecdoche for Britain; the collections invariably include British and Irish saints as well as English ones, although the titles frequently insist on England as the organizing rubric. The focus of this essay, the *Lives of Women Saints of Our Contrie of England*, addresses this tension directly: following medieval legendaries like the *Kalendar of the New Legend of England*, it justifies the inclusion of Scottish and Irish saints in an "English" collection by virtue of political alliance and territorial overlap in an idealized past. Scotland is included, the hagiographer claims, because it is "part of this isle" and because much of it belonged to the kings of Northumberland (10). Ireland is included because it has belonged to the English crown for four hundred years and because there was great friendship between the two countries in "Saxons time" (11). Britain, as we will see in the legend of St. Helen, is understood primarily in historical terms, as the prior name and cultural identity of England itself.

5. Osbern Bokenham, *Legendys of Hooly Wummen*, ed. Mary Serjeantson, Early English Text Society, o.s., 206 (London: Oxford University Press, 1938).

6. The author may be Ralph Buckland (1564–1611), whose works included a translation of six volumes of Laurentius Surius's *Lives of Saints*; see *Dictionary of National Biography*, ed. Leslie Stephen and Sidney Lee (London: Oxford University Press, 1937–38), 3:205–6. Both Wilson and Roscarrock cite Buckland's collection, as does Philippus Ferrarius, *Catalogus generalis sanctorum qui in Martyrologio romano non sunt* (Venice, 1625). The latter citation is recorded in the *Acta sanctorum* in reference to the Scottish virgin Mechtild; see *Acta Sanctorum Full Text Database*, http://acta.chadwyck.com, *April*, vol. 2 (Cambridge: Chadwick Healy, 2000), "XII April,"

"Praetermissi et in alios dies reiecti." I am grateful to H. A. Kelly for help in identifying this text.

7. The unique manuscript of the *Lives of Women Saints of Our Contrie of England*, British Library Stowe 53, is dated to 1610–15 by the text's editor, Carl Horstmann, on the basis of the script and watermark. The date of composition cannot be much earlier: Horstmann notes internal references to the third and fourth volumes of Baronius's *Annales ecclesiastici* (1591–92). See Carl Horstmann, ed., *The Lives of Women Saints of Our Contrie of England*, Early English Text Society, o.s., 86 (London: Trübner, 1885), xii–xiii. All citations are to this edition and are given parenthetically in the text. It should be noted that Horstmann mistakenly identifies the manuscript as BL Stowe 949. The manuscript apparently provides little information about its provenance before the eighteenth century, when it was owned by the antiquary Thomas Astle (d. 1803); see *Catalogue of the Stowe Manuscripts in the British Museum* (London, 1895), 1:30–31, 2:16.

8. The manuscript also contains seven non-native female saints' lives taken from the writings of church fathers. This section is clearly separate from the *Lives of Women Saints of Our Contrie of England*: the conclusion of that text is marked with a "finis" at the close of the legend of Mechtild and with an alphabetical index of the legendary's contents. The non-native saints' lives are indexed in a separate table.

9. Frances Dolan, *Whores of Babylon: Catholicism, Gender, and Seventeenth-Century Print Culture* (Ithaca: Cornell University Press, 1999). See also Huston Diehl, *Staging Reform, Reforming the Stage* (Ithaca: Cornell University Press, 1997); and Arthur Marotti, "Alienating Catholics in Early Modern England: Recusant Women, Jesuits, and Ideological Fantasies," in Marotti, *Catholicism and Anti-Catholicism*, 1–34. Claire McEachern also remarks the "absolutely fundamental quality of gender to national identity in this period" (a statement she highlights with italics) in *The Poetics of English Nationhood, 1590–1612* (Cambridge: Cambridge University Press, 1996), 29.

10. See Caroline Hibbard's essay on Henrietta Maria in chapter 4 of this volume.

11. Alexandra Walsham, *Church Papists: Catholicism, Conformity, and Confessional Polemic in Early Modern England* (Woodbridge: Boydell, 1993), 81.

12. Frances Dolan, "'The Wretched Subject the Whole Town Talks of': Representing Elizabeth Cellier (London, 1680)," in Marrotti, *Catholicism and Anti-Catholicism*, 218–58.

13. Important examples of recent scholarship on the role of religious discourses in fashioning national community include the last chapter of Richard Helgerson, *Forms of Nationhood* (Chicago: University of Chicago Press, 1992), and the essays collected in the first section of *Religion and Culture in Renaissance England*, ed. Claire McEachern and Debora Shuger (Cambridge: Cambridge University Press, 1997), es-

pecially Patrick Collinson's "Biblical Rhetoric: The English Nation and National Sentiment in the Prophetic Mode," 15–45, and Shuger's "'Society Supernatural': The Imagined Community of Hooker's *Laws*," 116–41. On the use of classical myth to establish England's authority as nation and empire, see Heather James, *Shakespeare's Troy: Drama, Politics, and the Translation of Empire* (Cambridge: Cambridge University Press, 1997).

14. See Homi Bhabha's introduction to *Nation and Narration* (London: Routledge, 1990), 3; Bhabha borrows the idea from Thomas Nairn, *The Break-up of Britain* (London: Verso, 1981), 348.

15. On gender and nationalism, see Nira Yuval-Davis and Floya Anthias, *Woman-Nation-State* (London: Macmillan, 1989); Nira Yuval-Davis, *Gender and Nation* (Thousand Oaks, CA: Sage Publications, 1997); and Tamar Mayer, ed., *Gender Ironies of Nationalism: Sexing the Nation* (London: Routledge, 2000). Recent work emphasizes women's participation in and exclusion from national politics, often from a comparative perspective: for example, Ida Blom, Karen Hagemann, and Catherine Hall, eds., *Gendered Nations: Nationalisms and Gender Order in the Long Nineteenth Century* (Oxford: Berg, 2000); and Rada Ivekoviç and Julie Mostov, eds., *From Gender to Nation* (Ravenna: Longo Editore, 2002).

16. On the Helena legend, see Antonina Harbus, *Helena of Britain in Medieval Legend* (Cambridge: Brewer, 2002).

17. In this, it offers an analogue to Protestant negotiations of England's "elect" status and a supranational community. See, for example, Jesse Lander's work on how different editions of the *Book of Martyrs* emphasize either a national or an international community: "'Foxe's *Books of Martyrs*: Printing and Popularizing the *Acts and Monuments*," in McEachern and Shuger, *Religion and Culture*, 68–92.

18. The legendary's use here, and throughout, of aristocratic figures to define England distinguishes its form of nationalism from modern nationalist discourses, of course, which—in Benedict Anderson's influential formulation—define all citizens as equal participants in the national community. Benedict Anderson, *Imagined Communities: Reflections on the Origin and Spread of Nationalism* (London: Verso, 1991).

19. This allegorical substitution is facilitated by other metaphoric representations of motherhood: thus Ermenilde is described as "a mother to all in any kind of necessite or miserie, thoroughe christian compassion desiring and studying to helpe all" (58). Christian compassion is here designated as the origin of a motherly impulse to care for others.

20. Julia Kristeva, *The Portable Kristeva*, ed. Kelly Oliver (New York: Columbia University Press, 1997).

21. As such, it produces what Kristeva calls a "diagonal" relationship: the category of identity conferred by cyclical time—that is, one's place in relationship to modes of reproduction (she mentions both age and sex here)—links one to others,

outside one's own national community, who share that identity. Although this is not only true of women (she gives European youth as another example), Kristeva suggests that women's more alienated or attenuated relation to the nation makes their participation in a supranational community a more conspicuous challenge to the nation as the context for identity and the structure of time it organizes.

22. Homi Bhabha, "DissemiNation: Time, Narrative and the Margins of the Modern Nation," in *Location of Culture* (London: Routledge, 1994), 153. Bhabha revises Kristeva's terminology, offering *pedagogical* and *performative* in place of *monumental* and *cursive*. This revision is part of the larger revision of the place of gender in the paradigm. In particular, he elides the idea of reproductive or cyclical time altogether, reducing Kristeva's three categories of time to two; the missing one surfaces only metaphorically, in association with linear or performative time, to which it was originally opposed. So for Bhabha the performative aspect of national identity is "that sign of the *present* through which national life is redeemed and iterated as reproductive process" (145). For a compelling analysis of the centrality of gender to the "temporal anomaly within nationalism," see Anne McClintock, "'No Longer in a Future Heaven': Nationalism, Gender, and Race," in *Becoming National*, ed. Geoff Eley and Ronald Grigor Suny (New York: Oxford University Press, 1996), 260–84. See also Kathleen Davis, "Time behind the Veil: the Media, the Middle Ages, and Orientalism Now," in *Postcolonial Middle Ages*, ed. Jeffrey Jerome Cohen (New York: St. Martin's Press, 2000), 105–22, who discusses Kristeva and Bhabha and suggests that premodern (specifically medieval) studies can help reopen the question of gender and nationalism.

23. Periodization in Foxe is explicitly structured by the onset and cessation of persecutions. If Foxe makes little direct claim for England's status as an "elect nation," this historiographic structure does confer on England a prominent and special role: Constantine—here, as in the *Lives of Women Saints of Our Contrie of England*, son of the British Helen—presides over the chaining of the Antichrist, while the persecution of Wyclif marks his renewed activity and Elizabeth's reign marks the last days. Alison Chapman provides a fascinating account of Foxe's use of a prefatory calendar to "signal a new Protestant investment in linear history" as opposed to a Catholic understanding of time in terms of the cyclical structure of the liturgy. Alison Chapman, "Now and Then: Sequencing the Sacred in Two Protestant Calendars," *Journal of Medieval and Early Modern Studies* 33 (2003): 91–123.

24. That is to say, rather than ordering the legends according to the calendar (and so foregrounding the liturgical celebration of their feast days), the *Lives of Women Saints of Our Contrie of England* sets them in chronological order. This is a departure not only from medieval legendaries (like the *Legenda aurea* and the *South English Legendary*) but also from other recusant collections of native saints: both Porter and Wilson use a calendrical organization, though Wilson replaces the prefa-

tory calendar with an alphabetical list of saints in the St. Omer 1640 edition of the *English Martyrologe*. Interestingly, there is evidence that another all-female legendary, Buckland's *Vitae sanctae mulierum Angliae*, was also organized chronologically rather than calendrically: Wilson's citations of Buckland for Elflede (January 20, 950), Kineswide (March 6, 666), and Edburge of Kent (December 13, 616) are, respectively, to pages 242, 177, and 115; the collection was ordered, that is, by the historical date, rather than the day, of the saint's death.

25. Henry Bradshaw, *The Life of Saint Werburge of Chester*, ed. Carl Horstmann, Early English Text Society, o.s., 88 (London: Trübner, 1887), 2:758.

26. The *Lives of Women Saints of Our Contrie of England* does not, however, positively exclude a female readership. Although the initial emphasis and rhetorical force focus on the responsibilities of a male audience, the first chapter of the introduction concludes with an acknowledgment of male and female readers: "By these now may we playnlie see the power of Christian vertue, the might of grace, the force of faith, when the weakest portions of nature by them are so inabled, to strong if not strange enterprises: that hence the slouth and pride of the perfecter sex may be more confounded, being so outgone by their inferiors, and the weaker also may be more emboldened and comforted in Christ, seeing their infirmitie made so potent by him, aboue sondrie by nature superiour" (10).

27. The text here seems to offer a neat example of Pierre Bourdieu's concept of "habitus," an intimate performance of cultural codes in ordinary behavior that does not, on the surface, seem to have ideological content but that generates a specific cultural (or class) identity. At the same time, the passage reminds us that the link between such activities and categories of identity can itself be a rhetorical construct in the service of a particular political position.

28. On the use of the figure of the miraculously intact body as an image of national identity, see Robert Stein, "Making History English: Cultural Identity and Historical Explanation in William of Malmesbury and Layamon's *Brut*," in *Text and Territory: Geographical Imagination in the European Middle Ages*, ed. Sylvia Tomasch and Sealy Gilles (Philadelphia: University of Pennsylvania Press, 1998), 97–115.

29. Dolan, *Whores of Babylon*, 90–91.

30. This revised story relies heavily on the story of Conanus Meridiadocus in book 5 of Geoffrey of Monmouth's *History of the Kings of Britain*. Horstmann identifies as the legend's immediate source Herman Flien, *Historia SS. Ursulae et Sociarum Virginum brevissime conscripta*, printed in Zachary Lippeloo, *Vitae sanctorum* (Cologne, 1596).

31. Cf. Bhabha's argument that nationalist discourses are structurally incoherent because fantasies of a nation's past are antithetical to the vigorous contemporary expression of national identity, what he calls the "prodigious, living principles of the people as contemporaneity" ("DissemiNation," 145).

32. Wilson, whose copious citations of Buckland make clear his interest in and access to the tradition of all-female legendaries, provides the most interesting comparandum. His *English Martyrologe* is very much concerned with the relationship between past and present: it comprises a legendary of ancient saints organized according to the calendar and a list of Catholics martyred in England since Henry VIII, organized chronologically. Both parts of the text include both men and women. The prefatory material generally avoids gendering its audience by addressing the reader directly in the second person: for example, "at last I thought it most conuenient, that YOW, whose hartes and myndes are firmely fixed in the honour and veneration of so glorious and elected wightes, and for the inbracing wherof yow daily suffer so great and many persecutions, should take vpon yow this Protection, for whose comfort and consolation principally (next after the honour of the Saintes themselues) the same is published" (fol. 2).

11

Anthony Munday's Translations of Iberian Chivalric Romances

Palmerin of England, Part 1 as Exemplar

Donna B. Hamilton

As early as 1580, in the midst of Elizabeth's negotiations with the Duke of Anjou and before the reaction to Edmund Campion's arrival was full-blown, Anthony Munday announced in the dedication of *Zelauto* to the Earl of Oxford that his translation of *Palmerin of England* was under way.[1] This initial activity turned into a commitment and enterprise that lasted nearly forty years and involved most of the major Iberian romances, with printing and reprinting taking place during the years 1588–92, 1595–96, 1598, 1602, 1609, and 1615–19 and, after Munday's death, in 1637 and 1639. While these translations have been little studied, Munday's expansion of romantic elements, humorous additions, and excisions or alterations of religious references have been discussed. Most recently, Helen Moore has especially commended Munday's style, skill, and accuracy as a translator.[2] Certainly the number and length of these romances and the absence of modern editions have been deterrents to further study. Older habits of dismissing romances as material for popular reading, and specifically for women readers whose interests were imagined as limited to private topics such as love, in combination with dismissive descriptions of Munday as a hack writer, have all discouraged attention. Such habits eliminate the possibility both of taking his work as a translator seriously and of considering his romance projects as ideologically and politically engaged. Further, within early modern English literary studies, there has been relatively little interest in England's relation to early modern Europe and so in the literature of Europe; frequently referred to within English literary contexts of humanism, rhetorical imitation, and theories of genre, the national epics of Spain, France, and Italy have served primarily as points of reference or departure.[3] The most significant disabler, however, has been the absence of any narrative that takes overall account of Munday in relation to the dominant narratives of early modern English literary history.[4]

Involved in the complexities of local and national chivalric culture, Munday's romances spanned a period that coincides closely with the time frame of the Accession Day tilts, 1580–1612, the dates J. S. A. Adamson used to date early modern English chivalric culture.[5] The tilts and other chivalric entertainments performed during the reign of Elizabeth provided an opportunity to celebrate her rule and court by means of the appropriation of pre-Reformation pageantry.[6] Usually expressive of favor and loyalty, and enacted by noblemen such as Leicester, Sir Philip Sidney, and Robert Devereux, Earl of Essex, chivalric displays also exercised the autonomy of the nobility[7] and became sites of contest. At Kenilworth in 1575, when Elizabeth and Leicester were at odds over international policy, each insulted the other.[8] While it is possible to write about a decline in chivalry by 1612[9] and certainly to discard any notion that chivalric forms were monolithic, forms and language of chivalry nevertheless had great staying power, especially for a culture attuned to the acquisition and representation of place and privilege.[10] As central as "forward" Protestant militancy was to this chivalric investment, Catholic gentry eager to defend their nobility against their loss of prestige also valued heraldry and lineage.[11] With chivalric forms as vulnerable to cultural change as other genres, in the early 1620s the attention to chivalry associated with the proposed Spanish match triggered a satiric anti-Catholic backlash and an equally virulent anti-Puritanism, effectively ending English chivalry as it had been known. We are generally familiar with the mixture of these cultural and political agendas as they found representation in Philip Sidney's *The Countesse of Pembrokes Arcadia*, Edmund Spenser's *The Faerie Queene*, and Mary Wroth's *The Countess of Pembroke's Urania* (1621). In addition to Munday's translations, other romances merit better integration into these discussions, including Margaret Tyler's *The Mirror of Knighthood* (1578), John Harington's

Orlando Furioso (1591), and Thomas Shelton's *Don Quixote* (1612, 1620), all of the latter being by translators with strong Catholic ties.

If the English heroic and chivalric romances by Sidney, Spenser, and Wroth were as a genre central to the developing literary system, that development occurred alongside warnings of the spectacular dangers lurking in the continental romances, routinely described as tainted by Catholic origins and steeped in sin, sex, and frivolity. In *The Schoolmaster* (written in the 1560s, printed in 1570), Roger Ascham traced the genre's origin to Catholicism: "In our forefathers tyme, whan papistrie, as a standyng poole, covered and overflowed all England, fewe bookes were read in our tong, savyng certaine bookes of Chevalrie . . . which . . . were made in Monasteries, by idle Monkes, or wanton Chanons." In *Palladis Tamia* (1598), a work that praises Munday as "our best plotter" for drama, Francis Meres cited the authority of Huguenot Lord de la Noue, who "censureth of the bookes of Amadis de Gaule," and then listed other romances to avoid, including *Palmerin de Oliva*, *Primaleon of Greece*, *Palmendos*, *Palladine*, and *The Mirror of Knighthood*—all of which were translated by Munday except *The Mirror of Knighthood*.[12] In a somewhat different construction, Arthur Golding—in his dedication of *The Psalms of David and Others. With J. Calvins Commentaries* (1571) to the Earl of Oxford, his nephew—juxtaposed the chivalric with the religious in order to emphasize the value of right religion to political and social life (*iir–*iiv). Related to these concerns, proclamations—dating especially from 1569, 1570, 1573, years of the Northern Rebellion, the papal bull excommunicating Elizabeth, and Leslie's *Treatise of Treasons*—against bringing foreign seditious books into the country always had as the focus of their concern the importation of Catholic materials.[13] In 1582 books written in defense of Campion and in 1584 *Leicester's Commonwealth* were similarly targeted as seditious.[14] Making translation from French a mainstay of his career, Munday's choice to translate Iberian romances from French translations involved him directly in such importation—smuggling, as it were, material that carried foreign ideologies.

Unlike Catholic books written by contemporaries and imported for subversive purposes, the foreign books that Munday was bringing into the country were of earlier dates, and their vogue in Europe was past. In Spain and Portugal, some fifty chivalric romances were published "almost one a year between 1508 and 1550; nine were added between 1550 and the year of the Armada; only three more came out before the publication of *Don Quixote*."[15]

Thus the period of greatest concentration coincided with the life of Charles V (1500–1558), and with his reigns as king of Spain and as Holy Roman Emperor. In France, where the Iberian romances were introduced under "princely auspices" and "royal patronage," they appeared first in folio for the aristocracy and later in less expensive quarto editions. In Italy they were prepared first for the popular market and later for both markets simultaneously, with quarto editions in italic typeface for the more learned and affluent reader and octavo editions in black letter for the less affluent.[16] Throughout these years of publication, European nations were confronted by Protestant and Turkish challenges to the dominance of Catholic powers, as well as by efforts to redraw the balance of power held by "composite monarchies," that is, monarchies ruling more than one state.[17] In addition to the universal appeal of lively stories, the romances Munday translated entered England during years when England was experiencing a high level of conflict with the Catholic nations of Europe, including reactions abroad to the execution of Catholics; the execution of Mary Queen of Scots; Spanish plotting to invade England and the defeat of the Spanish Armada; the voyage to Cadiz; voyages to and competition with Spain for wealth and power in the New World; the Gunpowder Plot and the Oath of Allegiance controversy; negotiations for a Spanish or French Catholic match for Prince Charles; and the beginnings of the Thirty Years' War. Munday's translations of Spanish and Portuguese romances provided an alternative means through which England's place within this international scene might be imagined and reconsidered.

Overturning earlier views of English identity by writing what would become the central narrative of early modern Protestant England, Foxe, Sidney, Spenser, and others imagined England as a world whose power and safety depended on remaining distinct from Catholic contamination and standing up against Catholic hegemony. Whatever differences existed within this viewpoint, including disagreements with particular issues of Elizabethan Protestant policy as well as varying degrees of disaffection from conservative perspectives on ceremonies and doctrine, anti-Catholicism and antipapalism remained at the core of this perspective. According to Blair Worden, the *Old Arcadia,* written on the heels of Sidney's politically damaging objections to Elizabeth's match with Anjou, encapsulated the program of the "forward" Protestants who preferred that England eschew alliance with both France and Spain and "stand alone." Diplomatically isolated, England needed to "make a virtue of it," taking advantage and glorying as they could in the knowledge that Catholic France and Spain "lived under the curse of God's displeasure."[18] Writing from a vantage point of virtual exile and "complex immersion"[19] in Ireland and Irish culture, and continually interrogating the role of the central Elizabethan government, Spenser nevertheless relied on Protestantism to define England's role in the world.[20] Representing in book 1 of *The Faerie Queene* Queen Elizabeth's glory in having secured Protestant holiness for her country, an accomplishment the nobility were to protect, Spenser embellished that representation with sequences in books 2 and 3 where he traced the Tudor line from Brutus to Elizabeth. As David Armitage has emphasized in his study of the ideological origins of the British empire, those sections of *The Faerie Queene* conceptualize English identity as Briton, a signifier under which the Scots, Welsh, and Irish could all be "reunited into a unitary British monarchy under Elizabeth."[21] That insularity had been central as well to the national identity constructed by John Foxe in *Acts and Monuments*, where he classified foreign peoples—including the Anglo-Saxons—alongside the pope as the threatening and usurping enemy.[22]

"Conceptualised within a wider western European framework" that concentrated on keeping "foreign powers out of the British periphery,"[23] British policy displayed different characteristics depending on what was happening to reformations in religion. During the 1550s and 1560s, when England's chief ally was Spain, France was regarded as the dangerous enemy. Beginning in the 1570s, when the pope's excommunication of Elizabeth and the Spanish alliance with the Netherlands resulted in English military involvement with Protestants in the Netherlands and Huguenots in France, both Leicester and Walsingham wanted "a general anti-Habsburg alliance with France."[24] Another threat from Spain had materialized when, in the wake of the death of King Sebastian of Portugal in 1578, Philip II acquired that kingship and with it all possessions of the Portuguese overseas empire, control of the entire Iberian peninsula, and possession of the "best warfleet in the western world."[25] The fear of what this combination would mean for England and other Protestant countries was palpable from the moment Philip's succession became apparent. When English policy makers were not worrying about Spain's activities in the Netherlands, they were watching Spain's activities in Ireland that were associated with threats on Elizabeth's life and attempts to put Mary Stuart on the English throne.[26] In 1588, the defeat of the Spanish Armada made England's autonomy seem more secure, but in fact what had begun was a war with Spain that would continue until 1604. Efforts to compete internationally with Spain also manifested themselves globally in England's explorations of the New World. According to David Sacks, Richard Hakluyt's "view of empire as a defense against Antichrist" furnished the governing idea for both his *Discourse of Western Planting* (1584) and *The Principal Navigations, Voyages and Discoveries of the English Nation* (first edition 1589, second 1598–1600). Within the context of that endeavor, a concept of an isolated England standing alone against Spain and the pope was exchanged for a vision of English imperial and Protestant expansion.[27] Whichever construction was more at play at any point in time or by any English author, Protestantism remained central to representing English or British identity as something that stood apart from that of Spain and much of Europe.

In contrast to the clarity with which these values justified England's later sixteenth-century policies, Munday's romance represented other models of religious triumphalism. Taking as their baseline the conversion of Constantine to Christianity, the sixteenth-century Iberian romances celebrated a world in which the unity of Christendom defined, coexisted with, and was identical to Catholicism. Having translated the seat of the emperor from the Rome of Augustine to Constantinople meant also, in the words of Anthony Pagden, "the transformation of a Roman *princeps* into a theocratic Hellenistic monarch."[28] Insofar as the tradition that emanated from that transformation contrasted the pagan and classical Roman empire with the Christian empire—the two being "spatially co-extensive"[29]—this Christian empire was conceptualized as an empire under Christ, one head and "one set of beliefs,"[30] with the emperor and the pope claiming "to hold *imperium* over the whole of the Christian world." Most importantly, the notion that a single system embraced "the whole of Christendom" became "one of the strongest elements in the political thought of the period,"[31] an element that the Reformation and English Protestantism had challenged. British insularity and British imperial goals now stood in opposition to a system driven by "inclusiveness" that had operated on the assumption that "there might be many kingdoms—but there could be only one empire."[32]

In the first edition of *Actes and Monuments* (1563), Foxe had bypassed the first one thousand years of the church, including the reign of Constantine, to concentrate on the past five hundred and the impurities introduced into the church during that time. Attacking Foxe, Catholic polemicists were eager to show that later elements of Catholicism—matters of belief, ceremony, and church government—had existed in those earlier days of the church, arguments to which Constantine was central. Answering Foxe with his translation of Bede's *Ecclesiastical Historie of England* (1565), Thomas Stapleton set forth in his dedication to Elizabeth the internationalized model Constantine had provided for kings and emperors, who were to "maintaine the only Catholike faith in their dominions, and to chase eftesoones all schismes and heresies that from time to time sprange up amonge." Noting Constantine's contribution in putting down the Arian heresy, he related how Constantine sent Osius, bishop of Corduba in Spain, to the churches of Egypt, with letters exhorting a reconciliation among those where religious division had arisen. He wrote to Arius and Alexander, bishop of Alexandria, to persuade them to come to accord and held a general council at Nice, where he himself represented any who could not attend, afterwards banishing Arius and others "of that secte." Describing next how Constantine dealt with Donatus by turning the problem over to the pope of Rome, Stapleton concluded by citing Constantine's contribution to church unity: "Thus laboured that vertuous and Christen Emperour Constantin the great to maintaine the unite of Christes church, and to abolish all heresies in the provinces of the whole world then subject unto him. This glasse he lefte to . . . other Christen Princes to looke on" (*5r). Continuing his attack in *A Counterblast to M. Hornes Vayne Blaste against M. Fekenham* (Louvain, 1567), Stapleton argued that while Constantine, like other emperors, had been an important supporter of the church, taking action that would eliminate heresy, he was never supreme governor of the church, having neither the power nor the desire to assume any authority over it.[33]

Explaining in the 1570 edition the need to reply to these "Lovanian bookes" (1:*i verso), Foxe announced that he would now present the "Image of both Churches, as well of the one, as of the other," beginning with the time of the apostles and continuing through the early years of English history (1:iiir). This change resulted in adding not only the Anglo-Saxon material for which Foxe is well known but also a lengthy treatment of Constantine as an example to all princes for the "zeale and care they ought to beare toward the Church of Christ" (1583, I4r); granting this important role, Foxe disputed the notion that from the time of Constantine the bishop of Rome had "supreme dominion" over the "spiritual governement of all . . . partes of the world" (1583, I4v). Claimed as an exemplar by Catholics and Protestants, Constantine had become both an icon of church unity and a focal point for religious-political dispute that would become common as well in the works of John Dee and Edmund Spenser, as they appropriated for the queen the Catholic imperial iconography of Constantine and Charles V.[34] Inscribed visually and verbally, this association of Queen Elizabeth with Constantine represented Elizabeth's authority over the church as similar to the power held by Constantine as he rid the world of heresies.[35] We are so familiar with this inscription that it is difficult to see it as anything but a monolith.

Nevertheless, in recuperating the romances of Spain and Portugal, Munday transferred into the English-language narratives in which the Constantine of Catholic ideology provided one of the organizing principles. Whatever the neutralizing effect of Munday's having excised details of Catholic religious practice—knights attending Mass and praying to the Virgin Mary, for example—those changes did not eliminate the plot elements that represent the normative as a world unified politically and religiously by way of Catholicism. Normally we consider an act of translation to involve appropriating material to the purposes of the target culture and its language, an act that often involves erasing aspects of the original in order to adjust the work to the ideology of the target.[36] Thus, while Munday certainly sanitized the original by eliminating a great deal of the Catholic religious material, he bypassed the opportunity either to remake the works as Protestant—Spenser's choice in adapting Ariosto and other continental forerunners for *The Faerie Queene*—or to disparage or revise the ideology of the Iberian works. In this instance, in which the translation into English of a narrative that represented a Catholic worldview was not adjusted to take on the ideology of the dominant and current culture, the task of translation constituted a preservationist move, a means of retaining and restoring the presence of an alternative—in this case, a "Romanizing"—view.[37] Thus, for Munday's romances, being able to notice how much is the same becomes more important than noticing what has been changed. In this program of "vernacular cultural enhancement,"[38] overall, the plots are the same, and usually book number matches book number, chapter number matches chapter number. Analogous but not identical in aim to such Catholic translations into English as Thomas Stapleton's *Bede's Ecclesiastical History*, Gregory Martin's *Rheims New Testament* and *Douay Old Testament*, and numerous devotional works, Munday's romances helped create a public sphere in which the Catholic perspective remained a competing voice and offered a counternarrative that represented the larger Catholic world positively as advantageous to England's safety and identity. Such views were thoroughly consonant with Catholic loyalism, that is, with loyalty to the

English nation and monarch coupled to a simultaneous disaffection with the loss of Catholicism as the national religion.

Many complications confront any study of Munday's romances. Their vexed bibliographic record adds to the challenge, with no list of titles and dates telling the complete story. Some of the romances announced as forthcoming did not appear, such as the *Orlando Furioso* promised in *Archaioplutos, or the Riches of Elder Ages* (1592) and *Amadis,* books 5 through 8, announced in book 1 (1619).[39] While an array of printer's rights were assigned for various volumes at different times, many volumes were never printed. Munday frequently made disclaimers attributing translating discrepancies to the contingencies of haste, distraction, and printers' errors. In the dedication of *Gerileon,* Munday also described how his work has been delayed and interrupted by his duties as messenger of the queen:

> I have been divers and sundrie times countermanded by her Majesties appointment, in the place where I serve, to post from place to place on such affaires as were enjoyned mee, so that not having fully finished one sheete, and the Printer beginning almost so soone as my selfe; I have been greatly his hinderaunce, and compelled to catch hold or such little leasures, as in the morning ere I went to horse-backe, or in the evening comming into mine Inne, I could compasse from companie. That I fable not herein, you are my witnesse; in that at your owne house I wrote a sheete or two, and elsewhere in your companie, as occasion served: and sithence in a long lingring journey, I have knit up the rest, sending leafe by leafe unperused to the Printer, which must needes yeelde doubyt of a perfect Translation. (A2r–A2v)

Some sections were translated by others; in the dedication to *Primaleon, Part 2* (1596), Munday remarked, "It was not my hap to doo the first part of *Primaleon,* (but onely the first foure sheetes thereof) by reason of my urgent occasions at that time."[40] Finally, his work contains advertising pitches, from announcements that a volume is forthcoming to his remark in *Palmerin D'Oliva* that he published his romances in segments because a smaller book sold more readily than a larger one and the promise of a sequel enticed the reader (A4r).[41]

While Munday's romances merit many discussions,[42] this essay deals only with selected sections of *Palmerin of England, Part 1,* sections that nevertheless illustrate some of the range of his engagement.

Palmerin of England, Part 1

Although we are used to thinking of English romance from Sidney through Wroth as part of a self-contained Protestant cultural project, that picture suffers some adjustment if we factor into it certain details of the continental chivalric romances that were translated into English during this period. Margaret Tyler dedicated *The Mirror of Knighthood* (1578) to Thomas Howard, first Earl of Suffolk and second son of Thomas, fourth Duke of Norfolk, executed in 1572 for his involvement in the plan to marry Mary Queen of Scots and in the subsequent rebellion of the Northern earls. Acknowledging to the reader that Spain was the work's country of origin—"in which nation by common report the inheritaunce of worldlye commendation hath to this days rested"—Tyler initiated a series of romance publications dedicated to people in England who were of or close to the Catholic party. Munday's romances included dedications to the Earl of Oxford and two of his children, as well as to the recusant Ralph Marshall. Thomas Shelton, who provided a commendatory verse for Richard Verstegan's *A Restitution of Decayed Intelligence* (1605), dedicated *The Historie of Don-Quixote* (1612)—an antichivalric romance—to Theophilus Howard, son to Thomas, first Earl of Suffolk. Different from these works, John Harington's *Orlando Furioso* was commanded by and dedicated to Queen Elizabeth, but his connections to Romanism remained strong, as is clear from his epigrams, some aspects of his translation of *Orlando Furioso,* and other works.[43]

These details shift just enough attention away from the Protestant program to make room to consider that Catholic romances were being placed in dialogue with their Protestant counterparts and, in the case of Tyler and Munday, were regarded suspiciously for religious and political reasons.[44] In 1582, *The Second Part of the First Booke of the Mirror of Knighthood* was licensed to Thomas East "to be printed, condiconally notwithstandinge that when the same is translate yt be brought to them [Barker and Coldock] to be perused, and yf any thinge be amisse therein to be amended."[45] While in *Zelauto* (1580) Munday had promised Oxford that *Palmerin of England* would be forthcoming, a Stationers' Register entry for February 13, 1581, specifies its license to Charlewood, "uppon Condicon that if there be anie thinge founde in The booke . . . worthie of Reprehension . . . then all the Bookes shalbe put to waste and Burnte."[46] In its request for freedom from control, the epilogue to the 1602 edition of *Palmerin* seems to confirm that this work caused suspicion:

"[I]f you finde the translation alterd, or . . . impaired, let this excuse answere his default. . . . A worke so large is sufficient to tire so simple a workeman as himselfe: and beside the Printer may in some place let an error escape. So between these two reasons, let the Author passe uncontrowled." In 1589, permission to John Wolfe to print *Amadis of Gaul,* books 2–5, specified that the bishops reserved the right to look at every book prior to printing.[47] Analogously, a remark Munday made in the prefatory material to *Primaleon,* book 1 (1619), seems to confirm that what had been at issue with *Primaleon* and other romances was Munday's persistent effort to get material into print that others had recognized as running against official policy. Dedicating *Primaleon* to Henry de Vere, Oxford's son, in the years of negotiations for the Spanish match, Munday noted that the several parts of *Primaleon* had long slept in oblivion but was "by favour of these more friendly times comming once more to be seene on the world's publiche theatre." In 1619, a moment had arrived that provided a more hospitable climate for voicing certain views in public.

While editions of *Palmerin of England, Part 1* appeared in 1596, 1602, 1609, and 1616, the fact that the romance had been planned for publication in 1581 especially warrants discussion of it within the context of that early date. The topic of royal succession stands at the center of the narrative of *Palmerin of England, Part 1,* a book in which that fixation participates in the larger concern for an ideology and politics based in a united Christendom. Such a narrative could have had acute applicability for the dates of both thwarted and successful publication, during the period of the Anjou marriage negotiations in 1578–81, following the publication in 1595 of Parsons's *Conference about the Next Succession,* at the end of the Nine Years' War and English defeat of the Irish and Spanish in 1601, and at the start of the negotiations for the Spanish match in 1616. In 1596, the date of the expanded *The Faerie Queene,* attention was also drawn to Spain and Cadiz. In 1609, when *The Faerie Queene* was again reprinted, the operable contexts may have included both the Oath of Allegiance controversy and the possibilities for England's future as represented by Prince Henry, the chivalric exemplar, on the eve of his investiture as Prince of Wales.[48] Whatever the valence of this work at later moments, the political circumstances of the years when it was first announced and entered, 1580–81, offer a compelling earlier context. In the first half of *Palmerin of England, Part 1,* the crisis in the kingdom of "Great Britain" (Munday's term, which constitutes a verbatim translation of the French version) has to do with England's loss of its heirs to the throne, a situation that throws the country into great sorrow. When the news of England's plight spreads abroad, knights of other countries come to Great Britain to lend assistance, circumstances that represent England not in isolation but as part of an international community of support that includes the emperor of Constantinople. If such a narrative could conceivably represent the tenets of Protestant internationalism, the second half of *Palmerin* argues for a different reading. For there, the action shifts to the Continent, to actions primarily in Spain and France, and, most centrally, to Miragarda, the Spanish princess whose beauty and worth are tested and proven to exceed those of any lady in the world. With the resources of the Catholic world so attractively presented, *Palmerin* would have been, by any measure, a challenging narrative for an Elizabethan readership.

Proceeding from the premise that England belongs to a European community to which she can turn in time of trouble, the *Palmerin* narrative begins with the catastrophe that has befallen the English King Frederick; the enchantress Eutropa has imprisoned his son Don Edward, who is married to the emperor's daughter. With the news that Don Edward, as well as Don Edward's twin sons Palmerin of England and Florian du Desert, have disappeared, and with his people now mourning this loss and fearful for their future, King Frederick sends a messenger to the emperor Palmerin D'Oliva of Constantinople to tell him of England's misfortune. Having gathered in Constantinople to celebrate the birth of the daughter of Prince Primaleon and now hearing news of England's distress, knights from many nations decide to go to England's aid. Primaleon departs first, followed by the king of Thessaly; two sons of the king of Hungary; the prince of Germany; Armedes, who is king of France; Recinde, who is king of Spain and soldan of Niquee; and "many princes more." Presenting an image directly opposite that of an England barricading itself against European enemies,[49] this narrative represents France, Spain, and others coming to lend a hand, even temporarily abandoning their own countries to go to the aid of Great Britain. The implications of this rescue mission include acknowledgment that England knows her dependency on stranger princes and an assumption that stranger princes have an investment in protecting the future of Great Britain. Both notions have something in common with Hiram Morgan's observation that England was not the only nation with a "British policy"; European nations also had British policies.[50]

As the narrative progresses through accounts of the knights' adventures in Great Britain, several plot elements repeat. Knights do battle with each other, and then, recognizing that their opponent is someone with whom they value alliance, stop fighting and embrace, as when Don Edward realizes he is fighting with Primaleon (ch. 10). Some knights go on to France and Spain to try their fortune and courtesy. Frequently, knights assume other names: Palmerin of England goes by the name Knight of Fortune; Florian by the name King of the Savage Man. To the Knight of Fortune falls the difficult task of having to rescue the many knights who came to help King Frederick but who one by one are nearly all imprisoned by Eutropa's nephew, Dramusiande. Other episodes represent the transfer of power from one group to another. At issue in one case is an enforced change in religion; at issue in others is English conquest of Ireland. Both are rich in political and religious valence for the 1580s.

The section that acknowledges the destruction of an ancient religion—and that invites a reading that relates to the Protestant takeover in England—occurs at a point when, after many adventures, this Knight of Fortune (Palmerin) arrives in London and, going first to a chapel, is astonished to find that many tombs have been ruined. A hermit informs him that the tombs were spoiled thirty-four years ago when the infidels invaded the land (ch. 36). Written by the Portuguese Francisco de Moraes, *Palmerin of England* was first printed in Portugal in approximately 1544, and in France in French translation in 1553,[51] dates that place the writing during the reign of Henry VIII, after the break with Rome and dissolution of the monasteries, and that place the French translation near the beginning of the reign of Mary Tudor, who would shortly become the wife of the king of Spain. The romance is thus not only Catholic in its origins but historically positioned in relation to the English break from Catholic universalism. Newly relevant in 1580, the reference to thirty-four years could then also have encompassed the reign and iconoclasm of Edward VI.[52]

Whatever the reader's initial point of reference, Eutropa has continued an analogous form of spoliation, although in her case the ruin is not of tombs but of place, identity, and concord—a situation that matches the experience of displaced and disenfranchised Catholic nobility. Under Eutropa's guidance, the pagans have become lords over kingdoms and countries, with the result that the knights who previously defended the country must now disguise their identities for safety. Hoping not to be recognized, they alter their armor and the devices on their shields. Eutropa has even succeeded in lining up the competing groups in such a way that no one is able to tell which side anyone is on, with the result that son has fought against father, brother against brother, and friend against friend (ch. 37). This situation has caused enmity not only at home but through all Christendom. Finally, in a utopian version of what might yet come to pass in England, the Knight of Fortune (Palmerin) arrives, conquers Dramusiande, and frees all the knights, thereby ending Eutropa's enchantment (ch. 41). With this victory accomplished, all of the stranger knights can finally leave England to return to their own kingdoms.

In the first fifty chapters of *Palmerin,* two sequences involving Ireland offer an analogous counternarrative. While again a variety of contexts may have given these episodes added relevance at different times, in 1544 and 1553 the relevant contexts would likely have been events in Ireland connected to Henry VIII's break with Rome, Cromwellian reform in England and Ireland, the dissolution of Irish monasteries, and the offense to Katherine of Aragon and thus to Charles V that these events represented.[53] The situation in Ireland had been exacerbated by Henry's move in 1534 to strip the Fitzgeralds of power; in response, Thomas Fitzgerald, soon to become tenth Earl of Kildare, led 140 horsemen to St. Mary's Abbey, denounced Henry VIII, and tried to take Dublin and Dublin castle, while boasting that he anticipated the assistance of Spanish troops. Meanwhile, "reports reaching Spain, France and Rome . . . presented the upheaval in Ireland as a crusade against an excommunicated ruler."[54] Henry's destruction of Kildare's power and subsequent executions represent well the kind of event on which Catholic Europeans would not have seen eye to eye with England's central authorities.

In 1581, however, later contexts that would have been relevant included the massacre at Mullenghast (1578), the effort of Thomas Stukeley to invade Ireland in 1577 under a papal banner, the attempt of James Fitzmaurice Fitzgerald and Nicholas Sanders to instigate in 1579 an Irish Catholic revolt against Elizabethan rule, and the related massacre at Smerwick in 1580. As W. G. Palmer has emphasized, "Fitzmaurice's landing represents something of a watershed in early modern Irish history," for with his landing the rumors of foreign invasions of Ireland "actually came true" and proved to be "the most visible manifestation of the power politics of the Counter Reformation coming to bear on Tudor policy in Ireland."[55] Part of the English response to this threat was massacre; another was general repression. In July 1580, after Campion's arrival in England, Elizabeth issued a proclamation that attributed current dangers in England to "English rebels and traitors overseas, and their accomplices at home, who were seeking to induce foreign princes to invade

England and had already provoked a papal invasion of Ireland" and announced that the queen had "mustered the strength of her realm . . . to withstand all hostile attempts by land or sea."[56]

As we might expect, the Irish episodes in *Palmerin* mimic the European Catholic view of England-Ireland relations. Rather than representing Ireland as under threat from a foreign continental power, the narrative tells of an Ireland that has been taken over by cruel giants with connections in England, in effect a reversal of the rhetoric English Protestants used to define and justify their methods in Ireland as an effort to civilize and purify.[57] In *The Faerie Queene,* Spenser would represent the English effort to defeat Spanish control of Ireland by way of Artegall, who is duty-bound to rescue Irena from Grantorto.[58] In the case of *Palmerin,* however, the rescuer is the Knight of the Savage Man (Florian); driven to Ireland by a storm, he discovers the Giant Calfurnien, who kills any who come his way and who, we learn later, is brother to a giant in England. Arriving at Calfurnien's castle, built by the king of Ireland but taken from him by force, the Knight of the Savage Man finds the ground littered with broken swords and armor and four knights on their knees being held in subjection. After defeating Calfurnien, the Knight of the Savage Man meets three women, daughters of the Marquesse Beltamor, whose father once met with the displeasure of the king of England. As a result the women have the castles their father built for them but have not inherited his wealth and so are left to abide other men's reversion. The entire sequence on how the women have been wronged seems to depend on an acknowledgment of the centrality of Irish women—wives and daughters—to the network of alliances in Irish cultural and political life, and more particularly to their struggle to maintain or regain control over their inheritances in the face of English-Irish conflict.[59] Further, the narrative projects the ultimate solution as available and originating in England itself, not from a foreign land. In the sections at issue, the Knight of the Savage Man (Florian), the English heir to the English throne, eventually destroys the giants. Initially, the Knight assures them that he can help them repossess their lands, that his influence with the king of England is strong, and that he regards the offense of their noble father as small (ch. 28). Many chapters later (ch. 65), the thread of this narrative resumes when Florian is in the English court entreating the king on behalf of the women's lost "patrimonie." Taking a position that the Elizabethan Catholics hoped to experience from their monarch and one that may even acknowledge generational differences,[60] the English king decides that although their father pursued a treasonable enterprise against him, the innocent daughters should not suffer for another's crimes: "since he hath sustained Law according to desert and his whole possessions are fallen into our hands, we returne them to the use and profite of the Damsels. . . . I will that the eldest of them be married to Don Rosiran my cousin and your great friend Argolant. . . . [F]or the third, we restore her to the Marquisate of her father, and will joyne her in marriage with Beltamor, brother to the fare-named Don Rosiran." Thus the daughters are not only restored to their inheritances but integrated into the society by marriage. This sequence of episodes is potentially applicable to any number of more specific interpretations.[61] And given the ease with which Harington personalized his readings of *Orlando Furioso*,[62] we can assume that *Palmerin* and others Munday translated were available for similarly topical readings, most of which would contrast sharply with Spenser's and others' recommended strategies of violence for recovering Ireland.[63]

Finally, the Irish material in *Palmerin* includes a separate incident that recalls the first English invasion of Ireland by Richard de Clare, second Earl of Pembroke, otherwise known as Strongbow, in 1170, as well as other invasions.[64] In chapter 32, the Knight of Fortune meets up with a ship carrying the giant Camboldam of Mulzella, the Lord of Penebroque, known as one of the cruelest tyrants in all the world and now seeking the knight who slew his brother Calfurnien. (In chapter 32 in the French edition, printed in Lyon in 1553, the name is "Camboldan de Mulzella, seigneur de Penebrocque"). The Knight of Fortune kills Camboldam and heads toward Great Britain to right yet other wrongs. In linking the first moment the English came to Ireland to cruelty later perpetrated on it, the narrative again characterizes England as the source of tyranny.

While the first half of *Palmerin* includes fictional narratives about the harm that has come to England with the abandonment of an old religion and the harm that England's oppressive measures have brought to Ireland, in the second half that harm is felt across the world. There the action moves out of Great Britain and to the Continent, with focus primarily on Spain but also on France. Throughout this half, the constant point of reference is Constantinople, from which vantage point it is clear that the disruptive situation in Great Britain has weakened the entire Christian world: the soldan of Babylon now has designs upon the empire. In succeeding chapters, the contest centers on a series of episodes aimed at proving the superiority of the Spanish princess, Miragarda, and thus also on proving her superiority over Targiana, the daughter of the Turk. Such material, which originally would have represented Spain's nationalism and goal of European and world domination, would have had great resonance in the years following Spain's defeat of the Turk at Lepanto in 1571, a defeat that seemed to signal that Christendom was successfully united against the Turk.[65] But the emphasis on knights from different countries trying to identify and claim as their own the best princess would have continued to carry topical meanings when Mary Tudor was married to Philip II, when Elizabeth was negotiating a match with Anjou, when Catholics were hoping that Mary Stuart or the Spanish Infanta would succeed Elizabeth, and when James was hoping for a Spanish match for Prince Charles, all moments when there was support for a policy that would prevent England from being isolated against a united Catholic Europe.

Given these contexts, such an idealized representation of a Spanish princess remains, for a publication in England and even by a Catholic loyalist, rather startling. The praise of Miragarda virtually knows no bounds. First Florendos and next Palmerin travel to Spain, where each learns of the beautiful princess Miragarda. While Florendos falls in love with her, Palmerin seeks to prove that his lady Polinarda (the lady featured in *Zelauto*) is superior to her. Continuing on his journeys, Palmerin comes to Navarre in the dominion of France (ch. 64), where giants imprison him in the castle. In the next chapter, the Princess Arnalte, daughter of the king of Navarre and a princess in love with Palmerin, is jealous of Miragarda. When all of the knights assure her that Miragarda is indeed superior, she gives in and releases Palmerin. A few chapters later, Targiana, the Turk's daughter, challenges Miragarda's superiority by sending Albayzar, the soldan of Babylon, to fight on her behalf. Recognizing Miragarda's beauty, Albayzar makes off in the middle of the night with the shield that has her picture on it and later uses it to argue that Targiana, the Turk, is more fair (ch. 82), an action that shows he is "blinded in love" (ch. 83). Finally Florendos, now going by the name the Black Knight, fights Albayzar to prove that Miragarda is superior.

As the story progresses, there exists the threat of continued war, along with increasing attention to the challenges offered by the leaders of Babylon, Persia, and the Turks. Although the emperor refuses to submit to the pagan demands, the tests include the soldan of Persia's request that Polinarda, daughter of Primaleon, be sent to marry him and that Florendos marry Armenia, daughter to Albayzar, the material Munday appropriated to different ends in

Zelauto. When the emperor replies that he would rather engage in perpetual war than hold league with them in these ways, heathen giants declare that they will reduce the empire to a desolate wilderness, the infant will be torn from the mother's breast, the channels of the streets shall pour forth the blood of their murdered subjects, the city now standing in wealth and pride shall be confounded, and people will say, "[H]ere sometimes stood the Cittie of Constantinople" (ch. 93). In the ensuing war, the emperor's knights defeat the giants, but in another part of the story Primaleon defends Albayzar, explaining that, while the Turks offer injury to his knights, Albayzar is not guilty of injuring them, and his alliance is needed. Similarly, Primaleon goes to the defense of Targiana, and Florendos travels with Albayzar in the dominions of Spain. At the end, Palmerin is again sent on his way for yet another adventure. Insofar as these last details primarily narrate Spain's success in curbing the Turk, they also present the Turk—not the Catholic—as the Other and represent Catholic Spain and Catholic Europe as the protectors of the unity of Christendom. The original delay in printing *Palmerin of England, Part 1*, its much later appearance in 1596, and its reprinting in the context of negotiations for the Spanish match are all made more understandable by a reading of the romance that takes account of its recuperative and aggressive ideological stance.

There are many questions that we can put to this material, including whether the argument I have made here can be sustained across other romances. The simplest, although rather totalizing, answer to that question is that the Catholic worldview is ever present whether or not we draw historical parallels and whether or not details of Catholic worship are omitted. A more limited but also more specific answer has to do with the degree to which the reprinting of several of Munday's romances at the time of the Spanish match negotiations confirms their and Munday's agenda. But once comfortable with the basic thesis, we may conclude that one significance of identifying these translations as representing a Catholic ideology put in circulation by a Catholic loyalist lies in what this combination suggests about the persistence of the Catholic narrative in England throughout the 1590s and into the reign of James. Further, with the example of Munday, we have some of the best evidence of the way a Catholic did and did not accommodate himself to Protestant culture and at the same time some suggestive material for considering how the wider culture accommodated the Catholic loyalist. Surely Munday was known in his time for what he was.

Notes

1. See Donna B. Hamilton, "Anthony Munday and *The Merchant of Venice*," *Shakespeare Survey* 54 (2001): 89–99, and *Anthony Munday and the Catholics, 1560–1633* (Aldershot: Ashgate, 2005). I am grateful to Ashgate for permission to publish a section from a chapter of my book.

2. John J. O'Connor, *Amadis de Gaule and Its Influence on Elizabethan Literature* (New Brunswick: Rutgers University Press, 1970), 131–47; Helen D. Moore, ed., "The Ancient and Honourable History of Amadis de Gaule: A Critical, Modern-Spelling Edition of Anthony Munday's Translation of Book One (1589; 1619) with Introduction, Notes and Commentary," 2 vols. (PhD diss., University of Oxford, 1996), vol. 1. See also Henry Thomas, *Spanish and Portuguese Romances of Chivalry: The Revival of the Romance of Chivalry in the Spanish Peninsula, and Its Extension and Influence Abroad* (Cambridge: Cambridge University Press, 1920), 149–55; Celeste Turner, *Anthony Mundy: An Elizabethan Man of Letters* (Berkeley: University of California Press, 1928); Mary Patchell, *The Palmerin Romances in Elizabethan Fiction* (New York: Columbia University Press, 1947), 15–23, 93, 127, 134.

3. Nabil Matar, *Turks, Moors, and Englishmen in the Age of Discovery* (New York: Columbia University Press, 1999), 13.

4. In Hamilton, *Anthony Munday,* I read Munday as a conformed Protestant and Catholic loyalist.

5. J. S. A. Adamson, "Chivalry and Political Culture in Caroline England," in *Culture and Politics in Early Stuart England,* ed. Kevin Sharpe and Peter Lake (Stanford: Stanford University Press, 1993), 165.

6. See Frances A. Yates, *Astraea: The Imperial Theme in the Sixteenth Century* (Boston: Routledge and Kegan Paul, 1975), 108–11.

7. Richard C. McCoy, *The Rites of Knighthood: The Literature and Politics of Elizabethan Chivalry* (Berkeley: University of California Press, 1989).

8. Susan Frye, *Elizabeth I: The Competition for Representation* (New York: Oxford University Press, 1993), 56–96.

9. Arthur B. Ferguson, *The Chivalric Tradition in Renaissance* (Washington: Folger Shakespeare Library, 1986), 140.

10. See William Rockett, "*Britannia,* Ralph Brooke, and the Representation of Privilege in Elizabethan England," *Renaissance Quarterly* 53 (2000): 474–99.

11. Richard Cust, "Catholicism, Antiquarianism and Gentry Honour: The Writings of Sir Thomas Shirley," *Midland History* 23 (1998): 40–70.

12. Thomas, *Spanish and Portuguese Romances,* 264, 265.

13. See Paul L. Hughes and James F. Larkin, eds., *Tudor Royal Proclamations,* vol. 1, *Royal Proclamations of King James I, 1603–1625* (New Haven: Yale University Press, 1964), 312–13, 341–43, 347–48, 376–79.

14. James F. Larkin and Paul L. Hughes, *Tudor Royal Proclamations,* vol. 2, *The Later Tudors (1553–1587)* (New Haven: Yale University Press, 1969), 488–91; D. C. Peck, "Government Suppression of Elizabethan Catholic Books: The Case of *Leicester's Commonwealth,*" *Library Quarterly* 47 (1977): 163–77; Cyndia Susan Clegg, *Press Censorship in Elizabethan England* (Cambridge: Cambridge University Press, 1997), 92–93.

15. Thomas, *Spanish and Portuguese Romances,* 147–48.

16. Ibid., 199–208; Paul F. Grendler, "Form and Function in Italian Renaissance Popular Books," *Renaissance Quarterly* 46 (1993): 470–83.

17. See J. H. Elliott, "A Europe of Composite Monarchies," *Past and Present* 137 (1992): 48–71.

18. Blair Worden, *The Sound of Virtue: Philip Sidney's "Arcadia" and Elizabethan Politics* (New Haven: Yale University Press, 1996), 115–16.

19. Christopher Highley, *Shakespeare, Spenser, and the Crisis in Ireland* (Cambridge: Cambridge University Press, 1997), 15.

20. Ibid., 17.

21. David Armitage, *The Ideological Origins of the British Empire* (Cambridge: Cambridge University Press, 2000), 54.

22. See Donna B. Hamilton, "Catholic Use of Anglo-Saxon Precedents, 1565–1625: Thomas Stapleton, Nicholas Harpsfield, Robert Persons, Richard Verstegan, Richard Broughton and Others," *Recusant History* 26, no. 4 (2003): 537–55; Anthony Pagden, *Lords of All the World: Ideologies of Empire in Spain, Britain and France, c. 1500–c. 1800* (New Haven: Yale University Press, 1995).

23. Hiram Morgan, "British Policies before the British State," in *The British Problem, c. 1534–1707: State Formation in the Atlantic Archipelago,* ed. Brendan Bradshaw and John Morrill (New York: St. Martin's Press, 1996), 66, 87.

24. R. B. Wernham, *The Making of Elizabethan Foreign Policy, 1558–1603* (Berkeley: University of California Press, 1980), 41; Wallace T. MacCaffrey, *Queen Elizabeth and the Making of Policy, 1572–1588* (Princeton: Princeton University Press, 1981), 302–23.

25. Geoffrey Parker, *The Grand Strategy of Philip II* (New Haven: Yale University Press, 1998), 87, 167.

26. Ibid., 161–91.

27. David Sacks, "Discourses of Western Planting: Richard Hakluyt, Europe's Wars of Religion, and the Beginnings of the British Empire," paper presented at the Early Modern British History Seminar, Cambridge University, November 21, 2001. I am grateful to David Sacks for allowing me to read this paper, the materials from which will appear in Sacks's forthcoming book *To Restore the Distracted Globe: Richard Hakluyt and His World.*

28. Pagden, *Lords of All the World,* 15.

29. Ibid., 24.

30. Ibid., 25.

31. Ibid., 27 (quoting J. H. Burns).

32. Ibid., 17.

33. Thomas Stapleton, *A Counterblast to M. Hornes Vayne Blaste against M. Fekenham* (Louvain, 1567), Y1r–Dd2v. See also Thomas Harding's *A confutation of a booke intituled An apologie of the church of England* (Antwerp, 1565), YY3v–YY4r, RRR1r, and *A detection of sunndrie foule errours, lies, sclaunders, corruptions, and other false dealinges, touching doctrine, and other matters, uttered and practized by M. Jewel, in a booke lately by him set foorth entituled, A defence of the Apologie* (Antwerp, 1568), a4v–b1r.

34. Yates, *Astraea*, 38–59; John N. King, *Tudor Royal Iconography: Literature and Art in an Age of Crisis* (Princeton: Princeton University Press, 1989), and *Spenser's Poetry and the Reformation Tradition* (Princeton: Princeton University Press, 1990).

35. See Yates, *Astraea*, 41–44; see also King, *Spenser's Poetry*.

36. See Daniel Russell, "Introduction: The Renaissance," in *The Politics of Translation in the Middle Ages and the Renaissance*, ed. Renate Blumenfel-Kosinski, Luise Von Flotow, and Daniel Russell (Ottawa: University of Ottawa Press, 2001), 31.

37. See Hugh Lloyd-Jones, "Erasmus, Dolet and the Politics of Translation," in Blumenfel-Kosinski, Von Flotow, and Russell, *Politics of Translation*, 37–56.

38. Ibid., 52.

39. Turner, *Anthony Mundy*, 89–90, 183.

40. Patchell, *Palmerin Romances*, 17. This remark may refer to the time he was in the Netherlands on a passport issued October 10, 1595, for six months; see Willem Schrickx, "Anthony Munday in the Netherlands in October 1595," *Notes and Queries* 44 (1997): 484–85.

41. See Thomas, *Spanish and Portuguese Romances*, 249–50; H. S. Bennett, *English Books and Readers, 1558–1603: Being a Study in the History of the Book Trade in the Reign of Elizabeth I* (Cambridge: Cambridge University Press, 1965), 253.

42. In Hamilton, *Anthony Munday*, I discuss other Munday romances.

43. Steven W. May, *The Elizabethan Courtier Poets: The Poems and Their Contexts* (Asheville, NC: Pegasus Press, 1999), 151–61; Jason Scott-Warren, *Sir John Harington and the Book as Gift* (New York: Oxford University Press, 2001). For Harington's defense of Ariosto, see Townsend Rich, *Harington and Ariosto: A Study in Elizabethan Verse Translation* (New Haven: Yale University Press, 1940), 41–45. For Harington's sympathetic representation of Ireland in his translation, see Clare Carroll, *Circe's Cup: Cultural Transformation in Early Modern Writing about Ireland* (Notre Dame: University of Notre Dame Press, 2001), 69–90. See also Ruth Hughey, ed., *The Arundel Harington Manuscript of Tudor Poetry*, 2 vols. (Columbus: Ohio State University Press, 1960).

44. Bennett, *English Books and Readers,* 62–63. Bennet mentions the Stationers' Register notations for the second part of Tyler's *Mirrour* (1582) and for Munday's *Palmerin* and *Amadis*; see discussion below. For more extensive discussion of these issues, see Hamilton, *Anthony Munday.*

45. Edward Arber, ed., *A Transcript of the Registers of the Company of Stationers of London, 1554–1640 A.D.,* 5 vols. (Gloucester, MA: P. Smith, 1967), 2:414.

46. Ibid., 2:383; Turner, *Anthony Mundy,* 47–48.

47. Bennett, *English Books and Readers,* 63; Arber, *Transcript of the Registers,* 2:607.

48. Ben Jonson's *Speeches at Prince Henry's Barriers* (1609) was prepared for a tournament played on January 6, 1610; see Helen D. Moore, "Jonson, Dekker, and the Discourse of Chivalry," *Medieval and Renaissance Drama in England* 12 (1999): 126. Munday's *London's Love,* an entertainment to celebrate Prince Henry's investiture, is dated 1610.

49. See Worden, *Sound of Virtue,* 115–24.

50. Morgan, "British Policies."

51. Thomas, *Spanish and Portuguese Romances,* 110–13, 147–48.

52. Eamon Duffy, *The Stripping of the Altars: Traditional Religion in England, c. 1400–c. 1580* (New Haven: Yale University Press, 1992), 379–477. See also Susan Brigden, *London and the Reformation* (Oxford: Clarendon Press, 1991), on the tombs specifically, 429, on the reign of Edward VI, 421–57.

53. Colm Lennon, *Sixteenth-Century Ireland: The Incomplete Conquest* (New York: St. Martin's Press, 1995), 103–4; Henry A. Jefferies, "The Early Tudor Reformations in the Irish Pale," *Journal of Ecclesiastical History* 52 (2001): 34–62.

54. Lennon, *Sixteenth-Century Ireland,* 107–9.

55. W. G. Palmer, "Ireland and English Foreign Policy in the 1570s," *Historian* 58 (1995): 100, and *The Problem of Ireland in Tudor Foreign Policy, 1485–1603* (Woodbridge: Boydell Press, 1994). For an overview of the history of Ireland relevant to this romance, see chapters by G. A. Hayes-McCoy in *A New History of Ireland,* vol. 3, *Early Modern Ireland, 1534–1691,* 10 vols., ed. T.W. Moody, F.X. Martin, and F. J. Byrne (New York: Oxford University Press, 1976–91), 3:39–141.

56. Conyers Read, *Lord Burghley and Queen Elizabeth* (New York: Alfred A. Knopf, 1960), 244, 244–47; Worden, *Sound of Virtue,* 76, 116.

57. Capitalizing on prejudicial notions that Irish Catholics were barbaric and anthropologically inferior infidels supporting a tyrannical and usurping pope, English political rhetoric cast the program for achieving domination in Ireland as an effort to civilize and purify. See John McGurk, *The Elizabethan Conquest of Ireland: The 1590s Crisis* (New York: Manchester University Press, 1997), 16; Nicholas Canny, *The Elizabethan Conquest of Ireland: A Pattern Established, 1565–76* (New York: Barnes and Noble, 1976), 125–36.

58. See Highley, *Shakespeare, Spenser,* 123.

58. For the situation in Ireland as represented in this paragraph, and especially on the policy of surrender and regrant by which Irish land was surrendered to English authorities and then given back as from the king of England, see Canny, *Elizabethan Conquest of Ireland,* 33–34, 62–63; McGurk, *Elizabethan Conquest of Ireland,* 3–28; Ciaran Brady, "Political Women and Reform in Tudor Ireland," in *Women in Early Modern Ireland,* ed. Margaret MacCurtain and Mary O'Dowd (Edinburgh: Edinburgh University Press, 1991), 67–90.

60. See Norman Jones, *The English Reformation: Religion and Cultural Adaptation* (Malden, MA: Blackwell, 2002), 33–57.

61. See also Brady, "Political Women."

62. See Carroll, *Circe's Cup,* 71–76.

63. Worden, *Sound of Virtue,* interprets similarly Sidney's representation of the firm dealings of Euarchus with the external enemy Macedon (250–51).

64. See R. F. Foster, ed., *The Oxford History of Ireland* (Oxford: Oxford University Press, 1998), 48–49; "Clare, Richard fitz Gilbert de, or Richard Strongbow," in *Dictionary of National Biography.*

65. For Spain's continued conflict with the Turks in the 1570s and for English encouragement of trade with the Turks, see Andrew C. Hess, "The Battle of Lepanto and Its Place in Mediterranean History," *Past and Present* 57 (1972): 53–73; and Pauline Croft, "Fresh Light on Bate's Case," *Historical Journal* 30 (1987): 523–39.

Contributors

RONALD CORTHELL is Professor and Chair, Department of English, Kent State University. He is the author of *Ideology and Desire in Renaissance Poetry: The Subject of Donne* (Wayne State University Press, 1997) and editor of the journal *Prose Studies: History, Theory, Criticism.* His current projects are a book on poets, patrons, and daughters in early modern English poetry and a study of Robert Southwell's *Saint Peter's Complaint.*

PETER DAVIDSON is Professor of Renaissance Studies in the University of Aberdeen. His most recent books are *The Idea of North* (Reaktion, 2005) and *The Universal Baroque* (Manchester University Press, 2007). With Jane Stevenson, he edited *Early Modern Women Poets, 1520–1700* (Oxford University Press, 2001). His edition of the *Collected Poems of S. Robert Southwell,* prepared in collaboration with Dr. Anne Sweeney, will be published by Carcanet Press in March 2007.

FRANCES E. DOLAN is Professor of English at the University of California, Davis. She is the author of *Whores of Babylon: Catholicism, Gender, and Seventeenth-Century Print Culture* (Cornell University Press, 1999; paperback edition with new preface from University of Notre Dame Press, 2005) and *Dangerous Familiars: Representations of Domestic Crime in England, 1550–1700* (Cornell University Press, 1994). *Marriage and Violence: Our Early Modern Legacy* is forthcoming from the University of Pennsylvania Press.

DONNA B. HAMILTON is Professor of English at the University of Maryland. Her publications include *Virgil and The Tempest: The Politics of Imitation*

(Ohio State University Press, 1990), *Shakespeare and the Politics of Protestant England* (University of Kentucky Press, 1992), and *Anthony Munday and the Catholics* (Ashgate, 2005).

Christopher Highley is Associate Professor of English at The Ohio State University and author of *Shakespeare, Spenser, and the Crisis in Ireland* (Cambridge University Press, 1997). He is currently working on a study of Catholics and national identity in early modern Britain.

Caroline Hibbard is Associate Professor of History at the University of Illinois at Urbana-Champaign. She is the author of *Charles I and the Popish Plot* (University of North Carolina Press, 1983) and of a number of articles on early Stuart Catholicism and on her current research focus, the court of Henrietta Maria.

Sophie Holroyd has a PhD in English literature from the University of Warwick.

Gary Kuchar is Assistant Professor of English at the University of Victoria. He is the author of *Divine Subjection: The Rhetoric of Sacramental Devotion in Early Modern England* (Duquesne University Press, 2005) and several articles on the relations between early modern literature and post-Reformation culture.

Arthur F. Marotti is Professor of English at Wayne State University, where he teaches courses in early modern English literature and culture. He is the author of three scholarly monographs: *John Donne, Coterie Poet* (University of Wisconsin Press, 1986), *Manuscript, Print, and the English Renaissance Lyric* (Cornell University Press, 1995), and *Religious Ideology and Cultural Fantasy: Catholic and Anti-Catholic Discourses in Early Modern England* (University of Notre Dame Press, 2005). He has also edited or coedited several books, including *Catholicism and Anti-Catholicism in Early Modern English Texts* (St. Martin's Press, 1999). His current projects include a collection of essays on early modern English Catholicism and a study of the personal anthologizing of poetry in manuscript in early modern England.

Molly Murray is an Assistant Professor of English at Columbia University, where she specializes in the nondramatic literature of the English Renaissance.

She is the author of articles on poetry and cultural history in *ELH* and *SEL*, and her current book manuscript is a study of religious conversion and its poetic refractions in early modern England.

ANNE M. MYERS is Assistant Professor of English at the University of Missouri-Columbia. She is currently completing a book on the relationships between literature and architecture in seventeenth-century England.

MARK NETZLOFF is Associate Professor of English at the University of Wisconsin-Milwaukee. He is the author of *England's Internal Colonies: Class, Capital, and the Literature of Early Modern English Colonialism* (Palgrave Macmillan, 2003). His current book project examines the writings of English travelers, confessional exiles, and state agents in early modern Europe.

CATHERINE SANOK is Assistant Professor of English at the University of Michigan. Her research focuses on late medieval religious and literary culture. She is currently completing a book manuscript on vernacular saints' lives and female audiences in late medieval England.

JANE STEVENSON is Professor of Latin at King's College, Aberdeen. She has published extensively both on aspects of post-Classical Latin literature and on women and education. Her books include *Women Latin Poets* (2005) and *Early Modern Women Poets* (2001, edited with Peter Davidson), both for Oxford University Press. She has also published four novels and two collections of novellas.

HEATHER WOLFE is Curator of Manuscripts at the Folger Shakespeare Library. She has edited *The Literary Career and Legacy of Elizabeth Cary, 1613–1680* (Palgrave Macmillan, 2007) and *Elizabeth Cary, Lady Falkland: Life and Letters* (RTM Publications, 2001) and has written numerous essays on manuscript culture in early modern England.

Index